DATE DUE			

The Role of Speech in Language

Proceedings of a conference entitled "The Role of Speech in Language" in the series "Communicating by Language" sponsored by the National Institute of Child Health and Human Development, National Institutes of Health.

The MIT Press   Cambridge, Massachusetts, and London, England

The Role of Speech in Language

EDITED BY JAMES F. KAVANAGH AND
JAMES E. CUTTING

408
R64
124347
apr. 1983

This book was set in Linotype Baskerville
by Bi-Comp, Inc.,
printed on Mohawk Neotext Offset
and bound in Columbia Millbank Vellum
by The Maple Press Company
in the United States of America .

Library of Congress Catologing in Publication Data

Main entry under title:
The Role of speech in language.
    Proceedings of the 5th of a series of meetings; proceedings of the 4th are entered under the title: Language by ear and by eye.
    Held at the Urban Life Center, Columbia, Md., Oct. 7–10, 1973.
    Includes bibliographies and index.
    1. Language and languages—Congresses. 2. Speech—Congresses. 3. Nonverbal communication—Congresses. I. Kavanagh, James F. II. Cutting, James E. III. United States. National Institute of Child Health and Human Development. IV. Title.
P23.R6   408   75–12561
ISBN 0–262–11059–8 (hardcover)

Contents

IV. Reflections on the Conference   313

Preface

This book reports the proceedings of the conference entitled "The Role of Speech in Language" sponsored by the Growth and Development Branch of the National Institute of Child Health and Human Development (NICHD). The conference was organized by the Cochairmen, Dr. James F. Kavanagh of the Growth and Development Branch and Dr. Alvin M. Liberman of the Haskins Laboratories and the University of Connecticut, and was held October 7 through October 10, 1973, at the Urban Life Center, Columbia, Maryland.

Within the Public Health Service of the Department of Health, Education and Welfare there are ten mission-oriented National Institutes of Health. The NICHD was established in 1963 as one of these ten Institutes. As part of its mission, the NICHD has stimulated and supported basic biological and behavioral research in communication. This research is intended to elucidate the processes by which individuals acquire and develop the ability to communicate and to lead to a better understanding of the role of communication in growth and development.

In connection with its interest in communication, the NICHD has sponsored a conference series, "Communicating by Language," to determine existing and potential directions for research as well as to identify the roles of the various disciplines in human communication. The first meeting was held at Princeton in 1964 and was an interdisciplinary exchange between scientists who are actively investigating the speech process. (The edited transcript is available through the ERIC Documentation Service: ED 059 200.) The second conference met at Old Point Comfort, Virginia, in 1965; it explored language development in children. (The proceedings were published by the MIT Press as *The Genesis of Language*.) Interdisciplinary experts on the reading process met in New Orleans in 1968 for the third conference. (The proceedings were published by the Government Printing Office as *Communicating by Language: The Reading Process*.) The fourth of the series was convened at Elkridge, Maryland, in 1971 to compare and contrast the processes of speech and reading. (The proceedings were published by the MIT Press as *Language by Ear and by Eye: The Relationships between Speech and Reading*.)

As a report on the fifth conference in this series, the present volume explores the function of speech in language. It is directed to the questions of how and within what limits the acoustic signal, the articulation that produces it, and the phonetic message it conveys are related to the rest of the language system. The aim is to describe what is known about this relationship and to pose fundamental questions that may stimulate further useful research.

The participants in this fifth conference were:

Ursula Bellugi
The Salk Institute
La Jolla, California

James F. Bosma
Oral and Pharyngeal Development Section
National Institute of Dental Research
Bethesda, Maryland

James E. Cutting
Department of Psychology
Wesleyan University
Middletown, Connecticut

Peter D. Eimas
Department of Psychology
Brown University
Providence, Rhode Island

Jerry Fodor
Department of Psychology
Massachusetts Institute of Technology
Cambridge, Massachusetts

Gordon Hewes
Department of Anthropology
University of Colorado
Boulder, Colorado

Ira J. Hirsh
Research Department
Central Institute for the Deaf
St. Louis, Missouri

Janellen Huttenlocher
Department of Education
University of Chicago
Chicago, Illinois

James J. Jenkins
Center for Research in Human Learning
University of Minnesota
Minneapolis, Minnesota

James F. Kavanagh
Growth and Development Branch
National Institute of Child Health and Human Development
Bethesda, Maryland

R. Paul Kiparsky
Department of Foreign Literatures and Linguistics
Massachusetts Institute of Technology
Cambridge, Massachusetts

Edward S. Klima
Department of Linguistics
University of California at San Diego
La Jolla, California

Alvin M. Liberman
Haskins Laboratories
New Haven, Connecticut

Philip Lieberman
Department of Linguistics
Brown University
Providence, Rhode Island

Peter Marler
Institute for Research in Animal Behavior
Rockefeller University
New York, New York

Ignatius G. Mattingly
Department of Linguistics
University of Connecticut
Storrs, Connecticut

David S. Palermo
Department of Psychology
Pennsylvania State University
University Park, Pennsylvania

David Premack
Center for Advanced Study in Behavioral Sciences
Junipero Serra Boulevard
Stanford, California

Peter C. Reynolds
Department of Hearing and Speech
Stanford Medical Center
Stanford, California

John Robert Ross
Department of Foreign Literatures and Linguistics
Massachusetts Institute of Technology
Cambridge, Massachusetts

William C. Stokoe, Jr.
Linguistics Research Laboratory
Gallaudet College
Washington, D.C.

Michael Studdert-Kennedy
Department of Communication Arts and Sciences
Queens College
Flushing, New York

Dr. Eimas was unable to attend the conference, but his research was summarized by Dr. Cutting.

At the time of the conference Dr. Cutting was attached to Yale University; Dr. Huttenlocher to Teachers College, Columbia University; and Dr. Lieberman to the University of Connecticut.

Dr. Studdert-Kennedy's work was supported in part by a grant to Haskins Laboratores from the National Institute of Child Health and Human Development. He wishes to express appreciation to Drs. Alvin Liberman, Ignatius Mattingly, and Donald Shankweiler for comments and criticisms.

Drs. Jenkins and Shaw acknowledge the support of the Center for Research in Human Learning at the University of Minnesota. The Center is supported by grants from the National Science Foundation (GB 17590), the National Institute of Child Health and Human Development (HD 01136), and the Graduate School of the University of Minnesota.

The research of Drs. Bellugi and Klima was supported by research grant NS 09811 from the National Institutes of Health and National Science Foundation Grant P4S 0132. They are also grateful to the more than 100 deaf people who worked with them in aspects of the research on sign language. In particular, they wish to thank Bernard Bragg, Carlene Canady, Henry Chen, Lou Fant, Lawrence Fleischer, Elizabeth Lay, David McKee, and Steve Turner, and the many students at Gallaudet College and California State University at Northridge who participated in their studies. Dr. Bellugi and Dr. Klima also appreciate the ingenuity and artistry of Frank A. Paul, who provided most of their illustrations of signing.

The preparation of Dr. Huttenlocher's paper was supported in part by a Career Development Award HD 21979 and in part by Grant HD 03215, both from the National Institutes of Health. She also thanks Deborah Burke, Susan Meadow, and Robert Schwartz for their helpful comments on the manuscript.

Dr. Marler's research was supported by grants from NSF (GB 33102) and NIMH (MH 14651). He is indebted to Drs. Jack Bradbury, Peter Eimas, Steven Green, Mark Konishi, George Miller, Fernando Nottebohm, William Stebbins, and Thomas Struhsaker for criticism and access to unpublished material. Dr. Marler is also grateful to Dr. Michael Studdert-Kennedy who read and criticized his manuscript and to other participants in the conference for their comments.

Dr. Ross' work was supported in part by a grant from the National Institute of Mental Health (5 PO1 MH 13390-08). He is grateful to Paul Kiparsky, Terry Langendoen, and Dave Stampe for helpful comments, and to Jim Cutting for general assistance.

Finally, the editors would like to thank Kathryn Kavanagh and Christine Donnelly for their assistance during the conference, Daphene Cave, Sharon Kennelly, Sharon Mariotti, and Marian Young for their careful typing of parts of the manuscripts in this volume, and above all, Christine Smith for her invaluable help both in the preparation for the conference and for this book.

James F. Kavanagh
James E. Cutting

The Role of Speech in Language

Introduction to the Conference

ALVIN M. LIBERMAN

Our topic—the role of speech in language—is not an established one: no one has made it the direct and primary object of his research. It is the more appropriate, therefore, that one of the chairmen of this conference say what we had in mind as we made our plans.

Our point of departure was a question: do we increase our understanding of language when we take into account that it is spoken? Obviously, we chairmen would answer in the affirmative; otherwise, we would have organized a different conference, or none at all, but certainly not this one. We hope, therefore, that you will want to answer similarly. If so, your aim will be to consider how we might increase our understanding of language by relating it to speech; you will want to count the ways. It is not my place, of course, to answer for you, or to try to bias the direction your discussion will take. I should only say why we think the question is a reasonable one and likely to trigger a productive discussion.

Our belief in an organic connection between speech and language comes, improbably, from some loose assumptions about grammar and the fit of grammatical form to grammatical function. The function of grammar is surely to connect sound to meaning, as linguists tell us. But how is it relevant to such an apparently simple function that the grammatical connection should be so complex? What is it about the capacities and limitations of creatures like us that makes the peculiar complications of grammar advantageous?

To provide a basis for discussing these questions we should consider the kinds of difficulties that might arise when a connection between sound and meaning is established. For that purpose, it is useful, first, to replace the words "sound" and "meaning" with the structures to which they are presumably related. Sound is no problem for us; it is produced by the apparatus of the vocal tract and received by the ear. Those sound-producing and sound-receiving structures are one end of the connection that grammar makes. Let us call it, for want of a better term, the transmission terminal. What, then, is at the other end? What structure serves similarly for meaning, and what shall we call it? Mincing no words, we shall suppose that the other terminal is an intellect, the place where our cognitive apparatus is housed. Fortunately, we need not speculate here about the nature of that intellect or its associated machinery, except to suggest that it is not linguistic and that communication within it is carried out in some unknown code. Fodor, Bever, and Garrett [1974], whose view of this matter is similar to ours, have called this code "mentalese." In any case, we have at one end a source—the intellect—that generates and understands linguistic messages, and at the other end a transmission terminal—the vocal tract and the ear—that produces and receives the sounds in which the messages are carried. Our question now takes the form: what is the function of a grammatical connection between source and transmitter?

In trying to answer our question, it is helpful to consider what communication would be like if grammar did not exist. In such agrammatic communication each message would be represented straightforwardly by a signal. The rule governing the flow of information would describe a one-to-one relation between a list of all possible messages and a corresponding list of signals. Moving back and forth between source and transmitter, the information would be converted—for example, from a neural representation to an acoustic one—but not in any way restructured. Surely that kind of communication would work well if there were reasonable agreement in number between the potential messages and the holistically different signals that can be efficiently produced and perceived. But there is the rub. Though we don't know exactly how many different sounds we can manage, the number is surely quite small. As to the potential messages, we can't even make a reasonable estimate; if we are to include all that our stored experience and cognitive machinery can generate, however, the number must be enormously large. This is to say that the intellect on the one hand and the vocal tract and ear on the other are not well matched to each other. But that is hardly to be wondered at. After all, those structures developed in evolution long before the appearance of language and in connection with biological functions that had nothing to do with language or, to any considerable extent, with each other. If, nevertheless, those disparate structures became connected for the purpose of communication, then, so long as the connection was agrammatic, the number of messages that the most prolific intellect could send was severely limited by the very small number of distinctively different signals that a poor transmission system can cope with. We see then a need for grammatical restructuring if information is to be made differentially appropriate for intellectual processing and for transmission through a vocal tract and ear [see Liberman, Mattingly, and Turvey, 1972; Liberman, 1974]. Thus, it may be, as Mattingly [1972] has suggested, that grammatical processes evolved as a kind of interface. If so, we should suppose that its function is to match the potentialities of an intellect to the limitations of our devices for producing and perceiving sounds, and thus vastly to increase the efficiency with which we can communicate ideas.

It is possible, of course, that other important changes might also have occurred in the evolution of language. Thus, the nonlinguistic structures that grammar connects might themselves have been modified in the direction of reducing the mismatch. Indeed, in the case of the vocal tract, at the one end of the system, such modifications did occur: our vocal tract differs anatomically from other primate vocal tracts, and in ways that appear to make it possible for us to produce a greater variety of sounds [See Lieberman, Crelin, and Klatt, 1972]. If we had to speak with the vocal tract of an ape, the grammatical interface would have a larger matching job to do; accordingly, it would have to be that much more complex if it were to work efficiently. As to what might have happened to the intellect, at the other end of the system, we hardly know how to ask the question. We can only speculate that our intellectual processes might have undergone evolutionary changes that made it more compatible with language. But such considerations, important though they may be, do not require an essential modification in our assumption about grammar and its function; we may still believe that grammar serves to reshape information so as to make it meet the very different requirements of an intellect and a transmission system.

We come now to the basis for our assumption that speech is an organic part of language. Taking grammar as the most distinctive characteristic of language, and assuming that it (or its underlying physiological processes) evolved as a matching interface, we find it reasonable to suppose that its form would somehow reflect the characteristics of the two nonlinguistic structures—intellect and transmitter—that it connects. Just how the grammar reflects those characteristics, and how the strength of the reflection varies with the distance from either of the nonlinguistic terminals, are empirical questions. But if our view of the function of grammar and of its evolution is at all correct, then we should suppose that important aspects of language are as they are because language is normally spoken and heard.

To look at grammatical processes from that functional point of view, we could begin either at the intellectual end and work downward, or at the speech end and work upward. Beginning at the intellectual end has its attractions: we are closer there to the semantic and syntactic activities that have traditionally been thought of as the essence of language. But starting at the speech end, which is what we propose to do in this conference, does not necessarily lead us away from the distinctive characteristics of language, and it has the great advantage that the processes we will be concerned with are more readily available to scientific investigation. Taking speech to comprise the part of language that extends from the phonetic message to the sound, we can frame our questions quite pointedly and reasonably hope to find some interesting answers. Thus, we can ask about the shape of the phonetic message and wonder, with some hope of satisfying our curiosity, whether there is anything like it in nonhuman communication. We can ask, further, What is required of the vocal tract and the ear if the phonetic message is to be efficiently communicated? Can these requirements be met straightforwardly, given the characteristics of the vocal tract and the ear, or is there a need for grammatical interfacing—a kind of speech grammar—even at this first, lowest stage of the system? If such a grammatical interface does in fact exist between sound and phonetic message, what is its form and how well does the form fit the function? In the evolution of this system did the auditory components change, as the vocal tract apparently did; if so, did the changes help the ear to meet the requirements of phonetic communication, thus making the grammatical interface less complicated than it otherwise would have been? Are speech production and perception unique to man and, if they are, what are their unique attributes? What are the conditions for the development of speech production and perception in the human infant, and what evidence, if any, do we find there for a species-specific, innate predisposition to language? What happens to grammar when human beings who have normal intellectual apparatus must interface, not to the vocal tract and ear, but, as in the case of deaf mutes, to visible gestures? What can we learn, in other words, about the grammar of spoken language by studying the grammar of sign? And when we look most generally at the more abstract components of spoken language—phonology, syntax, and semantics—do we see any formal resemblances to speech or any other evidence of accommodation to the limitations of the vocal tract and the ear?

To provide a structure that might properly contain questions like those, and the better ones you will raise, we will divide our conference discussions into three parts. In the first you will say what you want about the development of speech in the race and in the child. The second will offer an opportunity to consider what happens to grammar in the absence of speech; for that purpose, the most relevant evidence comes from studies of the sign language of the deaf. Broadening our view in the third part, we will examine aspects of semantics, syntax, and the more abstract parts of phonology to see if we can detect there the effects of speech and thus observe most generally the role of the speech in language.

References

Fodor, J., T. Bever, and M. Garrett. 1974. *The Psychology of Language.* New York: McGraw-Hill.

Liberman, A. M., I. G. Mattingly, and M. T. Turvey. 1972. Language codes and memory codes. In *Coding Processes in Human Memory*, A. W. Melton and E. Martin (eds.), 307–334. Washington, D.C.: V. H. Winston.

Liberman, A. M. 1974. The specialization of the language hemisphere. In *The Neurosciences: Third Study Program*, F. O. Schmitt and F. G. Worden (eds.), 43–56. Cambridge, Mass: The MIT Press.

Lieberman, P., E. S. Crelin, and D. H. Klatt. 1972. Phonetic ability and related anatomy of the newborn and adult human, Neanderthal man, and chimpanzee. *American Anthropologist*, 74: 287–307.

Mattingly, I. G. 1972 Speech cues and sign stimuli. *Am. Sci.*, 60: 327–337.

I. The Development of Speech in Man and Child

On the Origin of Speech from Animal Sounds

PETER MARLER

Speech as a Graded Signal System

One of many findings emerging from recent linguistic research is the graded nature of many speech sounds [see, among others, Lisker and Abramson, 1967; Kewley-Port and Preston, 1974; Wood, 1973; Studdert-Kennedy, this volume]. Although we perceive spoken words as being organized out of discrete, nonoverlapping segments, in fact sound spectrographic analysis reveals that many speech sounds we treat as discrete and categorically distinct, actually intergrade in their acoustical structure. This implies that segmentation is often imposed by the hearer rather than the speaker. Furthermore the acoustic patterns signaling different phonetic segments often lie along a continuum. The results of experiments with synthetic sounds, presenting a continuously varying series of intergradations, show that listeners segmentalize such speech continua and find it difficult even to discriminate between sounds that fall on the same side of the normal boundary between two speech sounds, such as [ba] and [pa]. Eimas and his colleagues have discovered that a predisposition to segmentalize such speech continua is present even in young infants. [Eimas et al., 1971; Eimas, in press; Cutting and Eimas, this volume].

These two findings, the graded nature of sounds of speech and the tendency of listeners to impose a discrete organization on them, are relevant to understanding how speech originated in the course of primate evolution. Considering these two discoveries together with recent findings on the vocalizations of birds and nonhuman primates permits the formulation of new hypotheses about the origin of speech.

Graded and Discrete Signals in Nonhuman Primates

A review of what we know of the vocalizations used by nonhuman primates under natural conditions shows that while the vocal repertoires of some are organized in acoustically discrete fashion, others show graded continua. I shall first document this point, and speculate that a graded system is perhaps most likely to have given rise to speech. A survey of the relationship between vocal repertoires, social organization, and ecology shows this speculation to be plausible in the sense that the emphasis on graded repertoires occurs in species showing some of the same evolutionary trends as early man.

First I shall consider four monkeys that live in the rain forests of East Africa. Two are *Cercopithecus* monkeys, the blue monkey *Cercopithecus mitis,* and the red-tailed monkey *Cercopithecus ascanius.* The other two are colobine monkeys, the black and white colobus *Colobus quereza,* and the red colobus *Colobus badius.* The first three live in small groups of about ten to twenty-five animals with a single adult male [Marler, 1969a; Aldrich-Blake, 1970; Struhsaker and Oates, in press; Rudran, Struhsaker, and Torre Bueno, pers. comm.]. As indicated in Table 1, they all defend a portion of their home range as a territory against adjacent troops. Unlike some other primate inhabitants of the same forests, such as baboons and chimpanzees, they rarely go to the forest floor, and are viewed as strictly arboreal species.

The red colobus provides a striking contrast. Troop size is much larger, consisting of fifty animals or more, with several adult males [Marler, 1970a; Struhsaker, in press]. Unlike its relative the black and white colobus, and the two cercopithecines, this is a nonterritorial species. It shares these characteristics, nonterritoriality and a large group size, with the other two species I shall mention, one also African, the chimpanzee *Pan troglodytes,* the other living in Asia, the Japanese macaque *Macaca fuscata.* Their troops, or "communities" in the case of chimpanzees, are of the order of fifty to one hundred members or more, with many adult males in the group, and they are nonterritorial. They show a much stronger tendency than the species mentioned earlier to go to the forest floor for moving from place to place, and a propensity to invade open areas, making them among the most terrestrial of nonhuman primates [Lawick-Goodall, 1969a, 1969b, 1971; Miyadi, 1965; Kawanaka, 1973; Green, in press].

We are thus dealing with two groups of species: one territorial, living in the forest in small groups, and the other nonterritorial, living in larger groups either in forest or more open country. In the three territorial species the initiative for defense and maintenance of intergroup spacing is taken by the adult male, and in all three there are vocalizations, among the loudest in the repertoire, which are unique to the adult male and used especially in communication between groups. In closely related, cohabiting species, such as the red-tailed and blue monkeys, these sounds are distinctively different both in internal form and in pattern of delivery, as shown in Figures 1 and 2. Specific distinctiveness in vocalizations is not, however, universal. Living closely together, these two cercopithecine monkeys are subject to the same predators and engage often in the interspecific communication of danger. It is no accident that the "chip" alarm calls of adult females and juveniles of these two species are exceedingly similar, as shown in Figure 3, and indeed rather stable throughout the entire genus *Cercopithecus* [Gautier and Gautier-Hion, 1969; Struhsaker, 1969, 1970; Marler, 1973a].

Table 1. Summary of the Social Organization, Territoriality, and Vocal Behavior of Some African and Asian Primates

Species	Group Size	Terrestrial	Territorial	Communication Emphasis	Sexual Dimorphism	Vocal Repertoire
Blue monkey	small	no	yes	between troops	yes	discrete
Red-tailed monkey	small	no	yes	between troops	yes	discrete
Black and white colobus	small	no	yes	between and within troops	yes	mixed
Red colobus	large	no	no	within troop	no	graded
Japanese macaque	large	yes	no	within troop	no	graded
Chimpanzee	large	yes	no	within troop	no	graded

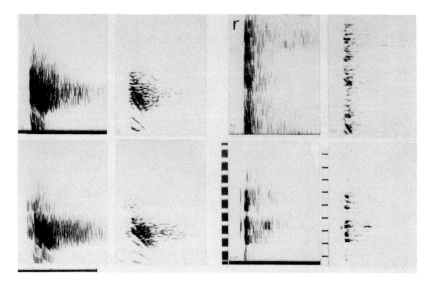

Figures 1, 2. Adult male loud calls of the African blue monkey (left) and the red-tailed monkey (right). Two individuals are illustrated for each. Wide (300 Hz) and narrow (40 Hz) band displays are given of each sound, side by side. Frequency markers—500 Hz intervals. Time marker (bottom left)—0.5 sec. [After Marler, 1973a]

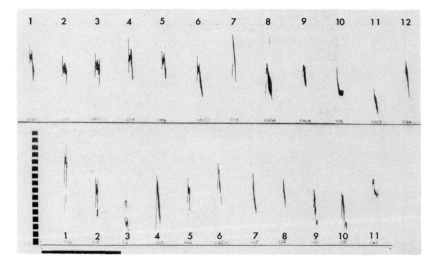

Figure 3. Selections traced from sound spectrograms of many different recordings of "chip" alarm calls of female red-tailed (top, 1–12) and blue monkeys (bottom, 1–11), illustrating variations in acoustical morphology. Scales as in Figure 2. [After Marler, 1973a]

As investigation proceeds through field observations and subsequent laboratory analysis of the sounds of red-tailed or blue monkeys, the classification is a relatively easy process. A series of categories is gradually derived, and each new sound heard subsequently is placed in one or another of them. There is rarely any confusion caused by sounds intermediate in morphology between existing categories. Figure 4 presents a summary of the vocal repertoire of blue monkeys, arranged to indicate that, with the exception of the "growl"–"pulsed grunt" continuum, the categories defined thus far are discrete. There is also a high degree of sexual dimorphism in vocal morphology, with three sounds unique to the adult male. The repertoire of the red-tailed monkey also shows a significant degree of discrete organization [Marler, 1972, 1973a].

Note that I am not asserting that fine variation in acoustical morphology has no communicative significance in these species. It probably does, and not only where there is conspicuous grading as in the pulsed grunts and growls of the blue monkey. Considering intensity, frequency, morphology, and timing, the variation within a category such as the "chip" alarm call probably has the potential for conveying information to others, though presumably animals will be less *sensitive* to within-category variations than to variations between categories. In speaking of a discrete

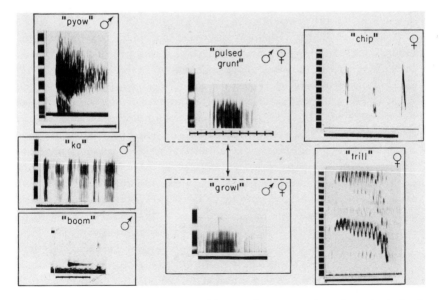

Figure 4. A summary of calls of the blue monkey arranged to show the lack of intermediate forms between major categories other than those between "pulsed grunts" and "growls." [After Marler, 1973a]

repertoire, I am drawing attention to the prominence of discrete organization in the basic acoustical patterns that make up the repertoire as a
whole, while still allowing for the likelihood that variations within categories, or in some cases between categories, may occur, and may be significant to listeners.

The point is illustrated by the vocalizations of the black and white
colobus. Figure 5 presents the main items in the repertoire. The roaring
of the male probably serves the same functions as the male loud calls
of *Cercopithecus*, namely, the maintenance of territorial spacing and
rallying of group members. The adult male "snort" introduces roaring
and is also given separately in a number of variants, one serving as a
threat, another as an alarm call. A further nonvocal sound not shown
is a tongue click used as a close-range threat. Then there are two other
systems of sound, one a squeak-scream used by adults and juveniles, varying along a number of dimensions, the other what I call "cawing," which
also varies considerably. These are two cases of grading in acoustical
morphology and temporal delivery, and these sounds are used primarily
for communication within the troop. This is also the case with the
"growl"–"pulsed grunt" continuum of the blue monkey. Conversely
those sounds which fall into discontinuous categories make up that part
of the repertoire especially concerned with distance communication,
whether within or between troops [Marler, 1972].

If a species living in dense forest is socially organized in territorial
groups, with a significant part of the vocal repertoire addressed to problems of intertroop communication, signaling must take place over appreciable distances in environments noisy from wind and sounds of insects,
birds, and other primates. In such circumstances there must be strong selection pressure for a discrete type of signal organization as the most efficient
means of unequivocal conveyance of information to an adjacent troop.

Under these conditions, any potential that graded signals might otherwise have for communication of more refined information would surely
be lost. Pressures for specific distinctiveness would also favor discrete
acoustical morphology and patterns of delivery. Within the troop circumstances differ. Here signaling is often over a shorter range. Even in the
forest, full of obstacles, communicants in the same troop can often see as
well as hear one another, and visual signals emitted in parallel with sounds
may aid in detecting and identifying the subtleties of graded signaling.

A similar argument can be brought to bear on the vocal behavior of
the second group of species. With the absence of territoriality, a
greater group size, and more complex troop organization resulting from
the presence of several adult males, we see a shift in emphasis toward

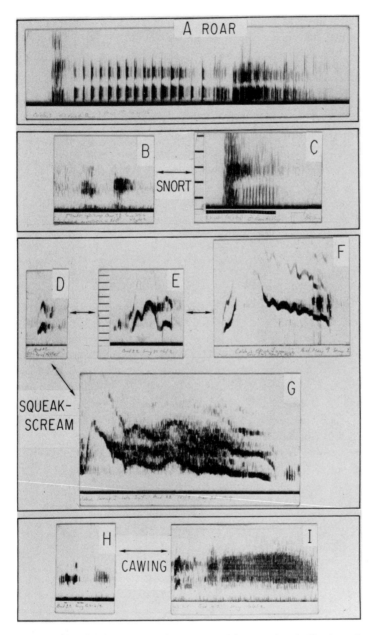

Figure 5. Calls of the black and white colobus monkey indicating where intermediate forms occur. [After Marler, 1972]

within-troop communication and an increase in the degree of grading of
vocal repertoires. The first example is the red colobus, living in the same
forests as the three other species we have discussed. The striking difference in their social organization is accompanied by an equally dramatic
difference in their signal repertoire. A provisional examination revealed
no discrete elements in the vocal repertoire at all [Marler, 1970a], as indicated earlier by Hill and Booth [1957]. In a detailed study, Struhsaker
[in press] has confirmed that the entire vocal repertoire of this species
seems to consist of a single continuously graded system. An example of the
way in which calls grade into one another is shown in Figure 6.

The chimpanzee provides another illustration of a graded vocal repertoire [Marler, 1969b]. There are independent variations among different
acoustical dimensions, such as duration, the fundamental frequency, the

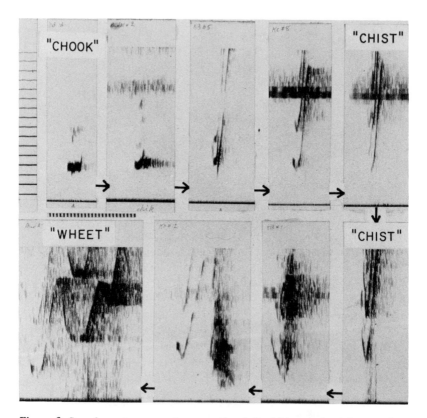

Figure 6. Sound spectrograms of some calls of the African red colobus monkey arranged to show how forms grade into one another. [After Marler, 1970a]

presence or absence of a vibrato, and the degree of emphasis on different parts of the acoustical spectrum, to say nothing of variations in patterns of delivery.

An even more extreme example is the Japanese macaque. Given its multimale social organization, with troops ranging upwards of fifty to one hundred animals, and a large undefended home, the hypothesis we are developing would predict the graded vocal repertoire which it does in fact possess.

What are we to make of the extensive variation found in the vocal repertoires of such primates as these? The weakest hypothesis would be that it represents disorderly and erratic variation, as though from relaxation of the relationship between vocal morphology on the one hand and ongoing behaviors and their physiological substrates on the other. There is in fact ample evidence of a degree of order. In the vocal repertoire of the chimpanzee, for example, Lawick-Goodall [1968a, 1968b] readily established correlations between type of vocalization and motivational state as inferred from circumstances and the accompanying behavior. That precision of vocal control can be achieved is implied by pant-hooting, one of the more stereotyped chimpanzee vocalizations, in which consistent individual differences are maintained in the face of involvement of pant-hooting in a graded relationship with other vocalizations such as screaming [Marler and Hobbet, in press].

Careful analysis of another graded system, that of the talapoin monkey in West Africa by Gautier [in press] suggest that variations along one or another acoustical dimension are by no means random but match other characteristics of the situation. Perhaps the most elaborate attempt to map continuous vocal gradations against the accompanying natural context of the vocalizing animal was conducted by Green [in press] on the Japanese macaque.

During a 14-month field study extensive recordings of vocalizations were compared with assessments of the social situation associated with each utterance. Sound spectrographic analyses were subjected to a systematic taxonomy on the basis of physical properties, resulting in a division into 10 classes. A summary of the distinctive features used shows that some relate to the temporal pattern of delivery, some to the mechanism of phonation, and some to more or less arbitrary acoustical properties. Table 2 lists the 10 classes, each characterized by a term conveying some impression of how they sounded to the observer.

We can illustrate the method with one of the groups, the class II "coos." These were divided into 7 types according to the features shown in Figure 7. In a separate analysis the circumstances of each were assessed

Table 2. Synopsis of Ten Major Classes of Vocalizations in the Japanese Macaque

Class	Name	Some Distinguishing Features
I	Girneys	Articulations alone or superimposed on voiced sounds
II	Coos	Simple, nonplosive, uniformly tonal
III	Whistles and warbles	Nonplosive, modified tonal, and predominantly tonal: duration > 0.18 sec
IV	Squawks and squeaks	Duration ≤ 0.18 sec, plosive tonal; rich harmonic structure; complex, predominantly tonal
V	Chirps and barks	Duration ≤ 0.18 sec or multiunit; plosive or noisy, predominantly tonal compound, some with clicks or dropouts
VI	Squeals and screeches	Duration > 0.10 sec, may be multiunit; noisy, predominantly tonal compound or complex, predominantly tonal; dominant frequency above 2400 Hz
VII	Shrieks and screams	Duration > 0.10 sec; simple or modified atonal, or predominantly atonal; dominant energy above baseline (ca. 80 Hz) and below 2400 Hz
VIII	Whines	Complex, predominantly tonal; duration > 0.18 sec; overtones more intense than fundamental; major energy ≤ 2400 Hz
IX	Geckers	Simple atonal, or complex, predominantly atonal, or plosive modified atonal; duration of units ≤ 0.10 sec
X	Growled sounds and roars	Pulsed and/or uniformly atonal, or complex, predominantly atonal with dominant energy at baseline

From Green [in press].

COO TYPE		DISTINGUISHING CRITERIA			
	Name	Midpoint pitch	Position of highest peak	Duration	Other features
	Double	≤ 510 Hz	N.A.	N.A.	Two overlapping harmonic series
	Long Low	≤ 510 Hz	N.A.	≥ 0.20 sec.	N.A.
	Short Low	≤ 590 Hz	≠ 1	≤ 0.19 sec	N.A.
	Smooth Early High	≥ 520 Hz	< 2/3	N.A.	No Dip
	Dip Early High	≥ 520 Hz	< 2/3	N.A.	Dip
	Dip Late High	≥ 520 Hz	≥ 2/3	N.A.	Dip
	Smooth Late High	≥ 520 Hz	≥ 2/3	N.A.	No Dip

N.A. = not applied for separation of types

Figure 7. A key for the arbitrary classification of one type of call (coo) of Japanese macaques into seven arbitrary types. [After Green, in press]

Table 3. Synopsis of Social Circumstances in which *Coo* Sounds Are Uttered by the Japanese Macaque

None of the contact circumstances are agonistic; none of the directed utterances accompany gestures or expressions of threat. All animals appear relatively calm as compared with the agitated demeanor and arousal observed in situations characteristic of other sound classes.

a. Separated Male
An adult male alone, calmly following the main troop concentration at a distance of at least 50m, directing vocalizations towards the troop or its straggling members

b. Female minus Infant
1. An adult female who has not returned to normal intrafamilial clustering after the death of her infant; shows demeanor of lethargy and depression; vocalizations directed at the body, or as apparently searching
2. A mature female, nulliparous or nonparous, showing similar demeanor, vocalizing while alone rather than at or within a family clustering typical of the birth season

c. Nonconsorting Female
In the copulatory season, a sexually active female who is neither consorting nor soliciting at the moment. She sits or lies calmly alone while vocalizing. She may have just completed a consort relationship, or abandoned pursuit of an unresponsive male, or was herself solicited but unresponsive

d. Female at Young
1. A mother vocalizing to her youngster (or adult daughter) while with or near it
2. A mother vocalizing while her youngster is not at hand as she moves from place to place apparently looking for it; her behavior changes on its appearance
3. A mature female without an infant approaching to join a huddled grouping in the birth season and vocalizing at it; the grouping is of a different matriliny and contains at least one infant
4. A mature or immature female alone near an infant-containing family grouping vocalizing as her visual attention is focussed on the infant

e. Dominant at Subordinate
1. A dominant in proximity to a subordinate, approaching it, or in affinitive contact with it
2. A dominant initiating activity which leads to affinitive contact or behaving in the fashion usually leading to such "friendly" contact, for example, grooming
3. Within consortship, sitting calmly with female or grooming between mounts

f. Young Alone
A yearling or juvenile sitting very calmly, looking around; not near or with its mother, siblings or playmates

g. Dispersal
Scattered individuals, or subgroupings out of visual contact with the main part of the troop, for example, during troop progression or while in foraging parties

h. Young to Mother
Calm youngster to its mother as near her, with her, or following her

i. Subordinate at Dominant
In calm approach or during affinitive contact or during behavior usually yielding such contact; not including youngster to mother or sexual solicitation

j. Estrus Female
1. During earliest stages of solicitation, that is, long-distance following of a dominant male
2. During later stages of solicitation of a dominant male or female as closely following or as seated or lying nearby after a close approach
3. During consortship as pursuing closely a male (copulatory) or female (pseudo-copulatory homosexual) partner or between mounts as the partner leaves

After Green [in press].

and classified, along the lines illustrated in Table 3. The two sets of information were then put together to see whether the subtle variants into which the sounds had been classified bore orderly or random relationships to the circumstances of production. As may be seen from Figure 8, the relationship was by no means random. Instead, each variant was highly correlated with one situation or a cluster of related circumstances. Thus there can be no doubt that the graded repertoire of the Japanese macaque has the potential for conveying subtle and complex information about the circumstances of sound production. Further work is required to establish whether or not these variants are in fact responded to differentially.

It is evident, then, that some nonhuman primates share with man a vocal system which is largely graded rather than organized into discrete, nonadjacent categories. The constellation of behavioral and ecological traits that tends to characterize those species with a graded repertoire— large, nonterritorial, multimale groups with a tendency to move on the forest floor and to invade open country—is consistent with speculations about the probable ecology and social organization of early man [Washburn, 1961; Campbell, 1972]. Notably, the list of primates with a predominantly graded vocal system includes the chimpanzee, probably the closest of all other surviving primates to human ancestry in its behavior, whether in social organization and temperament, tool preparation and use, or the habit of hunting and eating mammalian prey [Lawick-Goodall. 1972; Teleki, 1973].

Some Ethological Principles
Notwithstanding the insistence of Konrad Lorenz that ethological principles derived from studies of vertebrates are germane to understanding human behavior, many have tended to restrict their relevance to fish, reptiles, and nonprimate mammals. At best, human applications of ethological theory are usually countenanced only in such aspects of behavior as aggression, nonverbal signaling, or infant reflexes. Relevance of zoological findings in ethology to understanding speech behavior may seem implausible. Nevertheless, Mattingly [1972] has suggested that the ethological concepts of sign stimuli and social releasers are illustrated by our tendency to focus responsiveness on certain abstracted properties of the complex of stimuli that speech presents.

I suggest that another ethological concept, that of the innate release mechanism, is also useful in understanding speech perception and development. The underlying notion, originating with von Uexkull and developed fully by Lorenz [1935, 1950] is that sensory mechanisms evolved to preordain an individual's responsiveness to particular patterns of external

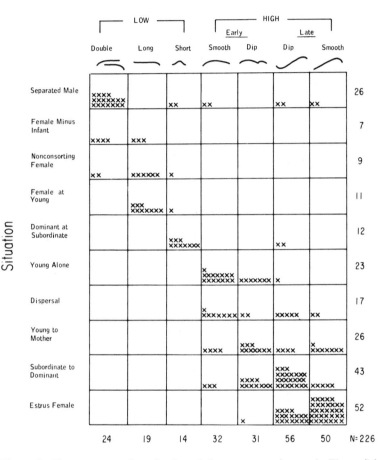

Figure 8. Circumstances of production of the seven sound types in Figure 7 by the Japanese macaque.

stimulation with special relevance in the history of a species, though perhaps not of the individual. The stimuli may be from the physical environment from other animals or from other members of the species. The term was coined especially to epitomize the finding in many animal species that individuals are responsive to specific stimuli from members of their own species without having had previous experience of them.

The concept of innate release mechanisms can be brought to bear on the process of vocal learning, but with two changes. Whereas ethologists have tended to view these mechanisms as primarily genetically fixed and unmodifiable, they are in fact sometimes labile, with the capacity for change as a result of learning. Secondly, I suggest that the concept is as useful in understanding certain kinds of motor development as it is in dealing with problems of responsiveness to the environment. I propose that in the evolution of man, as in the evolution of some other organisms, there was a change in the strategy of motor development from primarily endogenous control to control by sensory feedback.

Genetic programs for motor outflow seem to generate the motor activities of some animals [Bentley and Hoy, 1972; Wilson, 1972]. They may be modified in form and timing by proprioceptive feedback, but many basic patterns are endogenously generated [Doty, 1968]. The change I propose is from this endogenous control to a strategy in which motor development is guided primarily by sensory control, still providing opportunity for the influence of genetic information, but also allowing for extensive modification by individual experience. These two changes in ethological theory, the use of innate release mechanisms in motor development, and their potential modifiability, prepare the concept of the innate release mechanism of incorporation in what could prove to be a general model for the evolution of vocal learning [see Nottebohm, 1972a]. I suggest that it may be general in application because I find many parallels in avian vocal development with the development and perception of human speech [Marler, 1970b].

The Role of Templates in Bird Song Development

Birds, like man, rely heavily on communication by sounds in maintaining the structure of their societies. Certain vocalizations of many birds are learned in much the same way as speech, thus providing a basis for a comparative approach to systems of vocal learning. The effects on its vocal development of surgically deafening a bird early in life are especially revealing. I shall confine my remarks to just one aspect of their vocal behavior, the most complex of avian vocalizations, the "song" of the male.

A dove or chicken, deafened soon after birth, vocalizes at the normal time, and analysis of the sounds reveals a normal morphology [Konishi, 1963; Nottebohm and Nottebohm, 1971]. Thus a dove or a chicken needs no access to an external model to develop normal vocalizations. Nor does such a bird need to hear its own voice to generate the normal song.

The second condition I want to consider is characterized by the song sparrow. Young males of this species taken from the nest and reared alone in a soundproof chamber in social and acoustical isolation will develop song, notwithstanding its greater complexity as compared with the calls of doves and chickens. Like them, male song sparrows have the capacity to generate the complex motor output of singing without the prerequisite of an external model. However, if a young male song sparrow is deafened early in youth, and then reared under identical conditions, his singing, unlike that of doves and chickens, will be highly abnormal. All of the fine morphology is lost, and instead there is a burst of about two seconds of very noisy, erratic, pulsed sound with a rather insect-like quality, as shown in Figure 9. The song sparrow must hear his own voice if normal development is to occur [Mulligan, 1966].

In the third class of birds, most relevant to our present concern, a young male taken from the nest and reared in isolation in a soundproof chamber will develop a highly abnormal song. Although this song is outside the set of normal patterns for the species, certain qualities of the species-typical song persist, as I shall mention. Using the white-crowned

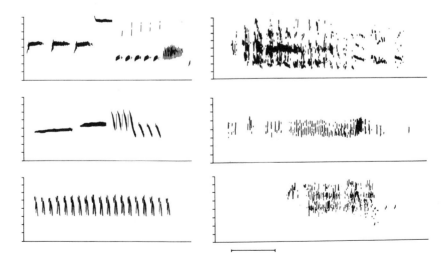

Figure 9. A comparison of songs of three bird species, song sparrows (top), white-crowned sparrows (middle), and Oregon juncos (bottom) as sung in nature (left) and by birds deafened in youth (right). [After Konishi, 1965; Mulligan, 1966]

sparrow as an illustration, playback of a recording of normal song to a young male at a certain critical phase of his life, the period between 10 and 50 days of age, results in the subsequent production of a close copy of the external model presented [Marler, 1970c].

What if a male white-crowned sparrow is surgically deafened early in youth? The song he develops is rather like that of a deafened song sparrow. The point of interest is that the song of a male deafened early is much more abnormal than that of an intact male reared in social isolation. All species-specific characteristics are lost, including those few retained by an intact isolate [Konishi, 1965]. Deafened, the male behaves as though his song were reduced to the lowest common denominator, perhaps the basic output of the passive syringeal apparatus with a flow of air through it. This interpretation is reinforced by the similarity of songs of early deafened white-crowned sparrows, song sparrows, and another relative, the Oregon junco [Konishi, 1964], three species whose normal songs are highly divergent. We can infer that hearing is involved in the divergence of the normal paths of development of these three species, not only to permit them to hear external models, but also to enable them to hear their own voices.

This discovery, that species differences in sparrow songs seem to originate with sensory mechanisms rather than motor mechanisms, led to speculation about the existence of auditory templates. I visualize these as lying in the neural pathways for auditory processing, embodying information about the structure of vocal sounds, with the capacity to guide motor development. As such they are conceived as having a more dominant influence on vocal development than structure of the sound-producing equipment or the characteristics of hearing in general, although these too can have an influence [Konishi, 1970]. According to this view, as the young male begins to sing he strikes a progressively closer match between his vocal output and the dictates of the auditory template. This is just the impression you get listening to a young male as he passes through the stages of subsong, plastic song, and finally full song.

In the song sparrow the template is presumably adequate to guide normal song development. In the white-crown, however, the template of a naive male is presumably less than adequate, although the same mechanism may suffice to focus the male's attention on an appropriate class of external models, thus explaining the finding that a male will reject inappropriate models while learning [Marler, 1970c]. While the selectivity of learning might depend on a different mechanism, it is economical to assume that the same one achieves both effects. We presumably see in the song of an intact but socially isolated male white-crown a picture of what the unimproved template embodies.

Given access to an appropriate external model during the critical period, the template presumably becomes more highly specified, now embodying instructions for normal song, including the characteristics of the particular dialect to which the male was exposed. Note that this learning precedes singing by 100 days or more, permitting Konishi [1965] to deafen male white-crowns both before and after learning, but before singing. The outcome was the same in either case, the very simple song of the trained and then deafened bird revealing no trace of the auditory learning that had taken place. Hearing is still required for the information incorporated in the improved template to be translated into motor activity, as suggested in Figure 10.

These findings are consistent with the hypothesis that an auditory template mediates between the external model on the one hand and the male's own singing behavior on the other. In contrast with the classical innate release mechanism the template does more than just control responsiveness to a set of external stimuli. That function is still served, both in the male, by focusing his attention on an appropriate set of external models, and probably also in the female, who does not normally sing, but who is responsive to the male song at the time of sexual pairing [Milligan and Verner, 1971]. Konishi [1965] demonstrated that the female induced to sing by injecting her with male sex hormone is in possession of the same information about song as the male. Exposed to normal song during early life, she will sing that same dialect under the influence of testosterone as an adult.

While we can conceptualize song templates as single functional mechanisms, they may involve several physiological components that together serve as stimulus filters. Components that are modifiable might be separate from those which underlie the selective perception of a naive, untrained male. The two sets might operate in series, or in parallel, with control shifting from one to the other after training. There may be species differences in the nature, number, and mode of coupling of templates. As with other "feature detectors" one should be prepared for the likelihood that similar behavioral ends may be achieved by different physiological mechanisms.

In the present case there is elegant economy in a physiological mechanism that serves both to guide the female in proper choice of a mate and to guide the process of male song development. If our interpretation is correct, the template serves as a kind of innate release mechanism which

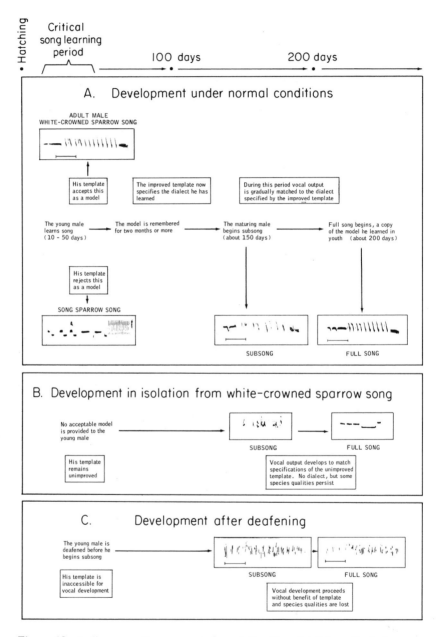

Figure 10. A diagrammatic representation of the "template" hypothesis for song learning in white-crowned sparrows, as applied to development (A) in a normal male, (B) in a social isolate, and (C) after early deafening. [After Marler, 1970c]

is also modifiable through experience, "innate" in this context implying that it develops initially without exposure to an exemplar from another animal [but see Marler, 1973b]. The modifications can then be incorporated into the mechanism to guide subsequent behavior of both male and female.

Thus, as Nottebohm [1972a] has pointed out, the incorporation of modifiable templates in motor development opens up new ontogenetic possibilities. It has been exploited as a fruitful developmental strategy by one group of organisms, birds, that rely heavily on vocal behavior in their social biology. It is conceivable that a similar revolution in ontogenetic strategy took place in the ancestors of man.

Speculations on the Origin of Speech

In both natural and synthetic speech we perceive the components of words as discretely different from one another even when they are not. Although one may speculate that paralinguistic variations in pitch, intonation, loudness, and tempo, those aspects of speech that so subtly convey variations of the speaker's mood and intent, are perhaps more likely to be processed in continuous rather than categorical fashion [Eimas, in press], much of the content of speech is obviously processed segmentally. The studies of Eimas and his colleagues [Eimas et al., 1971; Eimas, in press] have shown that such segmental processing of speech sounds occurs in infants as young as four months or even one month, long before they have begun to speak or even babble. Listening to related speech sounds such as [pa] and [ba], or [bæ], [dæ], and [gæ], distinguished in adults by acoustical criteria that are similar in all languages studied so far, infants are found to process them in essentially the same way as adults. This result suggests that human infants possess auditory templates for certain speech sounds. While they may have heard a lot of speech by four months or even one month, the early age at which this ability is manifest raises the possibility that certain speech sounds can be processed appropriately without the need for prior exposure to them. The analogy with innate release mechanisms is suggestive.

Auditory templates for certain speech sounds could serve a child well in two respects. First they would focus an infant's attention on an appropriate class of external stimuli for social responsiveness, much as the auditory templates of some birds restrict responsiveness to members of their own species when they are living in a community with many others present. Secondly, they provide an orderly frame of reference for the infant's developing responsiveness to the speech of others, drawing attention to the particular subset of speech properties that retain valence into adulthood [Mattingly, 1972]. The templates are presumably modified and multiplied, in the very process of aiding the infant's perception and analysis of the sounds of the language in which it participates.

Thus far the parallels with the role of auditory templates in birdsong are close, though birds use the ability for selective auditory perception we have discussed here to distinguish between acceptable and nonacceptable models for vocal development, while children use them both for this and for classifying acceptable sounds into subcategories as well. Birds also seem to have specific auditory filtering mechanisms for conspecific sounds involved in different behavioral systems [for example, Gottlieb, 1971], but I don't know of a case where more than one is involved in development of the same vocal pattern, such as song. We may press the analogy further, and suggest that a third function for speech sound templates lies in the development of speaking. Evidently the development of sensory mechanisms for speech perception precedes motor development, as in the white-crowned sparrow. Improvements in a child's babbling, as with a bird's subsong, may reveal growing skill in matching vocal output to auditory templates by auditory feedback. These templates for the sounds of speech will then be much modified and enriched compared with those of early infancy, as a result of continuing experience.

In this view, the evolution of innate but modifiable auditory templates for speech sounds was perhaps the most critical single change in the developmental physiology of human vocal behavior, potent for both sensory and motor development. Those nonhuman primates most likely to parallel prehuman ecology and social organization have vocal repertoires that tend to continuous acoustical gradations in somewhat the same way as speech. How these species process their vocal sounds as they listen and respond to them we do not know. If, as seems to be the case, the sounds serve mainly to communicate variations of mood, permitting companions to adjust and orient their behavior to the prospects of future action and reaction of the vocalizer, we may speculate that continuous sensory processing might well be more efficient for them than segmentalization. Application of the same habituation technique Eimas has used, studying responses of nonhuman primates to their own vocal sounds, would be one way to answer this question. Another might employ the habituation of averaged evoked potentials in the brain, both to detect possible segmental processing, and to assess the extent of lateralization of brain function, as is done successfully with human subjects responding to speech [Wood, Goff, and Day, 1971; Wood, 1973]. A direct conditioning approach to sound discrimination and generalization, using recorded vocalizations as stimuli, might also be employed.

Categorical and Continuous Sensory Processing

Studies of the discriminability of artifically synthesized, graded speech sounds indicate that the gradations are difficult for us to hear without special training. This difficulty, presumably resulting from our tendency to process speech sounds categorically, must be shared by other organisms that engage in categorical stimulus processing. If the graded vocalizations of chimpanzees and macaques provide them with advantages that a discrete repertoire lacks for them, as I have speculated, it seems likely that they would have to process their graded vocalizations in noncategorical fashion for this advantage to be realized. In higher primates, an evolutionary change to continuous processing of vocal sounds, with concomitant sensitization of the macaque and chimpanzee to gradations in the vocalizations of its species, may have been a necessary counterpart to the evolution of graded vocalizations. Discrete vocal organization is more widespread, and might be thought of as a more primitive primate condition.

The intermingling of categorical and noncategorical processing of sound signals may have called for some radical changes in sensory physiology. Processing of a conspecific repertoire of discrete signals by a series of separate "stimulus filters," as implied by the ethologist's battery of "innate release mechanisms," is presumably categorical in nature. Thus the postulated shift from continuous to categorical speech perception in early man may have been a step back to an earlier condition, but with a novel application, to the processing of predominantly graded signals. The concomitant retention of continuous sensory processing of nonspeech sounds and perhaps of the paralinguistic aspects of speech, a primitive trait for man but an advanced one for other primates, may have created physiological problems.

It is important to discover how nonhuman primates process conspecific vocal stimuli, especially those species with graded vocal repertoires, and to find out whether they exhibit cerebral dominance. One might even entertain the speculation that cerebral dominance originated in advanced nonhuman primates, to facilitate emergence of what was for them the relatively novel accomplishment of continuous vocal processing, to be retained by us in activities that then became subordinate again to the categorical speech processing of the dominant hemisphere.

Nottebohm's discovery [1971, 1972b] that the neural control of some birdsongs is lateralized should alert us to the possibility of other nonhuman parallels to hemispheric dominance. One might even speculate that lateral specialization for different sensory functions is part and parcel

of the revolution in developmental strategy that accompanies incorporation of auditory templates in speech perception and development. There
is evidence that while responsibility for categorical processing, possibly
by modifiable templates, is relegated mainly to the dominant hemisphere,
continuous processing of nonspeech sounds, perhaps including paralinguistic aspects of speech, remains primarily in the subordinate hemisphere
[Kimura, 1961; Studdert-Kennedy, this volume]. It is important to find
out whether nonhuman primates, especially those with graded vocal
repertoires, show cerebral dominance, and if so, how vocal control and
sound processing differ in the two hemispheres.

One possibility to explore concerns an animal's ability to identify and
distinguish vocalizations from memory. Graded vocalizations of chimpanzees and macaques are often given in rapid trains with each sound slightly
modified from the preceding one. It might be that close temporal juxta-
position of graded sounds is a prerequisite for continuous sensory processing. Such sounds may be more concerned with denoting rates and directions of change in the probabilities of social interaction of the vocalizer
with others than with precise denotation of different categories of response that are likely. The potential value of a given variant of graded
vocalization may be much reduced if used in isolation from other variants,
with short-term memory no longer available to guide in its identification.
One might think of categorical processing of vocalizations with a finite
set of stimulus filters as an aid in identifying sounds from memory when
heard separately from other sounds so that immediate comparison is no
longer possible. That the size of such a set of categorical filters is subject
to physiological limits is suggested by the tendency of animal signal repertoire sizes to cluster between 15 and 35 [Moynihan, 1970]. Could it be
more than a coincidence that speech is constructed from a similar number
of basic distinctive features—about 40 in English, ranging from 20 to
about 60 in other languages [Jakobson, Fant, and Halle, 1952; Miller,
personal communication].

The Revolution in Motor Development
I wish to argue then that new sensory mechanisms for processing speech
sounds, applied first, in infancy, to analyzing sounds of others, and somewhat later in life to analysis of the child's own sounds, were a significant
evolutionary step toward achieving the strategy of speech development
of *Homo sapiens*. There were also changes on the motor side. We are
lamentably ignorant of the course of vocal development in early deafened
nonhuman primates. We know that deafening of both adult and
infant squirrel monkeys [Talmage-Riggs et al., 1972; Ristau, personal

communication] leaves the major types of vocalization intact, but this is a species with mainly discrete vocalizations [Winter, Ploog, and Latta, 1966]. The outcome of deafening experiments might be different with a primate that has graded vocalizations.

A required addition on the motor side is the neural circuitry necessary to modify patterns of motor outflow so that sounds generated can be matched to preestablished auditory templates. Further analyses of the neural mechanisms employed in the motor control of learned birdsongs may provide guidance as to the *kind* of physiological processing that is required, so aiding the search for analogous functions in the human brain.

I propose, then, that critical steps in the evolution of human speech, from a primate already possessing a graded vocal repertoire, such as the chimpanzee [Marler, 1969b] were the incorporation of modifiable auditory templates both to reintroduce the categorical perception of conspecific vocalizations, and as elements in individual motor development. The revolution in motor development that this implies is not unique to man. We have evidence that some of the components have arisen in birds, perhaps several times [Nottebohm, 1972a]. It may represent a general mechanism for vocal learning, employed similarly by different species, albeit for different ends. The order in which the postulated changes in vocal perception and development might have occurred in the evolution of early man will be clarified when we learn more about how nonhuman primates perceive and process their own vocalizations, and about their dependence on auditory feedback in vocal development.

Categorical Perception and Syntax
In birds the developmental process is typically rapid and ends with the emergence of full song, which usually remains more or less fixed for life. While certain birds continue to modify their vocal behavior throughout life, there is no evidence that birds or any other species than man continue to recombine qualitatively different vocal units, separately meaningful, into new messages with new meanings. In other words, they have no syntax. For the child the first stages of vocal development are only a prelude to the long, elaborate process of achieving competence with the deep structure of his language, where a different set of special, universal predispositions seem to be involved [Chomsky, 1965; McNeill, 1966].

The capacity of our speech to encode information about potentially unlimited numbers of objects, operations, and concepts, often very complex, depends on the ability to change and rechange the order of information-bearing words, each with its own meaning. In animals the tendency is rather to pack as much information as possible into single, indivisible signals [Marler, 1961]. Thus a bird alarm call is at once a symbol for a predator and a directive to escape. The "rough grunting" of chimpanzees announces the discovery of food and also invites others to come and share. This incorporation of noun and verb functions in the same indivisible signal greatly limits the possibilities of syntactical rearrangement of sounds to create new messages.

The substitution of categorical for continuous processing of speech sounds may have directly facilitated the introduction of syntax as a radical innovation in primate communication. Once having accomplished the assemblage of discrete clusters of elements or words by recombinations of the same limited set of minimal sound segments, it is a natural step to recombine words in new ways. The two kinds of recombination may even employ similar kinds of physiological processes.

If this line of theorizing is correct, the introduction of auditory templates into the perception and development of speech at a critical stage in human evolution not only led to speech development by vocal imitation and the segmentation of continuously varying speech sounds, but also prepared the way for the syntactical openness that made our speech such a powerful force in social evolution. The comparative studies I have reviewed suggest that speech arose not just from a general increase in human intellectual capacity, but from a distinctive concatenation of specific physiological abilities on the one hand, and behavioral and ecological opportunities on the other, pressing the exploitation of these abilities to the utmost. Though human in detail, none of the basic physiological mechanisms is in principle unique to man. Perhaps what was lacking in other species was the coincidence between the appropriate physiological equipment and the right ecological opportunity, provided in the human case by the competitive force of the discovery and exploitation of tools in cooperative hunting. This constituted an ecological revolution as radical as that which followed the evolution of air-breathing lungs or the cleidoic egg. Developments in speech and in tool making must have interacted synergistically, with the advances in conceptual thought that speech made possible playing a direct role, as in the use of tools to make tools [Hewes, this volume; Lieberman, this volume]. With such immediate and fruitful applications, selective forces for new patterns of vocal behavior must have been strong. Functions that may initially have been simple, perhaps to mark local populations distinctively with learned behaviors, as in birds [Nottebohm, 1969; Nottebohm and Selander, 1972; Baker, in press], will quickly have been supplemented by other functions. Examples would be the naming of new objects or operations and recalling and discoursing about them in their absence while freed, by increasingly complex social organization, from the overwhelming need for quick, incisive individual action that is such a severe constraint on the communication systems of animals. The emergence of syntax achieved a new level of signaling complexity, far beyond anything evolved by animals, perhaps the culmination of the train of changes initiated by the evolution of modifiable auditory templates for the processing and development of speech.

References

Aldrich-Blake, F. P. G. 1970. Problems of social structure in forest monkeys. In *Social Behavior in Birds and Mammals*, J. H. Crook (ed.). New York: Academic Press.

Baker, M. C. In press. Song dialects and genetic differences in white-crowned sparrows (*Zonotrichia leucophrys*). *Evolution*.

Bentley, D. R. and R. R. Hoy. 1972. Genetic control of the neuronal network generating cricket (*Teleogryllus gryllus*) song patterns. *Anim. Behav.*, 20: 478–492.

Campbell, B. 1972. Man for all seasons. In *Sexual Selection and the Descent of Man, 1871–1971*, B. Campbell (ed.). Chicago: Aldine.

Chomsky, N. 1965. *Aspects of the Theory of Syntax*. Cambridge, Mass.: MIT Press.

Cutting, J. E. and Eimas, P. D. Phonetic feature analyzers and the processing of speech in infants. This volume.

Doty, R. W. 1968. Neural organization of deglutition. In *Handbook of Physiology—Alimentary Canal IV Motility*, C. F. Code (ed.). Washington, D.C.: Am. Physiol. Soc.

Eimas, P. D. In press. Speech perception in early infancy. In *Infant Perception*, L. B. Cohen and P. Salapatek (eds.). New York: Academic Press.

Eimas, P. D., E. R. Siqueland, P. Jusczyk, and J. Vigorito, 1971. Speech perception in infants. *Science*, 171: 303–306.

Gautier, J-P. In press. Field and laboratory studies of the vocalizations of talapoin monkeys (*Miopithecus talapoin*). *Behaviour*.

Gautier, J-P. and A. Gautier-Hion. 1969. Les associations polyspecifiques chez les Cercopithecidae du Gabon. *La Terre et la vie*, 2: 164–201.

Gottlieb, G. 1971. *Development of Species Identification in Birds*. Chicago: University of Chicago Press.

Green, S. In press. Communication by a graded vocal system in Japanese monkeys. In *Primate Behavior*, L. Rosenblum (ed.). New York: Academic Press.

Hewes, G. Comments on Mattingly's paper and on Levallois flake tools. This volume.

Hill, W. C. O. and A. H. Booth. 1957. Voice and larynx in African and Asiatic colobinae. *J. Bombay Nat. Hist. Soc.*, 54: 309–321.

Jakobson, R., C. G. M. Fant, and M. Halle. 1952. *Preliminaries to Speech Analysis*. Cambridge, Mass: MIT Press.

Kawanaka, K. 1973. Intertroop relationships among Japanese monkeys. *Primates*, 14: 113–159.

Kewley-Port, D. and M. S. Preston, 1974. Early apical stop production: a voice onset time analysis. *J. Phonetics*, 2: 195–210.

Kimura, D. 1961. Cerebral dominance and the perception of verbal stimuli. *Canad. J. Psychol.*, 15: 166–171.

Kimura, D. 1964. Left-right differences in the perception of melodies. *Q. J. Exp. Psychol.*, 16: 355–358.

Konishi, M. 1963. The role of auditory feedback in the vocal behavior of the domestic fowl. *Z. f. Tierpsychol.*, 20: 349–367.

Konishi, M. 1964. Effects of deafening on song development in two species of juncos. *Condor*, 66: 85–102.

Konishi, M. 1965. The role of auditory feedback in the control of vocalization in the white-crowned sparrow. *Z. f. Tierpsychol.*, 22: 770–783.

Konishi, M. 1970. Comparative neurophysiological studies of hearing and vocalization in songbirds. *Z. vergl. Physiol.*, 66: 257–272.

Lawick-Goodall, J. van, 1968a. A preliminary report on expressive movements and communication in the Gombe Stream chimpanzees. In *Primates: Studies in Adaptation and Variability*, P. Jay (ed.). New York: Holt, Rinehart and Winston.

Lawick-Goodall, J. van, 1968b. The behavior of free-living chimpanzees in the Gombe Stream Reserve. *Anim. Beh. Monogr.* 1.

Lawick-Goodall, J. van, 1971. *In the Shadow of Man*. London: Collins.

Lieberman, P. The evolution of speech and language. This volume.

Lisker, L. and A. S. Abramson. 1967. Some effects of context on voice onset time in English stops. *Lang. Speech,* 10: 1–28.

Lorenz, K. 1935. Der Kumpan in der Umwelt des Vogels. *J. Ornithol.,* 83: 137–213, 289–413.

Lorenz, K. 1950. The comparative method in studying innate behavior patterns. *Symp. Soc. Exp. Biol.,* 4: 221–268.

Marler, P. 1961. The logical analysis of animal communication. *J. Theoret. Biol.,* 1: 295–317.

Marler, P. 1969a. *Colobus quereza:* territoriality and group composition. *Science,* 163: 93–95.

Marler, P. 1969b. Vocalizations of wild chimpanzees. *Rec. Adv. Primatol.,* 1: 94–100.

Marler, P. 1970a. Vocalizations of East African monkeys. I. Red colobus. *Folia Primat.,* 13: 81–91.

Marler, P. 1970b. Birdsong and speech development: could there be parallels? *Am. Sci.,* 58: 669–673.

Marler, P. 1970c. A comparative approach to vocal development: song learning in the white-crowned sparrow. *J. Comp. Physiol. Psychol.,* 71: no. 2, part 2, 1–25.

Marler, P. 1972. Vocalizations of East African monkeys. II. Black and white colobus. *Behaviour,* 42: 175–197.

Marler, P. 1973a. A comparison of vocalizations of red-tailed monkeys and blue monkeys *Cercopithecus ascanius* and *C. mitis* in Uganda. *Z. f. Tierpsychol.,* 33: 223–247.

Marler, P. 1973b. Learning, genetics and communication. *Social Research,* 40: 293–310.

Marler, P. and L. Hobbet. In press. Individuality in long range vocalization of wild chimpanzees. *Z. f. Tierpsychol.*

Mattingly, I. G. 1972. Speech cues and sign stimuli. *Am. Sci.,* 60: 327–337.

McNeill, D. 1966. Developmental psycholinguistics. In *The Genesis of Language,* F. Smith and G. A. Miller (eds.). Cambridge, Mass.: MIT Press.

Milligan, M. and J. Verner. 1971. Interpopulation song dialect discrimination in the white-crowned sparrow. *Condor,* 73: 208–213.

Miyadi, D. 1965. Social life of Japanese monkeys. In *Science in Japan,* A. H. Livermore (ed.). Washington, D.C.; Am. Ass. Adv. Sci.

Moynihan, M. 1970. Control, suppression, decay, disappearance and replacement of displays. *J. Theor. Biol.,* 29: 85–112.

Mulligan, J. A. 1966. Singing behavior and its development in the song sparrow, *Melospiza melodia.* University of California, Berkeley, Publications in Zoology, 81: 1–76.

Nottebohm, F. 1969. The song of the chingolo, *Zonotrichia capensis,* in Argentina: description and evaluation of a system of dialects. *Condor,* 71: 299–315.

Nottebohm, F. 1971. Neural lateralization of vocal control in a passerine bird. I. Song. *J. Exp. Zool.,* 177: 229–262.

Nottebohm, F. 1972a. The origins of vocal learning. *Amer. Nat.,* 106: 116–140.

Nottebohm, F. 1972b. Neural lateralization of vocal control in a passerine bird. II. Subsong, calls, and a theory of vocal learning. *J. Exp. Zool.,* 179: 35–50.

Nottebohm, F. and M. Nottebohm, 1971. Vocalizations and breeding behaviour of surgically deafened ring doves, *Streptopelia risoria. Anim. Behav.,* 19: 313–328.

Nottebohm, F. and R. K. Selander. 1972. Vocal dialects and gene frequencies in the chingolo sparrow (*Zonotrichia capensis*). *Condor,* 74: 137–143.

Struhsaker, T. T. 1969. Correlates of ecology and social organization among African cercopithecines. *Folia primat.,* 11: 8–118.

Struhsaker, T. T. 1970. Phylogenetic implications of some vocalizations of Cercopithecus monkeys. In *Old World Monkeys,* J. R. Napier and P. H. Napier (eds.). New York: Academic Press.

Struhsaker, T. T. In press. *Behavior and Ecology of Red Colobus Monkeys.* Chicago: University of Chicago Press.

Struhsaker, T. T. and J. F. Oates. In press. Comparison of the behavior and ecology of red colobus and black and white colobus monkeys in Uganda; a summary.

Talmage-Riggs, G., P. Winter, D. Ploog, and W. Mayer, 1972. Effect of deafening on the vocal behavior of the squirrel monkey (*Saimiri sciureus*). *Folia primat.,* 17: 404–420.

Teleki, G. 1973. *The Predatory Behavior of Wild Chimpanzees.* Lewisburg, Penna: Bucknell University Press.

Washburn, S. L. (ed.). 1971. *Social Life of Early Man.* New York: Wenner Gren Foundation.

Wilson, D. W. 1972. Genetic and sensory mechanisms for locomotion and orientation in animals. *Am. Sci.,* 60: 358–365.

Winter, P., D. Ploog, and J. Latta. 1966. Vocal repertoire of the squirrel monkey (*Saimiri sciureus*). Its analysis and significance. *Exp. Brain Res.,* 1: 359–384.

Wood, C. C. 1973. Levels of processing in speech perception: neurophysiological and information-processing analyses. Unpubl. Ph.D. thesis. Yale University.

Wood, C. C., W. R. Goff, and R. S. Day, 1971. Auditory evoked potentials during speech perception. *Science,* 173: 1248–1251.

Comments on Marler's Paper

PETER C. REYNOLDS

Laboratory workers may not realize how important the acoustic communication of nonhuman primates can sometimes be. However, if you try to observe primates in a rain forest, the undergrowth is so thick that most of the contact you get with the animals is through their vocalization. I never appreciated the need for acoustic classifications until I found myself in a situation where sounds were pretty much all of the social information available to me. The problems of making visual contact are probably experienced by the monkeys themselves, since their eyes are very similar to ours. With arboreal monkeys, the acoustic communication may normally function in isolation from other communicative channels. This is in contrast to macaques and other terrestrial monkeys, where a purely acoustic classification system may be less satisfactory.

One of the most interesting things to come out of these spectrogram classifications is that the systems segregate by ecological niche and social organization rather than by taxonomy. The acoustic signals of the black and white colobus and the red colobus are very different from each other, yet these two species are in the same morphological genus. Another contrast would be the gibbon and the chimpanzee. Although both are apes, they are about as different as different can be in terms of their social organization, and I imagine gibbon communication would be more like that of the black and white colobus. I would like to see Peter Marler expand his chart (Table 1) to include more species, especially those that would be good test cases, like the squirrel monkey. This generalization is good news to the language origin theorist. It suggests that we should focus our attention on the changes in social organization that characterized hominids and not get too depressed by the absence of homologs of linguistic communication in man's closest relatives.

Another interesting point which was stressed is the role of individual variation in communication. In our eagerness to classify, we have tended to ignore this. Yet when you get to know a monkey group well, you eventually learn which vocalizations go with which individuals. Who says it is a major determinant of how it is responded to. Some individuals, for example, who are known to be nervous nellies, consistently have their alarm barks ignored. The social organization of monkeys is not reducible to age, sex, and rank categories. Propinquity and kinship affiliations determine who associates with whom, and these associative networks in turn determine how groups fission and combine. If, as has been claimed, the pragmatics and the semantics of animal communication are identical, so that the meaning of a message is not discriminable from its effect on other individuals, then "who calls" is an important factor in the interpretation of the call, and must be included in the description. It is known that individual recognition has an important place in the communication of certain birds, and we should not be surprised to find it in primates.

Marler has distinguished between graded and discrete call systems. Ultimately, the "psychological reality" of such classifications will have to be assessed. Capranica [1969] assesses this in bullfrog communication, but directly analogous experiments are impossible in primates because of their reluctance to respond to tape recordings in any repeatable way, although it may be possible with visual signals [MacLean, 1964]. However, single-cell electrode work may give us some information [Wollberg and Newman, 1972], and it may be possible to use cognitive tests to tap the animal's classificatory system, such as same-difference discrimination learning sets, utilizing both natural and modified cells as discriminanda. One reason for doing such experiments is that a graded system does not necessarily imply graded percepts. If one examined the spectrograms of human speech, one would see continuous intergrading of categories, at least to the naive observer. Yet there is a great deal of evidence that people in fact do not hear analogic signals but segment them on the basis of discrete criteria. In any case, on the basis of superficial similarity, it seems likely that human speech evolved from an acoustic system that was more like that of contemporary macaques and chimpanzees than like that of the black and white colobus.

The reluctance of monkeys to answer tape recorders brings me to another issue: the place of rationality in primate communication. The response of a primate to a call is not simply a function of the innate characteristics of the call but appears to involve a great deal of additional information: who said it, the hearer's relationship to him, the circumstances in which it was uttered. What makes primate communication interesting, in my opinion, is that it is probably integrated with these advanced neural functions we like to think are reflected in the expansion of intrinsic neocortex. In sum, an adequate description involves us not only in stimulus and response but in the animal's knowledge of the world.

Now such an approach makes the descriptive task very much harder, but it also yields information that makes more sense. Green's analysis [in press] is interesting because it suggests that the "monkey's world" may also be encoded in the acoustic form of the vocalization. While the exact ordering of the behavioral contexts, as far as I know, is original with Green, all of the contexts themselves have been established as socially relevant ones by other investigators: the categories of infant versus adult, male versus female, estrous versus anestrous female, dominant versus subordinate, mother versus child, consort versus nonconsort female, and separated versus nonseparated infant are all categories that have a long history in the study of macaques. This suggests that it may be possible to examine categories based on signal morphology and categories based on relevant social distinctions and relate the two in more meaningful taxonomies than has been done to date. Such a model may in fact be very close to a distinctive feature model of how or under what circumstances a particular combination of acoustic parameters or particular values of acoustic parameters are used.

Such close integration of signal properties with social categories is to be expected. In contrast to language, where the signal properties can be systematized independently of social categories, the systems of nonhuman primates are much less autonomized. In early language too—early in both a phylogenetic and ontogenetic sense—the system has less autonomy, and a linguistic description would presumably have to incorporate much more of what the linguist would call nonlinguistic contextual information. If the communication systems of nonhuman primates are less autonomous than language, the descriptions would have to include many distinctions that the linguist would categorize in the realm of paralinguistic and sociolinguistic phenomena. From an evolutionary point of view, the interesting thing to study is how communication that is highly dependent upon nonlinguistic context for interpretation of the signal comes to be less dependent upon it by providing internal communicative contexts. I think more detailed studies of context in monkeys may aid us here.

References

Capranica, R. R. 1969. A model system: vocalization in frogs. In *Primate Communication*, D. Ploog and T. Melnechuk (eds.). *Neurosciences Research Program Bulletin*, 7 (5): 427–436.

Green, S. In press. Communication by a graded vocal system in Japanese monkeys. In *Primate Behavior*, L. Rosenblum (ed.). New York: Academic Press.

MacLean, P. D. 1964. Mirror display in the squirrel monkey, *Saimiri sciureus*, *Science*, 146: 950–952.

Wollberg, Z. and Newman, J. D. 1972. Auditory cortex of squirrel monkey: response patterns of single cells to species-specific vocalizations, *Science*, 175: 212–214.

Open Discussion of the Papers of Marler and Reynolds

The Sound Spectrograph as a Display Tool

The necessity of presenting *visual* transformation of *auditory* information is a very interesting one. In western cultures information-by-eye is much more trusted than is information-by-ear; for example, one may believe an eyewitness, but who would believe an earwitness? Scientific presentations are not exempt from this overwhelming trend, one which might be called visual chauvinism. Moreover, in a journal article or in a book such as this one, it is not feasible or practical to attach a tape recording or bind a record into the pages of the text. Thus, when one writes an article about a subject in which auditory information plays a primary role, he or she is forced to transform that auditory diaplay into a visual display. Peter Marler has done so in his paper.

The particular visual display used by Marler is the sound spectrogram, and one could hardly imagine a better auditory-to-visual transform. The sound spectrograph, however, is an instrument which has unique and peculiar qualities: essentially, it was built to display the acoustic variation in the speech of adult male speakers with a low-frequency fundamental. The spectrogram is notoriously incapable of yielding a high-information acoustic display of a speaker with a relatively high fundamental. Philip Lieberman noted that this includes many men, most women, and all young children. If one insists that the hallmark of human speech is the existence of very rich spectral lines at intervals of about 100 Hz, the optimal characteristics for the sound spectrograph, about 80 percent of the human population would not have speech. Moreover, if the sound spectrogram is unjust to the bulk of the human population, it is likely to be more unjust to nonhuman populations and their vocal systems. Thus, one must take care in assuring that theoretical statements are not based primarily on the analysis of spectrograms.

Marler defended the use of the spectrograph as the best visual transform available, and emphasized that graded and discrete signaling systems in nonhuman primates are not based on spectrographic analysis, but are based on the social situations in which the calls occur [see also Green, in press]. However, Lieberman noted that graded continua particularly risk being linked too closely to the spectrograph. Because humans may not be able to hear precise differences between certain primate calls, we may then look to the spectrograph for supportive evidence. The graded nature of some visual transforms may be an artifact of the limitations of the display device. Thus, our ears and our machines may trick us into falsely categorizing a signaling system as being graded. Marler responded with assurance that graded and discrete call systems sound different to the trained human ear, and that they are used by different primate groups in readily observable, socially different ways.

Sexual Dimorphism

The vocal tract of the adult male human is typically somewhat longer than that of the adult female, and his fundamental frequency averages about an octave lower because of the growth of the thyroid cartilage. Alvin Liberman asked Marler if such differences occur in nonhuman primates as well. Marler noted that sex differences in fundamental frequency are common. For example, female colobus monkeys pant-hoot at a higher pitch than males, and thus appear to operate in a different register just as in humans. Nevertheless, the differences are probably not as great. As for vocal tract length, there does not appear to be any direct evidence. Certainly in some primates the differences in vocal apparatus are quite clear. The males of several varieties of *Cercopithecus* develop large, accessory, prethoracic vocal sacks, while the females do not.

Philip Lieberman suggested that one approximation of vocal tract differences is the difference between male and female body weight. In humans, adult males tend to be 4 to 12 percent heavier than adult females, and their vocal tract lengths appear to be related in a similar proportion. These two percentages do not appear to be indicative of the range found in different genetic pools, but appear to be two different modes. Certain people appear to belong to the 4 percent group, such as those of Southeast Asia, whereas others belong to the 12 percent group, such as those of most areas of the United States. Sex differences in the body weight of nonhuman primates appear to vary from about 2 percent for the gibbon to perhaps 15 percent for the baboon. Marler noted that, in general, sexual dimorphism in body weight occurs often in primates who live in large groups, who are terrestrial, and who use graded call systems, but may not occur for arboreal primates who live in small groups and use discrete calling systems.

Auditory and Visual Signaling Systems Together

Gordon Hewes asked Marler if there was any correlation between graded and discrete call systems and the extent to which the different call-system users have facial mask stereotypy. Marler suggested that there might be, and noted that the mandrills are an interesting case with respect to this point. They are members of the macaque lineage which have gone back to the forest to some extent. Presumably they reentered the forest with bare faces. Because eye contact is so limited in the dense foliage of the forest, they appear to have developed bizarre coloration on the face to aid in communication by sight. This bizarre coloration might be regarded as a discrete communication device, unlike the plastic and graded facial gestures which are used by the chimpanzee.

Marler speculated that the development of visual signaling systems may be stronger in those species which tend toward large groups, possibly also toward terrestriality and graded vocal signaling. When one watches monkeys in the wild, he finds that the first reaction to a vocalization by one of the members of a troup is for the others to look at it. The impression is that their subsequent behavior is as much modulated by what they see as by what they hear. Perhaps where visual and auditory systems work in concert at a close range there is a much reduced likelihood of error in the perception of the signal, or there is opportunity for more refined information.

Later, Ira Hirsh commented that auditory and visual signals interact in human communication all the time. For example, if one can watch the face of a speaker whom he otherwise cannot quite understand, word intelligibility increases dramatically. Lipreading is quite obviously a help for the near deaf.

Reference

Green, S. In press. Communication by a graded vocal system in Japanese monkeys. In *Primate Behavior*, L. Rosenblum (ed.). New York: Academic Press.

Symbols Inside and Outside of Language

DAVID PREMACK

The meat begging of the wild chimpanzee resembles preverbal requests in the child, a parallel which might encourage a sanguine interventionist to suppose that with human tutelage the chimp could be taught some degree of language. It is a small datum from which to extrapolate, however. Especially as the begging goes on in the presence of meat, the behavior tells more about communication than about representational processes. If, in requesting meat, the chimp were to draw a picture in the air (with its finger) of the animal being eaten—and perhaps accompany the picture with vocal imitations of the species' alarm call—this would be a richer commentary on representational processes. Yet even this might be dismissed as merely an iconic representation, a process which, according to some experts, is categorically different from the arbitrary symbolization that underlies language.

The whole topic of representational process or symbolization is in a highly unsatisfactory state and seems likely to remain so until some relevant operational criteria are provided. The emphasis must be on relevant, of course, since operationism alone will not cure anything. On what basis do we decide that the subject is using one item to stand for another and how do we measure the degree to which the representation is iconic as opposed to arbitrary?

In the context of our artificial language [Premack, 1971], the main question translates, When is a piece of plastic a word? The standard answer is that a piece of plastic is a word when it is used as a word. An item is a word when it is used in grammatically appropriate locations on semantically appropriate occasions. For instance, we may begin to suspect that a small blue triangular piece of plastic is the name for apple if (1) it is used consistently when the subject requests apple—for example, "Mary give Sarah apple"—as opposed to other fruits, and (2) it is the answer given when the experimenter points to an apple and asks, "What is the name of that?" and so on. These questions do not comprise an exhaustive test but are of the kind that can be used to get at the issue of use. In addition, we can obtain a second kind of evidence, corroborative of the first kind, by giving the subject only the putative word and asking it to describe the referent of the word. For example, we have given Sarah (a language-trained female chimpanzee), and more recently Elizabeth and Peony (new chimpanzee language trainees), a small blue triangle and asked them to match it to one member in each such pair of alternatives as: red versus green, round versus square, square-with-a-stem versus square-without-a-stem, and so on. On these tests they consistently assigned to the word all the features they independently assigned to the referent [Premack, 1971]. It would be a mistake to interpret this concordance as indicating confusion between word and referent. Not only do they not try to eat the word, but Sarah, the only one so far tested in this manner, passed a formal test on the distinction between word and referent. When told on some trials "Sarah insert cracker (in) dish," and on other trials "Sarah insert name of cracker (in) dish," she responded appropriately, putting a cracker in the dish on one occasion, an appropriate piece of plastic on the other [Premack, 1975].

Results from tests like those above are highly encouraging with regard to the chimpanzee's ability to use arbitrary items in wordlike ways. But they are of little help in assessing the animal's capacity for symbolization before language training is begun. To realize that objective we need tests that can be applied at an earlier stage. Ideally we need observations on field behavior of a kind that could hint strongly as to the species' representational capacities.

We can justify the hope for such evidence by joining a number of others in assuming that symbolization is not confined to language but occurs broadly. There is no difficulty in finding adherents of this view or would-be examples of the behavior. Piaget and Inhelder [1971], for example, discuss symbolic play in the child. Kohts [1937] reported similar behavior in her own child, the representation being somewhat more abstract since, not dolls as in the Piaget-Inhelder examples, but large and small sticks were used to stand for the child's father and mother respectively. But it is in Freud that all restrictions on the possibilities for nonlinguistic symbolization are lifted. In his theory of dreams, he attempts to tease out what today would be commended as the rules by which one element may stand for some combination of other elements [Freud, 1943]. Dreams are not separated off from other experience in Freud but are joined to all other experience; for it is not only in dreams that one element can stand for other elements, but every act, verbal and nonverbal, is accorded this capacity. The difficulty in Freud, for even a part-time operationist, is that ultimately there are no nonsymbols.

Suppose that symbolic play were observed in wild chimpanzees. As matters stand there are few if any such reports. Kohts, for example, looked closely at her one animal and though obviously ever-hopeful of finding such behavior found none. Nevertheless, suppose that the failure proved to be technical—Kohts's scrutiny fell only upon one animal—and that selective attention to an appropriate sample of wild chimpanzees disclosed incontrovertible evidence of symbolic play. To what extent would this entitle the view that chimpanzees can be taught some degree of language? On the surface, the finding would seem highly encouraging. Words— names of objects, agents, and actions—refer, and thus presuppose a representational process. If they did not we could not have sentences, at least not those of a kind with which we are familiar. Yet what evidence do we have that the representational process in the linguistic and nonlinguistic cases are the same or even similar? Specifically, when we say in the context of the child's play that *doll stands for father,* and in the context of its speech that *"doll" stands for doll,* does the critical phrase "stands for" have the same meaning in the two claims?

This question can be answered only insofar as the criteria applied in the two cases are the same. And in attempting to answer the question the first thing we find is that the criteria which serve nicely in the case of language—which clearly tell us when a piece of plastic is a word—are of doubtful value outside of language. They deal on the one hand with how a word is used, and on the other with the subject's ability to describe the referent of a word from the word alone. One has only to try applying these criteria outside of language to appreciate the difficulty.

Let us bypass dreams, however reluctantly, and concentrate upon play only because it is more amenable to uncomplicated observation. Although there is already a tradition which finds the origins of language in play [for example, De Laguna, 1963; Bateson, 1968; Reynolds, 1972], and some of the arguments are compelling, I am not sure any of them harden into serviceable criteria. For example, can we say of any item in play that it either is or is not used in an appropriate position in a sequence of items and is used on semantically appropriate occasions? A judgment of this kind presupposes, first, a syntax of play, and second, that the main function of play is or can be the same as that of language—communication of nonlinguistic states of affairs. One need not deny the possibility of a grammar of play, in order to reject the burden of working it out. Yet it is clear that nothing short of this will serve. The criteria that serve to identify symbols in language can be applied in nonlanguage only if the apparatus which the criteria presuppose—grammar and semantic functions—are also found in nonlanguage.

In addition, all the possible symbols we are likely to encounter outside of language will be heavily iconic in one way or another, rendering the second criterion nil. When the subject is able to describe the referent in the presence of the word alone, it is noteworthy, exactly because word and referent are not physically alike, any more than are, say, an apple and a small blue triangle. But outside of language, all symbols and referents will be physically similar, making the ability to describe the one given the other inconsequential. In effect, the criteria which serve so well in language will be useless in play and presumably other nonlinguistic domains as well. If we are to retain our objective we must find other criteria. But the new criteria cannot be relevant merely to nonlanguage symbols as the old criteria are not, or are not in an untroubled way. Comparison between symbols inside and outside of language is possible only if the new criteria are relevant to both cases. We turn to the pursuit of such a criterion.

Magic Circles

In considering the general relation between language and prelanguage structures, we have recently studied specifically the relation between the subject's likelihood of engaging in a behavior, its preference for the behavior, and the ease with which it can subsequently be taught names for the behavior. Elsewhere we have noted the correspondence between Elizabeth's preference for washing, cutting, and inserting, and the comparable order in which she learned names for these acts [Premack, 1975]. Another of the cases studied involves the contrast between *in, on,* and *under.* Recent data from children indicate that they acquire these prepositions in a definite order [Clark, 1974]. Between the ages of two and four, children are reported to respond more accurately to instructions involving "in," next most to "on" and least accurately to those involving "under." But the interpretation given these data is marred by the absence of a control: what is the probability that the child will carry out an act of *in, on,* or *under* independent of verbal instruction? If these probabilities are equal then the obtained outcome could be attributed to linguistic factors. But if they are not equal, then attempts to explain the data on linguistic grounds confront the problem of prelinguistic response biases. Moreover, the data we have recently obtained with the chimps strongly suggest that the corresponding response dispositions in children are unlikely to be equal.

We tested both Elizabeth and Peony for their preferences regarding *in, on,* and *under.* A small desk top was placed on the work table along with the subject, who customarily sat on the table while carrying out her lesson. There was ample space under the desk top as well as a bowl on top of it. The subjects were given a variety of familiar objects—clay, chalk, keys, toy animals, and so on—one at a time and allowed to place the object where they chose. In two sessions of this kind, Elizabeth put objects *in* the bowl, *on* the desk, and *under* the desk the following number of times: 12, 8, and 0. Corresponding figures for Peony were 9, 4, and 0.

Given these data, one can ask either of two questions. One is our original question, How readily will the subject learn linguistic markers for *in, on* and *under?* which we have continued to explore in a variety of cases. But there is also another quite different question: What is the basis of these preferences? Why is the animal apparently more interested in putting things in a container than in putting them under a structure?

In a first attempt to understand the subject's predilection for *in,* we left the bowl on the desk and with a piece of chalk added a circle, four inches in diameter, on the desk top. Both subjects inspected the circle, using tongues first, fingers next, which seems to be the customary receptor-order at least in young laboratory chimps. The inspection over, the circle proved to have for Elizabeth almost as much motive force as the bowl. Given the same objects as were used in the first test, Elizabeth put them in the bowl, in the circle, on the desk (but not in the circle), and under the desk the following number of times: 10, 20, 0, and 0. Peony found the circle less compelling; for her the corresponding figures were 20, 0, 2, and 8. This phase of the study is now continuing with variation in shape (for example, circle versus square), size, and location of both the bounded space and of the test objects.

In a second approach to this problem we drew a chalk circle, not on the desk top but in the center of the chimp's home cage, larger than the first one, approximately 3½ feet in diameter. All other movable objects were removed from the cage, and the chimp was brought back to the cage and observed there for a 10- to 15-minute period. Peony's behavior consisted largely of tasting the circle, either bending over and licking the chalk directly or sniffing and tasting her fingers after first rubbing them on the chalk. But after one session she began to use the circle in other ways. She placed herself inside it, some of the time just sitting there staring up at the trainer. But other times she rolled about, made sweeping motions on the floor with her arms, and scratched herself all over.

Elizabeth "used" the circle from the second session. On the first session, she too inspected the circle, mainly by direct licking, after which she ignored it. On the second session, she responded in a way that is best conveyed by the observer's notes. ". . . licked the circle after being in the cage 1½ minutes, but then ignored it until the 11th minute. Sitting on the table doing heavy breathing, though very calm, then suddenly jumped into the middle of the circle, rubbing all around herself (in a circle) with the back of her hands. Then sat down in circle for maybe 5 seconds (calm again) ; then started rubbing again. Total time in circle 35 seconds; then she got up and walked away like nothing had happened." Table 1 gives the duration each animal has seated itself inside the circle in the nine sessions so far given.

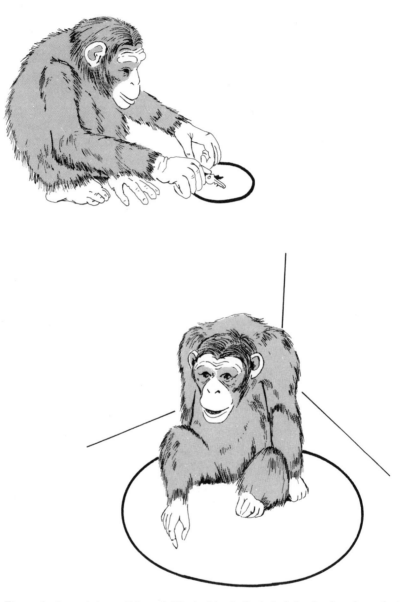

Figure 1. An artist's rendition of Elizabeth's chalk-circle behavior based on photographs.

Table 1. Time Spent in Circle in Home Cage

	Time in Circle (sec)	Session Time (min)
Elizabeth	3	6
	45	15
	3	20
	5	15
	15	15
	22	15
	23	15
	3	15
	17	15
Peony	0	6
	21	10
	6	15
	205	15
	40	15
	156	15
	65	15
	78	15
	52	15

There are two principal relations that we would like to understand. First, what if any is the relation between putting an object into a circle and putting oneself into a circle? Second, what is the similarity between that relation (between nonlinguistic entities) and the relation between a linguistic entity, sentence or word, and its designated state of affairs or referent? The two cases cannot be identical if only because of the wide differences in social purpose that are served by play and speech. Yet both cases may involve a representational process, and the question is whether the processes in the linguistic and nonlinguistic cases have anything in common.

Substitutability
In a less interesting though more neutral context we have used a procedure that can be applied to the present question [Jacobson and Premack, 1970]. The subjects were rats, and the responses were turning a running wheel in a clockwise and counterclockwise direction. The question was simply, to what degree are these two acts alike? In the mind of the human observer they are very alike, though partly perhaps because of the labels he applies to them. Are they equally alike in the mind of the rat?

To measure response similarity from the point of view of the actor rather than the observer, we defined similarity in terms of substitutability. We identified one or more functions in which an act A can be either an independent variable, a dependent variable, or both. After determining the effect of A upon itself, we determined the effect of a second response B upon A. If the two events have the same effects, then at least for the function in question, B is completely substitutable for A and the two acts are equivalent. The effect of B may be different from that of A in magnitude, sign, or both; then one can determine the effects of C and make at least ordinal statements about the similarity between A, B, and C. Similarity may be complicated by the fact that events are not mutually substitutable in like amount in all functions, but that is not a problem we need cope with here.

In the rat study we measured similarity with both a choice and habituation measure—and found them to give comparable results—but for present purposes the latter alone will suffice. Habituation concerns the effect of one member of a response class upon other members of the same class. The effect of eating upon eating is a classical example. Ultimately, as is well known, the effect is decremental, although there is an initial incremental transient, which shows up as a short ascending arm in a rate-time plot, a kind of appetizer effect. In the rat study, we first determined the effect of clockwise running upon itself and that of counterclockwise running upon itself. Next we determined the effect of each upon the other. In brief, one direction of running was found to be about 50 percent substitutable for the other, and the effect was roughly symmetrical. Eight minutes worth of counterclockwise running produced about 50 percent of the change that eight minutes worth of clockwise running produced in itself, and vice versa. In a second step, by arranging for both directions of running to produce an equal opportunity to drink, we answered a further question, What is the effect of a common "goal" upon different responses? Similarity increased notably: the two directions of running were then about 90 percent substitutable for each other.

Are putting objects in a circle and putting oneself in a circle functionally related? Presumably these acts will habituate like essentially all acts. If so, we can ask whether putting an object in a circle will reduce the tendency to put oneself in a circle and vice versa. If the frequencies of these acts do covary, so that one can be substituted for the other, we can determine the degree of their substitutability, and also, whether the substitution is symmetrical; for the effect of A on B need not be the same as that of B on A. We will need at least one other act as a control. A positive outcome will require not only that putting an object in a circle substitutes in part for putting oneself in a circle, but also, that the substitution effect is greater than it is for, say, putting the same object *on* a surface or *under* a surface, and so on.

Even if putting oneself in a circle and putting an object in a circle proved to covary, so that either could partially substitute for the other, we are not likely to rest content. Both acts will remain mysterious until we can relate them to some other act of more obvious biological significance. The patent candidate in the present case is *nesting*. Chimps in the wild build a nest each night and sometimes also in the day for a nap. The chimp seats itself in the crotch of a tree and then knits the branches below itself into a more or less circular mat. Elizabeth had no opportunity to nest, and her rubbing and circular thrashing about with her arms *may* be analogous to the seizing of branches which ordinarily would lie about her if the bounded space in which she placed herself were not concrete and chalk but the crotch of a tree. Of course, at this time we do not know whether there is any underlying biological act that will demystify the chimpanzee's tendency to seat itself excitedly in a chalk circle (or whether nesting is the specific demystifier). The mystery may simply have to be tolerated, or pursued along entirely different lines. But at least we know how to answer the question. Substitutability can be applied in this case too. Will a wild chimp with abundant opportunity to nest also seat itself excitedly in chalk circles?

Before leaving this topic consider an alternative to the explanation in terms of nesting behavior. One might wish to regard all explanations given in terms of biologically significant acts as a kind of myth with which we deceive ourselves, and the legitimate explanation as lying in a set of (blind) perceptual principles. One could say that with such myths we conceal from ourselves the fact that we are more robotlike than is comfortably considered. For example, the principle applicable to the present case might be, roughly: always enter a bounded versus an unbounded space, and take the center rather than the edge of that space. If the space were also bounded on the vertical, the organism might be led to go to the edge of the horizontally bounded space, but we need not be concerned with the accuracy or details of the principle at this time, only with the way in which explanation of this general kind differs from the usual kind. Given such a principle, we would regard it, and not the act of nesting, as the primary determining force. Both nesting and the chalk-circle behavior would be seen as instances of the perceptual principle. Perhaps we could differentiate between the biological and perceptual explanations by determining which parameters were the more forceful in controlling behavior. The substitution effects between nesting and chalk-circle behavior might not be symmetrical; if the effect of nesting on chalk-circle behavior were stronger than the reverse, this might be considered to favor the biological explanation. On the other hand, if per-

ceptual parameters were the main determinants, so that chalk-circle behavior took priority over nesting whenever the chalk formed a more per-
fect circle than the nest, this would seem to favor the perceptual account.
Also in favor of the latter is the fact that such principles use only physical
terms and therefore attain a higher level of abstraction than principles
stated in terms of biological or psychological parameters.

Notice that we do not equate substitutability with symbolization but
make a substantially weaker claim. If X stands for Y then each will be
substitutable for the other to a degree greater than if X did not stand
for Y. (We formulate it this way rather than compare the intended effect
with a base level of substitutability, for at this time we cannot assert that
the base level of substitutability is zero or that it is not produced by other
relations than "stands for.") The claim is that if two items stand in the
relation of symbol and referent, they will be mutually, though not necessarily symmetrically, substitutable in the habituation function, and this
holds both and perhaps equally for linguistic and nonlinguistic cases.

Consider four objections to this claim. The first objection strikes at
the heart of the argument, questioning the relevance of the habituation
claim specifically to the linguistic case. The whole relation between speaking or reading about an act, or even thinking about it, and the act itself
needs clarification. The commonsense understanding of that relation certainly does not suggest that one can be substituted for the other, and
thus does not suggest that the habituation model is the appropriate one
to use in attempting to decide whether or not X is a symbol of Y. For
example, no one proposes to solve even temporary hunger by speaking,
reading, or thinking about food. Likewise one is not advised to solve sexual deprivation by symbolic means. In fact, it is usually supposed that
engaging in the symbolic version of an act will have a facilitative effect,
not a decremental one. Movies which depict sex and books which describe
it are held to be concupiscent; society has never objected to a book on
the grounds that if the husband or wife is allowed to read it, he or she
will be less likely to carry out his or her marital obligation. Nor has reading books or seeing movies that depict lavish eating scenes ever been proposed as a form of dieting.

Yet the very fact that participation in the symbolic version of X may
have a concupiscent effect upon X is itself highly suspicious, and, as such,
not incompatible with the habituation model. Many habituation functions
have an initial ascending arm. The first bite or even first few bites of
food increase rather than decrease the probability of subsequent eating.
Likewise the frequency probability function for sex is not a simple decreasing one. There is an ascending arm there, too, early members of

a series of sexual bouts increasing the probability of later members. Ultimately the function for eating, sex, and presumably all acts, are decreasing ones, the outcome we have in mind when speaking of habituation. But the initial facilitative effect of an act upon subsequent occurrences of the same act is apparently no less genuine, though it is less widely reported.

Now it may be possible to interpret the facilitative effect of symbolic acts upon real acts as an instance of the ascending arm of the curve—and to argue that if symbolic participation were carried out long enough the effect would become decremental. Then, taking commonsense evidence seriously—for it suggests that the effect is always concupiscent—it becomes a matter of explaining why the symbolic participation is always brief, never long enough to produce a decremental effect. Of course, it is unfortunate that we have no actual laboratory evidence as to the effect of an eating scene, visual or verbal, upon eating; or the corresponding effect in the case of sex. Incidentally, the apparent absence of such evidence in the case of sex is the more interesting in view of its clear relevance to the legal issues concerning pornography. But, if common sense is sustained by measurement, and the characteristic effect of symbolic participation is incremental, we would have to answer why.

The first thing that comes to mind is that typically we do not engage in symbolic participation for "long" intervals. There are several reasons for this. First, when we find ourselves made hungry by a symbolic act and are in an unrestricted environment we are likely to put down the book and return with an apple, sandwich, or whatever. We do not read the passage over and over—until the effect may become decremental—but quit the symbolic version to participate in the direct one. Second, the amount of material of a constant thematic kind put into a book or movie is calculated not to produce a decremental effect. True, the decremental effect the writer seeks to avoid is not that of the reader's participation in the direct version of the acts in question, but of a decrement in the reader's likelihood of continuing the book. Nevertheless, in carefully attempting to ward off the first effect, writers may indirectly prevent the second effect, that is, may never permit an amount of material sufficient to produce a decremental effect in the real act.

The thrust of the argument is thus twofold. In any symbolic act two processes go on concurrently. The first is the effect of the symbolic act upon itself; the second is its effect upon the real or nonsymbolic version of the act. Why do symbolic acts tend to have a concupiscent rather than soporific effect upon real acts? Because, even though the ultimate effect of a symbolic act upon a real one may be negative, the symbolic act habituates before occurring in sufficient amount to have a negative effect. To make this argument persuasive we need further to assume that the curves for the cases differ, that the habituation function is steeper for symbolic acts and/or has a shorter ascending arm.

The best proof of this argument would consist in actually showing that symbolic acts can have an habituative or decremental effect on real acts. To do this we must overcome the problem noted above and arrange for the symbolic act to occur often enough for its effect on the direct act to get beyond the ascending arm to the descending arm of the curve. This might be done by (a) rewarding the subject for engaging in the symbolic act more than it would otherwise, (b) punishing the subject for not engaging in the symbolic act, or (c) by using neither reward nor punishment but simply presenting a continually changing symbolic input, not one eating scene or one sexual scene but a series of different scenes. Changing the visual or written scene might reduce the habituation effect at the level of the symbolic act, and allow a sufficient cumulative buildup of symbolic participation to have a decremental effect upon the real act. In brief, we are arguing that if people would think more consecutively, whether about eating, sex, or anything else, thought could have a decremental effect upon the act represented in thought. As it is, thought and other forms of symbolic representation tend to have a concupiscent effect. But this positive effect, which is manifestly different from no effect, needs explanation and a possible one is that it represents the ascending arm of the habituation function.

The second objection is somewhat fanciful. It may be a mistake to view chalk-circle behavior as an isolated event. In man, events of this kind are likely to occur as part of a system, specifically as elements in myths. Chimpanzees do not have myths, which could be explained by the lack of language, or even ritual dance, which could not be so explained. They do attain extraordinary arousal levels, and on these occasions engage in rhythmic maneuvers which are both frightening and exciting to the human observer. In the field, they career down hillsides, drag uprooted trees behind them, brandish limbs, holler [Lawick-Goodall, 1965]. In the laboratory, where there may be nothing to uproot or brandish, the animal circles the periphery of the cage, faster and faster, drums on resonant surfaces, beats its chest, hollers, and may end up flinging itself at the front of the cage where the observer is standing.

One cannot observe the rhythmic ascending pattern of this behavior—which may grow from a few opening shuffles to an airborne leap ending in a spread-eagle landing—without speculating that in man, behavior of comparable intensity and recurrence would be a ritual dance, the visual or nonlinguistic enactment of a myth. And this may be true in primitive man. But it is apparently not true of modern man. For in him analogous scenes can be observed that appear to be as devoid of ritual significance as they are in the chimpanzee; as though now all basic symbolization in man were confined to language.

But what is the point of this digression? The point concerns what a myth is, the role it may play, and the bearing this could have on the substitutability argument. According to standard theory, myths are abstractions or simplified versions of key relations in the individual's social life, necessarily done up in a dramatic or expressive form. The role assigned to them is that of helping the individual discover the invariances in his life; as he participates in the myth he comes better to understand his own life, the key relations of which are symbolized by the myth. In view of the evident difficulty in testing such a theory, the lack of supporting or refuting evidence is no surprise.

To complete the argument let us now expand on nest building so as to pretend that it may not be a skimpy event in the chimp's life but a basic one, the chimp's instance, in fact, of the general concept *shelter*. Every species shelters itself in some fashion, either by occupying existing caves or cliffs, for example, the baboon; building elaborate and permanent houses, as does man; or by recurrently assembling a temporary nest, like the chimpanzee's. Let us assume that in all cases the event is replete with significance of a kind that will not be necessary to go into here. In a language-competent species we would anticipate that the basic role of shelter in an individual and group's life would be brought out in one or more myths.

Would we anticipate that the tendency to participate in such myths—to listen to them, watch their enactment in a drama, to be an actor in the drama—would be reduced by actual participation in the acts represented in the myths? For instance, which (hypothetical) chimp is more likely to participate in the shelter myth? Elizabeth, who has been cut off from nesting, or her identical twin, who has been living in the wild with every opportunity to nest? The answer varies depending on whether one views the symbol as an element in a system or as an isolated event; the myth theory applying in the first case, the habituation argument in the second. But even if chimps were to have not only symbols but also systems of symbols—which seems highly unlikely—the conflict in points of view may not be serious. Our tests will lift the symbol from its usual context. Isolated from other symbols with which it may normally form a system, the individual symbol will be cut off from whatever may be the basic function of myth or ritual dance, giving the operational definition a chance to work.

The third objection concerns the fact that in language, symbolization is asymmetric. "Apple" is used to stand for apple but not vice versa; whereas in the nonlinguistic domain, even though one act might be primary, each act is likely to stand for the other. For instance, putting oneself in a circle might have a greater effect upon putting objects in a circle than vice versa, yet if an effect could be shown in the one direction, it is almost certain to be shown in the other direction. How basic is the difference between the asymmetry of symbolization in language and its likely symmetry in nonlanguage?

Language is used for communication, whereas play (for lack of a better word) is not. The difference in question is more likely to be a consequence of that fact than of any difference in the representational process itself. We could test that claim in the laboratory, where, to get at the full scope of the representational process, we can arrange to use language in other than the usual ways. For example, suppose it is shown that sufficient participation in the linguistic representation of an act does reduce the likelihood of engaging in the act itself. We can then test the opposite effect. Participating in various acts may be found to affect, say, the recognition time for sentences which describe these acts; the initial effect being, one might guess, incremental, the ultimate effect decremental. In any case, the asymmetric use of symbols in language is a comment on the nature of communication, and does not itself establish that the representational process is any more asymmetric in language than in nonlanguage.

A fourth objection concerns the fact that symbols in language are arbitrary whereas in nonlanguage they are iconic. In fact, the sign-symbol distinction is at least partly misleading, for it is not difficult to reconstruct that distinction in terms of a continuum and to show, at least in principle, how easily the icon can slide into the nonicon. But that is too interesting a story to treat curtly, and here we have no need of the story at all, not even a shortened version. Instead, let us suppose that the traditional sign-symbol distinction is fully correct. The question still remains whether or not there are shared functional relations between the icon and its referent and the arbitrary symbol and its referent. That must be settled on operational grounds such as those proposed here. If the two relations prove to share properties, we may note that this is so despite the fact that the form of the relation is iconic in one case and noniconic in the other. Alternatively, a substantive demonstration of shared properties in the two cases may encourage us to reexamine the sign-symbol distinction.

The Question of Units

What units do we have in mind on the linguistic side, words or sentences, and what units on the nonlinguistic side? A part of the time we have spoken as though the unit in question were the word and its referent, but on other occasions, as though it were the sentence and its designated state of affairs. Actually, the unit per se is not critical; more important is the manner in which the language is *used*, though this does turn out to be an indirect consequence of the unit. For instance, we have speculated about the relation between, say, reading about eating and the subsequent likelihood of engaging in eating. When one reads he reads sentences, not words. Therefore, if language should prove to be substitutable for nonverbal behavior, the relation seems far more likely to hold at the level of the sentence than at the level of the word.

The argument is sound in one respect, yet misleading in another. It is sound in urging that the effect in question is most likely to be found when language is used at the level of the sentence, that is, in multiples of sentences units—paragraphs or stories—which is the normal level of use. But it is misleading in suggesting that because the sentence is the normal pragmatic unit, the effect could not be measured at the level of the word. In fact, the effect can be measured at any level we like provided the experiment is done properly.

Suppose we sought to examine the substitutability of the word "tomato" for tomato, or the word "blonde" for blonde. An improper or at least inadequate test would be one in which the subject was required to repeat "tomato" or "blonde" some predetermined number of times. In a proper test the subject would be required to read such sentences as, "John sliced the large red tomato into thick slices. . . . His friends called out for some; he gave handfuls to all of them. No one bothered to slice them. They munched them whole. . . ." Then we would examine the subject's tendency to eat specifically tomatoes, in contrast to foods not mentioned in the sentences. A similar test in the case of "blonde" would use that word in appropriate sentences, and would then examine the subject's tendency to behave sexually toward blondes in contrast to other categories not mentioned in the sentences. In brief, proper tests require the arrangement of stories which differ only in the individual words whose effect we want to test. The word is treated as a feature of the sentence or story, and the stories as minimal pairs.

Consider now applying the same minimal features approach to the nonlinguistic case. Putting oneself into a circle, putting an object into a circle, or building a nest are all units of behavior analogous to the sentence; an adequate description of each would require a sentence and not a word. More direct evidence for the parallel comes from the fact that each behavior sequence can be decomposed into independently manipulable parts in a manner logically analogous to the division of the sentence into its independently manipulable parts, or words. To evaluate the effect of single elements or wordlike units in the nonlinguistic case, we might resort to visual representations, pictures, and arrange minimal pairs with them. For example, the effect specific to agent would require contrasting pictures of, say, the subject putting itself into a circle versus another organism putting itself into the same circle. Corresponding contrasts could be made for the object, for example, putting oneself into a circle versus a square, as well as for the act, for example, putting oneself into a circle versus, say, urinating into the same circle.

The parallel between action or immediate experience and the linguistic representation of that experience brings out one last point of interest. Earlier we commented on the fact that words are used primarily in sentences rather than alone. Why? An answer is suggested by looking at actual experience. The primary unit of experience is the act—which is analogous to the sentence—and not the elements of acts. The elements of acts no more occur in isolation than do the words which are the names of the elements.

Recapitulation
This article deals with the claim that symbols inside and outside of language may share basic processes. We have provided no data to support the claim but an argument which, if equipped with appropriate data, would support the claim. Briefly, we have speculated about the relation between immediate experience and the linguistic representation of that experience, focusing on the possibility that to a degree each may be substitutable for the other. The likelihood of engaging in an act may be affected by experiencing the linguistic representation of the act. Conversely, the recognition time for a sentence, for example, may be affected by previous participation in the act designated by the sentence. The experimental paradigm for measurement of substitutability is thus based upon the habituation function and involves two steps: First, determining the effect of X upon itself and Y upon itself, and then determining the effect of each upon the other. There seems little question that any act, linguistic as well as nonlinguistic, will affect itself; initially perhaps incrementally—the appetizer effect—in the long run decrementally. The only real question—and one of theoretical interest—is the effect of "unlike" acts upon each other, specifically linguistic acts upon designated real acts and vice versa.

The argument is completed by raising the same question of substitutability with regard to two nonlinguistic acts that bear an iconic relation to one another, such as putting an object into a circle and putting oneself into a circle, both of which are found in the chimpanzee. Can these acts substitute for each other? Suppose substitutability is shown to hold between iconically related real acts on the one hand and between linguistic acts and their designated real acts on the other. In this case, it would seem reasonable to hold that the phrase "X stands for Y" has a significant overlap in meaning when applied in the linguistic and nonlinguistic domains.

References

Bateson, G. 1968. Redundancy and coding. In *Animal Communication: Techniques of Study and Results of Research*, T. A. Sebeok (ed.). Bloomington: University of Indiana Press.

Clark, E. 1974. Some aspects of the conceptual basis for first language acquisition. In *Language Perspectives—Acquisition, Retardation and Intervention*, R. L. Schiefelbusch and L. L. Lloyd (eds.). Baltimore: University Park Press.

De Laguna, G. 1963. *Speech: Its Function and Development*. Bloomington: University of Indiana Press. 1st ed. 1927.

Freud, S. 1943. *A General Introduction to Psychoanalysis*. New York: Garden City Publishing Company.

Jacobson, E. and Premack, D. 1970. Choice and habituation as measures of response similarity. *J. Exp. Psychology*, 85: 30–35.

Kohts, N. N. L. 1937. The behavior of a small chimpanzee and a human infant. *J. Psychol. Norm. Path.*, 34: 494–531.

Lawick-Goodall, J. van. 1965. Chimpanzees of the Gombe Stream Reserve. In *Primate Behavior*, I. Devore (ed.). New York: Holt, Rinehart and Winston.

Piaget, J. and Inhelder, B. 1971. *Mental Imagery in the Child*. New York: Basic Books.

Premack, D. 1971. Language in chimpanzee? *Science*, 172: 808–822.

Premack, D. 1973. Cognitive principles? In *Contemporary Models of Learning and Conditioning*, J. McQuigan (ed.). Washington, D.C.: V. H. Winston.

Premack, D. 1975. *Intelligence in Ape and Man*. New York: Holt, Rinehart and Winston.

Reynolds, P. C. 1972. Play and the evolution of language. Ph.D. dissertation (anthropology). Yale University.

The Human Aspect of Speech

IGNATIUS G. MATTINGLY

Underlying the recent work of many of us at this conference is the question I would like to consider today. It may at first seem strange and unnecessary, but I hope to persuade you of its relevance and importance. My question is, what aspects of speech, if any, are peculiarly and distinctively human?

At one time, it would have been enough to answer that speech is the vehicle for language, and only human beings have language. Both of those propositions are now in dispute. Some people seriously question whether there is really any justification for reserving the term "language" for human communication: Premack [1971] and Lieberman [1973] suggest that chimpanzees have language. Students of sign and gesture point out that early man may have communicated linguistically without benefit of speech [Hewes, 1973], and that many deaf persons certainly do so [Bellugi and Fischer, 1972; Stokoe, this volume]; speech is perhaps only one of several vehicles for language. Moreover, there is reason to believe that speech evolved independently of language: structural parallels have been noted between speech and various animal communication systems that no one would call languages [Mattingly, 1972]. Thus we should not attach undue significance to the fact that speech is specific to man; its peculiarities might prove on closer observation to be of a not very profound kind, like the details that distinguish the courtship display of one species of gull from that of another [Tinbergen, 1951]. But in the face of these considerations, I would maintain that there is a truly human aspect of speech, something that marks it unmistakably as a product of man's cognitive powers.

Let me begin my pursuit of the human aspect of speech with a very general account of linguistic capacity. We suppose, with the generative grammarians, that the speaker-hearer has to deal with two significant versions of an utterance: a phonetic representation and a semantic representation [Chomsky, 1965]. The phonetic representation of the utterance is in a form suitable for transmission by the vocal apparatus; the semantic representation is in a form suitable for storage in long-term memory [Lieberman, Mattingly, and Turvey, 1972]. It is convenient to conceive of both of these representations as n-dimensional arrays of features. The features of the phonetic representation are few in number and refer to the properties of the vocal tract [Chomsky and Halle, 1968], while those of the semantic representation are presumably far more numerous and refer to the whole of human experience. In the course of speaking or understanding an utterance, the speaker-hearer forms both of these representations. He can do so because he knows, tacitly, how the phonetic representation relates to the acoustic speech signal, how the semantic representation relates to the contents of long-term memory, and how the two representations relate to one another. This way of describing linguistic capacity suggests that phonetics, grammar, and semantics exhibit significant parallels, and this is just the impression I am striving to create. Let me try to bring out the parallelism by looking at each of these forms of cognitive activity in turn.

Speech differs in interesting ways from other natural communication systems. To be sure, some animal communication systems share many "design features" [Hockett and Altmann, 1968] with speech, and there are striking parallels between the perception of speech and the perception of "sign stimuli" [Mattingly, 1972]. But for none of these systems is it difficult to imagine how the perceptual powers of the users can cope with the amount of information known to be contained in the signal. The messages are typically very simple indeed. They are central to the survival of individuals and species, but their information content is low. With speech, however, the problem is to explain how the system can convey as much information as in fact it does, without overwhelming the ear. Most of us will recall Liberman's account [Kavanagh, 1968, pp. 119–141] of the obstacles encountered in developing various alphabets composed of discrete sounds to be used in a reading machine for the blind. As in speech, linguistic information was being communicated by an acoustic signal. Yet none of the sound alphabets could be understood at information rates comparable to that of natural speech. At a considerably lower rate, the individual alphabet sounds merged in a buzz [Liberman et al., 1967].

Again, consider the difference between speech and various possible gesture systems that might conceivably convey linguistic information. The comparison is the more appropriate because speech itself is a system of articulatory gestures. Perhaps the simplest possible gesture system would be one consisting of gross bodily movement—shrugging one's shoulders, tossing one's head, turning one's back. Such gestures, we know, can convey attitudinal meaning either alone or in conjunction with speech [Eibesfeldt, 1970]. But obviously the repertoire is not large and the semantic possibilities are limited. However, if we allow independent movements of the arms, the potential repertoire of gestures increases. If the two hands work together, and can point to or touch the various parts of the upper body, a still larger repertoire is available, and the perceiver can concentrate his attention on a fairly small part of his visual field.

This is the method of sign language. Finally, consider facial gestures. The various physiognomic features can move independently and quite rapidly, and they are collocated in a fairly small visual area. Nonhuman primates communicate with facial gestures and human beings use them expressively, exploiting the extreme mobility of the face to express an extraordinary range of attitudes. One could even conceive of a form of sign language in which linguistic information would be transmitted by rapid and quasi-independent motions of brow, eye, nose, mouth, and chin. Such a physiognomic communications system might in principle carry more information than a manual system. However, it would be difficult or impossible to track the concurrent movements of the various facial features. Perhaps the motion of two hands is as much as the eye can comfortably follow.

But speech apparently offers a way of overcoming this kind of limitation. This is in a way rather surprising, for speech would not seem to be a highly efficient communication system. In certain respects it resembles our imaginary physiognomic system: a group of collocated articulators—larynx, tongue, velum, jaw, lips—are moving quasi-independently, and the perceiver has the difficult task of following these different movements. But there is a further problem. The perceiver of physiognomic gestures has a direct and continuous display, whereas the display available to the perceiver of speech is partial and indirect: it consists of the sounds that happen to be made as air passes through the shifting cavities and passages formed by the moving articulators. Yet from the indirect record contained in the acoustic signal, the listener can extract without difficulty the information carried by the articulatory gestures.

Speech can circumvent the limitations on both ear and eye because, unlike human gesture systems and animal communication systems, it is "encoded" [Liberman, et al., 1967]. To clarify what this means, consider the mapping of the phonetic representation on the speech signal. Most of the information is carried by a few prominent acoustic features: the fundamental frequency, the first two or three formants, the plosive bursts, and the patches of fricative noise. The rest of the signal can be discarded with little or no loss in intelligibility. Moreover, the acoustic signal does not consist of temporal segments corresponding to successive phones. Rather, the acoustic features typically carry information about two or more phones in parallel. These economies mean that the load on the input channel is much lighter than it would be if the perceiver had to attend to separate acoustic units, or to a visible array of gestures. Thus, phonetic information can be transmitted at a much higher rate.

The price for this gain at the input is the complexity with which the cues that are the basic data for speech perception are represented by the acoustic features [Mattingly and Liberman, 1969]. Thus we find that the cues for two or more successive phones may be carried simultaneously by the same acoustic event: a second-formant transition cues the place of articulation of a stop, and the place of the adjacent vowel. On the other hand, different cues for one phone may be far apart: when two vowels are separated by a consonant, the place of the second vowel may be cued not only by the quasi-steady state of its second formant, and the adjacent transition, but also by the second-formant transition between the first vowel and the consonant. Finally, quite different cues will signal the same phone in different environments: the alveolar consonant is cued by a rising second formant before a front vowel and a falling one before a back vowel. Indeed, the dispersal of information in time and frequency offers ample justification for Hockett's comparison of the speech signal to smashed Easter eggs [Hockett, 1955, p. 210].

When we investigate the sources of this complexity, we find that a restructuring of information occurs in at least three different ways. The most obvious restructuring is an acoustic one. Variation in the spectrum of the speech signal is determined in part by the changing shapes of the vocal tract cavities [Fant, 1960]. The relation of cavity shape to spectrum is hardly straightforward and sometimes ambiguous, but it is the movements of the articulators that are significant, and these are only indirectly reflected in the changes in cavity shapes over time. However, the matter is even more complicated. If an articulator consistently moved in such a way that, as a consequence of each motion, it attained a target position associated with some phonetic value, it would be possible to relate to each phone a target articulatory configuration, and hence a target shape and a target spectrum. But while such targets can be hypothesized, they are actually attained only in simple cases. More commonly, targets are merely approached, and the different articulators participating in the production of one phone do not generally come closest to their targets at the same time [Lindblom, 1963]. Furthermore, the motion of an articulator is ordinarily complex, determined by preceding and following phones as well as by the current one [Ohmann, 1966]. With electromyographic techniques, the different gestures underlying complex articulatory motion can frequently be distinguished at the neuromotor level [K. S. Harris, personal communication] as commands from different muscles. Yet restructuring can take place even at this stage of production; the muscle commands themselves are sensitive to phonetic context [MacNeilage and DeClerk, 1969].

Thus the task of speech perception is even more complicated than we originally suggested. What the listener has to recover from the acoustic data is not the mere physical motion of the vocal organs but the articulatory plan that is realized in this motion. How can he do this? At least part of the answer is that he is able to bring to his task information that severely constrains his perceptual hypotheses. My colleagues at Haskins Laboratories have argued that the listener has tacit knowledge of certain properties of the vocal tract, and they have proposed a "motor theory of speech perception" [Liberman et al., 1967]. Rather than reviewing their arguments, let us take it that the theory is essentially correct, and consider the kind of knowledge the theory imputes to the listener. Certainly, it is not the kind of knowledge that could be deduced from communication theory, or even from an analysis of the acoustic speech signal alone. The vocal tract is a highly eccentric collection of disparate structures with distinct primary functions. Though it has undergone some remodeling to make it a more serviceable signaling device [Lieberman, 1968], it is essentially a bizarre arrangement that can be rationalized only in evolutionary terms. Nor is it the kind of knowledge that the listener might be supposed to derive from his own experience as a speaker. Experience in speaking is neither necessary, as is known from clinical cases in which damage to, or congenital deformation of, the vocal tract does not interfere with speech perception [Lenneberg, 1967], nor sufficient, since it would not be adequately generalized knowledge. We need to assume that the listener's tacit knowledge is of a more abstract character if we are to account for his ability to recover phonetic information from the output of vocal tracts of different shapes and sizes. We might imagine his knowledge as the equivalent of a dynamic vocal tract model, an ideal speech synthesizer.[1] With a few adjustments, the model is good for any speaker. It is a highly selective model, enabling the processes of perception to extract information from the signal received by the ear, even though this signal is a complexly encoded record of articulation.

If such a model seems overly elaborate consider that it is required also to constrain the articulatory plan of an utterance if the speaker is not to make inconsistent or impossible demands on his articulators, and to monitor the utterance as it is being produced. Production and perception are regulated by the same tacit knowledge. The model is also needed to account for the fact that the infant must deduce the phonetic rules of his language from speech produced by adult vocal tracts very different

---

[1] I do not mean by these comparisons to suggest a "process" model. Neither the proposed model nor any synthesizer actually recapitulates the processes of production; rather, they demonstrate the relationship of selected phonetic variables to acoustic output.

from his own [Lieberman, Crelin, and Klatt, 1972], and must learn to manipulate his own vocal tract, accommodating to its individual variations and to its changes in shape and size as it matures.

Speech perception, then, is a very powerful process because it applies to the analysis of a certain kind of very complex data a profound, specialized knowledge about such data. This cannot be said of sign language, or of the gestural communication systems imputed to early man.

Let us turn now, adopting the conceptual framework of generative grammar, to the relationship between the phonetic and semantic representations. If we compare these two representations for some utterance, we find that in the phonetic representation, the elementary propositions of the semantic representation ("deep structure") are internally reordered and combined with one another, that some lexical morphemes have been deleted or anaphorically replaced, and that other morphemes have been introduced, any one of them perhaps representing two or more semantic or syntactic elements. At morpheme boundaries, as well as within morphemes, there is extensive phonological revision: sounds have been inserted, deleted, changed in one or more distinctive features or transposed with one another. In short, the phonetic representation is an encoding of the semantic representation [Mattingly and Liberman, 1969]. The effect of the encoding is to make the syntax of the utterance as compact and the articulation as efficient as possible. The speaker-hearer's ability to produce appropriate phonetic representations, as well as his ability to reconstruct the semantic representation from the phonetic representation, is dependent upon his competence: his internalized knowledge of the grammatical rules of his language. This grammar is so highly specified that he is able to judge the grammaticality of any utterance and to recover its deep structure. The grammar is generative; that is, the grammatical analysis of an utterance is its derivation from deep structure according to rules. Infinitely many such utterances can be derived.

A generative grammar plays a role in the production and the understanding of sentences similar to the role played by the vocal tract model in speech production and perception. It embodies the knowledge that enables the encoding to be correctly imposed and removed. The parallel may not seem immediately obvious because our way of knowing grammatical facts is very different from our way of knowing phonetic facts. Phonetic activity is to some extent observable, but grammatical activity is not. On the other hand, we have considerable intuitional insight into grammar and little or none into phonetics. Grammar is customarily presented as a system of formal rules rather than as a neurophysiological model.

This formalism, however, brings out certain interesting restrictions: the division of the grammar into components with different types of rules, the nonoccurrence of certain transformational patterns, the type of context that must be stated in a phonological rule, and so forth [Chomsky, 1957]. These restrictions are not functional; they reflect indirectly the idiosyncrasies of the underlying neurophysiological apparatus, though we cannot observe it directly as a flesh and blood reality, as we can the vocal tract. Moreover, such formalism is what we would expect of our articulatory model if it is to be the abstract thing we have suggested, independent of particular vocal tracts yet capturing their essential common features.

Our claim, then, is that the listener's grammatical analysis and his phonetic analysis are really quite similar forms of cognitive activity.[2] In each case, the listener brings to a complex array of data tacit knowledge sufficiently well-specified for him to determine the underlying structure of the array and to remove the encoding.

Consider finally the question, how does the speaker get the semantic representations that he encodes linguistically? This is of course a special case of a problem central to cognitive psychology: how is information stored in and recovered from memory? We know that the capacity of long-term memory must be enormous, but we do not know how we thread our way through the labyrinth so readily. Yet some inferences useful to our present purposes are prompted by the familiar phenomenon of paraphrase [Liberman et al., 1972]. If someone is asked to recall a sentence he has previously heard, he responds, typically, with a sentence that probably differs semantically (and also grammatically and phonetically) from the original, though probably also remaining semantically consistent with it. In fact, we would find it strange if on a certain day A were to say to B, "I'm coming tomorrow," and B were to report this the following day saying, "A said that I'm coming tomorrow," without indicating by appropriate intonation that he was quoting A directly. We would expect rather a paraphrased response that takes into consideration changes in the time, the speaker, and the world ("A said that he's coming today."). The phenomenon of paraphrase suggests that the semantic representations of the sentences one hears are not ordinarily preserved in memory as separate items. Indeed, this would be a most inefficient way of storing information, given the redundancy of human discourse. Rather, the

---

[2] Lieberman (1973) thinks that the encodedness of speech is peculiarly human, just as I do, but that the cognitive ability underlying language differs only quantitatively from the "logical" ability underlying the conditioned responses of lower animals.

semantic content of the sentence is somehow incorporated into a more general record of experience that is the basis of both paraphrases and newly created sentences. In fact, the two cannot logically be distinguished.

Bartlett [1932] has suggested that experience is represented in memory by "schemata." A schema is not a chronological record of previous perceptions, each separately preserved, but rather an integration of these perceptions into an "organized setting" relating to a particular sort of experience. A new perception is drastically influenced by the schemata, and also modifies the schemata themselves. The same, presumably, can be said of the semantic representation of a newly heard sentence. It does not seem likely that there can be any simple mapping of parts of the semantic representation onto parts of the schema. The schema is the product of a great many semantic representations and, of course, of percepts of other kinds. On the other hand, a single semantic representation may conceivably modify many different aspects of the schema, and the nature of the modification may depend on the state of the schema itself. If we had available some convenient visual display of a schema in memory—an enormous spectrogram, as it were—we would doubtless find it very difficult to identify unambiguously the correlates of a particular sentence. Memorial processes are neither directly observable nor intuitively accessible, but we suspect that the integration of a semantic representation is a kind of encoding. It is similar in principle to the other encodings we have discussed, though differing both in the content of what is encoded and in its scale, for the schema is an encoding not of one but of many sentences.

But if old sentences are lost, where do new sentences come from? The general affinity between perception and recall, and Bartlett's shrewd comment about remembering, are suggestive: ". . . The organism would say, if it were able to express itself: 'this and this and this must have occurred, in order that my present state should be what it is' " [Bartlett, 1932, p. 202].

Putting this in the terms we have been using, to recover semantic information is to produce a semantic representation that if encoded would prove to be consistent with the current state of the schemata. Moreover, for independent linguistic reasons, we want the semantic representations underlying the sentences the speaker produces to be formally similar to the semantic representations of the sentences he hears: there is only one kind of deep structure. What is needed, therefore, both for storage and for recall, are rules that relate semantic representations to schemata: a sort of generative grammar of memory. These rules must reflect the nature of human experience that can be remembered. They must also reflect any purely nonfunctional properties of memory attributable to its evolutionary history. And since we would not expect the processes of recall to vary markedly depending on the schemata of the individual, the rules must be abstract and general enough to transcend such individual differences. The storage and recovery of semantic information in memory is thus a further instance of the kind of cognitive operation that we have already observed in speech and language.

To recapitulate, I have tried to trace a cognitive pattern common to the processes of language, speech, and memory. In each of these processes information is thoroughly reorganized for functional reasons. The relationship of the original information to its reorganized form is complex: we have termed it encoded. Recovery of the information is accomplished with the help of a grammar which specifies the relationship between the unencoded and the encoded form of the information, and whose formal properties consequently reflect the nature of the encoding device. We cannot say that this cognitive pattern is unknown in lower animals: for example, the spider's knowledge of his web seems not dissimilar. But surely only in man is the pattern so highly developed and so diversely manifested. Of these manifestations, speech is of special interest. It is not as complex a system as language or memory, and it does not claim our attention so immediately when we reflect on the character of our knowledge. But it exemplifies nonetheless a thoroughly and peculiarly human kind of knowing.

References

Bartlett, F. C. 1932. *Remembering*. Cambridge, England: Cambridge University Press.

Bellugi, U. and S. Fischer. 1972. A comparison of sign language and spoken language. *Cognition*, 1: 173–200.

Chomsky, N. 1957. *Syntactic Structures*. The Hague: Mouton.

Chomsky, N. 1965. *Aspects of the Theory of Syntax*. Cambridge, Mass.: MIT Press.

Chomsky, N. and M. Halle. 1968. *The Sound Pattern of English*. New York: Harper and Row.

Eibesfeldt, I. 1970. *Ethology*. New York: Holt, Rinehart and Winston.

Fant, C. G. M. 1960. *Acoustic Theory of Speech Production*. The Hague: Mouton.

Hewes, G. 1973. Primate communication and the gestural origin of language. *Current Anthropology*, 14: 5–24.

Hockett, C. F. 1955. *A Manual of Phonology*. Memoir 11, *International Journal of Linguistics*. Baltimore: Waverley Press.

Hockett, C. F. and S. A. Altmann. 1968. A note on design features. In *Animal Communication: Techniques of Study and Results of Research*, T. A. Sebeok (ed.). Bloomington, Ind.: Indiana University Press.

Kavanagh, J. F. 1968. *Communicating by Language: The Reading Process.* Bethesda, Md.: U.S. Department of Health, Education, and Welfare, National Institutes of Health, Government Printing Office.

Lenneberg, E. H. 1967. *Biological Foundations of Language.* New York: Wiley.

Liberman, A. M., F. S. Cooper, D. P. Shankweiler, and M. Studdert-Kennedy. 1967. Perception of the speech code. *Psychological Review,* 74: 431–461.

Liberman, A. M., I. G. Mattingly, and M. T. Turvey. 1972. Language codes and memory codes. In *Coding Processes in Human Memory,* A. W. Melton and E. Martin (eds.). Washington: V. H. Winston.

Lieberman, P. 1968. Primate vocalizations and human linguistic ability. *J. Acoust. Soc. Amer.* 44: 1574–1584.

Lieberman, P. 1973. On the evolution of language: a unified view. *Cognition,* 2: 59–94.

Lieberman, P., E. Crelin, and D. H. Klatt. 1972. Phonetic ability and related anatomy of the newborn, adult human, Neanderthal man and the chimpanzee. *American Anthropologist,* 74: 287–307.

Lindblom, B. 1963. Spectrographic study of vowel reduction. *J. Acoust. Soc. Amer.,* 35: 1773–1781.

MacNeilage, P. and J. DeClerk. 1969. On the motor control of articulation in CVC monosyllables. *J. Acoust. Soc. Amer.,* 45: 1217–1233.

Mattingly, I. G. 1972. Speech cues and sign stimuli. *Am. Sci.,* 60: 327–337.

Mattingly, I. G. and A. M. Liberman. 1969. The speech code and the physiology of language. In *Information Processing in the Nervous System,* K. N. Leibovic (ed.). New York: Springer.

Ohmann, S. E. G. 1966. Coarticulation in VCV utterances: spectrographic measurements. *J. Acoust. Soc. Amer.,* 39: 151–168.

Premack, D. 1971. Language in chimpanzee? *Science,* 172: 808–822.

Tinbergen, N. 1951. *A Study of Instinct.* Oxford: Clarendon Press.

Open Discussion of the Papers of Premack and Mattingly

The Grammar between Mind and Mouth

Peter Reynolds suggested that the notion of grammar as the interface between the organ of the vocal tract and the organ of the mind is a fruitful line of thought. It makes sense that the constraints of the structure of the mind would filter down from the top, so to speak, and the constraints of the vocal tract filter up. The properties of the nonhuman primate mind, such as those shown in the work of Premack, could shed a good deal of light on the extent of the downgoing constraints. Also, the differences and commonalities of spoken language and sign language could afford some clues as to the structure of the mind rather than just the structure of the channel in which they are used.

Jerry Fodor continued this line of argument by suggesting that we look for linguistic universals of sign and speech. For example, properties of syntactic rules which are shared in both modalities should reflect the structure of the intellect behind them. Moreover, perhaps we have over-estimated the mismatch of mind and mouth. Once the individual has perceived sign or speech and obtained a morphological representation of it, perhaps less computation and reshuffling is needed than linguists and logicians have thought. That is, perhaps the mind so constrains both sign and speech as to make the comprehension of signed and spoken language a moderately easy task.

Articulation Comprehension by Ear and by Eye

Ira Hirsh elaborated on the intelligibility of auditory and visual displays of speech. Of course the ear is the best perceiver of spoken language, but when it is deafened we look for other ways to get the information into the system. Spectrograms have proved to be of only limited worth in this regard, because the information is presented in an indigestible, or rather undecodable, manner. Rather than presenting acoustic features of the signal, Hirsh has been attempting to display to the eye the articulatory features behind speech, those normally seen by the lip reader and those unseen except by the use of fluoroscopes and x-ray photography. Thus, if one can bypass the acoustic signal perhaps there is little of the speech grammar to worry about [see Liberman et al., 1967].

Mattingly agreed that this display system may work to a limited extent but he suggested that it may be difficult if not impossible to process all that articulatory information in anything approaching real time. Fodor added that much of the literature that has come out of the Haskins Laboratories seems to indicate that the correspondence between phone and articulation is not very great, perhaps no better than that between phone and acoustic structure. Michael Studdert-Kennedy concurred with Fodor in that there appears to be extensive encoding in the formation of a speech gesture.

Studdert-Kennedy elaborated on the question of rate in decoding. It does not seem that the rate at which the phonetic information is extracted from the acoustic signal is at all peculiar. A reasonable estimate appears to be about 40 bits per second [Liberman, Mattingly, and Turvey, 1972], a rate which also appears to be found in the reading of music by a skilled pianist or perhaps the return of a volley by a skilled tennis player. The peculiarity of speech appears to be in the fact that it is remembered. Rate in speech only partly depends on the tremendously skilled output and interpretive devices. Another constraint lies in remembering.

James Jenkins then noted that the visual system tends to be just as picky about what it likes to process as the auditory system. For example, in the films of Johanssen [1973], where small lights are placed at joints such as the wrist, elbow, knee, and ankle and then all other external lights are turned out, one can identify maleness, femaleness, approach, receding, and many other aspects of the actor. However, when the lights are placed off the joints, one cannot perceive anything but a jumble of moving lights without human referents. Perhaps the eye cannot perceive, or infer information about, unnatural displays. Lighted joints display ecologically valid motion seen everyday. Lights "at the joints of the tongue," or at articulatorily important points of the vocal tract may be unnatural and as undecodable as the speech spectrograms of Potter, Kopp, and Green [1947].

At this point William Stokoe commented that if the smearing of articulatory and acoustic features of speech is really that great, "speech appears to be more like sign language than we thought." Mattingly and Lieberman countered by suggesting that the recoding in speech is not mere stylization, as in the difference between printed and cursive writing, but was much more drastic.

Levallois Flake Tools

Philip Lieberman suggested that the complexity of grammars underlying speech and language may not be unique in man's development. Perhaps the "grammars" underlying other accomplishments are equally complex. For example, when man first made tools-to-make-tools, as in the case of the Levallois flake instruments, the "surface structure" of the finished implement is often as far removed from its "underlying structure" as spoken sentences are from their underlying sources. In fact there is a very precise grammar in tool making. Gordon Hewes agreed with this view, and incorporated it in his comments which follow. Alvin Liberman concurred that there is a grammar in tool making, but suggested that what is unique to language, if indeed anything is unique, is not the nature of the grammar but the application of it, conceivably for the first time, to communication.

References

Johanssen, G. 1973. Visual perception of biological motion and a model for its analysis. *Perception and Psychophysics,* 14: 201–211.

Liberman, A. M., F. S. Cooper, D. P. Shankweiler, and M. Studdert-Kennedy. 1967. Perception of the speech code. *Psychological Review,* 74: 431–461.

Liberman, A. M., I. G. Mattingly, and M. T. Turvey. 1972. Language codes and memory codes. In *Coding Processes in Human Memory,* A. W. Melton and E. Martin (eds.). Washington: V. H. Winston.

Potter, R. K., G. A. Kopp, and H. C. Green. 1947. *Visible Speech.* New York: Van Nostrand.

Comments on Mattingly's Paper and on Levallois Flake Tools

GORDON HEWES

First, I have been struck by frequent remarks of Ignatius Mattingly and others about the features of speech which seem to have been built into it to enhance the speed of its utterance or processing. My question is, just why has this been so important in the evolution of human language?

Humans can slow language down, without sacrificing too much information. Speech can be delivered quite slowly, as in certain very formal situations; language can be written, and read at exceedingly slow rates; and this is also true of Morse code, wigwag, and flag signaling. Yet "normal" speech is remarkably rapid, suggesting that there has been some kind of selective pressure for its acceleration over many millennia. Mattingly has described how initial and final consonants are folded in, over the intervening vowel, to produce a quick acoustic blip, which normal hearers can readily decompose into a consonant-vowel-consonant (CVC) syllable. Another, quite different aspect of the speed-up is embedding or encoding sentences, which compress several kernel sentences into a much shorter, more elegant and economical expression. The vocal calls of other mammals do not appear to exhibit such tendencies for compression. But what is the real function of these acceleration mechanisms?

The sign language of the deaf, of which we have heard much during this conference, seems to be slower than speech; but under optimal conditions, in the hands of an expert signer, such as a professional (hearing) interpreter for the deaf, delivery speed may approximate that of oral language. The amount of information loss may be only slightly greater than in simultaneous translation from one spoken language to another: sign language is certainly not as slow as flag signals or wigwag codes, or totally finger-spelled messages.

With regard to the explanation for the present speed of spoken language, I suspect that the explanation may turn out to be considerably more complicated than Zipf's principle of least effort, simply to conserve energy, or to prevent the listener from becoming bored, or even to prevent the listener from breaking into the speaker's message with a comment of his own. Instead, I think it possible that some of the pressure was endogenous, built up at the interface between the probably extremely rapid rate of cognitive integration of new and old information, from long-term memory storage, and the initially much slower processes required to receive and analyze acoustic inputs, and to convert them into the language code. Eventually these widely different rates would have reached a more balanced condition.

Next, Mattingly asks why the facial expression system has never been employed as the major channel for language, as against emotional communication. Several thoughts occur to me about this. The higher primates make considerable use of their faces in social interaction—especially direction of glance, eyelid and eyebrow movements, and various mouth displays. Even in man, with more complex facial musculature, a full-fledged language system limited to the face (including the eyes) has not emerged, I would guess, because it is so liable to interference from emotional messages. Effective propositional language requires, at times at least, emotional "decontextualization." This has not prevented the face from having a role in sign languages, such as American Sign Language (ASL), but this is usually in conjunction with manual gesture.

Mattingly has discussed the blending (encoding) of speech sounds at length, which involves problems both in speaking and speech-decoding. Sign language systems may exhibit comparable blending, as in ASL word-signs and also in finger spelling. The phenomenon may owe something, of course, to the fact that modern human sign-language users are fully equipped, even when they are deaf, with the neural mechanisms which permit the rapid handling of blended speech features. It is probably wrong to assume that a primordial gesture language, at an early hominid level, would have been delivered rapidly enough for much blending to occur. There is also something analogous to phonetic blending in written language, again both in performance and perception. This is present, but less striking in alphabetic scripts written cursively, but more obvious in ideographic scripts such as Chinese or ancient Egyptian, where highly cursive versions have arisen (in Chinese such writing is sometimes called "grass writing"). Something corresponding to the motor theory of speech perception may have to be postulated to explain how suitably trained readers can decode the more cryptic examples of very rapid Chinese calligraphy. Gestural or sign languages seem to reach similar levels of abbreviated delivery, suggesting that those who can decode them also operate with a motor perception system.

Two points which Mattingly did not bring up, but which occurred to me during his presentation, also may be worth mentioning. First, where does our human ability to produce vocal *imitations* of the calls of non-human animals fit into his schema? Peter Marler's very realistic imitations of both monkey calls and bird songs, used to illustrate his presentation, are at the expert extreme of a widespread human vocal ability. People all over the world make use of mammalian and avian calls, for hunting, for dealing with domestic animals, and for other purposes. Does the capacity to make such facsimiles of nonhuman sounds rest on our language capacity? Is it localized in the same hemisphere as the controls for speech, and other language-related abilities? Marler may have demonstrated an ability lacking in nonhuman primates, but possibly of great antiquity in the hominid line. We may have been too quick to rule out onomatopoeia as a factor in the emergence of human speech. Such limitations of sounds made by members of other species are obviously under voluntary cortical control, and are not triggered emotional cries. In modern times, in industrialized societies, many children imitate, in play, the noises made by various motors and mechanical devices. There is in this something akin to glossolalia, but with different functions, which deserves serious attention in the light of what is involved in speech production and speech decoding.

Second, I should like to add something of possible relevance, which may relate more to some of what Peter Marler was discussing than to Mattingly's remarks. Some monkeys have depigmented, whiteish eyelids, which they flash in certain expressive displays. Baby monkeys in several species start out with pinkish faces, ears, and volar (palm and hand) skin, which later get much darker. The Japanese macaque monkey has pinkish-brown facial skin which becomes very red when the animal is enraged. Many monkeys, notably the various colobine species, have striking, mask-like facial skin (and hair) patterns, which evidently function as species or subspecies markers. Young chimpanzees sport a small tuft of white hair near the end of the spine. Mandrills have brightly colored facial pigmentation. Rump skin coloration in many Old World monkeys is likewise very striking. These and many other facts show that in the primate order, pigmentation of both skin and hair has evolved to perform various social communicational functions.

In *Homo sapiens,* but in no other primate species, the volar skin is depigmented, no matter what the degree of pigmentation on the rest of the body surface. This light pigmentation also occurs beneath the finger and toenails in all racial groups. In nonhuman primates, the nails are usually dark brown to blackish. I suggest that volar depigmentation arose in the hominid line in order to maintain maximum visibility of the working surfaces of the hands and digits, as well as the nail-covered fingertips; the soles of the feet went along in this, so to speak, since the enzyme system dictating the absence of palmar melanocytes would act in the same fashion on the analogous specialized plantar skin, even though the latter surface did not function in hominid communication or to any significant extent in tool and weapon manipulation. Although this hypothesis may seem extravagant, I have yet to run across any other plausible explanation for volvar depigmentation in *Homo sapiens* alone among the primates. Furthermore, various aspects of the hypothesis are testable, at least in respect to the assertion that depigmented palms and fingernails enhance the decoding of messages transmitted by means of manual gesture, and the related claim that such depigmentation also facilitates the acquisition, by others, of observable manual skills involved in the manufacture and wielding of early tools and weapons.

We are concerned at this conference not only with speech behavior in modern man, but to some extent with its origins and connections with the communication systems of other animals. My digression about volar pigmentation was to suggest that this peculiar attribute of *Homo sapiens* may have some bearing on the antiquity of nonvocal communication, which many linguists have tended to regard as a recent and relatively unimportant back formation from spoken language.

Finally, this is a good place to add to what Philip Lieberman suggested about similarities between syntactic structure and early toolmaking. In Figure 1, I have illustrated two well-known Paleolithic stone tool types, which may make the point more clearly. Figure 1*a* is a hand axe or *coup de poing*, which was a standardized implement over a vast area of the Old World for about half a million years, down into the early part of the Middle Paleolithic, which began about 80,000 years ago. Tools of this kind suggest that hominid conceptual skills changed very slowly until the Middle Paleolithic. Even so, makers of such tools must have had some prior "mental image" of the finished product, from the point where they selected the raw stone nodules or chunks to the moment when they removed the final chip, and considered the tool finished.

Compared to the hand axe, the preparation of flakes from a prepared Levallois core (Figure 1, *a* through *e*) represents a much more complex work program. In the hand axe, the nodule is simply reduced to a core by striking off chips: the completed implement is the core. In the Levallois technique, a chunk of suitable stone is first reduced to a core which has the shape of a tortoise carapace (*b*), domed on one surface, flattish on the other. One end of this tortoise core is then struck off to produce a striking platform (*c*), often humped centrally in a shape called *chapeau de gendarme* by French prehistorians. A carefully aimed blow at the peak of this feature detaches a flake of fairly predictable size and shape (*d*, *e*), which is the purpose of the foregoing elaborate procedure. The core may be used to make further flakes, or it may be discarded. The syntax analogy lies in the prescribed order of the various steps in the technique, involving a preprogrammed series of precisely executed motor acts, of several different kinds. As with speech, an apraxic disturbance of the

GORDON HEWES   80

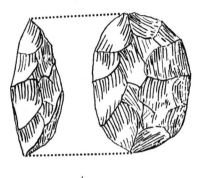

a.   b.

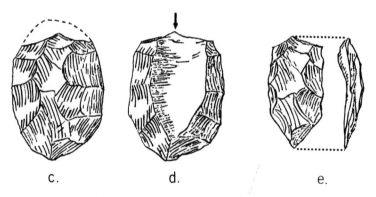

c.   d.   e.

Figure 1. Paleolithic stone tools to illustrate an analogy between early toolmaking
and syntax in language.
a. Hand axe or *coup de poing.* Lower Paleolithic of Africa, Europe, southwestern
and southern Asia. Length of average specimens approximately 10 to 15 cm.
Similarly chipped on opposite surface.
b–e. Stages in the manufacture of a Levallois flake from a prepared tortoise
core. Late Lower Paleolithic and Middle Paleolithic, in many of same geographic
areas as *a,* above. Approximately similar scale. *b.* The prepared tortoise core,
back and side view; the flattish underside is also chipped. *c.* One end of the
tortoise core is removed to produce a striking platform, in this case having the
chapeau de gendarme form. *d.* Arrow shows direction of the blow which has
detached a large central flake. *e.* Back and side view of the Levallois flake, the
object of the preceding operations. One edge of such a flake might be secondarily
chipped to improve its cutting or scraping function.

capacity to carry out such a series of programmed actions would lead to failure: the output would be meaningless. Tool making involving programmed activity of this kind did not emerge until the late Lower Paleolithic, at about the same time Lieberman and his colleagues suggest, from their studies of the reconstructed vocal tracts of fossil men, that articulate speech first became physically possible.

The Evolution of Speech and Language

PHILIP LIEBERMAN

Although the view that human language is "unique" and is disjoint from the communications systems of all other animals is still current [Lenneberg, 1967], the research of the past century has demonstrated that Charles Darwin's theory of evolution through natural selection is essentially correct. Human language can be no more disjoint from the communications systems of other living animals than human respiration or human locomotion. The apparent uniqueness of human language, like the apparent uniqueness of fully bipedal locomotion, merely reflects the fact that the intermediate forms are extinct.

Human locomotion and human language both can be viewed as the result of gradual processes that evolved from phylogenetically simpler hominid ancestors. A human characteristic like bipedal locomotion structures virtually all aspects of human behavior. Tool use and tool manufacture, for example, are possible in *Homo sapiens* because our hands are free. Tool use and tool manufacture, of course, crucially involve the presence of cognitive factors. Without the human brain, bipedal locomotion would not be that useful. The evolution of both bipedal locomotion and the human brain mutually reinforced the evolution of the behavioral patterns of tool use and tool manufacture which, in turn, placed greater selective advantages on both bipedal locomotion and enhanced cognitive abilities. It thus is both necessary and meaningful to discuss the evolution of human characteristics like bipedal locomotion and language in terms of the different factors that may have structured the selective factors resulting in the retention of the mutations that ultimately created *Homo sapiens*. These factors also are, and have been, operant in the evolution of other species. We thus can form and test hypotheses concerning the nature of human language and speech using data derived from other species.

I will discuss some of the factors that may be involved in the evolution of human language. These factors are necessarily linked; the presence of one particular factor is not, in itself, an explanation of the evolution of language. The absence, or lack of development, of one factor or another for modern *Homo sapiens* would imply the presence of intermediate grades of language relative to the language of present-day humans. As Darwin [1859] pointed out, evolution proceeds in small steps. I will propose a model involving the evolution of a number of interrelated factors that gradually derives hominid linguistic ability. I will necessarily have to limit the discussion of each factor, and the list of factors obviously will not be complete, but I will discuss some of the data that make each factor part of a scientific theory, a theory that can be tested and extended.

1. Speech and Language

Since the focus of this conference is the relationship between speech and language, I will start with these factors, though I do not intend to claim that language is impossible without speech. Human language appears to involve closely the constraints of human speech. However, as I will try to show in the discussion of some of the other factors, other forms of language are possible without the presence of the particular characteristics of human speech.

The special link between human speech and human language was recognized in the pioneering nineteenth-century studies of Broca [1861] and Wernicke [1874]. Broca found that lesions in a small area of the brain situated near the motor cortex in the left, dominant hemisphere of the brain impaired speech production and writing. The victims of the aphasia could still move their tongues, lips, and so on. In some instances they could sing, but they had difficulty when they either spoke or wrote. Lesions in the area of the brain that has come to be known as Broca's area essentially interfere with the organization of the articulatory maneuvers that produce speech, the "programs," as well as the written symbols that represent speech. Wernicke described and localized the complementary aspect of aphasia. He located an area of the brain near the auditory centers of the left dominant hemisphere. Lesions in this area produced an aphasia in which the victim left out words, used the wrong syntax, or "lost" the proper phonetic spellings of words. The victims of lesions in Wernicke's area essentially lose part of the "dictionary" and the grammar that every human carries about in his or her head. Both of these areas of the brain can be regarded as evolved additions to parts of the brain that deal with the production of sound (for Broca's area) and the perception of sounds (for Wernicke's area). Lesions in Wernicke's area clearly involve much more than the mere perception of sound just as lesions in Broca's area involve much more than the ability simply to move the tongue, lips, jaw, and so on. The total linguistic ability of the victim is impaired. The location of these areas near the parts of the brain that are directly concerned with auditory signals suggests that special neural mechanisms evolved matched to, and as a consequence of, vocal communication.

We can test this hypothesis with data derived from the study of other species. In recent years a number of electrophysiological and behavioral studies have demonstrated that various animals have auditory detectors that are tuned to signals of interest to the animal. Even simple animals like crickets appear to have neural units that code information about the rhythmic elements of their mating songs. The calling songs of male crickets consist of stereotyped rhythmic pulse intervals, and females respond to conspecific males by their songs [Hoy and Paul, 1973].

Similar results have been obtained in the squirrel monkey (*Saimiri sciureus*). Wollberg and Newman [1972] recorded the electrical activity of single cells in the auditory cortex of awake monkeys during the presentation of recorded monkey vocalizations and other acoustic signals. Eleven calls, representing the major classes of this species' vocal repertoire, were presented along with tone bursts, clicks, and a variety of acoustic signals designed to explore the total auditory range of these animals. Extracellular unit discharges were recorded from 213 neurons in the superior temporal gyrus of the monkeys. More than 80 percent of the neurons responded to the tape recorded vocalizations. Some cells responded to many of the calls that had complex acoustic properties. Other cells, however, responded to only a few calls. One cell responded with a high probability only to one specific signal, the "isolation peep" call of the monkey.

The experimental techniques necessary in these electrophysiological studies demand great care and great patience. Microelectrodes that can isolate the electrical signal from a single neuron must be prepared and accurately positioned. Most importantly, the experimenters must present the animals with a set of acoustic signals that explores the range of sounds that the animal would encounter in its natural state. Demonstrating the presence of neural mechanism matched to the constraints of the sound producing systems of particular animals is therefore a difficult undertaking. The sound producing possibilities and behavioral responses of most higher animals make comprehensive statements on the relationship between perception and production difficult. We can only explore part of the total system of signaling and behavior. Simpler animals, however, are useful in this respect since we can see the whole pattern of the animal's behavior.

The behavioral experiments of Capranica [1965] and the electrophysiological experiments of Frishkopf and Goldstein [1963], for example, demonstrate that the auditory system of the bullfrog (*Rana catesbeiana*) has single units that are matched to the formant frequencies of the species-specific mating call. Bullfrogs are members of the class of amphibia. Frogs and toads compose the order of anura. They are the simplest living animals that produce sound by means of a laryngeal source and a supralaryngeal vocal tract. The supralaryngeal vocal tract consists of a mouth, a pharynx, and a vocal sac that opens into the floor of the mouth in the male. Vocalizations are produced in the same manner as in primates. The vocal folds of the larynx open and close rapidly, emitting puffs of air into the supralaryngeal vocal tract, which acts as an acoustic filter. Frogs can make a number of different calls [Bogert, 1960]. These calls include mating calls, release calls, territorial calls which serve as warnings to intruding frogs, rain calls, distress calls, and warning calls. The different calls have distinct acoustic properties.

The mating call of the bullfrog consists of a series of croaks varying in duration from 0.6 to 1.5 sec. The interval between each croak varies from 0.5 to 1.0 sec. The fundamental frequency of the bullfrog croak is about 100 Hz. The formant frequencies of the croak are about 200 and 1400 Hz. Capranica [1965] generated synthetic frog croaks by means of a POVO speech synthesizer [Stevens, Bastide, and Smith, 1955]. This is a fixed speech synthesizer designed to produce human vowels. It serves equally well for the synthesis of bullfrog croaks. In a behavioral experiment Capranica showed that bullfrogs responded to synthesized croaks so long as the croaks had energy concentrations at either or both of these frequencies (200 and 1400 Hz). The presence of acoustic energy at other frequencies inhibited the bullfrogs' response of joining in a croak chorus.

Frishkopf and Goldstein [1963], in their electrophysiologic study of the bullfrog's auditory system, found two types of auditory units. They found cells in units in the eighth cranial nerve of the anesthetized bullfrog that had maximum sensitivity to frequencies between 1000 and 2000 Hz. They found other units that had maximum sensitivity for frequencies between 200 and 700 Hz. The units that responded to the lower frequency range, however, were inhibited by appropriate acoustic signals. Maximum response occurred when the two units responded to time-locked pulse trains at rates of 50 and 100 pulses per second that had energy concentrations at, or near the formant frequencies of bullfrog mating calls. Adding acoustic energy between the two formant frequencies at 500 Hz inhibited the responses of the low frequency single units.

The electrophysiological, behavioral, and acoustic data are complementary. Bullfrogs have auditory mechanisms structured to respond specifically to the bullfrog mating call. Bullfrogs don't simply respond to any sort of acoustic signal as though it were a mating call. They respond only to particular calls that can be made only by male bullfrogs, and they have neural mechanisms structured in terms of the species-specific constraints of the bullfrog sound producing mechanism. Capranica tested his bullfrogs with the mating calls of 34 other species of frogs. The bullfrogs responded only to bullfrog calls. They ignored all other mating calls.

The croaks must have energy concentrations equivalent to those produced by both formant frequencies of the bullfrogs' supralaryngeal vocal tract. The stimuli furthermore must have the appropriate fundamental frequency.

The bullfrog has one of the simplest forms of sound-making systems that can be characterized by the source-filter theory of sound production [Fant, 1960; to be discussed more fully below]. His perceptual apparatus is demonstrably structured in terms of the constraints of his sound producing apparatus and of the acoustic parameters of the Source-Filter Theory, the fundamental frequency and formant frequencies.

2. Plasticity and the Evolution of Human Speech

Frogs are rather simple animals, but they nonetheless have evolved different species-specific calls. Some of the 34 species whose mating calls failed to elicit responses from *Rana catesbeiana* were closely related. Others were more distantly related. Clearly, natural selection has produced changes in the mating calls of anuran species. The neural mechanisms for the perception of frog calls are at the periphery of the auditory system. They apparently are not very plastic since Capranica was not able to modify the bullfrogs' responses over the course of an 18-month interval. Despite this lack of plasticity, frogs have evolved different calls in the course of their evolutionary development.

Primates appear to have more flexible and plastic neural mechanisms for the perception of their vocalizations. Recent electrophysiological data [Miller et al., 1972] show that primates like the rhesus monkey (*Macaca mulata*) will develop neural detectors that identify signals important to the animal. Receptors in the auditory cortex responsive to a 200 Hz sine wave were discovered after the animals were trained by the classic methods of conditioning to respond behaviorally to this acoustic signal. These neural detectors could not be found in the auditory cortex of untrained animals. The auditory system of these primates thus appears to be plastic. Receptive neural devices can be formed to respond to acoustic signals that the animal finds useful.

3. Special Supralaryngeal Vocal Tract Anatomy

Modern man's speech-producing apparatus is quite different from the comparable systems of living nonhuman primates [Lieberman, 1968; Lieberman, Klatt, and Wilson, 1969; Lieberman, Crelin, and Klatt, 1972]. Nonhuman primates have supralaryngeal vocal tracts in which the larynx exits directly into the oral cavity [Negus, 1949]. In the adult human the larynx exits into the pharynx. The only function for which the adult human supralaryngeal vocal tract appears to be better adapted is speech production. Understanding the anatomical basis of human speech requires that we briefly review the source-filter theory of speech production [Fant, 1960]. Human speech is the result of a source, or sources, of acoustic energy being filtered by the supralaryngeal vocal tract. For voiced sounds, that is, sounds like the English vowels, the source of energy is the periodic sequence of puffs of air that pass through the larynx as the vocal cords (folds) rapidly open and shut. The rate at which the vocal cords open and close determines the fundamental frequency of phonation. Acoustic energy is present at the fundamental frequency and at higher harmonics. The fundamental frequency of phonation can vary from about 80 Hz for some adult males to about 500 Hz for children and some adult females. Significant acoustic energy is present in the harmonics of fundamental frequency to at least 3000 Hz. The fundamental frequency of phonation is, within wide limits, under the control of the speaker who can produce controlled variations by changing either pulmonary air pressure or the tension of the laryngeal muscles [Lieberman, 1967]. Linguistically significant information can be transmitted by means of these variations in fundamental frequency as, for example, in Chinese, where these variations are used to differentiate different words.

The main source of phonetic differentiation in human language, however, arises from the dynamic properties of the supralaryngeal vocal tract acting as an acoustic filter. The length and shape of the supralaryngeal vocal tract determines the frequencies at which maximum energy will be transmitted from the laryngeal source to the air adjacent to the speaker's lips. These frequencies, at which maximum acoustic energy will be transmitted, are known as formant frequencies. A speaker can vary the formant frequencies by changing the length and shape of his supralaryngeal vocal tract. He can, for example, drastically alter the shape of the airway formed by the posterior margin of his tongue body in his pharynx; he can raise or lower the upper boundary of his tongue in his oral cavity; he can raise or lower his larynx and retract or extend his lips; and he can open or close his nasal cavity to the rest of the supralaryngeal vocal tract by lowering or raising his velum. The speaker can, in short, continually vary the formant frequencies generated by his supralaryngeal vocal tract. The acoustic properties that, for example, differentiate the vowels [a] and [i] are determined solely by the shape and length differences the speaker's supralaryngeal vocal tract assumes in articulating these vowels. The situation is analogous to the musical properties of a pipe organ, where the length and type (open or closed end) of pipe determines the musical quality of each note. The damped resonances of the human supralaryngeal vocal tract are, in effect, the formant frequencies. The length and shape (more precisely the cross-sectional area as a function of distance from the laryngeal source) determine the formant frequencies. The situation is similar for unvoiced sounds where the vocal cords do not open and close at a rapid rate, releasing quasi-periodic puffs of air. The source of acoustic energy in these instances is the turbulence generated by air rushing through a constriction in the vocal tract. The vocal tract still acts as an acoustic filter but the acoustic source may not be at the level of the larynx as, for example, in the sound [s], where the source is the turbulence generated near the speaker's teeth.

The anatomy of the adult human supralaryngeal vocal tract permits modern man to generate supralaryngeal vocal tract configurations that involve abrupt discontinuities at its midpoint. These particular vocal tract shapes produce vowels like [a], [i], and [u], which have unique acoustic properties, as well as consonants like [g] and [k], which involve velar articulation. The acoustic properties of these sounds minimize the problems of precise articulatory control. A speaker can produce about the same formant frequencies for an [i], for example, while he varies the position of the midpoint area function discontinuity by one or two centimeters [Stevens, 1972]. They are also sounds that are maximally distinct acoustically. They, moreover, are sounds that a human listener can efficiently use to establish the size of the supralaryngeal vocal tract that he is listening to. This last property relates to factor 1, the specialized speech decoding that characterizes human language. The reconstructions of the supralaryngeal vocal tracts of various fossil hominids that Edmund S. Crelin has made [Lieberman and Crelin, 1971; Lieberman et al., 1972; Lieberman, 1975] indicate that some extinct hominids lacked the anatomical basis for producing these sounds while other hominids appear to have the requisite anatomical specializations for human speech.

4. Syntactic Encoding and Decoding

There are three interrelated aspects to the cognitive abilities that underly language: syntactic encoding and decoding, automatization, and "logical" ability. Syntactic encoding and decoding obviously involves the presence of neural mechanisms. We don't know very much about the workings of the brain but we don't have to know *how* the brain works to know *what* it does. A transformational grammar [Chomsky, 1957, 1964, 1968] is, among other things, a formal description of the syntactic encoding that is a characteristic of human language. Encoding in a more general sense seems to be a characteristic of other forms of human behavior.

A grammar to a linguist is not a set of prescriptive rules for writing sentences. A grammar is instead a formal description of some aspect of linguistic behavior. As Chomsky [1957, p. 11] puts it: "Syntactic investigation of a given language has as its goal the construction of a grammar that can be viewed as a device of some sort for producing the sentences of the language under analysis. More generally, linguists have been concerned with the problem of determining the fundamental underlying properties of successful grammars." The fundamental property of grammar that Chomsky revealed is its transformational syntax. Chomsky demonstrated that language must be viewed as a two-level process. Underlying the sequence of words that constitutes a normal, grammatical sentence is a "deep phrase marker" [Chomsky, 1964], which is closer to the logical level of analysis necessary for the semantic interpretation of a sentence. The transformational syntax is the "device" that restructures the deep, underlying level of language that is suited for semantic analysis into the actual sentence that a person writes or speaks. The aspect of transformational syntax that we want to stress is its encoding property, which is formally similar to the process of speech encoding [Liberman, 1970].

In Figure 1 we have presented a diagram that is essentially similar to the traditional parsing or constitutent analysis [Bloomfield, 1933] of traditional grammarians. The symbol S stands for sentence, NP for noun phrase, VP for verb phrase, V for verb, N for noun, and T for article.

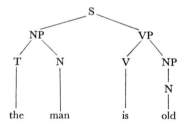

Figure 1

The diagram shows the syntactic relationships of the words of the sentence *The man is old*. The words *the man,* for example, constitute a noun phrase, the words *is old* constitute a verb phrase, which in turn is made up of a verb plus a second noun phrase. The word *old* constitutes the second noun phrase (the article of the second noun phrase reduces to an implied article). Diagrams of this sort are quite traditional. The first noun phrase could be called the subject of the sentence, the second, the object or predicate, etc. Semantic relationships are often "explained" by means of diagrams of this sort. The "actor-object" relationship, for example, is apparent in the diagram of the sentence *Joe hit the man.* The actor is the noun that precedes the verb, the object the noun following the verb.

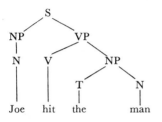

Figure 2

We have simplified these diagrams, and many of the details that a grammarian might find essential have been eliminated, but the essential facts and "explanatory" power of these diagrams have been preserved. Parsing is a "device" that formally "explains" some aspects of semantics; that is, it reduces semantic analysis to a mechanical procedure. The noun to the left of the verb is the actor, that to the right of the verb is the object, the noun acted on. The interesting thing about human language is that no one ever really utters sentences like *Joe hit the man* and *The man is old,* when they want to convey the information in the sentence *Joe hit the old man.* The two underlying, deep phrase markers that would result in the simple sentences *The man is old* and *Joe hit the man* are encoded, or scrambled together into one, more complex, sentence. The process is general and pervasive. The sentence *Joe hit the dirty old man who was wearing the red hat* would have underlying it a set of deep phrase markers that could have resulted in the sentences: *Joe hit the man. The man is old. The man is dirty. The man was wearing a hat. The hat is red.* It's much faster to utter the single complex sentence than the set of simpler sentences underlying it. The listener also doesn't have to keep track of the semantic referents and remember that you're talking about the same man in the first four simple sentences. All four repetitions of the word *man* are collapsed into a single *man* in the complex sentence. The two repetitions of the word *hat* are collapsed into a single *hat.* The complex sentence has fewer words and doesn't require keeping track of the semantic referents of the five "simple" sentences.

The transformational syntax can be regarded as the device that rearranges, deletes, and adds words to form the sentences of human language. The transformational syntax makes it impossible to sort out mechanically the semantic relationships of the words of complex sentences by using traditional sentence parsing. The "actor–acted on" relationship, for example, is semantically equivalent in the sentences *Joe hit Bill* and *Bill was hit by Joe,* though the words are on opposite sides of the verb. There are a number of reasons why traditional constituent grammars are not, in themselves, able to account for the properties of human languages [Chomsky, 1957, 1964; Postal, 1968], but it's enough to point out that they cannot account for the syntactic encoding that is characteristic of human language and for the complementary decoding that must take place when a listener or reader interprets a sentence.

5. Automatization

Human language involves rapidly executing complex sequences of articulatory movements or making equally complex perceptual decisions about the identity of particular sound segments. At a higher level, complex syntactic relationships must be determined. The speaker is, however, directly concerned with none of these processes. The semantic content of the message is the primary concern of the speaker or listener. The sending and receiving processes are essentially automatic. No conscious thought is expended in the process of speech production, speech perception, or any of the syntactic stages that may intervene between the semantic content of the message and the acoustic signal. It is clear that "automatized" skills are not unique to human language. Other aspects of human activity, such as dance, for example, involve similar phenomena. The novice dancer must learn the particular steps and movements characterizing a particular dance form. Once the steps have been learned, they become automatized. The dance itself involves the complex sequences. Playing the violin, skiing, or driving a car all involve automatized behavior.

The bases for the automatized behavior that is a necessary condition for human language may reside in cross-modal transfers from other systems of hominid and primate behavior. Tool use, for example, requires a high degree of automatization. You can't stop to think how to use a hammer every time you drive a nail in. Hunting is perhaps a still stronger case. A successful hunter must be able to thrust a spear or throw a stone without pausing to think about the mechanics of spear thrusting or stone throwing. Natural selection would quickly favor the retention of superior automatization. Automatized behavior pervades all aspects of culture. Indeed a cultural response is, to a degree, a special case of automatized

behavior. Electrophysiological data derived from rhesus monkey demonstrates that automatization in primates involves establishing special pathways in the animal's motor cortex as the animal "learns" to perform a
task [Evarts, 1973]. Evarts observed the electrical activity of motor cortex
neurons and the animal's muscles during the performance of learned hand
movements. The animal's muscular activity when it learned to perform
the task was extremely rapid. Its muscles acted within 30 to 40 msec,
about twice as fast as it could have responded if it had to "think about"
the task. Short response times like this usually are associated with reflex
actions but these short response times were the result of the animal's auto-
matizing a response. The learned automatized responses of simpler animals generally are not taken as tokens of the animal's "culture," but they
nonetheless exist. The function of play in animals may indeed be to learn
various patterns of automatized behavior that are germane to the animal's
"culture." Puppies spend a lot of time staging mock battles, kittens stalk,
and so on. It wouldn't be difficult to devise appropriate experiments to
explore the possible connection between play and automatization.

A special factor of automatized behavior may be that a "plastic" period
is involved. It is comparatively easy to shape behavior during the plastic
period. Afterward it is either impossible or more difficult for the animal
or human to learn the automatized behavior. Puppies thus can be trained
more readily than adult dogs. We're just beginning to appreciate some
of the critical periods involved in learning various activities. Human newborns, for example, can be trained to walk alone about two months earlier
than they normally do, if we take advantage of a critical period. Brief
daily exercise of the walking reflexes that exist in human newborns leads
to an earlier onset of walking alone [Zelazo, Zelazo, and Kolb, 1972].
If a newborn infant is held under his arms and his bare feet are permitted
to touch a flat surface, he will perform well-coordinated walking movements similar to those of an adult. This reflex normally disappears after
about eight weeks. However, if the infant is actively exercised throughout
this period, the reflex can be transferred intact from a reflex to a voli-
tional action. Latent periods are quite important in the acquisition of
human language [Lenneberg, 1967]. All humans can readily learn different languages in their youth. They all appear to retain this ability to
at least age 12 [Sachs, Lieberman, and Erickson, 1973]. Most humans,
however, can learn a foreign language only with great difficulty (or not
at all) during adult life. There are, of course, exceptions to this rule,
and some adults are quite fortunate in retaining the ability to learn new
languages with great facility. The same comments probably apply to

learning to play the violin or tightrope walking, though no definitive studies have yet been made.

6. Cognitive Ability

Cognitive ability is a necessary factor in human language. Linguists often tend to assume that cognitive ability *is* linguistic ability. Indeed, since the time of Descartes the absence of human language in other animals has been cited as a "proof" of man's special status and the lack of cognitive ability in all other species. Human language has been assumed to be a necessary condition for human thought. Conversely, the absence of human language has been assumed to be evidence of the lack of all cognitive ability.

The cognitive abilities traditionally associated with presumably unique human behavioral patterns like tool use and tool making have been observed in a number of different animals. Chimpanzees have often been observed using and making tools [Lawick-Goodall, 1972] but they are not the only primates who have been observed doing so. Beck [in press] reviews much of the evidence that shows tool use in other primates in their natural settings. Tool use has also been carefully documented in the sea otter [Kenyon, 1969]. Sea otters float on their backs and use stones as anvils against which they break the shells of crustaceans. They will hold onto stones that are suitable anvils, tucking the stone under a flipper as they swim between meals. The sea otter thus not only uses a stone tool, but preserves it for future applications.

Tool use and toolmaking under less natural conditions have even been observed in birds. Laboratory-raised Northern blue jays (*Cyanocitta cristata*) have been observed tearing pieces from pages of newspapers and using them as tools to rake in food pellets which were otherwise out of reach [Jones and Kamil, 1973]. The toolmaking techniques that can be observed in living nonhuman animals are rather simple. The stone tools associated with the earliest known fossil hominids are, however, also rather simple. We'll discuss the cognitive implications of different toolmaking techniques, but it is clear that the tool-using and toolmaking behavior of many living animals is a reasonable approximation to the initial base on which natural selection acted in the gradual evolution of hominid behavior.

The linguistic ability of chimpanzees also is evidence of a cognitive baseline present in living nonhuman animals. Chimpanzees do not have the speech-producing anatomy of modern *Homo sapiens* [Lieberman et al., 1972]. They could not produce human speech even if they had the neural devices, localized in Broca's area, that organize the complex articulatory gestures of human speech. Chimpanzees, however, can be taught to use a modified version of American Sign Language. American Sign Language is not a method of "fingerspelling" English words. It is instead a system that makes use of gestures each of which corresponds to complete words, morphemes (for example, past tense), or phrases [Stokoe, 1960]. It has a different grammar than standard English and really is a different language with its own linguistic history. Chimpanzees taught this sign language communicate in a linguistic mode with human interlocutors [Gardner and Gardner, 1969; Fouts, 1973]. They also can be observed communicating with other chimpanzees through sign language [Fouts, 1973]. Other experimenters have taught chimpanzees to communicate with humans by means of plastic symbols [Premack, 1971] and by means of a computer keyboard [Rumbaugh et al., 1973]. These experiments demonstrate that chimpanzees can communicate in a linguistic mode. Chimpanzees, for example, are aware of what constitutes a "grammatical" syntactic construction [Rumbaugh et al., 1973]. They conjoin words to form sentences, such as *I want apples and bananas,* and they understand the principle of negation [Premack, 1971]. They generalize the use of words, categorize in terms of semantic attributes, and use syntactic and logical constructs such as conditional sentences, *Lucy read book if Roger tickle Lucy* [Fouts, 1973]. The chimpanzee's cognitive linguistic abilities are, at worst, restricted to some subset of the cognitive abilities available to humans. Chimpanzees may lack the syntactic encoding that must be formally described by a transformational syntax in human language. Definitive experiments investigating the syntax of chimpanzee communications using sign language have yet to be done, and we don't really know whether their sentences are syntactically encoded. The difference at the cognitive level may, however, be quantitative rather than qualitative.

It is important to note, at this point, that quantitative functional abilities can be the bases of behavioral patterns that are qualitatively different. I think that this fact is sometimes not appreciated in discussions of gradual versus abrupt change. A modern electronic desk calculator and a large, general-purpose digital computer, for example, may be constructed using similar electronic logical devices and similar magnetic memories. The large, general-purpose machine will, however, have 1000 to 10,000,000 times as many logical and memory devices. The structural differences between the desk calculator and the general-purpose machine may thus simply be quantitative rather than qualitative. The "behavioral" consequence of this quantitative difference can, however, be qualitative. The types of problems that one can solve on the general-purpose machine

will differ in kind, as well as in size, from those suited to the desk calculator. The inherent cognitive abilities of humans and chimpanzees thus
could be quantitative and still have qualitative behavioral consequences.

An Interactive Model for the Evolution of Human Language

I have discussed some of the factors that I think are relevant to the evolution of language and speech. The first hominid "languages" probably
evolved from communication systems that resembled those of present-day
apes. The social interactions of chimpanzees are marked by exchanges
of facial and body gestures as well as vocalizations [Lawick-Goodall,
1968]. Chimpanzees also use tools, make tools, and engage in cooperative
behavior (for example, hunting). All of these activities have been identified as factors that may have placed a selective advantage on the evolution of enhanced linguistic ability [Washburn, 1968; Hill, 1972].

Australopithecus africanus essentially had the same supralaryngeal
vocal tract as present-day apes [Lieberman, 1973; 1975]. This, however, still would have allowed *A. africanus* to establish a vocal language
if other prerequisites were also present. *A. africanus* would have had to
have had the motor skills and automatization necessary to produce the
coordinated articulatory maneuvers that are necessary for the production
of speech. Australopithecines were more advanced in relative brain size
than any present-day ape, and, if external brain morphology means anything, they were more advanced in internal organization as well. Quantities of shaped stones associated with early hominids have been recovered.
These stones probably were used as projectiles, among other things
[Leakey, 1971]. The transference of patterns of "automatized" behavior
from activities like toolmaking and hunting would have facilitated the
acquisition of the motor skill necessary to make these sounds. Enhanced
communicative ability would, in turn, facilitate the use of tools. The process would be circular, a positive feedback loop in which each step en-
hances the adaptive value of the next step. Particular neural capacities
may initially not have been innately present. That is, they may not have
been in place at birth like the auditory detectors of frogs, which don't
appear to involve much, if any, learning. The plasticity of the australopi-
thecine auditory system, however, surely would have been at least as great
as that of present-day rhesus monkeys, dogs, chaffinches, and others.

The initial language of the australopithecines thus may have had a
phonetic level that relied on both gestural and vocal components. The
system may have become more elaborate as factors like tool use, toolmaking, and social interaction became more important. The ability to control
rage and sex is one of the factors that makes human society possible

[Hamburg, 1963]. Language is probably one of the most important factors in reducing the level of aggressive behavior in human society. Social control is as important a factor as hunting in the evolution of human society [Washburn, 1969]. The level of interaction between mother and child which can be noted in the vocal and gestural communications of chimpanzees, in which the mother is the primary agency of socialization [Lawick-Goodall, 1972], is a good example of this source for the increased selective advantage of communication. As hominid evolution diversified and larger-brained hominids appeared in the *Homo habilis/ erectus* lineage, the selective advantages of linguistic ability would have increased.

The final crucial stage in the evolution of *human* language would appear to be the development of the bent two-tube supralaryngeal vocal tract of modern man. Figure 3 shows a divergence in the paths of evolution. Some hominids like the classic Neanderthal fossils appear to have retained the communication system that was typical of the australopithecines, perhaps elaborating the system, but retaining a mixed phonetic level that relied on both gestural and vocal components [Lieberman and Crelin, 1971]. Other hominids appear to have followed an evolutionary path that has resulted in almost complete dependence on the vocal component for language, relegating the gestural component to a secondary "paralinguistic" function. The process would have been gradual, following from the prior existence of vocal signals in the linguistic communication of earlier hominids.

The bent supralaryngeal vocal tract that appears in forms like present-day *Homo sapiens* and the Es-Skhul V fossil allows its possessors to generate acoustic signals that (1) have very distinct acoustic properties and (2) are easy to produce, being *acoustically stable*. These signals are in a sense optimal acoustic signals [Lieberman, 1970; 1973; 1975]. If vocal communications were already part of the linguistic system of early hominids, the mutations that extended either the range or efficiency of the signaling process would have been retained. At some later stage (that is, later with respect to the initial appearance of the bent, two-tube supralaryngeal vocal tract) the neural mechanisms that are necessary for the process of speech encoding would have evolved. The humanlike supralaryngeal vocal tract would have initially been retained for the acoustically distinct and articulatory stable signals that it could generate. The acoustic properties of the vowels [i] and [u] and the glides [y] and [w], which allow a listener to determine the size of a speaker's supralaryngeal vocal tract, would have preadapted the communication system for speech encoding.

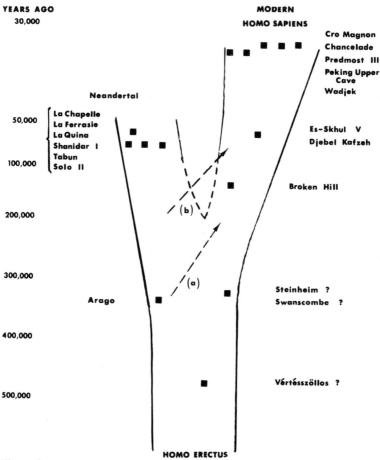

Figure 3

The process of speech "decoding" appears to involve crucially the left hemisphere of the brain. When isolated vowels are, for example, presented dichotically to a human listener there is no right ear advantage so long as the listener is responding to vowel stimuli that could have been produced by a single, unique vocal tract. If the vowel stimuli are instead derived from a set of different vocal tracts, a strong right-ear advantage is evident [Darwin, 1971]. The listener has to make use of a perceptual recognition routine that normalizes the incoming signals in terms of the supralaryngeal vocal tracts that could have produced the particular stimuli. The neural modeling of this recognition routine apparently involves the left-dominant hemisphere of the listener's brain. The traditional mapping of areas like Broca's and Wernicke's areas in the left hemisphere of the brain reflects the result of a coherent evolutionary process in which the human brain evolved special, unique mechanisms structured in terms of the matched requirements of speech production and speech perception.

The Uniqueness of Encoding

Although the speech of modern *Homo sapiens* is a fully encoded system, we can't assert dogmatically that other animals and, in particular, various fossil hominids had completely unencoded systems of vocal communication. The acoustic basis of speech encoding rests in the fact that the pattern of format frequency variation of the supralaryngeal vocal tract must inherently involve transitions. The shape of the supralaryngeal vocal tract cannot change instantaneously. If a speaker utters a syllable that starts with the consonant [b] and ends with the vowel [æ] his vocal tract must inherently involve transitions. The shape of the supralaryngeal vocal tract cannot change instantaneously. If a speaker utters a syllable that starts with the consonant [b] and ends with the vowel [æ] his vocal tract must first produce the shape necessary for [b] and then gradually move toward the [æ] shape. Formant transitions thus have to occur in the [æ] segment that reflects the initial [b] configuration. The transitions would be quite different if the initial consonant were a [d]. The nonhuman supralaryngeal vocal tract can, in fact, produce consonants like [b] and [d]. Simple encoding could be established using only bilabial and dental consonant contrasts. The formant transitions would all be either rising in frequency in the case of [bæ] or falling in frequency for [dæ]. It probably would be quite difficult, if not impossible, to sort the various intermediate vowel contrasts that are possible with the nonhuman vocal tract, but a simple encoding system could be built up using rising and falling formant transitions imposed on a general, unspecified vowel. The resulting language would have only one vowel, a claim that has often been made for the supposed ancestral language of *Homo sapiens* [Kuipers, 1960]. The process of speech encoding and decoding and the elaboration of the vowel repertoire could build on vocal tract normalization schemes that made use of sounds like [s], which also can provide a listener, or a digital computer program, with information about the size of the speaker's vocal tract. Vocal tract normalizing information could also be derived perhaps by listening to a fairly long stretch of speech and then computing the average formant frequency range. The process would be slower than simply hearing a token of [i] or [u], but it would be possible.

There might have been a gradual path toward more and more encoding for all hominid populations as social structure and technology became more complex. The preadaptation of the bent two-tube supralaryngeal vocal tract in some hominid populations would have, if this were true, provided an enormous selective advantage. In other words, there may not have been any single path toward the evolution of encoded speech. Fossil hominids like Neanderthal man may have had cognitive abilities equal to those of hominids like Es-Skhul V. However, the absence of a preadapted bent two-tube vocal tract would have prevented them from generalizing the encoding principle.

Tool Use, Grammar, and Encoding

As we noted earlier, linguists often tend to view human language as though it were disjoint from all other aspects of human behavior. A linguistic grammar is essentially a formal description, or rather a formal abstraction, of certain aspects of language. Linguists, in general, would not think of applying the formal apparatus of a linguistic grammar to some other kind of human behavior. However, it is apparent that other aspects of human, and indeed of nonhuman, behavior can be described using the same formal apparatus. Reynolds, for example, has studied the play activity of young rhesus monkeys [Reynolds 1972]. He found that rhesus monkeys have a number of stylized basic gestural patterns. These patterns are all quite short. They each consist of a particular body posture and facial expression. Some of the basic patterns involve movements and vocalizations. The basic play patterns are essentially "atomic" units that combine in certain regular ways to form play sequences. Some of the basic patterns occur only at the start of play sequences; they are "initiators." Others can occur only at the end of a play sequence; they are "terminators." Still other basic patterns occur within play sequences. The monkeys will break off play whenever a basic pattern occurs in the wrong position. There are, if we borrow the terminology of linguistics, "grammatical" play sequences, and we can describe these sequences by means of "grammatical" rules.

The "grammatical" rules that appear to be appropriate for the description of rhesus monkey play sequences are those usually associated with constituent analysis, or sentence parsing. Let's consider the following short example of sentence parsing, which is drawn from Chomsky [1957]. Consider the following set of grammatical "rules."

(1) $S \rightarrow NP + VP$
(2) $NP \rightarrow T + N$
(3) $VP \rightarrow V + NP$
(4) $T \rightarrow$ the

(5a) N → man   (5b) N → house   (5c) N → ball
(6a) V → hit   (6b) V → lost

Each rule $X \to Y$ is to be interpreted as the instruction "rewrite X as Y." We can call the sequence of operations that follows a "derivation" of the sentence *the man hit the ball* where the number at the right of each line in the derivation refers to the rule of the grammar used in constructing that line from the previous line.

S
NP + VP   (1)
T + N + VP   (2)
T + N + V + NP   (3)
the + N + V + NP   (4)
the + man + V + NP   (5a)
the + man + hit + NP   (6a)
the + man + hit + T + N   (2)
the + man + hit + the + N   (4)
the + man + hit + the + ball   (5c)

Thus, the second line of the derivation is formed from the first line by rewriting sentences as NP + VP in accordance with rule (1), the third line is formed from the second line by using rule (2), and so on. We could represent the derivation by means of the diagram in Figure 4.

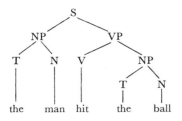

Figure 4

If we add a "filter" condition to the rules of the grammar it will mechanically derive a number of "grammatical" English sentences, for example, *The man lost the house* and *The man hit the house*. The filter condition states that no derivation shall be considered complete unless all of the alphabetic symbols are replaced by English words. The application of a particular rule in this grammar is contingent on only one fact—the left-hand symbol of a rule must be present on the last line of the derivation.

The grammar that we have discussed is what linguists call a "phrase structure" grammar. It is the formal embodiment of traditional sentence parsing. Phrase structure grammars in themselves cannot capture the encoded nature of the syntax of human language. Phrase structure rules, however, do have a role as a component of the grammar of human language [Chomsky, 1957, 1964]. They have one formal property that, though it superficially appears trivial, is an important limitation of their explanatory power. A phrase structure rule can be applied in a derivation whenever the alphabetic symbol on the left of the rule appears on the last line of the derivation. *A phrase structure rule thus can apply to a line of a derivation without considering its past history.*

After digressing on the play activity of the rhesus monkey and phrase structure rules, we can now return to the question of the language of Neanderthal hominids. In fact, we have not really been digressing, since the point that we want to make is that we can apply the rules of grammar to the analysis of some of the artifacts of Neanderthal culture, the stone tools and toolmaking techniques.

Stone Toolmaking Techniques and Encoding

The Paleolithic, or Old Stone Age, encompasses a period of perhaps almost three million years. There are important differences in the types of stone tools found in different parts of this era. The first tools, which are associated with the australopithecines and *Homo habilis,* are either unshaped stones or stones that have a flake or two taken off them. The tools become progressively more complex, and their manufacture ultimately involves taking many, many chips out of the piece of stone that the toolmaker started with. We might think of a process in which toolmakers continued to refine the process of tool fabrication, making the chips smaller as time went on. The basic technique, however, would be unchanged though new modifications would be introduced. The process would simply become more refined.

The technique involved in making these tools is conceptually similar to the process of whittling on a stick. You start by making an initial chip, then a second, a third, and so on. In making a particular chip you have to keep only two things in mind: (*a*) the last chip that you made, and (*b*) the final form of the tool that you're trying to make. The process formally reduces to the phrase structure grammar with a filter condition that we just discussed. The filter condition is formally equivalent to stating that you know what sort of tool you're aiming for. The phrase structure grammar formally embodies the fact that you only need to know the last "line of the derivation," that is, the state of the tool bank at the instant that you chip it. You don't need to have a memory of the operations involved in getting to that stage.

We would be wrong in thinking that all stone tools involved the same technology. About 600,000 years ago a radically different stoneworking technology started. The Levallois flake tools [Bordes, 1968] are the result of a multistage process. The toolmaker first prepares a core. The preparation of the core involves a number of steps itself to produce the basic shape shown in Figure 1 of Hewes [this volume]. Once the core is ready, the toolmaker switches his technique. He chips out complete flakes, each of which may serve as a completed tool, with every blow of his hammer. The Levallois toolmaking technique cannot be reasonably described by means of a phrase structure grammar. A transformational grammar which formally incorporates a memory is necessary. There is no simple invariant "last chip" at which the toolmaker abruptly stops preparing the core and switches to flaking off the final products. The toolmaker rather has to keep in mind a particular functional attribute of the striking platform, which involves the entire upper surface of the core [Bordes, 1968, pp. 27–28]. The formal "grammatical" description of the process must also reflect this degree of abstraction, which cannot be keyed to the appearance of a single "alphabetic" symbol that represents a particular chip of stone.

Phrase structure grammars cannot formally account for the syntax of human language [Chomsky, 1957, 1964]; they also cannot serve as grammars of the Levalloisian tool technique that is one of the characteristics of the culture of Neanderthal man. Transformational grammars, as we noted, introduce the concept of encoding into syntax. Although we cannot positively conclude that the grammar of the syntax of Neanderthal language had a transformational component, their Levalloisian stone tools suggest a degree of cognitive development that formally calls for a transformational grammar. Many other aspects of the culture of modern human populations need transformational descriptions if we attempt to derive a formal description. Marriage customs, for example, involve constraints on the lineages of both bride and groom that include a memory component. Death rituals involving funeral goods also implicitly require some knowledge of the former life and habits of the corpse.

The most likely assessment of the encoding abilities of Neanderthal man thus would be that language was encoded, but not nearly as encoded as in modern *Homo sapiens*. The development of the Neanderthal supralaryngeal vocal tract was not suitable for fully encoded speech. The neural structures of the brain that play so crucial a role in the perception of encoded speech in the dominant, left hemisphere of the brain would therefore probably not have been as well developed in Neanderthal man. Language, however, would exist though it would not be the language of modern *Homo sapiens*. Language, like other human attributes, appears to be the result of a gradual evolutionary process, and intermediate stages and common underlying factors are to be expected in the languages and communications systems of extinct earlier hominids and of other living species.

References

Beck, B. B. In press. Primate tool behavior. In *World Anthropology*, Proceedings of the Ninth International Congress of Anthropological and Ethnological Sciences, Chicago, 1973.

Bloomfield, L. 1933. *Language*. New York: Holt, Rinehart and Winston.

Bogert, C. M. 1960. The influence of sound on the behavior of amphibians and reptiles. In *Animal Sounds and Communication*, W. E. Lanyon and W. N. Tavolga (eds.). Washington, D.C.: Amer. Instit. Biolog. Sci.

Bordes, F. 1968. *The Old Stone Age*. World University Library. New York: McGraw-Hill.

Broca, P. 1861. Nouvelle observation d'aphémie produite par une lésion de la moitié postérieure des deuxième et troisième circonvolutions frontales. *Bull. Soc. Anatom. Paris*, 6 (series 2): 398–407.

Capranica, R. R. 1965. *The Evoked Vocal Response of the Bullfrog*. Cambridge, Mass.: MIT Press.

Chomsky, N. 1957. *Syntactic Structures*. The Hague: Mouton.

Chomsky, N. 1964. *Aspects of the Theory of Syntax*. Cambridge, Mass.: MIT Press.

Chomsky, N. 1968. *Langauge and Mind*. New York: Harcourt, Brace.

Darwin, C. 1859. *On the Origin of Species*. Facsimile edition. New York: Atheneum Publishers.

Darwin, C. J. 1971. Ear differences in the recall of fricatives and vowels. *Q. J. Exp. Psychol.*, 23: 386–392.

Evarts, E. V. 1973. Motor cortex reflexes associated with learned movement. *Science*, 179: 501–503.

Fant, G. 1960. *Acoustic Theory of Speech Production*. The Hague: Mouton.

Fouts, R. S. 1973. Acquisition and testing of gestural signs in four young chimpanzees. *Science*, 180: 978–980.

Frishkopf, L. S. and M. H. Goldstein, Jr. 1963. Responses to acoustic stimuli from single units in the eighth nerve of the bullfrog. *J. Acoust. Soc. Amer.* 35: 1219–1228.

Gardner, R. A. and B. T. Gardner. 1969. Teaching sign language to a chimpanzee. *Science*, 165: 664–672.

Hamburg, D. A. 1963. Emotions in the perspective of human evolution. In *Expression of the Emotions in Man*, P. Knapp (ed.). New York: International Universities Press.

Hewes, G. W. Comments on Mattingly's paper and on Levallois flake tools. This volume.

Hill, J. H. 1972. On the evolutionary foundations of language. *American Anthropologist*, 74: 308–317.

Hoy, R. R. and R. C. Paul. 1973. Genetic control of song specificity in crickets. *Science*, 180: 82–83.

Jones, T. B. and A. C. Kamil. 1973. Tool-making and tool-use in the Northern blue jay. *Science,* 180: 1076–1077.

Kenyon, K. W. 1969. *The Sea Otter in the Eastern Pacific Ocean.* Washington, D.C.: U.S. Government Printing Office.

Kuipers, A. H. 1960. *Phoneme and Morpheme in Kabardian.* The Hague: Mouton.

Lawick-Goodall, J. van. 1968. A preliminary report on expressive movements and communication in the Gombe Stream chimpanzees. In *Primates: Studies. in Adaptation and Variability,* P. Jay (ed.). New York: Holt, Rinehart and Winston.

Lawick-Goodall, J. van. 1972. *In the Shadow of Man.* New York: Macmillan.

Leakey, M. D., ed. 1971. *Olduvai Gorge, Vol. 3.* Cambridge, England: Cambridge University Press.

Lenneberg, E. H. 1967. *Biological Foundations of Language.* New York: Wiley.

Liberman, A. M. 1970. The grammars of speech and language. *Cognitive Psych.,* 1: 301–323.

Lieberman, P. 1967. *Intonation, Perception, and Language.* Cambridge, Mass.: MIT Press.

Lieberman, P. 1968. Primate vocalizations and human linguistic ability. *J. Acoust. Soc. Amer.,* 44: 1574–1584.

Lieberman, P. 1970. Towards a unified phonetic theory. *Linguistic Inquiry,* 1: 307–322.

Lieberman, P. 1973. On the evolution of human language: A unified view. *Cognition,* 2: 59–94.

Lieberman, P. 1975. *On the Origins of Language: An Introduction to the Evolution of Human Speech.* New York: Macmillan.

Lieberman, P. and E. S. Crelin. 1971. On the speech of Neanderthal man. *Linguistic Inquiry,* 2: 203–222.

Lieberman, P., E. S. Crelin, and D. H. Klatt. 1972. Phonetic ability and related anatomy of the newborn, adult human, Neanderthal man, and the chimpanzee. *American Anthropologist,* 74: 287–307.

Lieberman, P., K. S. Harris, P. Wolff, and L. H. Russell. 1972. Newborn infant cry and nonhuman primate vocalizations. *J. Speech and Hearing Research,* 14: 718–727. Also in Status Report 17/18 (1968), Haskins Laboratories.

Lieberman, P., D. H. Klatt, and W. A. Wilson. 1969. Vocal tract limitations on the vowel repertoires of rhesus monkey and other nonhuman primates. *Science,* 164: 1185–1187.

Miller, J. M., D. Sutton, B. Pfingst, A. Ryan, and R. Beaton. 1972. Single cell activity in the auditory cortex of rhesus monkeys: behavioral dependency. *Science,* 177: 449–451.

Negus, V. E. 1949. *The Comparative Anatomy and Physiology of the Larynx.* New York: Hafner.

Postal, P. M. 1968. *Aspects of Phonological Theory.* New York: Harper and Row.

Premack, D. 1971. Language in chimpanzee? *Science,* 172: 808–822.

Reynolds, P. C. 1972. Play, language and human evolution. Paper presented at 1972 meeting of Amer. Assoc. Adv. Sci., Washington, D.C.

Rumbaugh, D. M., T. V. Gill, and E. C. von Glaserfeld. 1973. Reading and sentence completion by a chimpanzee. *Science,* 182: 731–733.

Sachs, J., P. Lieberman, and D. Erickson. 1973. Anatomical and cultural determinants of male and female speech. In *Language Attitudes: Current Trends and Prospects*, R. Shuy and R. Fasold (eds.). Washington, D.C.: Georgetown University Press.

Stevens, K. N. 1972. Quantal nature of speech. In *Human Communication, A Unified View*, E. E. David and P. B. Denes (eds.). New York: McGraw-Hill.

Stevens, K. N., R. P. Bastide, and C. P. Smith. 1955. Electrical synthesizer of continuous speech. *J. Acoust. Soc. Amer.*, 27: 207.

Stokoe, W. C., Jr. 1960. *Sign Language Structure: An Outline of the Visual Communication System of the Deaf*. Studies in Linguistics Occasional Paper 8. Buffalo, N.Y.: University of Buffalo.

Washburn, S. L. 1968. *The Study of Human Evolution*. Eugene, Ore.: Oregon State System of Higher Education.

Washburn, S. L. 1969. The evolution of human behavior. In *The Uniqueness of Man*, J. D. Roslansky (ed.). Amsterdam: North-Holland.

Wernicke, C. 1874. *Der aphasische Symptomen-complex*. Breslau: Franck and Weigert.

Wollberg, Z. and J. D. Newman. 1972. Auditory cortex of squirrel monkey: Response patterns of single cells to species-specific vocalizations. *Science*, 175: 212–214.

Zelazo, P. R., N. A. Zelazo, and S. Kolb. 1972. "Walking" in the newborn. *Science*, 176: 314–315.

Comments on Lieberman's Paper

In considering the possibility of speech or speechlike communication within varieties of fossil hominids, Philip Lieberman has raised an issue which is familiar among the anthropologists. Successive generations of anthropologists have vociferously debated this issue.

But Lieberman and his associate, Edward Crelin of the Yale University Department of Anatomy, have more information about these fossil anthropoids. It is now possible to describe fully the skills of Neanderthal and of more "human" hominids, some of which were temporally coincident with Neanderthal. And continuing comparative anatomical study has provided a base for interpolation of the form of the pharynx and the mouth. These interpolations become less valid as they are extended to the larynx, as a structure farther from the portions of the fossil skulls which are available for study. But this is not critical to his concept, for it may be inferred that these fossil hominids had a phonatory larynx. Lieberman's inferences are relevant to supraglottal articulation. His advantage in these considerations, compared with earlier anthropologists, is that of greater understanding of the anatomical and performance requisites of verbal expression in normal modern man. He has been able to extrapolate from his own work in this topic to his current concepts of the possibilities of speechlike phonatory communication in fossil hominids.

I must offer a few caveats about this general matter of the interpretation of speech capabilities from peripheral anatomy. There are some risks in applying the descriptions of the speech performances of normal man to anatomically different persons. Those of us who work with subjects whose motor effector performance is distorted by malformation often marvel at the acoustically normal or near normal speech which can be accomplished by seemingly inappropriate anatomical structures. In the circumstance of cleft palate, for instance, control of the palatopharyngeal isthmus may be accomplished by exceptional action of the superior constrictor muscle, so that the resultant speech is normal or near normal in its pharyngeal resonance and in its oral articulation. The achievement of oral articulation of speech in the circumstance of severe hypoplasia of the tongue is even more remarkable. We studied a 12-year-old child with this malformation who employed alternative valving gestures of the mesopharynx and the lips to achieve certain speech articulations. Analogous compensations in speech articulation are found in adults who have undergone excision of portions of the palate or tongue for removal of cancer. A modern man who has adequate social experience of speech and an adequately sensient and motor mobile pharynx and mouth is generally capable of speech.

A correlate of this adaptability of the peripheral apparatus in accomplishing speech is that the actions of speech may have little role in the formation of the speech effector apparatus. We recognize that the motor effector structures are formed in intimate relation to their functions. This is as true of the pharynx and mouth as it is of the limbs. The muscles structure themselves by their actions. And, in some simplification, we may say that the motor skeleton, once formed in the fetus, is developed into its child and mature structure and shape in response to physical stresses imposed upon it by motor function.

But the quantity of the speech participation of the pharynx and mouth is almost incidental in the general motor activities. The principal sensory-cued motor performances of this area are those of position maintenance by the pharynx and the mouth, of pharyngeal participation in tidal respiration, of oral feeding and pharyngeal swallowing. Speech is infrequent, in comparison. And its actions are gentle. From such observations and reasoning, I would infer that speech is of little significance as a mechanism of effecting muscular and skeletal form.

Lieberman has expounded upon the strategic role of phonatory communication in the survival and perpetuation in pattern of a corporate group of hominids. But, again, this achievement does not depend upon the developmental genesis of the supraglottal articulatory system. I would rather expect that a hominid having the social orientation and the integrative competencies requisite to complex communication would be able to phonate or "speak" in an adequate variety of sounds with any approximately humanoid pharyngeal and oral effector system.

Open Discussion of the Papers of Lieberman and Bosma

Hunting in the Development of Man

There was much discussion about the aspects of man which might make him unique. Since the conference centered on language, since the extent if not the existence of language is certainly unique to man, and since language may have come late in man's development—he may have been unique in the animal kingdom before he acquired speech—there was a tendency to look elsewhere in man's repertoire of skills. One obvious and theoretically important skill is hunting.

Gordon Hewes noted that there are two types of hunting, one characterized by very loud vocalizations, as in stampede hunting, and the other characterized by silence, as in stalk hunting. In stampede hunting the hunters yell and scream and wave vegetation, and the cries have very little, if any, linguistic content. In stalk hunting, on the other hand, the few vocalizations that are used are discrete and meaningful signals such as the imitations of bird calls. Man hunts by both methods, but when hunting in large groups he invariably uses the stampede method. Peter Reynolds agreed with Hewes, and suggested further that hunting and its importance in man's development may have been greatly overemphasized. One of the characteristics of human behavior is that complicated tool use and complicated information about the purpose of learning tool skills is endemic to all aspects of human behavior. Perhaps hunting was singled out in the past because it was rigidly thought that it was one of the most distinctive things that man does. Now we know that this is not the case. Hunting is flashy, and for that reason it probably attracted much attention.

Reynolds went on to suggest that the cake, and cooking in general, are a much more subtle example of what makes man unique. Why not take Samuel Johnson's statement that man is a cooking animal as the first instance of why he stands apart from the rest of the animal kingdom? Lieberman added that hearths go back about three thousand years or more, and certainly first occurred after man acquired speech.

Reconstructing Early Speech

Several people were interested in how Lieberman and his colleagues reconstruct vocal tracts from fossil remains. Since the vocal tract is mostly soft tissue, and fossil remains are entirely "hard" tissue (bone), which generally surrounds but does not encase the area, there was some question as to how accurate modeling can be.

James Bosma noted that muscle shapes bone and bone shapes muscle in a functional relationship. Lieberman then noted that muscles leave marks on bones (and fossils), and that it is from these marks that one can infer where the muscles went. In working with fossils, a simple rule of comparative anatomy is helpful: one looks for a living animal with a skeleton structure similar to that of the extinct animal. If one wishes to model dinosaurs, for example, one looks to present-day, much smaller, lizards to get an idea of the skeletal morphology. In a similar manner the shape of vocal tracts in early man can be reconstructed. The human vocal tract is basically a tube which changes its shape according to the sound produced. If some gestures are anatomically and neuromuscularly impossible, the corresponding sounds can never be produced. This is how one can determine that Neanderthal man could not produce [i] and [u]. As Lieberman noted, one can pound brass tubes in various shapes and see what the resulting formant frequencies are, or one can use a computer to do the work digitally.

Peter Marler then asked Bosma if it were possible for skeletal differences to occur between two young organisms which have the same musculature but use it in a different fashion, and for such muscle usage to be reflected in the differences in adult skeletal morphology. Bosma concurred. As an example he noted that in some cases of polio of the tongue in a young human, the upper and lower jaws narrow considerably leaving a skeletal structure quite different from the normal adult human. The narrowing is entirely due to muscle inaction.

Lieberman noted that while there are such differences stemming from atrophy and hypertrophy, one cannot underestimate differences due to heredity. In a different domain, he gave the example of Genie, a girl who was strapped in a small chair in a small room at a very young age and left there for many years [see Fromkin et al., 1974]. She was never given the opportunity to walk until she was about twelve years old, and did so almost immediately after her release. In other words, she had the adult skeletal morphology requisite for walking and attained that structure entirely through maturation, not use of muscles. This is remarkable since the newborn infant does not have a morphology consonant with upright posture and walking. Lieberman's point is that such changes will occur whether or not the individual uses the muscles for the particular function that they were "intended" to be used for.

Marler found the analogy between locomotive function and vocal function a little hazardous. In the case of locomotion one may have a much clearer picture of the mechanical work that has to be done than in the case of speaking. It would appear that there are many more degrees of freedom in vocal signaling, and even more in speech. Lieberman replied by suggesting that this is not really the case. For example, the vowels [i, a, u] delimit, very nearly, the vowel space of human speech. Only a few more parameters are needed to specify the entire phonetic repertoire.

In summary, Lieberman's view of the evolution of speech is roughly that man first had something to say, second, had something to say it with, and third, became dextrous at maneuvering that apparatus. Bosma, in contrast, would reverse the order of the three steps.

Reference

Fromkin, V. A., S. Krashen, S. Curtiss, D. Rigler, and M. Rigler. 1974. The Development of Language in Genie: A Case of Language Acquisition beyond the "Critical Period." *Brain and Language,* 1: 81–108.

From Continuous Signal to Discrete Message: Syllable to Phoneme

MICHAEL STUDDERT-KENNEDY

All speech is syllabic. All languages constrain syllabic structure and base their constraints on the natural phonological contrast between consonant and vowel. Certainly, the human vocal tract is capable of producing an indefinite sequence of vowels, and even of certain consonants. But the choice of all languages has been to alternate consonants, or consonant clusters, and vowels. What is the communicative function of this choice? Mattingly [this volume] has sketched the broad outline. He has pointed to the complex encoding of discrete phonetic elements into a more or less continuous acoustic signal; he has shown how the code permits unusually rapid and efficient transfer of information; he has drawn striking formal analogies among phonetics, grammar, and memory. My purpose is to examine two aspects of the phonetic code in more detail: first, the structure and function of the syllable as reflected in perception; second, more briefly, the underlying cerebral mechanisms. Taken together, they suggest a natural system elegantly adapted to its role in linguistic communication.

Perceptual Structure and Function of the Syllable

Let me say, to begin with, that precise definition of consonant and vowel[1] is even more difficult than the definition of syllable. For, as Sweet [1877, p. 51] observed, "the boundary between vowel and consonant, like that between the different kingdoms of nature, cannot be drawn with absolute definiteness." Most of what I have to say deals only with stop consonants and relatively sustained monophthongal vowels. Our knowledge of speech perception comes largely from study of these two phonetic classes and their combination in a simple consonant-vowel (CV) syllable. But I believe this knowledge can furnish quite general insights.

The syllable is an articulatory and acoustic integer. Greek grammarians gave us the word for it: *sullabē*, "a taking together," syllable. Roman grammarians gave us words for the elements that are taken together: *littera vocalis*, "the voiced letter," vowel, and *littera consonans*, "the letter that sounds with" the vowel, the consonant. Into the syllable the speaker encodes, and from it the listener decodes, these discrete, phonetic segments. Among the evidence for the psychological reality of such segments is the corpus of spoonerisms gathered by Fromkin [1971]. Here, one aspect

---

[1] "Consonant" and "vowel" refer to elements in the phonetic message rather than to their correlates in the acoustic signal. I have used the terms for both meanings in what follows and trust that context will make clear which is intended.

of her data is of particular interest. Speakers may blunder by exchanging syllables for syllables, consonants for consonants, and vowels for vowels, but they never metathesize across classes. They may say, "I'll have a slice of [bost rif]," or even "of [rist bof]," but never "of [iost brf]." The syllable, itself a functional unit, is compounded of consonant and vowel, each fulfilling some syllabic function that forbids their metathesis.

Stetson [1951] gave us some understanding of these functions in production. He recognized the syllable as the fundamental unit of speech, the unit of stress contrast, of rhythm and meter. His motor definition of the syllable as a "chest pulse" has not stood up, at least for unstressed syllables [Ladefoged, 1967, Chapter 1]. But his description of the time course of the syllable is still useful. He described the consonant-vowel-consonant (CVC) syllable as "a single ballistic movement," composed of release, nucleus, and arrest. Similarly, Pike [1943] described speech as alternate constrictions and openings of the vocal tract.

One obvious acoustic correlate of the syllabic movement can be seen in the amplitude display of a spectrogram. The onset of an open (CV) syllable tends to yield a low, but rapidly rising, amplitude, the nucleus a relatively sustained peak. For a longer utterance we can make a crude syllabic count from the amplitude peaks. The count is crude because many utterances (the word *tomorrow*, [təmɔro], for example) may yield a single peak (due only in part to the sluggishness of the spectrograph's amplitude integrating response), even though we know they contain several syllables. Where amplitude fails to reveal syllabic structure, formant pattern may serve: the initial pattern tends to display a rapid movement, or scatter, of energy over the frequency domain, while the later portion tends to be relatively stable and sustained [see Malmberg, 1955]. Taken together, changes in amplitude and frequency offer an acoustic contrast between the beginning and the end of a CV syllable, between its onset and its nucleus. The event is unitary, but its character changes as it occurs. This ill-defined acoustic contrast provides the auditory ground for the perceptual consonant and vowel.

Let us turn, first, to the phenomenon of categorical perception. Experiments have repeatedly revealed differences between stop consonants and vowels in their patterns of identification and discrimination. Stimuli for these experiments consist of a dozen or so synthetic speech sounds distributed in equal acoustic steps along a continuum ranging across two or more phonetic categories (from, say, [b] to [d] to [g] or from [i] to [ɪ] to [ɛ]). In identification, listeners are asked to assign each of the stimuli, presented repeatedly and in random order, to one of the phonetic classes. They then assign consonants more consistently than they do vowels, particularly those tokens close to a boundary between phonetic classes. In other words, they identify consonants absolutely or "categorically," independently of the test context, while they identify vowels relatively or "continuously," with marked contextual effects [Liberman et al., 1961; Fry et al., 1962].

Here we have the first, and oldest, indication that listeners have a longer short-term auditory store for vowels than for consonants. Recently, Sawusch and Pisoni [1974] have elaborated with the finding that vowels, like nonspeech tones, are susceptible to psychophysical anchoring effects: the boundary between synthetic vowels along an acoustic continuum is shifted toward the vowel that occurs most frequently in the test. For consonants, the effect is absent: the listener relies on some internal standard, less readily subverted by test composition. Note, incidentally, that if a vowel, already assigned to its phonetic class, is to affect phonetic assignment of following vowels, the listener must retain an auditory image, or echo, of the vowel even after he has identified it. The process of identification does not therefore terminate auditory display: auditory store and phonetic store can exist simultaneously [see Wood, 1973b].

In the related discrimination task, typically administered in ABX format, a listener is called on to discriminate between pairs of tokens separated by one or more equal acoustic steps along the synthetic continuum. If these tokens are drawn from different phonetic classes, discriminative performance is high for both consonants and vowels. If they are drawn from the same phonetic class, discriminative performance drops slightly for vowels and considerably, to a point little better than chance, for consonants. In other words, a listener discriminates between vowels at a relatively high level whether he assigns them to different phonetic categories or not: his discrimination is more or less independent of identification, much as it is for nonspeech sounds [Mattingly et al., 1971]. But a listener can reliably discriminate between consonants only if he assigns them to different phonetic categories: his discrimination depends upon and, to a fair degree, can be predicted from, his phonetic assignments [Liberman et al., 1961; Studdert-Kennedy et al., 1970].

Early accounts of this phenomenon pointed to articulatory differences between consonants and vowels, but their acoustic differences have proved more crucial. Stevens [1968] remarked the brief, transient nature of consonantal acoustic cues, and Sachs [1969] showed that vowels were more categorically perceived if their duration and acoustic stability were reduced by CVC context. Lane [1965] pointed to the greater duration and intensity of the vowels and showed that they were more categorically perceived if they were "degraded" by being presented for discrimination in noise.

The role of auditory, or echoic, memory, implicit in the work of Stevens, of Sachs, and of Lane, was made explicit by Fujisaki and Kawashima [1969, 1970]. They argued that the listener's poor auditory memory for consonants forced him to rely, for ABX discrimination, on phonetic memory. They formulated a mathematical model of the process and showed that, if they reduced vowel duration sufficiently, their model would predict quite accurately the discrimination of both consonants and vowels from listeners' phonetic identifications.

Pisoni [1971, 1973] made a direct test of this account. He varied the intratrial interval in an AX "same"-"different" task. For vowels, an increase in the A-X interval (with a presumed decrease in clarity of A's auditory store) led to a decrease in the likelihood that a listener would judge two acoustically different, but phonetically identical, tokens as "different." For consonants, there was no significant effect. In several other experiments, Pisoni [1975] has shown that the degree to which vowels are perceived categorically (measured by the degree to which phonetic class predicts discriminability), may be varied by manipulating the degree to which auditory memory is made available in the experimental task. Note, however, that while a fair degree of categorical perception of vowels can be readily induced, continuous perception of consonants is much more difficult [Pisoni and Lazarus, 1974]. The listener's auditory memory for consonants is intrinsically short.

Consider next dichotic ear advantages. As is well known, Kimura [1961a, 1961b, 1967] showed that if different digits are presented to opposite ears at the same time (dichotically), those presented to the right ear are recalled more accurately than those presented to the left. She attributed the effect to specialization of the left cerebral hemisphere for language functions and to stronger contralateral than ipsilateral ear-to-hemisphere connections. The effect and her interpretation have been repeatedly supported.

Shankweiler and Studdert-Kennedy [1967] used Kimura's technique to probe the processes of speech perception. They showed that the right ear advantage did not depend on higher language processes, since it could be obtained with pairs of nonsense syllables differing only in an initial or final stop consonant. Furthermore, they showed that the effect did not appear if the competing syllables were steady-state vowels or CVC syllables differing only in their vowels [Studdert-Kennedy and Shankweiler, 1970]. Following Kimura and others [Milner, Taylor, and Sperry, 1968; Sparks and Geschwind, 1968], they assumed that ipsilateral ear-to-hemisphere connections were inhibited by dichotic competition, so that, while right ear inputs reached the left (language) hemisphere by a direct contralateral path, left ear inputs traveled an indirect route, contralaterally to the right hemisphere, then laterally across the corpus callosum to the left hemisphere. The ear advantage was due to loss of auditory information from the left ear signal as it traveled its indirect path to the language hemisphere. The consonant-vowel difference in ear advantage could then be attributed to the same acoustic factors as their differences in degree of categorical perception: the vowel portion of the signal, being more intense and of greater duration than the consonant, suffers less loss or "degradation" on the left-ear-to-left-hemisphere indirect path, and so yields no reliable right ear advantage. This is probably not the whole story, since nonacoustic, attentional factors have also been implicated [see, for example, Spellacy and Blumstein, 1970]. However, Weiss and House [1973] have played for dichotic ear advantages the role that Lane [1965] played for categorical perception: they have shown that a right ear advantage appears for vowels if the vowels are presented dichotically in noise.

Yet another experimental paradigm yielding stop consonant-vowel differences, this time directly in short-term memory, is due to Crowder [1971, 1972, 1973]. If subjects are given, one item at a time, a span-length list of digits for immediate, ordered recall, they recall the last several digits more accurately when the list has been presented by ear than when it has been presented by eye. This modality difference presumably reflects the operation of separate modality stores, the short-term auditory store being more retentive than the visual [Crowder and Morton, 1969]. This interpretation is supported by the fact that the advantage to the most recent auditory items (recency effect) is reduced or eliminated if the list ends with a redundant verbal item, as a signal for the subject to begin recall (suffix effect). That the suffix interferes with auditory store is suggested by the fact that the effect occurs for either backwards or forwards speech, is reduced if list and suffix are spoken in different voices, and is absent if the suffix is a tone.

The finding of interest in the present context is simply that while all three effects (modality, recency, suffix) are observed for lists of CV syllables differing in their vowels (for example, random repetitions of [gæ, ga, gʌ] or of [bi, bo, bu]), none of them is observed for CV or VC syllables differing in their initial or final stop consonant (random repetitions of [ba, da, ga] or of [ɪb, ɪd, ɪg]). Crowder [1971] concludes that vowels are included in precategorical, auditory store, but that stop consonants are excluded. Liberman, Mattingly, and Turvey [1972] agree with this conclusion, arguing further that phonetic decoding of the stops "strips away all auditory information," that phonetic classification terminates auditory display.

While this interpretation is unlikely to be correct [see Wood, 1973b], the difficulty of retaining auditory information about stop consonants is again suggested by results from a fourth experimental paradigm, devised by Dorman (1974). He synthesized three three-formant sounds: a 250-msec [bæ], a 250-msec [æ], and a "chirp," consisting of the first 50 msec of the synthesized [bæ]. The "chirp" contained all the acoustic information necessary for phonetic classification of the initial [b], but, separated from the following vowel, no longer sounded like speech. Dorman next varied the intensity of the "chirp" and of the first 50 msec of the two speech sounds in two steps: 0, —7.5, and —9 db. He then presented these stimuli in pairs, each member drawn from the same stimulus type, to ten subjects and asked them to judge whether the initial intensities of the pairs were "the same" or "different." The results were that every subject gave close to 100 percent performance on the vowels and "chirps" and close to 50 percent performance, or chance, on the CV syllables. In other words, asked to judge acoustic differences irrelevant to segmental classification, subjects could detect those differences in vowels or non-speech sounds, but not in stop consonants.

We must not exaggerate. Many experiments have demonstrated that listeners do retain at least some "echo," however rapidly fading, of stop consonants. All studies of categorical perception reveal some margin of auditory discriminability within stop consonant categories, and several experimenters have tested this directly. Barclay [1972], for example, showed that listeners could reliably judge variants of [d], drawn from a synthetic continuum, as more like [b] or more like [g]. Pisoni and Tash [1974] found that reaction times for "same" responses were faster to pairs of acoustically identical stop-vowel syllables than to pairs of phonetically identical, but acoustically different syllables.

Furthermore, Darwin and Baddeley [1974] have recently challenged Crowder's interpretation that stop consonants are excluded from precategorical store. They have shown that a moderate recency effect may be obtained with consonants if the syllables in the list are acoustically distinct [ʃa, ma, ga], even more if the consonants are in syllable-final position. They argue that listeners cannot make use of their auditory store of the later items in a list, if those items are acoustically similar and confusable as are [ba, da, ga]. They support their argument by demonstrating that the recency effect can be reduced or abolished for vowels, if the vowels are both very brief (30 msec of steady-state in a 60-msec CV syllable) and occupy neighboring positions on an F1-F2 plot. They conclude that "the consonant-vowel distinction is largely irrelevant," and they propose "acoustic confusability" as the determining variable.

However, among the determinants of "acoustic confusability" are the very acoustic factors that distinguish stop consonants from vowels, namely, energy and spectral stability. We have reviewed evidence from four experimental paradigms in which consonant and vowel perception differ. In three of these (and, no doubt, if one chooses in the fourth) the differences can be reduced or eliminated by taxing the listener's auditory memory for the vowel or by sensitizing it for the consonant. But these qualifications do not mitigate the consonant-vowel differences: they merely emphasize that the differences are there to be eliminated. There is little question that consonants are less securely stored in auditory memory than vowels. [For further discussion see Studdert-Kennedy, 1975; in press.]

Plausible communicative functions for these differences are not hard to find. Consider first, vowel duration. Long duration is not necessary for recognition. We can identify a vowel quite accurately and very rapidly from little more than one or two glottal pulses, lasting 10 to 20 msec. Yet in running speech vowels last 10 to 20 times as long. The increased length may be segmentally redundant, but it permits the speaker to display other useful information: variations in fundamental frequency, duration, and intensity within and across vowels offer possible contrasts in stress and intonation, and increase the potential phonetic range (as in tone languages). Of course, these gains also reduce the rate at which segmental information can be transferred, increase the duration of auditory store, and open the vowel to contextual effects, the more so, the larger the phonetic repertoire. A language built on vowels, like a language of cries, would be limited and cumbersome.

Adding consonantal "attack" to the vowel inserts a segment of acoustic contrast between the vowels, reduces vowel context effects, and increases phonetic range. The attack, itself part of the vowel (the two produced by "a single balistic movement") is brief, and so increases the rate of information transfer. Despite its brevity, the attack has a pattern arrayed in time and the full duration of its trajectory into the vowel is required to display the pattern. To compute the phonetic identity of the pattern, time is needed, and this is provided by the segmentally redundant vowel. Vowels are the rests between consonants.

Rapid consonantal gestures cannot carry the melody and dynamics of the voice. The segmental and suprasegmental loads are therefore divided over consonant and vowel—the first, with its poor auditory store, taking the bulk of the segmental load, and the second taking the suprasegmental load. There emerges the syllable, a symbiosis of consonant and vowel, a structure shaped by the articulatory and auditory capacities of its user, fitted to, defining, and making possible linguistic and paralinguistic communication.

Cerebral Specialization for Syllable Perception

The distinctive acoustic structure of the syllable into which the speaker encodes consonant and vowel seems to call for a specialized neurophysiological decoding mechanism in the listener. Evidence for the operation of such a mechanism first came from the dichotic listening studies mentioned above [Shankweiler and Studdert-Kennedy, 1967; Studdert-Kennedy and Shankweiler, 1970]. One question that these studies tried to answer was whether the mechanism was specialized for both auditory and phonetic analysis of the syllable or for phonetic analysis alone. I will not review the evidence here, but simply state our conclusion that "while the auditory system common to both hemispheres is equipped to extract the auditory parameters of a speech signal, the dominant hemisphere may be specialized for the extraction of linguistic features from these parameters" [Studdert-Kennedy and Shankweiler, 1970, p. 594].

As we shall see shortly, recent evidence suggests that this conclusion may not be correct: the left himisphere may be specialized for both auditory and phonetic analysis. First, however, we should note that Wood [1973a; also Wood, Goff, and Day, 1971] has provided impressive support for the conclusion in a study of the evoked potential correlates of phonetic perception. He synthesized two stop-vowel syllables, [ba] and [ga], which differ only in the extent and direction of their second and third formant transitions, the acoustic cues to their phonetic identities. He synthesized each at two fundamental frequencies: 104 Hz (low) and 140 Hz (high). From these syllables he constructed two types of test. In the first, fundamental frequency was held constant and the syllables were presented binaurally in random order: subjects identified each syllable phonetically, as fast as possible, by pressing one of two buttons. In the second type of test, phonetic identity was held constant, while fundamental frequency varied: subjects identified the fundamental frequency of each syllable as high or low. Both types of test therefore contained tokens of the same syllables, identified by pressing the same button with the same finger. During the tests, electrical activity was recorded from a central and a temporal scalp location over both left and right hemispheres. Evoked potentials were averaged and compared at each scalp location for the preresponse periods during presentation of identical syllables in the two tasks. Notice that the only possible source of variation in the EEG records compared was in the task carried out by the subjects while the records were taken. Statistical tests revealed significant differences between left hemisphere records for the phonetic and fundamental frequency tasks at both locations. No significant differences appeared for either of the right hemisphere locations. Furthermore, when the "speech" task called for identification of the isolated formant transitions of the two syllables—acoustic patterns which carry all the information necessary for phonetic identification, but which, lacking a following vowel, are not heard as speech—there were no significant left hemisphere differences between records for "speech" and nonspeech tasks. The previously observed differences cannot therefore have been due to auditory analysis of the information-bearing formant transitions, but must presumably be attributed to phonetic interpretation of the auditory patterns. The experiments leave little doubt that different neural events occur in the left hemisphere, but not in the right, hemisphere during phonetic, as opposed to auditory analysis of the same acoustic signal.

In other words, the language hemisphere does indeed appear to be specialized for phonetic interpretation (and, presumably, higher language functions), but not for auditory analysis of speech. This might seem to imply that the physical vehicle of the phonetic message is a matter of indifference. Superficial support for this view comes from two further sources. First, Papçun et al. [1974; also Krashen, 1972], have shown that experienced Morse code operators, identifying both individual letters and words presented dichotically, show a significant right ear advantage. Second, Kimura [see Kimura and Durnford, 1974] and others have repeatedly shown a right field (left hemisphere) advantage for tachistoscopically presented letters. If both Morse code and printed letters can invoke left hemisphere processing, there might seem to be little reason to claim any special status for speech.

Nonetheless, there are solid grounds for making this claim. First, several studies have suggested that the left hemisphere is specialized for extracting acoustic features important in speech. Halperin, Nachshon, and Carmon [1973] have shown that the dichotic ear advantage shifts from left to right as the number of transitions in brief, temporally patterned sound sequences increases. Among their stimuli were permutations of three long (400 msec) and short (200 msec) sound bursts similar to the patterns used in Morse code. Their results therefore fit neatly with those of Krashen [1972], who found that naive subjects have a right ear advantage for dot-dash sequences no more than seven units long. Taken together, the two studies suggest left hemisphere specialization for judging duration and temporal pattern. Both studies have the weakness that subjects were asked to label the sequences, a process that might well invoke left hemisphere control.

This objection is not decisive since arbitrary labeling of isolated formant transitions in Wood's [1973a] study did not evoke the left hemisphere potentials of phonetic labeling. Nonetheless, the weakness is avoided in some recent experiments by Cutting [1974]. In one of these he constructed two-formant patterns identical with patterns signaling [bV] or [dV] except that their first formant transitions fell rather than rose along the frequency scale, producing a phonemically impossible sound that subjects did not recognize as speech. In a nonlabeling dichotic recognition task with these stimuli, subjects gave a right ear advantage of the same magnitude as for the normal CV syllables also used in the study. Cutting concludes from this and other experiments that the left hemisphere may be specialized for auditory analysis of speech.

But why then did the isolated transitions of Wood [1973] yield no left hemisphere effect? The answer to this may be that the speech auditory analyzer is engaged not simply by acoustic features, but by features distributed over a signal of some minimum duration (such as that of a stressed syllable). Here the work of Wollberg and Newman [1972] on squirrel monkeys is suggestive. They made single-cell recordings from cortical neurons responsive to the species' "isolation peep." A normal pattern of neuronal response occurred only if the entire "peep" was presented. Perhaps it is not far-fetched to suppose that the human cortex is supplied with sets of acoustic detectors tuned to speech, each inhibited from output to the phonetic system in the absence of collateral response in other detectors.

Be that as it may, the evidence for specialized left hemisphere auditory analysis is, at best, preliminary and, in any case, not essential to the claim of special status for speech. Nor, indeed, is any form of speech-specific auditory analysis, whether unilateral or bilateral. Certainly, the accumulating evidence for specialized acoustic property detectors [Cutting and Eimas, this volume] is important and may even be decisive. But the initial strength of the claim comes from the distinctive structure of the syllable. The underlying phonological elements that determine this structure are common and peculiar to all languages. And recovery of those elements, whether from alphabet, optophonic light pattern, Morse code, or the neural display of an auditory system, engages mechanisms in the language hemisphere. The syllable is the structure on which the hierarchy of language is raised.

References

Barclay, J. R. 1972. Noncategorical perception of a voiced stop. *Perception and Psychophysics,* 11: 269–274.

Crowder, R. G. 1971. The sound of vowels and consonants in immediate memory. *J. Verbal Learning and Verbal Behavior,* 10: 587–596.

Crowder, R. G. 1972. Visual and auditory memory. In *Language by Ear and by Eye,* Kavanagh, J. F. and I. G. Mattingly (eds.). Cambridge, Mass.: MIT Press.

Crowder, R. G. 1973. Precategorical acoustic storage for vowels of short and long duration. *Perception and Psychophysics,* 13: 502–506.

Crowder, R. G. and J. Morton. 1969. Precategorical acoustic storage (PAS). *Perception and Psychophysics,* 5: 365–373.

Cutting, J. E. 1974. Two left-hemisphere mechanisms in speech perception. *Perception and Psychophysics,* 16: 601–612.

Cutting, J. E. and P. Eimas. Phonetic feature analyzers and the processing of speech in infants. This volume.

Darwin, C. J. and A. D. Baddeley. 1974. Acoustic memory and the perception of speech. *Cognitive Psych.,* 6: 41–60.

Dorman, M. 1974. Discrimination of intensity differences on format transitions in and out of syllable context. *Perception and Psychophysics,* 16: 84–86.

Fromkin, Voctoria. 1971. The nonanomalous nature of anomalous utterances. *Language,* 47: 27–52.

Fry, D. B., A. S. Abramson, P. D. Eimas, and A. M. Liberman. 1962. The identification and discrimination of synthetic vowels. *Language and Speech,* 5: 171–189.

Fujisaki, H. and T. Kawashima. 1969. On the modes and mechanisms of speech perception. *Annual Report of the Engineering Research Institute, University of Tokyo,* 28: 67–73.

Fujisaki, H. and T. Kawashima. 1970. Some experiments on speech perception and a model for the perceptual mechanism. *Annual Report of the Engineering Research Institute, University of Tokyo,* 29: 207–214.

Halperin, Y., I. Nachshon, and A. Carmon. 1973. Shift of ear superiority in dichotic listening to temporally patterned verbal stimuli. *J. Acoust. Soc. Amer.,* 53: 46–50.

Kimura, D. 1961a. Some effects of temporal lobe damage on auditory perception. *Canad. J. Psychol.,* 15: 156–165.

Kimura, D. 1961b. Cerebral dominance and the perception of verbal stimuli. *Canad. J. Psychol.,* 15: 166–71.

Kimura, D. 1967. Functional asymmetry of the brain in dichotic listening. *Cortex,* 3: 163–178.

Kimura, D. and M. Durnford. 1974. Normal studies on the function of the right hemisphere in vision. In *Hemisphere Function in the Human Brain,* S. J. Dimond and J. G. Beaumont (eds.). London: Elek Science.

Krashen, S. 1972. Language and the left hemisphere. *Working Papers in Phonetics,* 24. UCLA Phonetics Laboratory.

Ladefoged, P. 1967. *Three Areas of Experimental Phonetics.* New York: Oxford University Press.

Lane, Harlan L. 1965. The motor theory of speech perception: A critical review. *Psychol. Rev.* 72: 275–309.

Liberman, A. M., K. S. Harris, J. Kinney, and H. Lane. 1961. The discrimination of relative onset time of the components of certain speech and nonspeech patterns. *J. Exp. Psychol.,* 61: 379–388.

Liberman, A. M., I. G. Mattingly, and M. Turvey. 1972. Language codes and memory codes. In *Coding Processes in Human Memory,* A. W. Melton and E. Martin (eds.). Washington: V. H. Winston.

Malmberg, B. 1955. The phonetic basis for syllable division. *Studia Linguistica,* 9: 80–87.

Mattingly, I. G. The human aspect of speech. This volume.

Mattingly, I. G., A. M. Liberman, A. K. Syrdal, and T. Halwes. 1971. Discrimination in speech and nonspeech modes. *Cognitive Psych.,* 2: 131–157.

Milner, B., L. Taylor, and R. W. Sperry. 1968. Lateralized suppression of dichotically-presented digits after commissural section in man. *Science,* 161: 184–185.

Papçun, G., S. Krashen, D. Terbeek, R. Remington, and R. Harshman. 1971. Is the left hemisphere specialized for speech, language and or something else? *J. Acoustic Soc. Amer.,* 55: 319–327.

Pike, Kenneth L. 1943. *Phonetics.* Ann Arbor: University of Michigan Press.

Pisoni, D. B. 1971. On the nature of categorical perception of speech sounds. Unpublished Ph.D. thesis, University of Michigan, Ann Arbor.

Pisoni, D. B. 1973. Auditory and phonetic memory codes in the discrimination of consonants and vowels. *Perception and Psychophysics,* 13: 253–260.

Pisoni, D. B. 1975. Auditory short-term memory and vowel perception. *Memory and Cognition,* 3: 7–18.

Pisoni, D. B. and J. H. Lazarus. 1974. Categorical and non-categorical modes of speech perception along the voicing continuum. *J. Acoust. Soc. Amer.,* 55: 318–333.

Pisoni, D. B. and J. Tash. 1974. Reaction times to comparisons within and across phonetic categories. *Perception and Psychophysics,* 15: 285–290.

Sachs, R. M. 1969. Vowel identification and discrimination in isolation vs. word context. Research Laboratory of Electronics, MIT, *QPR* 93: 220–229.

Sawusch, J. R. and Pisoni, D. B. 1974. Category boundaries for speech and nonspeech sounds. *J. Acoust. Soc. Amer.,* 55: 436 (A).

Shankweiler, D. P. and M. Studdert-Kennedy. 1967. Identification of consonants presented to left and right ears. *Q. J. Exp. Psychol.,* 19: 59–63.

Sparks, R. and N. Geschwind. 1968. Dichotic listening in man after section of neocortical commissures. *Cortex,* 4: 3–16.

Spellacy, F. and S. Blumstein. 1970. The influence of language set on ear preference in phoneme recognition. *Cortex,* 6: 430–439.

Stevens, Kenneth N. 1968. On the relations between speech movements and speech perception. *Z. Phon. Sprachwiss. u. Komm. Fschg.,* 21: 102–106.

Stetson, R. H. 1951. *Motor Phonetics.* Amsterdam: North-Holland.

Studdert-Kennedy, M. 1975. Information processing in phonetic perception. In *Contemporary Issues in Experimental Phonetics,* N. J. Lass (ed.). Springfield, Ill.: Charles C Thomas.

Studdert-Kennedy, M. In press. The perception of speech. In *Current Trends in Linguistics,* T. A. Sebeok (ed.). The Hague: Mouton. Also in Haskins Laboratories Status Report on Speech Research. 1970. SR-23, 15–48.

Studdert-Kennedy, M. and Shankweiler, D. P. 1970. Hemispheric specialization for speech perception. *J. Acoust. Soc. Amer.*, 48: 579–594.

Studdert-Kennedy, M., A. M. Liberman, K. S. Harris, and F. S. Cooper. 1970. The motor theory of speech perception: a reply to Lane's critical review. *Psychol. Rev.* 77: 234–249.

Sweet, H. 1877. *Handbook of Phonetics.* Oxford: Clarendon Press. (Also, 1970. College Park, Md: McGrath.)

Weiss, M. S. and House, A. S. 1973. Perception of dichotically presented vowels. *J. Acoust. Soc. Amer.*, 53: 51–58.

Wollberg, Z. and J. D. Newman. 1972. Auditory cortex of squirrel monkey: response patterns of single cells to species specific vocalizations. *Science,* 175: 212–214.

Wood, C. C. 1973a. Levels of processing in speech perception: neurophysiological and information processing analyses. Unpublished Ph.D. dissertation, Yale University.

Wood, C. C. 1973b. Parallel processing of auditory and phonetic information in speech perception. *J. Acoust. Soc. Amer.*, 55: 435(A).

Wood, C. C., W. R. Goff, and R. S. Day. 1971. Auditory evoked potentials during speech perception. *Science,* 173: 1248–1251.

Phonetic Feature Analyzers and the Processing of Speech in Infants

JAMES E. CUTTING AND PETER D. EIMAS

Recently, Kaplan and Kaplan [1971] asked the question: "Is there such a thing as a prelinguistic child?" The traditional answer was a rather emphatic yes: for example, the first months of a child's life are generally characterized by nonlinguistic vocalizations [Jakobson, 1968; Lieberman, Crelin, and Klatt, 1972; Kewley-Port and Preston, 1974]. Recent work, however, indicates that the answer to this question might be no; in fact, must be no.

Certainly one must be impressed with the child's rapid mastery of complex speech utterances and the rules for generating them [see Bloom, 1970; McNeill, 1970; Slobin, 1971; Menyuk, 1971; Brown, 1973]. This research, however, has dealt with the speech production of children between the ages of 18 months and 5 years. Before that time, and certainly before the age of 12 months, the speech productions of a child are rather infrequent and erratic; semirandom babbling is the rule. Indeed, when the infant is very young there is evidence that his vocal tract is not even equipped to emit a repertoire of speech sounds that correspond to those found in the speech of normal adults [Lieberman et al., 1971]. Since the ontogeny of language production in the infant appears to be severely constrained by the ontogeny of the vocal apparatus, the answer to the Kaplans' question may lie in the realm of speech perception rather than speech production.

The mechanisms for auditory processing, like those for other sensory systems, are functional in the neonate. Wolff [1966] has shown that at two weeks the infant can tell the difference between a voice and other auditory sounds; Wertheimer [1961] has shown that neonates can localize sounds at birth, and there is evidence that the fetus responds to auditory stimulation several weeks before birth [Bernard and Sontag, 1947], perhaps even to the speech of the mother.[1] Since the young infant has a sufficiently tuned auditory apparatus, it seems reasonable to devise an experimental situation in which the infant is asked if he can perceive language events in a linguistic fashion. Two problems immediately arise: (*a*) what question should we ask, and (*b*) how should we ask it?

The Appropriate Linguistic Question
It would be somewhat ludicrous to ask the infant to disambiguate a syntactically ambiguous sentence. Instead, it would be more appropriate to

[1] J. Bosma and D. Baker, personal communication.

ask him about an earlier aspect of language processing [see Studdert-Kennedy, in press]. An infant, for example, might be able to make a discrimination at the phonological level; or, perhaps more likely, he might be able to perceive the difference between a pair of phonemes which differ along a single phonetic feature. Since this appears to be a reasonable level of language to ask the infant about, it is necessary to consider which phonetic features the infant might be able to perceive.

One prominent feature is voicing. This feature separates the consonant phonemes in the following nonsense syllables: [ba] (as in *bottle*) from [pa], [da] from [ta], and [ga] from [ka]. A second candidate is place of articulation, a feature which distinguishes [ba] from [da] from [ga], and [pa] from [ta] from [ka]. Nasalization is a third phonetic feature which, for example, distinguishes [ma] from [ba]. Frication is a fourth likely feature, a dimension roughly separating [sa] from [ta].

In our first study [Eimas et al., 1971], we selected the feature of voicing. Voicing is a very stable phonetic feature for particular individuals within a given culture [Lisker and Abramson, 1964, 1967]; it is universal in all languages, or nearly so [Lisker and Abramson, 1964, 1970; Abramson and Lisker, 1965, 1970]; and it is quite prominent in the acoustic stream [Jakobson, Fant, and Halle, 1951]. Also, voiced and voiceless consonants can be synthesized rather easily by a computer-driven parallel-resonance synthesizer, such as that available at the Haskins Laboratories [Mattingly, 1968]. Moreover, they can be synthesized along a continuum with equal increments of acoustic change between the members of the stimulus array.

Since more is known about initial consonants than final or medial ones, the stimuli used in the first experiment and all subsequent ones were initial consonants in consonant-vowel (CV) nonsense syllables. The voiced-consonant syllables were all perceived as [ba] by adult listeners, and the voiceless-consonant syllables were perceived as [pa]. In natural speech, syllable-initial [b] and [p] phonemes are distinguished by the timing relationship between the release of the constriction at the lips, and the onset of the pulsing of the vocal folds. For an American English [ba] these two events happen very nearly at the same time. For [pa], however, there is a slight lag in the onset of the action of the vocal folds. Thus, the release of the constriction may occur 40 to 70 msec before the onset of voicing at the glottis.

Our linguistic question must be redefined as two questions. First, can the infant tell the difference between members of a cross-phoneme-boundary pair of stimuli; for example, [ba] from [pa]? If the answer is yes, a more sophisticated second question must then be asked: like the adult, can the infant *not* tell the difference between members of a within-phoneme-boundary pair; that is, two tokens of [ba] that have different voice onset times, or correspondingly, two different tokens of [pa]? For adults this peculiar capability is called categorical perception [see, among others, Liberman, 1957; Liberman, Harris, Kinney, and Lane, 1961; Abramson and Lisker, 1965; Liberman, Cooper, Shankweiler and Studdert-Kennedy, 1967; Mattingly, Liberman, Syrdal, and Halwes, 1971; Pisoni, 1971, 1973]. Unlike most acoustic patterns, certain members of some speech continua appear to be discriminable only to the extent that the member stimuli can be labeled differently. If infants yield experimental results that are functionally parallel to those of adults, the inference is nearly irresistible that infants perceive speech.

The Linguistic Question Appropriately Posed

Knowing what to ask the infant is only half the battle; how to ask the question is the other and perhaps more difficult half. Here it is necessary to consider what the infant does, and what is important in his ecology.

Young infants sleep an inconvenient amount of time, and to find an awake and alert infant is in itself not a trivial problem. In order to measure his receptivity to events in his environment it is necessary to use one of the many indicants of the orienting response, some of which are found even in neonates [Kessen, Haith, and Salapatek, 1970]. Successful measures of the infant's awareness of the environment and of environmental changes include visual fixation [for example, Karmel, 1969], changes in heart rate [for example, Graham and Jackson, 1970], and systematic changes in the EEG pattern [for example, Molfese, 1972; Dorman, 1974].

Another response system, which has high ecological validity and which plays a dominant role in the infant's earliest encounters with his environment, is the sucking response. Moreover, unlike heart rate and EEG recordings, sucking responses are highly visible and easily measured. Siqueland and DeLucia [1969] have used this response to great advantage in assessing the visual perception of infants. We have also used the sucking response, but our interest has been to evaluate the infant's perception of acoustic events.

In this experimental situation the infant is given a hand-held nipple upon which to suck. Instead of transducing nutrients the nipple transduces pressure, which is in turn transformed into polygraphic and digital records of the sucking responses. Contingent on the sucking response is the presentation of an auditory stimulus, one of the members of the speech continua synthesized for the study.[2] Two different methodological criteria

---

[2] In actuality, only high-amplitude sucking responses resulted in auditory stimulation. The amplitude was set for each infant individually, such that it yielded a baseline sucking rate between 20 and 30 responses per minute.

have been used for stimulus presentations. In one method, used by Eimas et al. [1971], the *intensity* of the stimulus is contingent on the rate of the infant response. While the rate of presentation is held constant, stimulus intensity is increased for rapid responding from an inaudible level to as much as 75 db sound pressure level against 63 db background noise. If the infant is not sucking at a high rate, the amplitude of the stimulus is systematically decreased.

In the second method, which is currently being used, the *rate* of the stimulus presentation is contingent on the rate of sucking. Stimulus presentation and sucking response are nevertheless not always related one-to-one. Each stimulus is 500 msec in duration, followed by a compulsory period of silence which is also 500 msec in duration. Thus, there is an irreducible refractory period of one second; though the infant may respond at a rate faster than one per second, the items are not presented at a rate greater than that. If, however, the infant sucks at a rate less than once per second, stimulus presentation rate exactly corresponds to response rate.

The infant quickly learns the relationship between the presentation of the stimulus and his sucking response, and he is quite willing to make from 200 to 600 sucking responses to listen to a particular stimulus during the course of a 10-minute experimental session. This remarkable effort to obtain stimulation is an impressive testament to the curiosity that we are born with.

Stimuli, Procedure, and Results
Shown at the top of Figure 1 is a sound spectrogram of an extremely prevoiced [ba], a stimulus in which the vibration of the vocal folds began 150 msec before the lip release was initiated. Plotting time against frequency, we see that the signal is easily divisible into three temporal segments: an initial low-frequency, low-amplitude steady-state voice bar which immediately precedes the release of the constriction, a 40-msec segment of formant transitions which increase in frequency, and a considerably longer segment of three steady-state formants which correspond to the vowel [a]. To vary stimuli along the dimension of voice onset time (VOT), several acoustic parameters must be changed. When a stimulus is varied between −150 msec VOT and 0 msec VOT, only the voice bar is altered. The duration of the voice bar denotes the appropriate negative value on the VOT continuum.[3] When voice onset follows the

---

[3] Convention has it that when voicing onset precedes the release the interval is measured in negative VOT values, and when voicing onset follows the release the interval is measured in positive values [Abramson and Lisker, 1965].

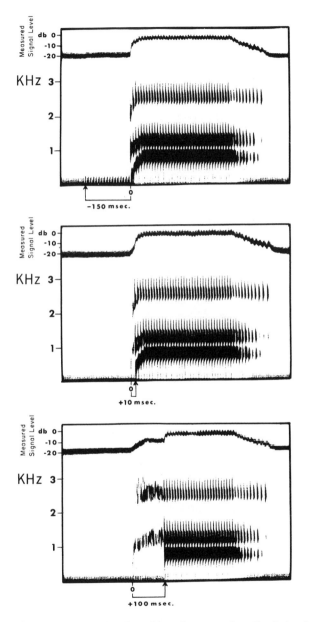

Figure 1. Three stimuli used in voice-onset time discrimination studies. In American English the first two are [ba], and the third is [pa]. (Adapted with permission from Abramson and Lisker, 1973).

release the acoustic manifestation of VOT is changed. The onset of the first formant is cut back by the amount of difference between release and voice onset. For example, if a stimulus has a +40-msec VOT, the onset of the first formant (F1) is precisely at the beginning of the steady-state resonance; that is, there is no F1 transition. Note that the lower spectrogram in Figure 1, the stimulus [pa], has no F1 transition.

Acoustic changes are also revealed in the upper formants for all positive value voice onsets. F2 and F3 retain their shapes and frequencies, but they are excited by a different sound source. Before voice onset an aperiodic, hissing sound is created by a local turbulence near the point of constriction in the mouth (in this case the lips). After voice onset the upper formants attain their more accustomed appearance, driven by the periodic glottal source. Figure 1 displays spectrograms of three stimuli from this type of continuum whose VOT values are —150, +10, and +100 msec. Also shown are the overall amplitude envelopes for each stimulus.

The stimuli used in the first study in this series were those from a [ba]–[pa] continuum synthesized by Lisker and Abramson at the Haskins Laboratories. The VOT values were —20, 0, +20, +40, +60, and +80 msec. Since the [b]–[p] phoneme boundary in English is at about +25 msec VOT [Lisker and Abramson, 1970; Abramson and Lisker, 1973], the pair of stimuli whose values are +20 and +40 lie within different phoneme categories; the +20 msec stimulus is typically identified as [ba], and the +40 msec stimulus is identified as [pa]. This pair is called the D pair since the members belong to different categories. Two other pairs of stimuli were S pairs since they belong within the same phoneme category. These pairs were —20 and 0, and +60 and +80. The members of the first pair are both identified by adults as [ba], and those of the second pair [pa].

Before the experimental session begins, a baseline sucking response rate must be obtained from each infant against which all subsequent response rates can be measured. Afterwards the experiment begins its preshift stage, and stimuli are presented contingent on the infant's sucking responses. Within a few minutes the infant learns the association between stimulus and response, and increases his response rate to approximately 50 or 60 responses per minute. After the response peak occurs the infant's responses typically decrease in a dramatic fashion, the hallmark of adaptation. At least two minutes after the peak rate and a decrease of at least 20 percent, the postshift experimental phase begins and the infant's response rates diverge according to the stimuli that are presented.

Members of Group *C,* the control group, continue to listen and respond to the same stimulus that they heard in the previous portion of the experiment. Regardless of which VOT stimulus the infants listen to, their response rate continues to decrease and approach an asymptote. Unlike those in the control group, Group *S* and *D* infants experience a shift in stimulation. Those in Group *S* listen and respond to a different stimulus, but nonetheless a stimulus whose initial consonant is from the same phoneme category. Their response rate, like that of the control group, typically continues to decrease toward zero.

Infants in Group *D,* on the other hand, listen and respond to a new stimulus whose initial consonant is a different phoneme. The response rate of this group is quite different from that of the other groups. Instead of continuing to decline, their response rate increases markedly. These infants often maintain a higher-than-preshift response rate throughout the four-minute postshift period. A schematic representation of the response rates typical of the three groups is shown in Figure 2. In the initial study [Eimas et al., 1971] there was no difference between the postshift response functions for Group *S* and Group *C.* Group *D,* however, showed a significantly higher response rate than either of the other two groups. Furthermore, one-month and four-month infants in this group yielded essentially identical response functions.

The implication of these results is compelling: since the infant and the adult perceive some speech events in a similar manner, and since the infant has had only a very limited exposure to language, the mecha-

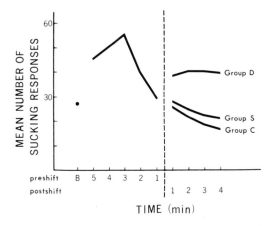

Figure 2. A schematic representation of the results of Eimas, Siqueland, Jusczyk, and Vigorito [1971] from tests in which infants were presented stimuli from a [ba]–[pa] continuum.

nisms by which he perceives speech must be innate. Perhaps they are phonetic feature analyzers, or property detectors.

Some Problems and Their Resolutions

Before amplifying this notion, however, it is necessary to consider a few problems. First, there are a few procedural difficulties. For example, in this type of experimental situation only about 40 to 50 percent of the infants make it through the entire session. Others cry or fall asleep, or their response rate decreases so rapidly before the experimental shift that it has fallen considerably below baseline. In this situation their data must be ignored. These difficulties, although trying for the experimenter, are minor. There is no reason to believe that infants would differ in the manner that they perceive these stimuli; that is, there is no evidence that infants who do not fulfill the requirements for remaining in the experiment possess analyzing systems of a markedly different nature. They are just fussier.

Another problem arises when considering the age of the infants that can be used as subjects. The first study used one- and four-month old infants for a very good reason. At younger than one month the infant will usually fall asleep before the 10- to 15-minute experimental session is complete. After four months the infant becomes too active, and begins to crawl out of the experimental apparatus and to pull at the surrounding paraphernalia. The limitations set by infant age, however, also appear to be rather minor. With respect to the younger infant in particular, there is no reason to believe that they have learned much, if anything, about their to-be-native language between birth and four weeks.

Other problems on a more theoretical level are not so easily dismissed. For example, it happens that the phoneme boundary at about $+25$ msec VOT is only one of two such boundaries. An additional boundary occurs in many languages at about -30 to -50 msec VOT. One language which uses this phonetic boundary is Thai; English, of course, does not. If, indeed, the results of the first study are explainable in terms of innate phonetic feature analyzers, we would expect that there would be another set of innate analyzers tuned for stimuli with VOT values greater than -30 to -50 msec. These phonetic detection devices would not be needed in English, and perhaps in the English-speaking adult they have become inoperable from lack of use. Nevertheless, all infants in all cultures might be expected to be born with such a set of phonetic analyzers.

This notion was examined in a paradigm identical to that of the previous study, except that here we looked at the infant's perception of the "Thai" boundary. D-pair stimuli had -70 and $+10$ msec values on the

VOT continuum. S-pair stimuli had values of -150 and -70 msec. Spectrograms of the -150 msec and $+10$ msec stimuli are shown in Figure 1. In this experimental situation Group D infants yield a response rate pattern similar to that of all infants who listen to cross-boundary pairs; their postshift response rate is significantly greater than their pre-shift response rate. Group S infants, however, show a somewhat atypical result. They too yield a postshift increase, although the increase is slight and nonsignificant. Nevertheless, the difference between the two groups is not significant; and thus there is only a suspicion that innate phonetic feature detectors exist in this range of the VOT continuum. Thus far, the "Thai" boundary results are neither supportive nor embarrasing for the phonetic feature detector hypothesis.

Another small theoretical hurdle arises when we reconsider the results of the initial experiment in light of what is known about the Spanish voiced and voiceless stop consonants. The Spanish VOT boundary for labials is at $+15$ msec VOT [Abramson and Lisker, 1973]. This fact is important here because in Spanish, the D pair stimuli of the initial study ($+20$ and $+40$ msec VOT) both lie within the [p] phoneme category. Would Spanish infants perceive these stimuli differently than American infants? Not likely.[4] It appears that, in terms of VOT boundary values, English is a much more reasonable language than Spanish; or, at least, it has a phonetic boundary which conforms to that of more languages than does Spanish. Since the English boundary value is about $+25$ msec VOT and the Spanish boundary differs from it by only 10 msec, the differences between the phonetic perceptions of labials in the two languages might be accounted for by perceptual tuning that occurs over time, shifting the boundary slightly according to the constraints of the culture that the individual is reared in.

The final and most serious theoretical problem concerns the nature of voice onset time as a true continuum. It takes only a brief glance at Figure 1 to see that, as stimuli vary in VOT from -150 to $+100$ msec, more acoustic change occurs within certain time domains than others. For example, there is little difference between stimuli of -150 and 0 msec VOT. All that separates them is a low-amplitude, low-frequency voice bar that barely registers on the amplitude display above the topmost spectrogram in Figure 1. Somewhat more acoustic change is manifested by differences in VOT from $+40$ to $+100$ msec as the first formant

---

[4] In a very recent study, Lasky, Syrdal-Lasky, and Klein [1975] have obtained evidence confirming our hypothesis that infants from Spanish-speaking environments perceive VOT differences in the same manner as infants in American English-speaking environments.

is cut back and the upper formants become aspirated. Nevertheless, the most prominent acoustic changes occur near the middle of this continuum between 0 and +40 msec VOT and it is here where the phonetic boundary lies. Along with changes in excitation of the upper formants, the first-formant transition is trimmed away piece by piece as stimuli increase in VOT, until at +40 msec there is no F1 transition. Imagine that, instead of phonetic feature detectors, there are auditory feature detectors that are triggered by low-frequency, rapidly rising frequency information [see Whitfield and Evans, 1965]. A +20 msec VOT stimulus has a brief transition, somewhat similar to that found in —40, —20, or 0 msec VOT stimuli. A +40 msec VOT stimulus, on the other hand, has no transition and is seemingly more like +60, +80, and +100 msec stimuli. Thus, there appear to be two categories of stimuli: those with and those without F1 transitions. Although this explanation cannot account for the adult data on categorical perception (consider for example the Spanish VOT boundary of +15 msec), Stevens and Klatt [1974] have suggested that it might account for the infant data in the initial study.

Herein lies an issue of major theoretical importance: do neonates come equipped with phonetic feature detectors or with speech-relevant auditory detectors which are later incorporated into the language system? Although the voice-voiceless distinction may be the most important phonetic distinction in all languages, it cannot easily be used to settle this issue. A phonetic dimension which is purer in an acoustic sense must be used. Place would appear to be such a feature, particularly with respect to stop consonants before front vowels.

Another Phonetic Feature: Place

We, along with others [Moffitt, 1971; Morse, 1972], have investigated the infant's perception of stop consonants which differ only in place of articulation. For the sake of generality we selected another vowel, [æ] as in *battle*. For the sake of simplicity of discussion we will consider here an experiment which used two-formant stimuli, [bæ] and [dæ]. Mattingly et al. [1971] used these exact stimuli in a previous speech perception experiment with adult subjects. Schematic representations of six stimuli selected for the present study are shown in Figure 3. All were 245 msec in duration, with 15 msec of prerelease voicing, 40 msec of formant transitions, and 190 msec of steady-state vowel. Stimuli differed only in the trajectory of the F2 transition: Stimulus 1, [bæ], had an F2 transition which increased in frequency from a value of 1232 Hz to 1620 Hz, while at the other extreme Stimulus 6, [dæ], had a steady-state F2 of 1620 Hz. Equal increments of change in the initial frequency of the F2 transitions arrayed the

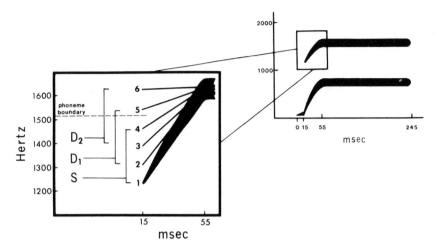

Figure 3. A schematic spectrogram of a two-formant [bæ] and the acoustic variation in the second-formant transition requisite for a [bæ]–[dæ] continuum.

six stimuli along an acoustic continuum. Since the [bæ]–[dæ] phoneme boundary occurs with a transition beginning at about 1500 Hz, Stimuli 1 and 4 were an S pair, while 2 and 5, and 3 and 6 were D pairs. Members of each pair differed by 230 Hz in the initial frequency of the F2 transition.

The experimental situation was the same as described earlier, and essentially so were the results.[5] As usual Group C and S infants continued to decrease their response rate in the postshift phase just as shown in Figure 2, while Group D infants increased their response rate with the advent of a stimulus beginning with a different phoneme. In this study, there was no difference between results of the D_1 and D_2 pairs. There was, however, a minor but interesting perturbation in the parallel between these results and those of the initial study represented in Figure 2. The postshift response function of the Group D infants differed slightly in shape. In Figure 2 the response rate for the first two minutes after the stimulus shift is approximately equal to that of the third and fourth minutes. In the present study this initial response rate was less than that of the third. However, in two other studies, the difference was even more pronounced and held for both the third and fourth minutes as well. In other words, the Group D infants in the place-of-articulation studies attained a postshift response peak later than those in the original VOT study. Enough data have been collected to consider this a real and signifi-

[5] See Eimas (1974) for a more detailed account.

cant difference. It is interesting, then, to consider the place distinction in light of what we already know about the voicing distinction. Miller and Nicely [1955] have shown that, in listening to syllable-initial consonant phonemes under conditions of white noise, voicing is preserved better than place. Also Shankweiler and Studdert-Kennedy [1967] found that voicing was a more prominent feature than place in the lateralization of speech as measured by the results of a dichotic listening task. We seem to have found a functional parallel to the results of the adult studies along a dimension which might be termed phonetic-feature strength.

Again, these results suggest that infants come into the world with bundles of *phonetic* feature analyzers. However, as with voicing, it remains possible that these discriminations could be made on the basis of auditory features alone. It happens that [dæ] syllables such as Stimuli 5 and 6 have very little, or no, second-formant transition, whereas [bæ] syllables such as Stimuli 1 through 4 have considerable F2 transitions. If infants had one auditory detector tuned to about 1500 Hz which was triggered by rapidly moving frequencies and another detector in the same range triggered by relatively constant frequencies, the results of the present study might easily be obtained.

Thus, in the present study we felt it necessary to include an additional experimental condition which considered this possibility. Instead of presenting the entire speech stimulus, the acoustic cue important for the phonetic categorization of the stop consonants, the F2 transition, was excised and presented by itself. Mattingly et al. [1971] have named these stimuli "chirps" because of their resemblance to the discrete elements of birdsong [see, for example, Marler and Mundinger, 1971]. Mattingly and his coworkers found that adults perceive these chirps differently in isolation than when they are part of a speech context. Would infants do the same? Yes, we found that, like adults, they perceive them differently.

The paradigm was again identical to that of previous studies, but there the stimuli were S-chirp and D-chirp pairs as represented in the inset of Figure 3, not the entire S and D pair stimuli. The results showed that infants *increase* their response rate during the postshift phase for *both* types of stimulus pairs.

The overall results of both the chirp and the full two-formant stimulus conditions of this study are represented in Table 1. The pattern is remarkably similar to that for adults found by Mattingly et al. [1971]. When the acoustic cue for a particular phoneme is part of the sound pattern of a speech utterance, infants can discriminate between items that lie across a phoneme boundary, but they cannot discriminate between items

Table 1. Perception of Variation in the Cue for Place of Articulation

	Can the Stimuli Be Discriminated?	
Speech Cue	D Pairs	S Pairs
Within the speech context	yes	no
Alone as nonspeech	yes	yes

from within the same phoneme category. However, when these acoustic cues are isolated and presented by themselves, all pairs become about equally discriminable. Such a pattern, whether in infants or adults, suggests that the isolated chirps are perceived in what can be described as a nonspeech mode, whereas the whole speech utterance (which necessarily includes the F2 transition) is perceived in a speech mode [Mattingly et al. 1971].

Auditory Feature Analyzers

Do these results invalidate the notion that acoustic feature analyzers (or, in a narrower sense, detectors) are involved in the infants' perceptions? Not at all. The question arises, however, as to how they contribute to the perception of speech.

Whitfield and Evans [1965] demonstrated that certain cortical neurons in the cat respond vigorously to glissandi, but not to steady-state tones. They also found single neurons which responded to specific direction of frequency change. For example, some units responded to frequency changes from low to high, but not for the reverse direction. Moreover, this type of detectors can be located in lower-than-cortical-level areas as well. Nelson, Erulkar, and Bryan [1966], for example, found frequency-change detectors at the level of the superior colliculus. We would expect that such auditory analyzers occur in humans as well.

Brady, House, and Stevens [1961] investigated adult human perception of sounds characterized by rapidly changing resonant frequencies, such as those found in the formant transitions of speech stimuli. Their results, like those of Mattingly et al. [1971], suggest that these nonspeech sound patterns are perceived differently than speech. However, the fact that they may be perceived in a different manner does not preclude the possibility that certain stages of auditory processing underlie speech processing. Consider the following example: Nabelek and Hirsh [1969] and Pollack [1968] found what could be described as two perceptual modes in the processing of frequency transitions in tone-like stimuli. The rules that govern the perception of long glissandi (those which last up to a second or more) are different from those for brief glissandi (those of less than

100 msec). More specifically, brief glissandi are more discriminable than longer ones with the same endpoint frequencies. Interestingly it is the brief glissandi which most resemble formant transitions in speech, and it is these which we found that two- and three-month-old infants could perceive and discriminate as brief chirps out of a speech context. Perhaps there are special auditory mechanisms for perceiving brief and rapidly changing auditory events, and these mechanisms contribute to speech perception by extracting from the acoustic signal speech-relevant information which can be used later in making a phonetic decision.

Cutting [1974] has elaborated this notion that there may be an intimate relation between the processing of speech and certain nonspeech sounds. It appears that transitional frequency information in complex nonspeech sounds is perceived in a manner similar to that of formant transitions in speech sounds. This inference stems from a result showing that, in dichotic listening, equal amounts of change in the transitions of both speech and nonspeech sounds appear to yield equal increments of perceptual change as measured by the right-ear advantage. In other words, adding formant transitions to vowel stimuli increases the magnitude of the right-ear advantage, and does so regardless of whether or not the transitions correspond to particular phoneme segments. Likewise, adding initial transitions to complex tone stimuli alters the resulting ear advantage in favor of the right-ear stimulus. Both results reflect an increase in the engagement of the processing mechanisms of the left-hemisphere system. Thus, the locus of speech-relevant acoustic processing may be intimately related to the locus of speech perception. It is clear, however, that phonetic decisions are not merely the end result of auditory processing [see also Liberman et al., 1967].

We have seen that the auditory feature analyzers by themselves cannot accommodate the infants' perception of speech. Perhaps auditory and phonetic feature analyzers function in a hierarchical way to determine in a direct sequential manner the results of the infant, and for that matter of the adult, studies of speech perception. Recent evidence, however, suggests that the contribution of the auditory analysis is not very directly involved in the infant's discrimination of speech sounds. Eimas [in press] has found that infants are insensitive to differences in VOT when D pairs of to-be-discriminated stimuli differ in the magnitude of their voice onset difference.

Whether the cross-boundary VOT difference is 20, 60, or even 100 msec, the relative increment in response rate does not change. Thus, stepping across the phoneme boundary is quantal and complete for the infant: there is no additive contribution of auditory analysis beyond that which is necessary for a phonetic decision. In this experimental situation auditory analysis appears to be too far removed from the phonetic decision making process to affect the results. The same conclusion appears to be true for the processing of cues for place of articulation. Thus, we conclude that, although it is necessary that some form of auditory analysis extract the speech-relevant information from the acoustic signal, this information merely provides the input to the special speech processing analyzers. It is not necessarily an immediate antecedent of quantal phonetic decisions.

Phonetic Feature Analyzers

A number of researchers have begun to consider and explore models of speech perception that are based on feature detectors and do not require knowledge of production processes [see, for example, Abbs and Sussman, 1971: Cole and Scott, 1972; Cooper, 1974; Cutting, 1974; Eimas and Corbit, 1973; Eimas, Cooper, and Corbit, 1973; Lieberman, 1970; Stevens, 1972]. Although these detector systems could be auditory or linguistic in nature, we believe that speech is analyzed by both auditory and phonetic feature detection. We further believe that these detector systems are arranged in a hierarchical manner, such that the perception of speech is mediated directly by phonetic feature detectors that are sensitive to relatively restricted ranges of complex acoustic energy.

There are numerous problems that remain unresolved in hypothesizing a phonetic feature detector model. For example, what number and how many kinds of detectors are needed, and what is the nature of the invariant acoustic information? Nevertheless, a model of this kind accommodates much of the data and, moreover, does so by means of mechanisms that are analogous to the detector systems known to exist for the processing of complex visual information in man [McCollough, 1965; Blakemore and Campbell, 1969]. The independent evidence for phonetic feature detectors is considerably less extensive than the evidence for visual detector systems. However, it is sufficient, we believe, to permit the inference that linguistic feature detectors exist and are the sole explanation for the results of the infant studies presented here.

In a recent series of experiments with adults, Eimas and Corbit [1973] obtained results which favor the existence of two phonetic feature detectors, one for the acoustic consequences of each of the two modes of voicing found in English and many other languages [Lisker and Abramson, 1964]. They used a selective adaptation procedure, whereby the voiced or voiceless member of a phonetic contrast, such as [b]–[p], could be adapted by the repeated presentation of a good exemplar of that voicing mode. To measure the effects of adaptation, identification functions for bilabial and apical series of synthetic speech sounds, each of which differed only in VOT, were obtained from the same listeners in both an adapted state and an unadapted state. If detectors existed for two voicing distinctions, it was reasoned, then repeated presentation of a particular phoneme exemplar would fatigue the detector underlying its analysis and reduce that detector's sensitivity. As a consequence, the identification functions for the series of synthetic speech sounds would be altered. The results confirmed our expectations. After adaptation with a voiceless stop, either [p] or [t], listeners assigned fewer stimuli to the voiceless category, especially those stimuli near the original phonetic boundary. Adaptation with a voiced stop, either [b] or [d], had the opposite effect—fewer stimuli were heard as voiced stops. Adaptation, in essence, resulted in a shift in the locus of the phonetic boundary toward the adapting stimulus. It is particularly important to note that the effects of adaptation were very nearly the same whether or not the adapting stimulus and the to-be-identified stimulus were from the same series of speech sounds. That is, adaptation with the voiced stop [d] altered the phonetic boundary for an array of bilabial stops nearly as effectively as did the bilabial stop [b]. It would appear, then, that the major effect of adaptation is to lower the sensitivity of the common voicing detector underlying the adapting stimulus and the members of the identification series.

Arguments are possible that the effects of adaptation are not sensory in nature, but rather reflect alterations in response decision factors. However, such explanations are difficult to defend given the fact that adaptation works across phoneme classes. Just how a response bias developed by the repeated presentation of [b], for example, might affect the tendency to assign the labels [d] or [t] to stimuli is not readily apparent. In addition, Sawusch and Pisoni [1974] have presented evidence that the identification functions for stop consonants are virtually unaffected by experimental manipulations that would be expected to produce marked changes in the assignment of phoneme labels according to the assumptions of both signal detection theory and adaptation-level theory. Such manipulations, however, do affect the identification of pure tones in a manner predicted by adaptation-level theory. [For other explanations of this phenomenon, see Ades, 1974; Bailey, 1973].

In a second experiment, Eimas and Corbit [1973] showed that selective adaptation could also alter the locus of the peak of discriminability in a series of bilabial stop consonants. This evidence strongly indicates that the discriminability of such an array of synthetic stops is based on the manner in which acoustic information is assigned to phonetic feature categories. Alterations in phonetic decision criteria, as measured by a shift in the locus of the phonetic boundary, were matched almost perfectly by the shift in the locus of the discriminability peak. Furthermore, Eimas, Cooper, and Corbit [1973] found that the site of adaptation was central and specific to the speech processing system. Presentation of the adapting stimulus to one ear and the identification series to the other unadapted ear did not alter either the direction or magnitude of the adaptation effects. However, when the voicing information, used for adaptation, was presented in a nonspeech context, there were no reliable or systematic effects of adaptation. This was true despite the exhortations of the experimenters, who suggested to some subjects that they might try to perceive the adapting stimuli as speech.[6]

Finally, Cooper [1974] has obtained evidence for the existence of phonetic feature detectors that mediate the perception of the three major distinctions for place of articulation. Using a selective adaptation procedure again and a series of synthetic speech sounds that varied in the starting frequency and direction of the second- and third-formant transitions, Cooper found marked shifts in the loci of the phonetic boundaries and peaks in the discriminability functions. All of these shifts were consistent with the assumption of three independent feature detectors.

A model of speech perception based on phonetic feature detectors yields a number of advantages as well as being able to accommodate much of the data on the perception of segmental units by both infants and adults. Eimas and Corbit [1973] have outlined a feature detector model that can account for the adult discrimination and identification data with and without adaptation. Eimas [in press] has extended the analysis to explain the data from infant studies of speech perception. It is with this extension that we will now be concerned. To explain the infant's ability to discriminate variations in the cues for voicing and place of articulation by reference to phonetic feature values, we need first to assume the presence of appropriate phonetic feature analyzers. These analyzers, by inference from our infant studies, must be operative shortly after birth, perhaps having been set in operation merely by experiencing speech. Given the passive nature of a feature detector analysis, the presentation of a signal with sufficient linguistic information to activate the speech processing mechanisms will excite each of the phonetic feature analyzers for

----

[6] More recent evidence from our laboratory [Tartter, 1975] indicates that it is possible to obtain reliable adaptation effects when the acoustic information is presented in a nonspeech context. Such findings clearly implicate an auditory level of analysis in addition to a phonetic level.

which there is an adequate stimulus. The repeated presentation of the same stimulus, which occurs in the infant studies, will result in the adaptation of the activated detectors [see also Eimas and Corbit, 1973]. Adaptation of the detectors, which presumably results in the diminution of their output signals, may well be related to the decrement in the reinforcing properties of novel stimuli and the subsequent decrement in the infant's response rate. The presentation of a second speech stimulus, which, although acoustically different, excites the same set of detectors, will not be experienced as a novel stimulus by the infant. Consequently, there will be no increased effort to obtain this stimulus. Introduction of a second stimulus that activates one or more different detectors, on the other hand, yields a different set of phonetic feature values and will be experienced as novel. Our notion is that the infant increases his response rate in order to obtain this new perception. From phonetic-feature detectability and from the infant's well-established appetite for novel stimulation, it can easily be predicted that infants in Groups S and C will, on the average, show continued decrement in the conditioned response rate during the final four minutes of the experiment. The infants in Group D, by contrast, will show a marked increase in the rate of response during the postshift minutes. This increment is unrelated to the amount of acoustic difference between the two stimuli. To explain the continuous discrimination of variations in second-formant transitions in a nonspeech context, we need to assume that there was not sufficient linguistic information in the stimulus to activate the speech processing mechanisms and that the processing of these sounds was limited to the more general, auditory mechanisms (see Eimas, Cooper, and Corbit, 1973; Mattingly et al., 1971).

We should consider why infants (and adults) are able to discriminate within-category variations of the second-formant transition in nonspeech settings and yet are unable to discriminate the same information in speech contexts. It seems reasonable to assume that an acoustic event, whether speech or nonspeech, undergoes much of the same auditory processing [see Cutting, 1974]. Hence, the failure to discriminate the same information in one context presents something of a paradox. Perhaps it is simply the case that the output of speech processing mechanisms takes precedence over the output of nonspeech auditory mechanisms. Or it is possible that phonetic processing requires more time than auditory analysis, and that at the conclusion of phonetic feature extraction, the relatively brief but complex auditory information, which signals consonantal features, has faded or in some other manner become unavailable to the response decision component [Fujisaki and Kawashima, 1968; Liberman, Mattingly, and Turvey, 1972]. The evidence to date does not permit us to choose among these and other explanations.

With regard to the advantages of linguistic detectors, the analysis of speech into phonetic features requires only that the acoustic event have sufficient linguistic information (phonetic information, for our purpose) to activate the speech processing mechanisms, and that the detectors be present and operative. This form of analysis does not require a decision on the listener's part that the acoustic signal is speech and, hence, in need of special processing. Analysis-by-feature detection is an automatic and passive process, and as such provides the infant with the means for the immediate recognition of speech and the means for parsing speech into discrete elements. These factors must surely hasten the acquisition of speech. Were it necessary for infants to learn that speech requires special processing and that speech is composed of discrete elements despite its continuous form, the acquisition of language would be a difficult and tedious process, if indeed language could be learned at all. Finally, the automatic analysis of speech into distinctive and invariant features provides the infant with a set of anchor points by which he can eventually come to recognize and master the considerable amount of context-conditioned variation found at all levels of language. That some of these anchor points might be more innate than others is not a serious problem. Without some degree of invariance in both the signal and processes of analysis, the acquisition of human languages would not be possible in the relatively short time that it takes a child to become a proficient user of language.

References

Abbs, J. H., and H. M. Sussman. 1971. Neurophysiological feature detectors and speech perception: a discussion of theoretical implications. *J. Speech and Hearing Research,* 14: 23–36.

Abramson, A. S., and L. Lisker. 1965. Voice onset time in stop consonants: acoustic analysis and synthesis. *Proceedings of the Fifth International Congress of Acoustics,* Liège, 1–4.

Abramson, A. S., and L. Lisker. 1970. Discriminability along the voicing continuum: cross-language tests. *Proceedings of the Sixth International Congress of Phonetic Sciences,* Prague, 1967, 15–25.

Abramson, A. S., and L. Lisker. 1973. Voice-timing perception in Spanish word-initial stops. *J. Phonetics,* 1: 1–8.

Ades, A. E. 1974. Bilateral component in speech perception? *J. Acoust. Soc. Amer.,* 56: 610–616.

Bailey, P. J. 1973. Perceptual adaptation for acoustical features in speech. *Speech Perception: Report on Research in Progress.* Queen's University, Belfast, Northern Ireland, 2: 29–34.

Bernard, J., and L. W. Sontag. 1947. Fetal reactivity to tonal stimulation: A preliminary report, *J. Genet. Psychol.* 70: 205–210.

Blakemore, C., and F. W. Campbell. 1969. On the existence of neurons in the human visual system selectively sensitive to the orientation and size of retinal images. *J. of Physiol.,* 203: 237–260.

Bloom, L. 1970. *Language Development: Form and Function in Emerging Grammars.* Cambridge, Mass.: MIT Press.

Brady, P. T., A. S. House, and K. N. Stevens. 1961. Perception of sounds characterized by a rapidly changing resonant frequency. *J. Acoust. Soc. Amer.,* 33: 1307–1362.

Brown, R. 1973. *A First Language, the Early Stages.* Cambridge, Mass.: Harvard University Press.

Cole, R. A. and B. Scott. 1972. Phoneme feature detectors. Paper presented at the meetings of the Eastern Psychological Association, Boston, Mass., April.

Cooper, W. E. 1974. Adaptation of phonetic feature analyzers for place of articulation. *J. Acoust. Soc. Amer.,* 56: 617–627.

Cutting, J. E. 1974. Two left-hemisphere mechanisms in speech perception. *Perception and Psychophysics,* 16: 601–612.

Dorman, M. F. 1974. Auditory evoked correlates of speech sound discrimination. *Perception and Psychophysics,* 15: 215–220.

Eimas, P. D. 1973. Linguistic processing of speech by young infants. Paper presented at the conference "Language Intervention with the Mentally Retarded." Wisconsin Dells, Wisconsin, June.

Eimas, P. D. 1974. Auditory and linguistic processing of cues for place of articulation by infants. *Perception and Psychophysics,* 16: 513–521.

Eimas, P. D. In press. Speech perception in early infancy. In *Infant Perception,* L. B. Cohen and P. Salapatek (eds.). New York: Academic Press.

Eimas, P. D., W. E. Cooper, and J. D. Corbit. 1973. Some properties of linguistic feature detectors. *Perception and Psychophysics,* 13: 247–252.

Eimas, P. D., and J. D. Corbit. 1973. Selective adaptation of linguistic feature detectors. *Cognitive Psych.,* 4: 99–109.

Eimas, P. D., E. R. Siqueland, P. Jusczyk, and J. M. Vigorito. 1971. Speech perception in infants. *Science,* 171: 303–306.

Fujisaki, H., and T. Kawashima. 1968. The influence of various factors on the identification and discrimination of synthetic speech sounds. *Reports of the Sixth International Congress on Acoustics,* Tokyo, August, B-95–B-98.

Graham, F. K., and J. C. Jackson. 1970. Arousal systems and infants' heart rate responses. In *Advances in Child Behavior Development,* vol. 5, C. C. Spiker and L. P. Lipsitt (eds.). New York: Academic Press, 59–117.

Jaksobson, R. 1968. *Child Language Aphasia and Phonological Universals.* The Hague: Mouton.

Jakobson, R., C. G. M. Fant, and M. Halle. 1951. *Preliminaries to Speech Analysis.* Cambridge, Mass.: MIT Press.

Kaplan, E. L., and G. Kaplan. 1971. The prelinguistic child. In *Human Development and Cognitive Processes,* J. Eliot (ed.). New York: Holt, Rinehart and Winston, 358–381.

Karmel, B. Z. 1969. The effect of age, complexity, and amount of contour on pattern preferences in human infants. *J. Exp. Child Psychol.,* 7: 339–354.

Kessen, W., M. M. Haith, and P. H. Salapatek. 1970. Infancy. In *Carmichael's Manual of Child Psychology*, 3rd. ed., P. H. Mussen (ed.). New York: Wiley, 287–445.

Kewley-Port, D., and M. S. Preston. 1974. Early apical stop production: a voice onset time analysis. *J. Phonetics*, 2: 195–210.

Lasky, R. E., A. Syrdal-Lasky, and R. E. Klein. 1975. Discrimination of VOT by four to six and a half month-old infants from a Spanish environment. *J. Exp. Child Psychol.* (in press).

Liberman, A. M. 1957. Some results of research on speech perception. *J. Acoust. Soc. Amer.*, 29: 117–123.

Liberman, A. M., F. S. Cooper, D. Shankweiler, and M. Studdert-Kennedy. 1967. Perception of the speech code. *Psychol. Rev.*, 74: 431–461.

Liberman, A. M., K. S. Harris, J. A. Kinney, and H. Lane. 1961. The discrimination of relative-onset time of the components of certain speech and nonspeech patterns. *J. Exper. Psychol.*, 61: 379–388.

Liberman, A. M., I. G. Mattingly, and M. T. Turvey. 1972. Language codes and memory codes. In *Coding Processes in Human Memory*, A. W. Melton and E. Martin (eds.). Washington, D.C.: V. H. Winston. 307–334.

Lieberman, P. 1970. Towards a unified phonetic theory. *Linguistic Inquiry*, 1: 307–322.

Lieberman, P., E. S. Crelin, and D. H. Klatt. 1972. Phonetic ability and related anatomy of the newborn and adult human, Neanderthal man, and the chimpanzee. *Amer. Anthopologist*, 74: 287–307.

Lieberman, P., K. S. Harris, P. Wolff, and L. H. Russell. 1971. Newborn infant cry and nonhuman primate vocalization. *J. Speech and Hearing Research*, 14: 719–727.

Lisker, L., and A. S. Abramson. 1964. A cross-language study of voicing in initial stops: acoustical measurements. *Word*, 20: 384–422.

Lisker, L., and A. S. Abramson. 1967. Some effects of context on voice onset time in English stops. *Language and Speech*, 10: 1–28.

Lisker, L., and A. S. Abramson. 1970. The voicing dimension: some experiments in comparative phonetic. In *Proceedings of the Sixth International Congress of Phonetic Sciences*, Prague, 1967. 563–567.

Marler, P., and P. Mundinger. 1971. Vocal learning in birds. In *Ontogeny of Vertebrate Behavior*, H. Moltz (ed.). New York: Academic Press. 389–450.

Mattingly, I. G., 1968. Synthesis by rule of general American English. Supplement to Status Report on Speech Research. Haskins Laboratories.

Mattingly, I. G., A. M. Liberman, A. K. Syrdal, and T. Halwes. 1971. Discrimination in speech and nonspeech modes. *Cogn. Psychol.* 2: 131–157.

McCollough, C. 1965. Color adaptation of edge-detectors in the human visual system. *Science*, 149: 1115–1116.

McNeill, D. 1970. *The Acquisition of Language*. New York: Harper & Row.

Menyuk, P. 1971. *The Acquisition and Development of Language*. Englewood Cliffs, N.J.: Prentice-Hall.

Miller, G. A., and P. Nicely. 1955. An analysis of perception confusions among some English consonants. *J. Acoust. Soc. Amer.*, 27: 338–352.

Moffit, A. R. 1971. Consonant cue perception by twenty- to twenty-four-week-old infants. *Child Development*, 42: 717–731.

Molfese, D. L. 1972. Cerebral asymmetry in infants, children, and adults: auditory evoked responses to speech and noise stimuli. Unpublished Ph.D. dissertation (psychology), Pennsylvania State University.

Morse, P. A. 1972. The discrimination of speech and nonspeech stimuli in early infancy. *J. Exp. Child Psychol.* 14: 477–492.

Nabelek, T., and I. J. Hirsh. 1968. On the discrimination of frequency transitions. *J. Acoust. Soc. Amer.,* 45: 1510–1519.

Nelson, P. G., S. D. Erulkar, and S. S. Bryan. 1966. Response of units of the inferior-colliculus to time-varying acoustic stimuli. *J. Neurophysiol.,* 29: 834–860.

Pisoni, D. B. 1971. On the nature of categorical perception of speech sounds. Unpublished Ph.D. dissertation (psycholinguistics), University of Michigan.

Pisoni, D. B. 1973. Auditory and phonetic memory codes in the discrimination of consonants and vowels. *Perception and Psychophysics,* 13: 253–260.

Pollack, I. 1969. Detection of rate of change of auditory frequency. *J. Exp. Psychol.,* 77: 535–54.

Sawusch, J. R., and D. B. Pisoni. 1974. Category boundaries for speech and nonspeech sounds. *J. Acoust. Soc. Amer.,* 55: 436(A).

Shankweiler, D., and M. Studdert-Kennedy. 1967. Identification of consonants and vowels present to left and right ears. *Q. J. Exp. Psychol.,* 19: 59–63.

Siqueland, E. R., and D. A. DeLucia. 1969. Visual reinforcement of nonnutritive sucking in human infants. *Science,* 165: 1144–1146.

Slobin, D. I. 1971. *Psycholinguistics.* Glenview, Ill.: Scott Foresman.

Stevens, K. N. 1972. The quantal nature of speech: evidence from articulatory-acoustic data. In *Human Communication: A unified view,* E. E. David, Jr. and P. B. Denes (eds.). New York: McGraw-Hill, 51–66.

Stevens, K. N., and D. H. Klatt. 1972. The role of formant transitions in the voice-voiceless distinction for stops. *J. Acoust. Soc. Amer.,* 55: 653–659.

Studdert-Kennedy, M. in press. The perception of speech. *In Current Trends in Linguistics,* T. A. Sebeok (ed.). The Hague: Mouton. Also in Haskins Laboratories Status Report on Speech Research, 1970, SR–23: 15–48.

Tartter, D. C. 1975. Selective adaptation of acoustic and phonetic detectors. Unpublished master's thesis, Brown University.

Wertheimer, M. 1961. Psychomotor coordination of auditory and visual space at birth. *Science,* 134: 1962.

Whitfield, I. C. and E. F. Evans. 1965. Responses of auditory cortical neurons to stimuli of changing frequency. *J. Neurophysiol.,* 28: 655–672.

Wolff, P. H. 1966. The natural history of crying and other vocalization in early infancy. In *Determinants of Infant Behavior,* Vol. 4, B. M. Foss (ed.). London: Metheun, 81–109.

Developmental Aspects of Speech Perception:
Problems for a Motor Theory

DAVID S. PALERMO

The infant data collected by Eimas and his colleagues [Cutting and Eimas, this volume] provide a major breakthrough in our understanding of certain aspects of language development and, in particular, speech perception. Add to that research the studies by Moffitt [1971], Morse [1972], Trehub and Rabinovitch [1972], and most recently Trehub [1973], and the conclusion may be drawn that infants in the first few months of life can make just those auditory discriminations among speech stimuli which may be important to the language environment in which they are reared.

Such data suggest a number of interesting and, perhaps, far reaching implications. First, they imply that the hypothesis advanced by Lenneberg [1967, p. 67] that "the lateralization of brain function is not present at birth" is incorrect. That hypothesis was investigated more directly in our laboratory by Dennis Molfese in his doctoral dissertation [1972]. Molfese attached electrodes to the left and right temporoparietal regions of the heads of subjects ranging in age from one week to twenty-nine years. Three groups of subjects were formed with mean ages of 5.8 months, 6 years, and 25.9 years. He recorded the auditory evoked potentials of these subjects in response to two syllables, two words, and two nonspeech stimuli. His results demonstrated clear lateralization effects in all age groups. Auditory evoked potentials were greater in the left hemisphere in response to both types of speech stimuli and greater in the right hemisphere in response to the nonspeech stimuli. Weitzman and Graziani [1968] have also provided some data on the latter point with premature infants.

Analyses of Molfese's data not only revealed that lateralization of brain function is present at birth but, and again in contrast to Lenneberg's hypothesis, the differential responsiveness of the two hemispheres was greater in infants than in adults. Thus, in terms of averaged evoked response indicators we have clear evidence of speech versus nonspeech discrimination, and we have the surprising finding of marked laterality effects to both kinds of stimuli at one week of age with a decrease in laterality as a function of age.

Finally, Lenneberg's argument that, with respect to speech, "the dominance phenomenon seems to come about through a progressive decrease in involvement of the right hemisphere" [1967, p. 15] is incorrect. In fact, Molfese found that proportionately greater involvement of the right hemisphere occurs with increasing age. Thus, the human organism begins with a strong hemispheric lateralization of function which, as a result of neurophysiological maturation and/or functional development required by environmental imposition, is modified in the direction of reduced lateralization as the organism gets older. The reduction of lateralization seems to take the form of increased participation by both hemispheres in processing both speech and nonspeech auditory signals. In any case, these data make it clear that the infant is actively processing incoming stimuli and that he processes speech stimuli in a manner different from nonspeech stimuli right from the start.

The fact that the infant is capable of such differential processing of speech makes it quite clear that traditional motor theories of speech perception are in some sense misnamed and that all of the "motor" activity must be limited to neural activity at some level independent of any neuromuscular activity. Perhaps such activity takes place at the highest levels in the form of motor plans. If the motor theory of speech perception is correct, then the cortical activity which is associated with it and related to subsequently developed production processes must be present at birth as well. It follows then that the period from birth to the end of the infant's first year, when the observable production of speech begins, must involve at least (a) the development or maturation of neuromuscular control of the production apparatus, (b) coordination of that production apparatus with the cortical-subcortical controls which operate in terms of plans, and (c) the cognitive substructure which relates the sound system to meaning.

Although one does not wish to place too much emphasis upon the dichotomy of speech perception and speech production—it is clear that they are closely interdependent—it seems to me that, since we have fairly well established the facts that speech sound discrimination occurs long before speech production and that lateralization of function is present just as early in life, we now need to provide some evidence for the cortical-subcortical activity associated with what will eventually govern the speech production capabilities of the child. If that kind of evidence cannot be found it would be worthwhile to examine the hypothesis that speech production is mediated by processes involved in the perception of speech rather than vice versa.

Advancing a perceptual hypothesis of speech production is stimulated by a variety of empirical evidence which is presently in the literature. Such an argument would, of course, begin first with the data of Eimas [see Cutting and Eimas, this volume] and those stimulated by his work in the area of infant speech perception as well as the neurophysiological responses of infants to speech and nonspeech stimuli which are beginning to come in.

Second, the work of Lieberman [1973] suggested that the production apparatus of the neonate, who is capable of speech perception, has not matured to the point which would allow speech production even if other prerequisites were met. It takes approximately another six months after birth before the supralaryngeal vocal tract assumes the bent shape which appears to be required for speech production.

Third, one could raise Lenneberg's [1962] clear case of the congenitally anarthric child who had full language capabilities except speech production without ever having uttered a word. Speech perception was present and language comprehension, but no speech production. As Lenneberg notes, perception and understanding of speech is possible without productive capacities but the reverse is never the case.

Fourth, we know that the congenitally deaf child does not develop normal speech (if he develops speech at all) although he acquires other aspects of language of the sign variety and, with difficulty, the written symbol variety. The deaf child's incapacity is not a result of motor disabilities, even at the cortical level, but of incapacities in the area of speech perception. Furthermore, if deafness occurs after speech is acquired, speech production gradually shows signs of disintegration, presumably because it is no longer supported by perception. Production ability does not disappear altogether since proprioceptive feedback remains intact. If the congenitally deaf child is given perceptual help through a hearing aid then he becomes capable of developing relatively normal speech.

Fifth, there are some data, albeit anecdotal, that speech perception precedes speech production even at later ages than infancy. The [fɪs]–[fɪʃ] (FISS–FISH) example given by Berko and Brown [1960] (which I have replicated) is perhaps the best example.

Sixth, we know that delayed auditory feedback markedly impairs speech production as a function of tampering with speech perception, that is, the feedback of one's own speech [Yates, 1963].

Seventh, there is evidence to suggest that second language learning requires that speech sound discriminations be made before linguistically appropriate speech sound production can take place [Leon, 1966]. In addition to the apparent dependence of production on perception which this observation implies, such a finding in this context could be interpreted to mean that the critical period hypothesis of Lenneberg [1967] may be viewed as a perceptual limitation.

It seems that a theory which argues that speech perception is related in a basic way to speech production even at the highest neural levels should speak to all these empirical issues because all of them suggest that speech perception is basic to speech production. Furthermore, interference with speech production even in aphasic cases where cortical involvement may occur does not necessarily impair speech perception. Thus, according to Lenneberg all receptive aphasia cases result in productive impairment but the reverse is not necessarily true.

My colleague Walter Weimer disagrees with me about raising the proposal and further makes the point that I will get into serious evolutionary-developmental problems if I carry this issue too far. He points out, and I resonate to the matter, that if perception is required for production then one must resort to teleological explanations of how perception came about evolutionarily, since the evolutionary adaptivity of perception would not occur if there were no production to perceive [see Weimer, in press].

Recognizing this philosophical pitfall (as well as the complementarity of the development of speech perception and production), let's push this analysis a bit further, if only to see how it might stimulate some research hypotheses and theoretical problems. Let's assume for the moment that speech perception is innate and that speech production develops by building upon the innate capacity to make appropriate speech sound discriminations. To say that speech perception is innate says nothing, of course, about the specific physiological mechanisms responsible for these abilities. It should also be clear that such a position does not argue that phonological rules are innate; they must be acquired within the context of the particular language community of the child. I will also ignore the question of how particular phonological strings become associated with particular meanings, if that in fact occurs.

If we assume that speech perception is innate and overt motor production develops from it, what kinds of guesses can we make about the acquisition of the production processes?

1. Lenneberg [1967] presents a variety of developmental neurophysiological data which suggest that a certain amount of maturational change must take place before language can be acquired. If we assume that the perceptual equipment is given, then those neurophysiological maturational factors must be interpreted to relate to production capabilities and the conceptual or cognitive substructures which support the use of language.

2. In terms of the babbling which precedes language there is evidence that infants can produce languagelike sounds from 6 to 12 months of age but in terms of spectrographic analyses the sounds are not speech insofar

as the adult model is concerned [Lynip, 1951; Lenneberg, 1967]. It may well be that at this stage the child has not developed conceptually to the point of relating his own productive capacities to those of others around him. Thus, he may make speechlike sounds but not try to produce speech because he fails to recognize the relation between the two and/or the relation between speech and meaning.

3. At about the age of one year the child does in fact begin to speak as well as babble. This just happens to be the time when the child reaches stage 5 of Piaget's sensory motor period which includes tertiary circular reactions characterized by experimentation with means which produce novel results. Probably the child experiments with speech sounds as well as other kinds of behaviors. During the preceding developmental stage (roughly 8–12 months of age), according to Piaget, the child has become able to imitate behaviors he could not see, and now at stage 5 he has reached the cognitive level which makes it possible for him to produce the sound differences he has long perceived. As Weir [1962] noted, at least some children spend a good deal of time actually playing with sound production in much the way Piaget describes tertiary circular reactions.

4. Speech acquisition thus becomes a matter of mapping motor production patterns, with auditory feedback, upon speech sound discriminations already innately available—and in turn of learning the phonological rules associated with one's own language.

5. In order to account for the order of acquisition of features as postulated by Jakobson [1968], and for which there is some empirical support [see Menyuk, 1971], we would have to develop some comparable hierarchy of perceptual feature saliency different from Jakobson's. The available data seem to support the general outline of Jakobson's ideas but not the specifics of the theory.

In summary, I find Eimas' work very exciting. It adds to the rapidly accumulating evidence of the amazing capabilities of the infant and child which we have so long ignored or at least theoretically softpedaled. Furthermore, for me, it raised one more question about the speech perception-production relationship, in general, and the motor theory of speech perception, in particular. While the issues raised here, and the implications they have suggested, may not be crucial to a motor theory, it does need to be made clear how the theory accounts for them. Consideration of the perceptual hypothesis of speech production suggested here may at least provide focus on these issues, raise further questions, stimulate research and, I hope, expand and clarify our theories of speech and language.

References

Berko, Jean, and R. Brown. 1960. Psycholinguistic research methods. In *Handbook of Research Methods in Child Development*, P. H. Mussen (ed.). New York: Wiley, 517–557.

Cutting, J. E., and P. D. Eimas. Phonetic feature analyzers and processing of speech in infants. This volume.

Jakobson, R. 1968. *Child Language Aphasia and Phonological Universals*, Allan R. Keiler (trans). The Hague: Mouton.

Lenneberg, E. H. 1962. Understanding language with ability to speak: a case report. *J. Abnorm. Soc. Psychol.*, 65: 419–425.

Lenneberg, E. H. 1967. *Biological Foundations of Language*. New York: Wiley.

Léon, P. 1966. Teaching pronunciation. In *Trends in Language Teaching*, A. Valdman (ed.). New York: McGraw-Hill, 57–79.

Lieberman, P. 1973. On the evolution of language: a unified view. *Cognition*, 2: 59–94.

Lynip, A. W. 1951. The use of magnetic devices in the collection and analysis of the preverbal utterances of an infant. *Genet. Psychol. Monogr.*, 44: 221–262.

Menyuk, P. 1971. *The Acquisition and Development of Language*. Englewood Cliffs, N.J.: Prentice Hall.

Moffitt, A. R. 1971. Consonant cue perception by twenty-to-twenty-four week old infants. *Child Development*, 42: 716–731.

Molfese, D. L. 1972. Cerebral asymmetry in infants, children and adults: auditory evoked responses to speech and noise stimuli. Unpublished doctoral dissertation, Pennsylvania State University.

Morse, P. A. 1972. Discrimination of speech and nonspeech stimuli in early infancy. *Journal of Experimental Child Psychology*, 14: 477–492.

Trehub, Sandra E. 1973. Infants' sensitivity to vowel and tonal contrasts. *Developmental Psychology*, 9: 91–96.

Trehub, S. E., and M. S. Rabinovitch. 1972. Auditory-linguistic sensitivity in early infancy. *Developmental Psychology*, 6: 74–77.

Weimer, W. B. In press. *Structural Analysis and the Future of Psychology*. Englewood Cliffs, N.J.: Prentice-Hall, chapter 14.

Weir, R. H. 1962. *Language in the Crib*. The Hague: Mouton.

Weitzman, E. D., and L. J. Graziani. 1968. Maturation and topography of the auditory evoked response of the prematurely born infant. *Developmental Psychology*, 1: 79–89.

Yates, A. J. 1963. Delayed auditory feedback. *Psychol. Bull.*, 60: 213–232.

On the Interrelatedness of Speech and Language

JAMES J. JENKINS AND ROBERT E. SHAW

The preceding papers move us to respond to the main theme of the conference with a mild caveat: *Speech and language may not be as separable as we readily assume them to be.* It is easy to lose sight of this potential difficulty because of our specialized training and the usual analytic approach that we make to problems in the laboratory.

Our reactions to these fascinating papers on speech perception demonstrate how impressive they are and, at the same time, illustrate the ease with which we (both as spectators and as researchers) can become deeply involved in one aspect of the speech-language-communication system. Obviously, we applaud these studies and the significant contribution that they make to our knowledge of speech perception. But being thrust in the discussants' role demands that we be cautious in relating the findings to the theme of the conference. The success of the studies, their inherent attractiveness, and the requirements that we must deal with one thing at a time, tempt all of us to believe that the divisions that we acknowledge in the subject matter are "natural" or "real" or "true." But we must not yield too readily to that temptation. In doing so, we may fail to take full advantage of the general implications of what we are learning in each specialized area and we may fail to reach a higher understanding of the general process we seek to study.

At this point in the conference it is clear that someone ought to make an appeal to holism. We have chosen to put ourselves in that position. We could merely say that we must remember "the big picture" and urge that everyone think about the relation of speech and language, but it seemed to us that it would be more effective if we could draw your attention to a field that has suffered considerable damage from fractionation and "overanalysis"—the field of aphasia research. The closeness of the subject matter makes the material relevant, and the findings that we will concentrate on making it obvious that speech and language do not necessarily separate themselves readily. In addition we will present a sketch of a *coalition* view of language function which emphasizes the interrelatedness of symbolic function.

As every student of language knows, the scientific study of aphasia began in the period of the "diagram makers" in neurology. Still under the influence of the phrenological movement, investigators of the central nervous system labored to assign particular functions to brain locations. The identification of the motor cortex, the auditory projection area, and

This paper reflects a position that is developed in detail in Jenkins et al., 1974.

the visual cortex (roughly one hundred years ago) lent strong support to the division of functions and their independent assignment to cortical areas. Discrete mental faculties were supposed to reside in the cells of specific areas.

Language and speech were particularly victimized by this kind of thinking. By 1887, Bastian (to choose a single example) had followed out the logical consequences of the separation of sensory and motor functions and added his analysis of the modes of language function to propose "pure word deafness," "pure word blindness," productive aphasia, receptive aphasia, and a variety of "conductive" aphasias to be associated with the breaking of connections between visual, auditory, and kinaesthetic areas. Research and theory in aphasiology have been hampered by such conceptions ever since.

Empirical research on large samples of brain-damaged patients over the last fifty years had failed to find evidence for even the gross productive-receptive or motor-sensory aphasias, much less the exotic special forms of aphasia frequently proposed [for example, Head, 1926; Weisenberg and McBride, 1935; Wepman, 1951; Schuell and Jenkins, 1959]. But the temptation to separate input from output and one language function from another continues nonetheless. We want to insist that we need an alternate model of the speech-language-communication system that explicitly recognizes its "all-of-a-pieceness" rather than emphasizing the componential differences.

In the past year in the course of revising Hildred Schuell's monumental contribution to aphasia research [Schuell, Jenkins, and Jiménez-Pabón, 1964] we have found it useful to work with a model or schema that tries to capture some of the interdependence of which we speak. Although Figure 1 may look more like a fertility goddess than a scientific model, it is our current representation of the interconnectedness of communications functions. The figure represents a *coalition* rather than a flow chart or hierarchical system. Each portion of the system can affect the functioning of each other part, though some portions are more intimately related than others. There is not room here to develop the model in any detail [see Jenkins et al., 1974] but it can be sketched sufficiently to indicate our views.

A Functional Schema for Communication

We identify that which is communicated as a *communiqué*. We recognize two broad types of communiqués, those which are *figural* (natural, nonlinguistic signs or behaviors) and those that are *symbolic* (conventionally or arbitrarily meaningful). The communicaton schema, of course, in-

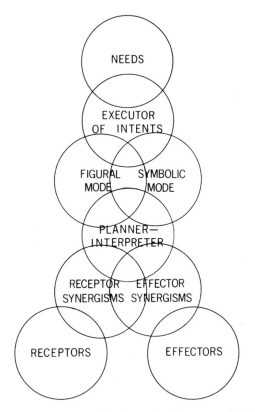

Figure 1. Schema for discussing the communication process.

volves both types of communiqués. Let us consider the functional components of the schema from top to bottom.

NEEDS

This component represents the source of purposes or goals that a person must continually satisfy if well-being is to be maintained. Some of the need states are biological in origin (for example, food, oxygen, sleep, activity, optimal stimulation,) ; other need states are probably acquired (love, communication, social dominance).

EXECUTOR OF INTENTS

This component executes all decisions required for formulating "means-ends" propositions directed toward the satisfaction of needs. Attitudes toward the indicative core of propositions are selected as well as the cognitive mode in which the proposition is to be formulated. One is already deciding as to whether the communiqué will be symbolic or figural.

FIGURAL MODE OF KNOWLEDGE

We regard this as the most primitive (basic) mode of cognition. Figural communiqués are formulated in this mode. It is also the repository of information gained from figural communiqués and from direct experience of objects and events. Definitions of symbols through pointing, acting out, demonstrating, and so on (*ostensive* definitions) must also be processed and stored in this mode.

Propositions formulated in this mode may be expressed by gesture, facial expressions, or actions. Such propositions are true or false by virtue of whether or not what they express is also a component of what they signify. For instance, a smile is a true expression of a happy mood, if it originates from such a mood, rather than being shammed. The expressed proposition is part of the meaning of what it signifies.

SYMBOLIC MODE OF KNOWLEDGE

This is the mode in which knowledge by description is processed and stored. Symbolic communiqués are formulated in this mode. It is the primary repository of knowledge derived from languages of all types, including mathematical, musical, and chemical notations, sign language, finger spelling, and artificial codes of any kind.

Propositions formulated in this mode are asserted via symbolic representations. These propositions have derivative meaning only. They are true or false by virtue of whether what they assert satisfies either *conventional* relations (for example, "A circle is round") or *ostensive* relations ("That is a dog").

The lower portion of our schema refers to the function of those components that make the implicit proposition evident to others. This deals with the appropriate patterns of activation of the effector systems of the body by which the proposition is enacted as either a signal or symbolic communiqué.

PLANNER-INTERPRETER

The planner is the first stage in a three-stage command system by which the effector organs are activated appropriately for the proposition formulated. Although we do not understand how, the implicitly formulated proposition provides a "model" or higher-order pattern by which complex sets of motor activities can be integrated into speech or other molar action sequences. The planner component, following directives originating from the means-end analysis performed by the executor of intents, has as its primary function the synthesis of a program by which the effector action is controlled. (It is difficult to draw the line between speech and language here.)

The interpreter functions similarly on the side of reception. Note that we assume here that higher-order plans for the analysis of incoming signals are necessary for comprehension of either symbolic or figural communiqués.

EFFECTOR SYNERGISMS

A synergism is a preprogrammed sequence of coordinated activities which, once initiated, runs off automatically to completion. Effector synergisms were once thought to be simple chains of reflexes, but since the manner in which they are executed can be varied by higher control processes (here, the planner), the reflexive definition is no longer appropriate.

The evidence for the existence of synergisms is abundant. The chief theoretical argument for assuming their existence arises from attempts to explain highly integrated, complicated motor activities, such as those involved in speech, playing musical instruments, dancing, and sports. The rapidity with which such activities must occur defies explanation in terms of voluntary response patterns or response sequences controlled by sensory or neural feedback. Preprogramming or "prepackaging" seems absolutely necessary.

RECEPTOR SYNERGISMS

Although the evidence for receptor synergisms is more indirect than for effector synergisms, we believe that analogous arguments can be made for their existence. The preceding papers constitute strong evidence for preprogrammed subroutines for the analysis of incoming auditory communiqués. Without such synergisms, it would be difficult to account for the efficiency with which rapidly occurring and incompletely specified signals are processed.

It is tempting to suggest that the receptor synergisms are closely related to the effector synergisms, although this cannot be demonstrated at the present time in any strong manner. We believe, in the case of speech at least, that the output of the receptor synergisms is "written in the same code" as the input to the effector synergisms.

EFFECTOR ORGANS

These are the systems of body action at the end of the production process. Their activation provides the instantiation of communiqués as an explicit enactment of publicly observable behaviors.

RECEPTOR ORGANS

These are the sensory systems involved in the pickup of the physical energy patterns supporting the manifest form of the communiqué.

OVERALL ORGANIZATION

The functional components listed above are not presumed to be related in a simple hierarchical form. Neither are they a disconnected set of independent parts. Taken together they form a *coalition* in which to varying degrees each functional component influences, and is influenced by, the others. This is a difficult notion to convey and is best understood in the context of examples of their interaction. Here we can only point out that the components are not only productively and receptively interrelated but also interconnected by a variety of forms of feedback and "feed-forward" controls.

It should be noted that the figure representing the schema is simplified in several important ways. The most important simplification is that the components in the lower half of the figure are represented by single structures on the diagram. Of course, the reader is expected to elaborate this flat schema into parallel layers of components. For example, when we are considering a speech act, the effectors involved are those of the speech musculature; when we consider an act of writing, the effectors are the arm, hand, and fingers. The effector synergisms are correspondingly different in the two cases. On the receptive side the same kinds of parallel structures exist. For reading, the visual receptors and visual analyzing systems are implicated; for listening, the auditory receptors and the auditory analysis systems are involved. One can imagine many special systems pressed into service of communication functions—gesturing in sign language, reading words by touching raised letters or Braille, writing with a pencil held in one's teeth or lashed to one's foot, and so on. We do not suppose that the specific aspects of these diverse systems are represented in the same functional component; thus the schema must not be so interpreted. Obviously, at some point the various systems converge on language and the analysis is in common. However, at the periphery in both production and perception the systems may be very different, alike only in performing the same kind of function for the overall communication system.

Problems in Interrelations

In 1951 Lashley posed the problem of serial order in behavior as a challenge to both psychological and physiological theorists. In this provocative paper he argued that the organization of complex motor events (speaking, typewriting, playing the piano) could not be explained by reflexes or associative chains of responses. The speed, the diversity, and the integrated assembly of the component responses simply prohibited the traditional interpretations. Since that time many other theorists have joined Lashley in urging the notion of some kind of higher-order planning component as a necessary part of any explanatory scheme [for example, Miller, Galanter, and Pribram, 1960; Lenneberg, 1967; Pribram, 1971]. Such a component must be capable of organizing individual effector synergisms into diverse programs for the control of complex motor activities.

Although most psychological theories have not yet progressed to the point of incorporating such planning components in a meaningful way, there appears to be little objection to the arguments for such a component. In the case of speech sound production, however, Wickelgren [1969] has argued that a proliferation of particular responses (up to the level of 1,000,000 or so) might save a separable associative production model. In reply, Halwes and Jenkins [1971] have argued that such a model is unsuitable and loses more in explanatory power than it gains in simplicity of production. Aside from this one instance, theorists in most fields seem to agree that such a productive component is required.

In regard to interpreter programs, the agreement is not so great because the phenomena are even less well understood. Yet it seems to us one must argue for such a component. The research on speech perception that has been summarized for us here has destroyed any hope of finding *simple* one-to-one correspondence between the acoustic signal and the linguistic elements that are crucial in the interpretation of that signal. In general, however, the interaction of the stimulus pattern and the context are predictable from higher-order rules using linguistic and articulatory constructs. This latter finding seems to argue for an interpreter component that is closely tied to the planner component, if not identical to it.

Some Findings from Aphasia Research

It seems to us that the most important findings from aphasia research from the point of view of this conference are those that reflect on the interconnectedness of speech and language. When one surveys a large population of aphasic patients, there is convincing evidence for a generalized language deficit [Schuell and Jenkins, 1959; Schuell, Jenkins, and Carroll, 1962; Jenkins and Schuell, 1964]. Intimately associated and highly correlated with the general deficit are the test findings on speech, auditory comprehension, reading, writing, and arithmetical calculation. Acuity of hearing, seeing, and feeling and gross movements of the speech musculature, on the other hand, are *not* associated with language deficit.

Careful examination of our cases does not turn up the classic divisions of aphasic diagnosis. We have no evidence in our data for the loss of language production without a nearly corresponding loss of language perception and no evidence for a loss of perception without a nearly corresponding loss of language production. We do not find a loss of vocabulary without a loss of grammatical structure nor do we find a loss of grammatical structure without a loss of vocabulary. While one can have deficits of receptors or effectors without much affecting language, once the disturbance perturbs the function of the planner-interpreter or the symbolic mode, generalized language effects begin to appear.

Many researchers who turn to the language pathologies for guidance as to the nature of language turn away in disappointment. They hope to find "experiments of nature" which will disassemble the language mechanism or show the ground plan of its functions. But aphasic language does not come apart into semantic, syntactic, and phonological components, nor does it come apart as a sequence of layers of development. It does not yield machine assembly components either. Most of the time, it shows rather diffuse, global "weakening" with lots of variation in salient symptoms depending on circumstances. We want to argue that the researcher should not turn away but should attempt to understand what he sees. The point that these "experiments of nature" are making is precisely the point that language does not split into subsystems under the impact of brain damage. And that surely is an important fact about language function that we had better assimilate (whether it fits our experimental biases or not). Even for the aphasic, such language as he has is pretty much all of one piece.

Indeed, if one does not start with a mosaic model of the cortex, or a mechanical model of the brain, or a computer model of processing, or a linguistic analysis of language levels, it is difficult to see why one would expect the speech-language-communication system to be anything other than unified. After all, natural language is learned all of a piece; semantics, vocabulary, syntax, production, and audition all are part of the one great experience that we call learning a first language. What *is* surprising is that the figural and symbolic functions are relatively separated in the cerebral hemispheres and that it is possible to lose considerable function in one without appreciable loss in the other [Bogen, 1969*a*, 1969*b*; Bogen and Bogen, 1969]. *That* surprising fact, however, may be responsible for the ease with which we have been misled in aphasia diagnosis.

The following case occurs in clinics and hospitals every day. The clinician reports that a patient is a severe aphasic. He neither comprehends sentences nor can he produce them functionally. It is common, however, to hear this same patient described by nurses on the ward as a "patient who can't talk, but who understands everything I say to him." Such a patient is usually responding to social and situational cues that he still understands perfectly (because they are *figural* information) even though he is unable to process *symbolic* information. When the nurse comes into his room at noon and the noises of the food cart and the smell of the hot lunch fill the air, the patient's response of getting ready for lunch may have nothing to do with the fact that the nurse tells him that it is time to eat.

An interesting documentation of just this kind of fact arose by chance in the course of another study. Shankweiler and Harris [1966] wanted to study speech production in aphasic patients who were supposed to have no comprehension difficulties. (They were interested in investigating a hypothesis about "linguistic regression" in aphasic speech errors and did not want the work clouded by the patient's lack of understanding of the word they wanted him to produce.) They were assigned a series of patients who were clinically regarded as having production but not comprehension difficulties. In careful preliminary testing of the patients' comprehension, they discovered that these patients could not correctly identify (by multiple-choice pointing) up to 50 percent of the common words that the investigators had planned to use in their tests!

Our conclusion from our studies of patients is that the speech-language-communication schema is a highly interrelated coalition of functions that interpenetrate each other in various ways and to various degrees. Rather than separate levels or separate machines, we tend now to think in terms of a dynamic left hemisphere that is working on language at all levels simultaneously. The aphasic has the problem that he is generating faulty signals somewhere in the system because of brain damage. The normal system probably has a very considerable capacity to adsorb faults and rectify errors by redundant processing and the use of many constraints. The aphasic system has more marked faults and far less capacity to correct them, so the faults that are characteristic of his damaged mechanisms are propagated throughout the system. The net result is not so much a specific type of error but rather a quantitative increase in errors of many sorts. The faults influence the perception of speech and the production of speech, the interpretation of what is heard and the formulation of what is to be said, the retrieval of vocabulary and the ordering of syntax.

One ubiquitous kind of fault that is characteristic of aphasia is marked reduction in auditory symbol span. This seems to reflect a strong limitation that brain damage puts on the aphasic patient when he tries to function in the symbolic mode. From the reports of our patients and their test data it is clear to us that the reduction in span affects such diverse activities as sentence understanding during reading and listening on the one hand, and retrieving infrequent vocabulary items for speaking on the other. The patient loses track of where he is and what he is doing in the symbolic sphere and diverse errors result.

Examples could be multiplied in great diversity and detail but perhaps the above statements are sufficient to make the point. There is little evidence to support the division of speech-language-communications functions into our favorite categories of the laboratories. It is important for all of us to be aware that strict concentration on our favorite areas may perpetuate the unfortunate notion that we are all dealing with different functions and different pieces of machinery that can be assembled later, component by component, into the finished machine. As far as we can see, the bets still ought to be made in the other direction.

References

Bastian, H. C. 1887. On different kinds of aphasia: their classification and ultimate pathology. *British Medical Journal*, 2: 931–936, 985–990.

Bogen, J. E. 1969a. The other side of the brain: I, Dysgraphia and dyscopia following cerebral commissurotomy. *Bulletin of the Los Angeles Neurological Society*, 34: 73–105.

Bogen, J. E. 1969b. The other side of the brain: II, An appositional mind. *Bulletin of the Los Angeles Neurological Society*, 34: 135–161.

Bogen, J. E., and G. M. Bogen. 1969. The other side of the brain: III, The corpus callosum and creativity. *Bulletin of the Los Angeles Neurological Society*, 34: 191–220.

Halwes, T., and J. J. Jenkins. 1971. Problem of serial order in behavior is not resolved by context-sensitive associative memory models. *Psychol. Rev.*, 78: 122–129.

Head, H. 1926. *Aphasia and Kindred Disorders of Speech.* New York: Macmillan.

Jenkins, J. J., E. Jiménez-Pabón, R. E. Shaw, and J. W. Sefer. 1974. *Schuell's Aphasia in Adults* (2nd ed.). New York: Harper & Row.

Jenkins, J. J., and H. Schuell. 1964. Further work on language deficit in aphasia. *Psychol. Rev.*, 71: 87–93.

Lashley, K. S. 1951. The problem of serial order in behavior. In *Cerebral Mechanisms in Behavior*, L. A. Jeffress (ed.). New York: Wiley.

Lenneberg, E. H. 1967. *Biological Foundations of Language.* New York: Wiley.

Miller, G. A., E. Galanter, and K. H. Pribram. 1960. *Plans and the Structure of Behavior.* New York: Holt, Rinehart and Winston.

Pribram, K. H. 1971. *Languages of the Brain.* Englewood Cliffs, N.J.: Prentice-Hall.

Schuell, H. and J. J. Jenkins. 1959. The nature of language deficit in aphasia. *Psychol. Rev.* 66: 45–67.

Schuell, H., J. J. Jenkins, and J. B. Carroll. 1962. A factor analysis of the Minnesota Test for the Differential Diagnosis of Aphasia. *J. Speech and Hearing Research*, 5: 349–369.

Schuell, H., J. J. Jenkins, and E. Jiménez-Pabón. 1964. *Aphasia in Adults*. New York: Harper & Row.

Shankweiler, D. and K. S. Harris. 1966. An experimental approach to the problem of articulation in aphasia. *Cortex*, 2: 277–292.

Weisenberg, T., and K. McBride. 1935. *Aphasia, a Clinical and Psychological Study*. New York: The Commonwealth Fund.

Wepman, J. M. 1951. *Recovery from Aphasia*. New York: Ronald.

Wickelgren, W. A. 1969. Context-sensitive coding, associative memory, and serial order in (speech) behavior. *Psychol. Rev.*, 76: 1–15.

Open Discussion of the Papers of Studdert-Kennedy, Cutting and Eimas, Palermo, and Jenkins and Shaw

Some Data, Some Chickens, and Some Eggs

Jerry Fodor remarked on some of his recent work in infant speech perception which is complementary to the Eimas work. He has been interested in whether or not infants perceive syllables as having an internal phonemic structure. Can they, for example, recognize the fact that two syllables which share an initial stop consonant but have different vowels are more similar than two syllables which share neither consonant or vowel? The answer is that they can: they can establish a head-turning response to a particular consonant in a high-vowel environment and transfer that response to the same consonant in a low-vowel environment.

Fodor then made a suggestion with regard to the difference between those who emphasize the importance of production, or motor, components of the language acquisition question [see Mattingly, this volume], and those who emphasize the perceptual component of language acquisition [see Cutting and Eimas, this volume; Palermo, this volume]. The extrapolation from these two different positions could go on forever unless someone calls for a halt to it. The point is that, both on theoretical and empirical grounds, the phone is neither a perceptual object nor a motor object. It is what gets exchanged in speech, and nothing more. It is the intended object of communication on the part of the speaker who by some algorithmic system transforms it into a waveform, and it is recovered when the listener recognizes what the intention of the speaker was. There is no more reason to think that it is decomposable into a batch of motor commands than there is to suppose that it is decomposable into a batch of perceptual features. Obviously both perception and production are relevant, as the chicken is relevant to the egg and vice versa, but there is no reason to oscillate between the extreme views as to which is primary. Therefore, Fodor concluded it is a false dilemma.

Lieberman noted that, while there was value in Fodor's perspective, the specific signals of speech are obviously constrained by both production and perception and constrained in different ways. The two systems are matched for what they can do best. For example, in the Eimas data [Cutting and Eimas, this volume] the prevoiced detector (at about −50 msec VOT) seems to be somewhat less efficient than the coincident-voice detector (at about +25 msec VOT). Perhaps, this is due to constraints of production. Moreover, in the acquisition of particular phonemes Lebanese-Arabic children and American-English children both appear to produce the coincident-voiced stop (our [b]) first. The Lebanese-Arabic children go on to produce the prevoiced-stop at a later point in time, the only other voicing-mode in their native language, while American-English children go on to produce the post-voiced stop later in their development, the only other voicing-mode in English. Thus there appears to be a hierarchy of naturalness in the production of voicing in stop consonants. On the other hand, perceptual/auditory constraints may come into play when one considers the difference in VOT of model productions of stop consonants. The absolute refractory period of the auditory system appears to be about 80 to 100 msec, a value found in many animals. Is it mere coincidence that the difference between prevoiced and coincident-voiced stops, and coincident-voiced and postvoiced stops is within this neighborhood? Lieberman thinks not.

Ignatius Mattingly added that, from Palermo's comments, it is clear the motor theory of speech perception has to be formulated much more carefully. In its current form of abstraction, the motor theory is one which does *not* depend on experience with production. In fact, it would probably be better to say that it guides both acquisition of production and acquisition of perception.

Aphasia and Sign Language

James Jenkins then spoke to the issue of aphasia and its probable effect on sign language. In general, aphasics cannot "do" sign language. It is tempting to think that one could take the aphasic who is having problems with speech and convert him to sign, bypassing those problems. This procedure, however, does not appear to work. All that aphasics can do is use conventional, highly frequent signs that were present in the culture and that they knew before, knowledge that is presumably deep in both the figural and symbolic modes. They cannot *acquire* sign language any more readily than they can acquire a new auditory language.

David Premack disagreed in part. Aphasics can learn the same plastic symbol system that chimps learn. In testing a half dozen "global" aphasics, Premack found that they could be taught names for concrete objects, agents, and actions, and they learned more rapidly than intact chimpanzees. Moreover, they learned relational ("same-different") notations which were then used to introduce the interrogative. They also transfer from one form of the interrogative to another form. Before testing, however, these patients could do one task only: they could recognize a word from a nonword, even though they could not make any match between the word and its referent. Afterwards they learned not only relational and interrogative forms, but also conjunctions and possessives. This work points to the conclusion that if one avoids the speech system in an aphasic, and if the knowledge and perceptual systems are intact, then the individual can form functional associations between the plastic-symbol language "markers" and existing cognitive events. This process is successful, in part, because a plastic system avoids memory problems—the pieces of plastic are permanent, not transient, symbols. Furthermore, they permit the number of alternatives to be controlled. Alvin Liberman suggested that further discussion of sign language wait until after the presentations of Bellugi, Stokoe, and Klima.

II. Language without Speech

Aspects of Sign Language and Its Structure

URSULA BELLUGI AND EDWARD S. KLIMA

Introduction

At a conference concerned with the role of speech in language it is appropriate to take a close look at a human language which has developed *without speech,* and in the absence of hearing, namely, the sign language used by most of the deaf in America, or American Sign Language (ASL). What is the form of a language which is produced by the hands through articulated gestures in relation to the body and is based on visual analysis? To put this question into focus, we shall quote from the letter of invitation which we received as an introduction to the central topic of this conference.

At this conference we want to talk about the function of speech in language. We use the term "speech" to include the transmission end of the language system—specifically the acoustic signal, the articulation that produces it, and the phonetic (and phonological) message it conveys. We want to know how and within what limits that end of language shapes the rest of the system, and in particular, how it relates to the further restructuring of the linguistic information that linguists call grammar.

Behind our thinking about the conference is the belief that the function of grammatical processes is to restructure information so as to make it differentially appropriate for several components that presumably arose separately in evolution and are badly mismatched. At the one end of the system is a nonlinguistic intellect and a long-term memory. Surely these must have existed in some form before the evolution of language, much as they exist now in nonspeaking animals. At the other end are the components most directly concerned with transmission—the ear and the vocal tract—which also existed long before they were incorporated as terminals in linguistic communication. So long as the contents of the intellect cannot be restructured to fit the transmission apparatus, creatures can communicate their ideas only by *signals that differ uniquely and holistically from each other.* Given the richness of the intellect and the obvious limitations on the production and perception of signals, that kind of nongrammatical system cannot take the animal very far. We have assumed that grammar may have arisen as a kind of interface, joining into a single system those components of intellect and transmission that were once quite separate and not very compatible. Such assumptions as these lead us to expect that grammatical processes might bear the marks of both components—intellect and transmission system—and that is the question that we want to talk about. [Kavanagh, personal communication, italics added.]

What is American Sign Language? What is the form of the visual-gestural communication used by the deaf? It might seem, at first glance, that the basic units, that is, the signs of the language used by the deaf in America, differ uniquely and holistically from each other. As Kavanagh suggests, this seems to be an appropriate characterization of the signals of animals. Indeed, it has been said, presumably by those lacking close acquaintance with American Sign Language, that the language *is* just such a loose collection of gestures—gestures which themselves have no systematic internal structure and which are strung together without hierarchical syntactic organization. It is our claim that this is *not* the case— that what may have begun at one time as a loose collection of pantomime or gestures has become over time and generations of use a *language,* with at least a considerable degree of the systematic character and hierarchical organization we have come to expect of human languages. The question becomes all the more intriguing when sign language is viewed as a language that has arisen apart from the mainstream of human evolutionary development. After all, there can be little doubt that modern man is well designed for learning, processing, and using spoken language analyzed by the ear. However, when we examine the special situation in which hearing is blocked from birth and in which a primary language composed of articulated gestures rather than speech is learned by eye instead of by ear, we may indeed be able to better isolate the special effects of the particular transmission system.

   In the following pages, we will describe some of the recent research we have been conducting that may elucidate such questions. Our basic concern is the structure and acquisition of a language in another mode: the visual-gestural language used by the deaf. As a way of examining the biological foundations of language in general, we chose to investigate this "experiment of nature." Our research questions have centered around the following theoretical issue: we are attempting to determine, on the one hand, the degree to which the "linguistic" function puts its distinctive stamp on the form of expression regardless of the particular *mode* of communication, and, on the other hand, the extent to which differences in the *mode* "predispose" essential differences in the form of expression. Our studies are concerned with: (*a*) the way in which signs of American Sign Language differ from "nonlinguistic" pantomimic gestures, as well as the way they differ from words in spoken language; (*b*) the degree to which the formational aspects of American Sign Language constitute a tightly constrained system; (*c*) the nature of this system from the point of view of its internal structure; (*d*) the nature of the grammatical processes (if any) which modulate the meaning of signs.

   We have been engaged in these studies for only three years now, and it must be clearly understood that studies of the structure and organization of sign languages are very much in their infancy. This paper will attempt to draw together some first thoughts on the organization of ASL, and should be considered as exploratory research. We will touch on results of controlled experiments and observational data. Our working group has included Susan Fischer, Adele Abrahamson, Patricia Siple, Robbin Battison, Nancy Frishberg, Richard Lacy, Krystina Hooper, Sharon Neumann, Bonnie Gough, and Shanny Mow.[1] The research has, to date, been a collaboration among linguists, psychologists, and articulate deaf people.

Background Studies of Sign Language

Serious *linguistic* interest in the study of sign languages is relatively recent, with the possible exception of Wundt, whose comprehensive works included a section on gesture. The single outstanding work in recent years is that of Stokoe in his "Sign Language Structure" [1960] and his publication with Casterline and Croneberg of the *Dictionary of American Sign Language* [1965]. Stokoe's work provided an important starting point for the investigations in our earlier studies. The *Dictionary* provides the first attempt to make a phonemiclike analysis of American Sign Language—to catalog signs according to some of the gestural characteristics that differentiate one sign from another. It provides information on more than 2000 signs of ASL; we refer to the *Dictionary* frequently in our research. Recently, I. M. Schlesinger with his colleagues in Israel has been developing a different notation system based on dance notation, which will be more at a level corresponding to "phonetic" descriptions [Schlesinger, in press].

There has been a great deal of research on the deaf with respect to memory and cognitive functions in terms of *written* English, but almost none in terms of the system of communication the deaf use among themselves. Some of the former is summarized in Furth [1971]. Furth's own work with the deaf, which emphasizes the cognitive (as separate from linguistic) functions, is described in detail in several excellent publications [Furth, 1966, 1972; Furth and Youniss, 1969].

To our knowledge, with few exceptions, there has been little linguistic or psychological research on the properties of the communication system which develops in the absence of hearing and in a visual-gestural mode. Our original objective in research was to understand better the human

---

[1] A book, *The Signs of Language,* by Edward S. Klima and Ursula Bellugi, Harvard University Press, is now in preparation. This will discuss and include research by several members of the group.

capacity for language through an examination of the child's acquisition of a language in a different mode, and to compare this process with the acquisition of spoken language. In order to pursue the investigation of the language learning process, it is, of course, necessary to understand a great deal about the structure of what is being learned: the target language. While studies in first-language acquisition of English abound now, such progress was possible only with the aid of an extremely sophisticated knowledge of the structure of English, and knowledge of speech perception and production. All of this sophistication was in the area of spoken language.

Faced with a form of communication in a different mode, we found ourselves confronted with a new and essentially different set of problems. Not only was there very little in the way of research on the language (with the exception of Stokoe's work); there was even considerable question as to whether this form of communication had the status of a "language" in the sense that English is a language.

From the outset, we decided to limit the scope of our inquiry, wherever possible, to those deaf people who had learned sign language as a natural language from deaf parents. We were able to locate three local deaf families with young deaf children, and we are nearing completion of the collection of raw materials for a study of the acquisition of sign language as a first language. The basic data base for our developmental study consists of monthly videotapes of the children with their parents, in our studio and in their homes. We have also begun an intensive investigation of the grammatical aspects of sign language. During the course of our investigations, we discovered fertile areas of exploration regarding other facets of the language and its use.

SIGN LANGUAGE IN AMERICA

A few words are in order about the subjects of our experiments and about the varieties of sign languages. By one recent census count there are about 450,000 profoundly deaf people in the United States, including people who have become deaf later in life. The number of deaf people who are either deaf from birth or deaf since the first two years of life is far smaller, and of these "prelingually" deaf, most were born to hearing parents. Perhaps 10 to 20 percent of deaf children are born to deaf parents, and this small group includes most of the deaf children who learn to communicate by gesture from their parents as a natural language.

There are different sign languages just as there are different spoken languages—differing from one another most obviously in the form of the signs which they use. British Sign Language, for example, is quite unrelated to American Sign Language despite their common written language.

We must point out that there are several varieties of gestural communication now in current use among the American deaf and that our studies are of one of these only. Beyond the immediate scope of the research described here are the various methods of rendering English in the hands often used in educational settings: (a) by finger spelling each letter of the words of English sentences; (b) by one of a number of sign systems developed in an effort to approximate English word order, morphology, and syntax; or (c) by speaking English and signing simultaneously. Our studies, instead, are of American Sign Language, a totally different language which is likely to be the communication prelingually deaf people use among themselves and the gestural communication used by deaf families.

Because there is very little general knowledge about American Sign Language, we find that there are frequent misunderstandings about its status. We refer to some of the major misunderstandings we have encountered:

1. American Sign Language is not a derivative or degenerate form of written or spoken English. It has a lexicon which does not correspond to English, and it must be considered as a different language. The grammatical principles which govern the modification of meaning of signs are different, both in form and in content, from grammatical processes in English and in spoken languages in general.

2. American Sign Language is in no way limited to expressing "concrete ideas." It is a full-fledged language with the possibility for expression at any level of abstraction. There is vocabulary dealing with religion, politics, ethics, history, and other realms of mental abstraction and fantasy [see Klima, this volume].

3. There are, of course, gaps in ASL vocabulary in various technical areas. Such gaps are typically filled in by on-the-spot finger-spelled borrowings from English. But this is, of course, a sociolinguistic phenomenon, common also in the case of spoken languages when two languages spoken in the same area have radically different sociocultural status positions. As items of technical vocabulary become more commonly used, new signs are invented for them. Then again, there are some areas—such as the vocabulary for vision—where ASL is richer than English.

4. American Sign Language is not a universal form of communication. It is, as we noted, a different language from British Sign, although the written form of the languages spoken in the two countries is essentially

the same. For all but the most rudimentary purposes, the two sign languages are mutually incomprehensible.

General Approach

When we consider the full range of possible speech sounds across spoken languages, it becomes clear that each individual language constrains itself to a small subset of this staggering variety. Each selects those sounds which will be phonemically the same; it further selects, from the various physically possible sequences of these, the particular combinations of sounds that will be permitted to occur in sequence within the structure of its words. Languages are not the same in the sounds they select, and the sounds which an individual language selects as its *language* sounds need not coincide with those that are used in other sorts of vocal communication within the same culture (speakers of English, for example, use sounds in the interjections "phew!" "'tsk! tsk!" and so on, which, though they count as language sounds in certain other languages, do not in English).

Modern linguistics has done more than catalog the sounds that individual languages select to form their words; it has shown that in an individual language there will be regular recurring relationships between the particular sounds chosen. Rather than a helter-skelter, arbitrary selection from the possible speech sounds, there tends to be symmetry in each particular system. Modern linguistics has also argued that there are certain universal constraints that hold across languages—constraints whereby the existence, in a given language, of a given type of sound implies the existence of another type of sound in that language. In spoken language, at every level we find a system—and a highly constrained one at that.

Modern linguistics has also shown the complexity of the coding between the continuum which is the acoustic signal and the discrete phonetic segments we perceive when we hear the signal but to which no individual isolable segments of the acoustic signal need correspond. A given stretch of acoustic signal often contains simultaneously information about more than one segment. This parallel transmission of information is, according to Mattingly and Liberman [1969], the most basic formal resemblance between speech and the higher levels of language.

One central notion within recent linguistic theorizing, at least along generative-transformational lines, is that in the description of a particular spoken language the domain of the phonological rules is not restricted to the finite set of morphemes of that language but includes also those strings of sounds which are phonologically regular in the language but

happen not to have a meaning. Within the system are not only the morphemes that actually *are* but also those stretches of sound which *might
be* morphemes were it not for certain accidents of history. Thus in current
American English [brɪk] ("brick") is an actual word and [blɪk] is a possible word, but not an actual one–an accidental gap in the system; whereas
[bnɪk] with an initial [bn-] is extrasystemic (impossible, as far as the English system is concerned), although the sequence occurs in other languages. It is assumed that a native speaker of English has appropriate
linguistic intuitions along these lines. The rules formulated by the linguist
are, according to this view, not just a tidy way of cataloguing the "facts";
rather, they are supposed to represent what the speaker-hearer has internalized regarding the structure of his language.

There is no reason, a priori, to assume that the characteristics of spoken
language just discussed should also appear in a primary language based
on gestures. In fact, sign languages clearly differ in at least one very obvious respect from spoken languages: the individual signs in sign languages are not analyzable as linear sequences of segments [see also Klima,
this volume]. Still open, however, are questions as to (a) whether there
is a system in the form of signs and (b) the nature of this system if there
is one.

Before we consider the evidence with respect to the internal structure
of signs, let us first consider briefly notational problems and a comparison
between pantomime and signs.

ON NOTATIONAL PROBLEMS

We shall use some notational devices we have developed to distinguish
the various forms of language that enter into the special problems our
experiments consider. In spoken language we must distinguish the actual
sound of the spoken word *name* from its phonological notation as [n e y m],
and from the written form in standard spelling: "name." In ASL we must
likewise distinguish the original gesture or some pictorial representation
of it from the attempt to provide a notational description of it: $[H_> H_{<}\overset{v}{x}]$
and distinguish these furthermore from a translation equivalent rendition
in English words (which has no relation to the actual form of the sign):
NAME. These distinctions are made in Figure 1.

ON PANTOMIME AND SIGNS

There are certain aspects of "deaf communication" in general that, we
believe, present some real problems when one attempts an analysis of
the signs of sign languages. In particular, when the deaf communicate

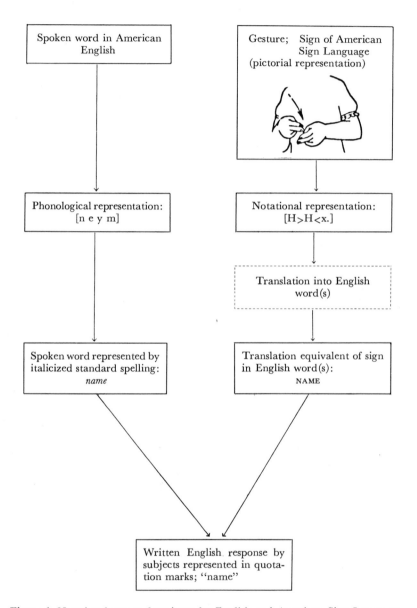

Figure 1. Notation forms and variants for English and American Sign Language.

with one another in colloquial or everyday narrative style, the "signing" is often interspersed with elements of pantomime. The amount of such pantomime in "deaf communication" varies, of course, from individual to individual and from situation to situation, but it far exceeds that generally found in communication by hearing speakers of standard American English. What is significant, however, is that in "deaf communication" the sign-symbolic (the "linguistic") and the pantomimic are, of course, in the same mode. In fact, the signs themselves may on occasion undergo clearly mimetic modification. From the point of view of signers, however, there appears to be a perceived difference between the extremes of what is clearly signing and what is clearly pantomiming. (We are currently attempting to develop criteria for differentiating the less clear area between the extremes.) In a preliminary study we have asked twelve people to convey in pantomime objects and actions for which there are common English words and also corresponding ASL signs. One of the words used was "egg." The majority of people did a pantomime something like the following: they gestured picking up a small oval-shaped object, hitting it on the edge of some imaginary surface; they held it so that when they gently gestured breaking it open and emptying the contents, they gave the impression of having a part of the shell in either hand; then most feigned putting the two parts in one hand and throwing them away. This is schematized in the first diagram.

Let us consider now what goes on in signing EGG in American Sign Language. The sign for EGG is clearly related to a part of the pantomimed act: namely breaking the eggshell and emptying its contents. The second diagram shows the sign for EGG in American Sign Language.

EGG

The correct sign for EGG in ASL requires a particular hand shape *and that hand shape only*. (We have seen mothers correct their children, if they signed in with the hands in the shapes shown in the third and fourth diagrams).

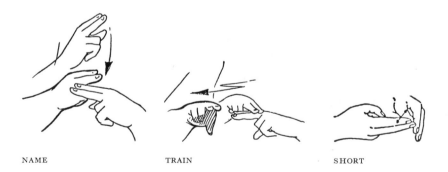

Incorrect Forms of EGG

The hand shape used in signing EGG in ASL is also used for SHORT, TRAIN, BUILD, WEIGH, NAME, BUTTER, FUNNY, MOOCH, and many other signs which, however, differ from EGG in other ways.

NAME   TRAIN   SHORT

When a nonsigner sees the sign EGG and is, at the same time, given its meaning, the relationship, for him, between the sign and a part of the pantomimed version we have described is certainly not entirely opaque. The critical question, however, is the relationship of this sign to other signs of ASL for a deaf native signer. That there is a recognizably adequate way to form the sign—that there are, in fact, conditions of well-formedness applying to it—is indicated by the mother's correction of the child's "mispronunciation." Clearly there are individual differences, differences between children's and adults' formations of the sign (because of differences in the hands) ; and there are differences from one rendition to the next in a single individual. Still, it seems to be the case that certain elements must remain constant if the gesture is to count as a recognizable rendition of *that* sign. In fact, if the handshape is otherwise the same, but with the two fingers spread, this would constitute a mispronunciation for an American signer. We have tried this, and native signers either look puzzled, or nod encouragingly and make the sign correctly, or openly show us our "error." And if, instead of making the motion as shown in the drawing, we stop at the point of contact of the two hands, the sign would be understood, not as EGG, but as NAME.

NAME

But in the pantomimed versions there are no conditions of well-formedness. The only restriction on the hands for steps 1 through 4 of the pantomime seem to be that the hand be shaped *as if* holding an egg. From one person to the next, from one version to the next, from one step to the next, the hands could and did change configuration. Each person "held" the imaginary egg in an individual way and cracked it in a different way; the only constant was the imagined shape of the egg.

We have asked some deaf people to communicate very complex information in pantomime (without using signs). The complexity of the information which can be successfully expressed seems to be limited primarily by the ingenuity and imagination of the individual. A languagelike system is obviously not necessary for communicating some kinds of cognitive information. (We are disregarding relative economy of means of communication). While there may be some conventional gestures in pantomime, there is no sense in which the gestures of pantomime overall are limited or restricted in form, to say nothing of being composed of a much smaller set of recurring shared features. With pantomime, the question of well-formedness does not arise, only the question of effectiveness.

HISTORICAL CHANGE IN ASL

It seems to us plausible that at least certain aspects of what is now American Sign Language originated from some form of pantomime or iconic representation. The language has, by now, lost a great deal of its transparency. What is the process by which this occurs? We can trace some aspects by investigating historical change over time.

There is evidence that some signs in American Sign Language have changed over the last fifty years. We have been fortunate enough to see some films (courtesy of the Gallaudet Archives Library) which were made in 1913 of some elderly and very eloquent signers. With these as a starting point, we have noted the changes in the formation of some signs. As another source, we have located a book published around the same date [Long, 1918] which describes signs. We also found some elderly deaf couples who are a rich source of information on change in formation of signs over time.

In the few examples we have already considered, the change is often from what seems iconic in the direction of somewhat more systematic aspects of the language. For example, in the 1913 film, the sign for BODY was made by moving both hands downward in parallel with the shoulders to the hips. The sign for BODY found in current use today is made with the flat hands in the same orientation as before, but instead of outlining the contours of the body from the shoulders to the hips, it is made with a touch at the chest, a slight movement away and downward, and another touch above the waist. There are a large number of signs which involve two contacts in an area, such as HOME, YESTERDAY, WE, QUEEN, BACHELOR. It seems possible that the older sign has become modified so that it is more like other ASL signs in movement.

Another example is the sign for SWEETHEART, which was made, according to our elderly informants; over the region of the heart, touching the body, the two hands coming together at the edge of the little fingers. The sign is now made without touching the body, centered, and with the two hands in contact in the same orientation as a number of other ASL signs (GAME, ACCIDENT, and so on).

SWEETHEART, 1913   SWEETHEART, 1973

As a method of further investigating what may be systemic pressure in ASL, we are now conducting more intensive studies of such historical changes in signs. We note that the direction of change is often toward some recurring element or aspect which appears in already existing signs of the language. That is, we begin to see that there are recurring shared aspects of signs to which new and old signs come to conform. [See Frishberg, 1973, for other examples of historical change.]

Experimental Study in Short-Term Memory

The types of errors that are made when information is retrieved from short-term memory have led toward an agreement that for hearing people short-term memory has a phonological basis. Conrad [1962] was the first to show that intrusion errors in a short-term memory task that involved remembering *visually* presented printed letters correlated with errors in perception of spoken letters unler noise. When given as a stimulus, the printed letter C is not remembered as the visually similar closed O, but rather as the phonologically similar voiced Z. By now there is abundant evidence, according to Conrad, that short-term memory thrives on a speechlike input [Conrad, 1972]. We shall suggest in this section that this might better be amended to languagelike input, so that it is not restricted to the speech mode. We have completed three experiments on short-term memory for signs, one of which is described here.

METHOD OF EXPERIMENT

Signs of American Sign Language were presented on videotape at the rate of one sign per second by a native signer in list lengths of three signs up to seven signs. Subjects were deaf college students of deaf parents who learned ASL as a primary natural language. Recall was immediate, ordered, and written. The experiment was preceded by a task in which the subjects saw and identified each sign separately made. In a parallel experiment, English words corresponding to the ASL signs were presented on audiotape at the rate of one per second in comparable lists to hearing college subjects with no knowledge of sign. Corresponding to the tasks for the deaf, there was a naming task, for hearing subjects, and recall of spoken words was also immediate, ordered, and written.

ON CHOOSING SIGNS FOR THE MEMORY EXPERIMENTS

We have already emphasized that ASL is a language very different from English. There are, of course, differences in the lexical structure of the two languages, just as there would be between any two different languages. Some signs require several English words in translation; and sometimes it is difficult to find a way to render the precise meaning of a sign in English without resorting to lengthy paraphrase. There are, of course, ASL signs which can be translated by more than one English word; for example, a sign which has as translation equivalent "gravy," "grease," or "greasy." This is similar to the difference in dictionary entries between any two languages.

Finally, just as any two distinct languages used by people in more or less similar cultures will have some pairs of lexical items which are near semantic equivalents across the two languages (that is, the two forms will commonly be intertranslatable), there are ASL signs and English words which form a fairly good match, as the sign represented by GIRL and the English word *girl*. Thus, although there are differences in lexical correspondence between ASL and English, we can make use of the *Dictionary of American Sign Language* and of the intuitions of native deaf signers to compile lists of signs with fairly direct translation equivalents into English. It is these signs which are used in our experimental studies in sign language. Thus, for this experiment we used some 135 common signs of ASL which were commonly intertranslatable with single English words. We chose signs which had nounlike functions in ASL, many of them from the vocabulary of the preschool deaf children of our acquisition studies. We eliminated compound signs or signs which seemed to us unusually long in time or large in space.

PROCEDURE

For this experiment there were eight deaf subjects who had had deaf parents and learned sign language as a primary natural language. The deaf subjects were students at Gallaudet College in Washington, D.C. Eight undergraduate hearing subjects at the University of California at San Diego, none of whom had any knowledge of sign language, were subjects for the parallel experiment presented in spoken English words. The lists were presented to the deaf in signs of ASL on videotape. They were made by a native signer, and were made without adding facial expression. (This is rather unnatural for ASL since facial expression ordinarily occurs concurrently with signing in the deaf. The absence of added facial expression allowed us to study the processing of ASL signs without other confounding factors.) The signs were made with what may be considered the equivalent of a "list" intonation. The test materials were prepared for hearing subjects in an analogous manner. As stimuli for the hearing subjects, the words (the English translation-equivalents of the signs) were spoken and presented on an audiotape recorder. The same words in the same order were used for list lengths three through seven, and a tape was made for identification and naming. The procedures on the test are analogous (stimuli were ASL signs for the deaf, English spoken words for the hearing) except that the deaf subjects responded by writing down what is for them the English translation equivalent of the sign whereas the hearing subjects responded by writing the alphabetic representation of the spoken word. In other words, an extra step—giving the translation equivalent in English for the signs—was required for the deaf subjects.

The details and results of this experiment have been written up in a working paper [Bellugi, Siple, and Klima, manuscript] and are not included here. We shall concern ourselves only with the intrusion errors made by deaf subjects.

INTRUSION ERRORS

Perhaps the most interesting outcome of our studies in short-term memory has to do with clues that we gain to the nature of the encoding processes used by deaf subjects when attempting to remember signs. We have said that intrusion errors are often used to investigate the nature of encoding in short-term memory with hearing subjects. In like manner, the intrusion errors in short-term memory for signs by deaf native signers will give clues to the nature of processing in a language in different modalities.

An intrusion error was considered to be any response given in a particular serial position which was different from any of the set of items considered correct for the item presented in that position, excluding repetition errors and errors which were carryovers from a previous list. There was no overlap between the intrusion errors made by deaf subjects and by hearing subjects to the same items. In other words, the errors made by the deaf subjects were in *no* instances the same as the errors made by the hearing subjects, although the correct answers would be the same.

In a previous memory experiment [Bellugi and Siple, 1974] we compared deaf subjects' responses in ASL signs with their responses in translations into written English words. Very significantly, we found that the
intrusion errors made by deaf subjects when responding in signs had considerable overlap with the errors made when deaf subjects responded in
the written English translation equivalents of signs. This suggests that
deaf subjects are using the same strategies for encoding and remembering
signs when the response required is in ASL signs and when the response
required is in a different language and a different mode. Again in that
experiment we found that the intrusion errors made by deaf subjects had
little or no overlap with the intrusion errors made by hearing subjects
(although a correct response for both might be the same). This indicates
that deaf subjects are using different strategies for encoding than hearing
subjects.

Let us consider some specific examples of intrusion errors for hearing
and for deaf subjects in this experiment. For a word that a hearing person
heard as *horse,* the intrusion error given was the written response "house."
For the American Sign Language gesture that a deaf person named as
HORSE, the intrusion error was the written response "uncle." There is
similarity in phonological form between the spoken words *horse* and
house; they differ only in the medial segments. Equally, there is a close
relationship in form between the signs represented by the English translation equivalents HORSE and UNCLE; that is, the signs are highly similar visually. The written response "tree" was given as an intrusion error for
the spoken word *tea* more than once by our hearing subjects. The written
translation equivalent "tree" was given as an intrusion error more than
once by our deaf subjects for the sign which they named NOON. In both

Sign on Test   Intrusion Error

NOON   "tree"

cases, the errors bear a resemblance to the original item: *tree* and *tea* are auditorily similar: the sign for TREE and the sign for NOON are visually similar. As we began analyzing the data we were struck by a number of cases in which there was clearly a relationship of visual similarity between the ASL sign presented on the test and the actual sign represented by the translation equivalent which our deaf subjects wrote as an intrusion error response. Although in the total number of errors which occurred there was much variation, nonetheless it seemed to us that in a surprising number of instances the sign presented on the test and the ASL translation equivalent of its written English word response were visually similar in form—visually similar but not in the broad pantomimic sense.

Our deaf subjects seemed *not* to be using a phonological form of the spoken word as a basis for remembering signs. If they had been, we would expect at least some overlap between the errors made by hearing and by deaf subjects. But what sort of code or codes could they be using? There are many other possibilities; a visual code based on the printed or written form of English word responses; a semantic code based on the *meaning* of the gestures, or a visual code based on the *form* of the original signs—on specific formational parameters. It was the frequency of the last type of errors that impressed us.

VISUAL AND AUDITORY SIMILARITY RATINGS

We wanted to measure the degree to which the errors made by deaf subjects were visually based (that is, the signed translation equivalent of the written word response was visually similar to the original sign presented) as compared with auditorily based intrusion errors made by hearing subjects. We decided to take an equal number of item and intrusion-error pairs made by hearing and by deaf subjects and to present them at one time as pairs of signs for visual similarity ratings and at another time as pairs of spoken English words for auditory similarity ratings.

For quantitative analysis, we selected all the intrusion errors which were made more than once for a single stimulus item. There were 26 of these multiple errors for the deaf with sign presentation and eight for the hearing subjects with auditory presentation. In order to have lists of equal length from the deaf and hearing subjects, 18 other errors were randomly selected from those which occurred once among the hearing subjects. The printed form of the item-and-intrusion-error pairs made by the deaf and the printed form of the 26 item-and-intrusion-error pairs made by the hearing subjects were combined into one list and randomized. These 52 pairs were then prepared in the two different modes; the pairs of stimulus items and intrusion errors (combined for the two groups) were recorded on audiotape in spoken form by a hearing person; the same pairs and intrusion errors were translated into signs of ASL and made on videotape by a native signer.

Ten hearing subjects with no knowledge of sign language were asked to rate the 52 pairs of signs for visual similarity. The subjects were not told the source of the pairs or the meaning of the signs. A scale of 1 to 5 was used with a 1 rating meaning "highly similar" and a 5 rating meaning "highly dissimilar." Ten other hearing subjects were asked to rate the set of items from the audiotape presentation in terms of acoustic similarity along the same scale. In each case, we gave examples of pairs not on the list that could be considered as "highly similar" or "highly dissimilar." A summary of the results is shown in Figures 2 and 3 and Table 1.

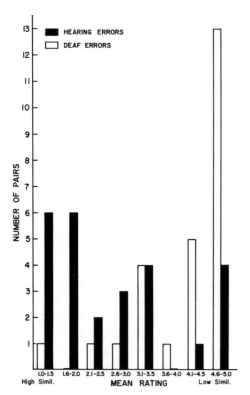

Figure 2. Mean auditory ratings by hearing subjects of sign or word and multiple-intrusion-error pairs.

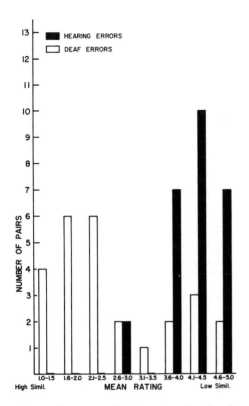

Figure 3. Mean visual ratings by hearing subjects of sign and word and multiple-intrusion-error pairs.

Table 1. Mean Similarity Rating from 1 "Highly Similar" to 5 "Highly Dissimilar"

Item and Intrusion Error Pairs	Auditory Presentation Pairs of Spoken Words	Visual Presentation Pairs of Signs
Hearing pairs	2.58	4.19
Deaf pairs	4.20	2.64

The table shows that when all item-and-error pairs were presented as spoken words and rated on the basis of auditory similarity, a large proportion of the errors made by deaf subjects were rated as low in auditory similarity, while the majority of the errors made by hearing subjects were rated toward the "similar" end of the scale. Conversely when all the pairs were presented as signs, and hearing subjects with no knowledge of sign language were asked to rate them for visual similarity, most of the hearing subjects' errors were rated as low in visual similarity and a large proportion of deaf item-and-error pairs were rated as visually similar. In fact, from the mean ratings, it seems that the errors made by the deaf were visually similar to the original item presented to the same degree that the errors made by the hearing subjects were auditorily similar to the original item presented. Not only was there no overlap in terms of actual intrusion responses made by the deaf and by the hearing, but we can now give evidence that the very nature of the errors made by hearing and deaf subjects is fundamentally different. The multiple intrusion errors made by the deaf for signs of ASL are demonstrably errors which are visually similar to the sign presented.

INTRUSION ERRORS AND LINGUISTIC SHARED PARAMETERS

Again, intrusion errors in ordered recall made by hearing subjects for spoken words were, as in previous experiments, words which resembled the original word presented in phonological form. Thus hearing subjects remembered "coat" for *coke*, and the two differ only in the final segment. Others remembered "bother" for *father*, and the two differ only in the initial segment. Other subjects remembered "cover" for *color,* and the two differ only in the medial segment. This suggests storage and retrieval based on sequential phonological segmentation of words.

When we examine the intrusion errors made by deaf subjects for signs, we find a totally different pattern of responses. We have established that the signs represented by the written word response are visually similar to the signs originally presented on the test. Now let us define more precisely the nature of the visual similarity. We shall see that it may well be based on an internal analysis of signs into simultaneously occurring parameters. Let us consider some typical examples of sign and error pairs, presented in Figure 4.

The sign presented on the test was NAME, and more than one deaf person remembered "egg" instead. The signs for NAME and EGG have the same hand shape and the same orientation, and both are made with two hands, in the same place of articulation. The two signs, in fact, differ only in *movement.* The sign for BIRD was presented on the test, and has

HOME

"Yesterday"

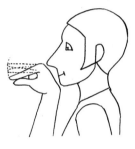

BIRD

"Print"

NAME

"Egg"

Sign Presented on Memory Test   Sign Translation of Intrusion Error

Figure 4. Examples of intrusion errors from memory experiment.

been said to be an iconic representation of the beak of a bird. The intrusion error made for BIRD was not some semantic or phonological error, but instead was "print." The signs for BIRD and PRINT have the same hand shape and orientation and the same closing movement, and both are made with one active hand. They differ only in *place of articulation,* since BIRD is made on the palm of the hand. The sign HOME was presented on the test, and the error made for it was "yesterday." Again the two signs share many aspects: HOME and YESTERDAY are both made on the cheek, both are made with one hand only, both are made with a movement involving a touch near the mouth, a movement away, and another touch on the upper cheek (what we call "two-touch" signs). The two signs differ only in *hand configuration,* since one uses a tapered "O" hand, and the other a closed hand with thumb and little finger extended. And finally, for the sign SOCKS more than one deaf subject remembered "star" instead. The signs for *star* and *socks* are highly similar: both

Sign on Test   Intrusion Error

SOCKS   "Star"

are made with two hands in the same hand configuration, and both are made in the space in front of the body, with a brushing motion backwards and forwards along the side of the index fingers. The two signs differ only in *the orientation of the hands* at the start of signing. These selected examples give us some clearer notion of the dimensions along which signs are stored in short-term memory.

We note that in each case the intrusion error was similar to the original sign presented in some formational aspects, but was not the same. We have discussed several aspects of signs, which we have called parameters: (a) the configuration of the hand or hands in making the sign; (b) the place of articulation of the sign, which may be a contact with the body, contact with another hand, or the space in front of the body; (c) the *movement* involved in making the sign, and (d) the *orientation* of the hands. With the exception of the last, these are the aspects of signs presented by Stokoe in the *Dictionary of American Sign Language* [see also Friedman, 1974, for further discussion of orientation]. The results of the experiments we have described would support the hypothesis that deaf subjects code and store signs not as holistic gestures, but rather in terms of formational parameters. Note that these are *simultaneously occurring aspects* of a sign, and not sequentially occurring segments, as in speech. For each parameter, we could list a set of elements, or *primes*. Among the hand configurations used in ASL, for example, are the closed fist, the pointing index hand, and a "V" hand. Among the location primes are the forehead, the nose, the chin, and wrist. Among the movement primes are opening of the fingers, movement away from signer, circling movement, contact, and so forth.

How strong is the evidence for the nature of the storage in short-term memory? We have completed three experiments in short-term memory for signs. Examining the ordered responses, we can list the intrusion errors which occurred more than once within each test. From this listing, for each experiment, more than two-thirds of the sign-error pairs differed in one parameter only. Most of the sign-error pairs, then, are highly similar formationally.

SUMMARY

Thus we have some experimental evidence suggestive of a systematic character in the form of recurring parameters of signs. Certain aspects of the results of these studies suggest possible ways of getting at deeper regularities in the formational aspects of ASL. The general question that interested us was how signs are coded in memory. The results from the memory experiments were consistent with a theory that signs are coded in terms of certain formational parameters. A similar claim had already been made about spoken language—in terms, of course, of the altogether different types of parameters characteristic of it: distinctive features, phonemes, and so on [Wickelgren, 1965]. According to our findings, thus, there was no reason to suppose a priori—as had been supposed—that signs are processed more in terms of meaning because of their "representational character" or are processed as "unitary wholes without internal analysis." These findings were based on the types of errors made by the subjects in ordered recall of lists of signs (in particular, intrusion errors made by more than one subject). These results support a model of short-term memory which include the coding of signs in terms of, for example, primes of the major formational parameters including hand configuration, place of articulation, movement, and orientation. The task of the subject in remembering a list of signs and their order of presentation would involve, according to this model, the storage of the particular primes of the major parameters (these would code the form of the sign), and their recall. The simplest error, according to this model, would be the recall of the inappropriate prime for a single major parameter.

Slips of the Hand
We have another important source of information on the organization of signs. We have begun to make a collection of errors that deaf people make in signing which are equivalent to slips of the tongue. It seems more appropriate to call them "slips of the hand." So far we have collected more than 80 such errors, all of them made by deaf people in sign language, and most of them on videotape. This work is being carried on in our laboratory by Sharon Neumann.

What units of organization are affected by slips of the hand? Sometimes entire signs are switched. Sometimes a prime of one sign is erroneously realized in another sign: hand configurations may be switched; a movement may persevere; or a location may be anticipated. This is striking evidence for the independence and reality of the parameters of ASL.

We find that sometimes the error results in something which is an actual sign of American Sign Language, although it was not the sign intended by the signer. For example, one person intended to sign MY MOTHER. Instead of using the correct hand configuration and orientation of the sign MY, she anticipated the hand configuration and orientation of the sign MOTHER. This resulted in what looks like the ASL sign for FINE instead of MY.

Most commonly, however, slips of the hand result in gestures which are not actual signs of ASL but seem to be "possible" signs of ASL, that is, the slip which occurs seems like a lexical gap in American Sign Language. In the same way, Victoria Fromkin [1971, 1973] has shown that slips of the tongue generally result in actual or possible sound sequences of spoken language.

In intending to sign DEAF WOMAN, a person made an anticipatory slip. She used the handshape for WOMAN with the movement and place of articulation of DEAF, with the results shown in the following diagram.

Slip of the Hand

Intended   Produced

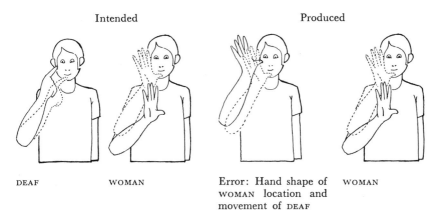

DEAF   WOMAN   Error: Hand shape of   WOMAN
                            WOMAN location and
                            movement of DEAF

The resulting slip is not a sign of ASL, but it could be a sign. That is, there are many signs with that particular hand shape and point of contact, as in TREE, FATHER, or DEER. There are many signs which are two-touch signs, as previously pointed out, as in HOME, FLOWER, BODY, or BACHELOR. There are many signs with the cheek as place of articulation, such as GIRL, TOMORROW, APPLE, and TELEPHONE. Thus, although the error just described is not a sign of ASL, it has recurring shared elements with other ASL signs and in that sense counts as a possible sign.

Most frequently, it is the hand shape that is exchanged, or switched, though we have found instances of errors involving movement only and of slips involving place of articulation. A slip of the hand in which move-

Slip of the Hand

Intended   Produced

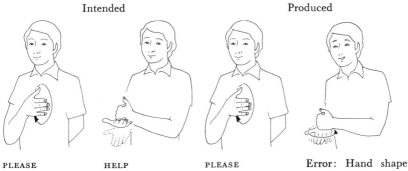

PLEASE   HELP   PLEASE   Error: Hand shape
                                           and location of
                                           HELP, movement
                                           of PLEASE

ment perseverated is shown in the preceding drawing. A deaf person intended to sign PLEASE HELP. PLEASE is signed with a circular motion and the circular motion perseverated also in the sign HELP.

The fact that we can identify and locate possible signs in ASL, with reference to recurring shared elements of the language, gives us further evidence for some kind of underlying system in the formation of ASL signs. Evidence from slips of the hand taken together with evidence from intrusion errors in short-term memory and with data from historical change in signs all point in a particular direction with respect to the question which we originally raised. It seems not to be the case that the signs of ASL differ uniquely and holistically from one another, or that American Sign Language is a loose collection of gestures. We are finding evidence for a psychologically real internal analysis of signs; a system based on recurring shared elements or aspects of signs. There is no tendency for these to be sequentially ordered elements as in speech. Rather, they seem to be primarily a *simultaneous* organization of parameters: unique hand configurations, unique places of articulation, unique movements, unique orientations, relationships between the hands, and so on. The phenomena involved in slips of the hand again suggest a performance model which crucially involves the major parameters as psychologically real, independent entities. In these slips, the prime of a major parameter of one sign in a sequence is substituted for (or interchanged with) that of another sign in the sequence.

A Comparison Between Two Sign Languages

The studies so far described suggest that there is a characteristic stamp to ASL. A much more fundamental question, however, is whether the system is such as to exclude certain gestures which are, nonetheless, physically possible. More specifically we want to ask whether there are actual signs in another sign language which would be extrasystemic (or "impossible") in ASL.

A language based on movements of the hands in space may have quite different characteristics from a language based on the vocal apparatus. Perhaps there are no particular restrictions on the form of signs within a sign language so that any imaginable gesture can become a sign in any sign language. Perhaps knowing one sign language, a person can rapidly learn another without the barrier that molds man's tongue. By examining two very divergent sign languages (American Sign Language and Chinese Sign Language) we hope to arrive at a deeper understanding of the nature of formational constraints within a sign language. Our next study will be of interference phenomena between the sign languages. This should help us identify critcal differences between the two divergent languages in a visual mode.

We have been able to locate a handbook of some 2000 Chinese signs [Goodstadt, 1970], and have had some contact with native deaf Chinese signers. Here we will present only one aspect of our findings. From some preliminary study of the book of Chinese signs and some videotapes we have made of Chinese signers, we can already isolate examples of what seem to be systematic differences between the two sign languages. For instance, there are many signs in ASL which use a particular hand shape prime in which the index fingertip touches the tip of the thumb and the middle, ring, and little fingers are raised. We can call it a "pinching" hand shape.

"Pinching" Hand Shape

Figure 5 presents some ASL signs which involve the pinching hand shape. Note that in these signs, it is the *thumb and index finger,* the

Figure 5. The pinching hand shape in American signs.

"pinching" part which is dominant in ASL. This is the part which makes contact, which joins, grasps, or leads, which is prominent in the action. Sometimes the contact is made with the side of the hand; even there it is the thumb and index side which is dominant, as in FOX and PROFIT in ASL. The other three fingers (middle, ring, and little) may be close together or spread; may be stiff or relaxed. These differences seem to be immaterial in ASL.

We have found a number of signs in Chinese Sign Language (CSL) in which the same hand shape prime is involved, but in a very different way (see Figure 6). In some CSL signs, the middle, ring, and little fingers are the dominant part of the sign or are acted upon. These three fingers are never acted upon nor active in ASL. Thus, in the CSL signs for GIVEN NAME, TOPIC, GOOD REPUTATION, CHOP, ENROLL, MENU, QUESTION, the

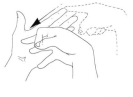

Figure 6. The pinching handshape in some Chinese signs.

"pinching" hand is used in a way that does not occur in ASL: the middle, ring, and little fingers can be the dominant part of some CSL signs, as shown in Figure 6. Until we looked at some Chinese signs, we had not noticed which features of this hand shape are dominant in ASL. It was only when we began to see differences between the ways in which this hand shape is used in two different sign languages that we realized something more about systematic regularities of ASL. We now see that two sign languages may have the same elements but different constraints on the use of these elements in signs. We also found signs which use elements not occurring in ASL and look forward to the opportunity of investigating these differences.

So far we have been able to find three categories of signs in Chinese Sign Language that may bear a particular relationship to American Sign Language. Some Chinese signs approximate the form of signs in ASL, although they have a different meaning (actual signs). Some Chinese signs *might* be signs of ASL, but are not actually realized. These could be considered as "lexical gaps" in American Sign Language, that is possible, but not actual signs. And finally, there seem to be some Chinese signs which are "impossible" in American Sign Language, that is, impossible as far as the system of primes and their combinations is concerned.

ACTUAL SIGNS

We have located a set of Chinese signs that are made by Chinese signers in such a way that they closely resemble signs in American Sign Language, but they have a different meaning in the two languages. The formation of the signs in the two different languages is sufficiently similar that American deaf signers perceived the Chinese sign as equivalent to a sign in ASL. For example, American deaf signers "recognize" the Chinese sign for EXPLAIN as their sign for *cook*. The Chinese sign for FATHER is equivalent to the ASL sign for SECRET. The Chinese sign for ONE WEEK is equivalent to the ASL sign for FALSE.

Chinese: FATHER

Chinese: ONE WEEK

Other such pairs are presented in Table 2.

These signs have approximately equivalent forms in two different sign languages, and there seems to be little or no relationship between the meanings associated with the signs in the two languages: (This is, incidentally, one argument against the pervasiveness of iconicity in signs.)

Table 2. Signs Formed in the Same Way in CSL and ASL

Gloss for Chinese Sign	Gloss for American Sign
tease	bachelor
help	push
teacher	myself
intelligent	suit yourself

POSSIBLE, BUT NOT ACTUAL SIGNS

We have found Chinese signs that "could be" American Sign Language signs but are not actual signs. We have already seen examples of such accidental lexical gaps from the slips of the hand referred to previously. The Chinese sign for DISTRACTED has the hand shape and orientation of the American sign for PLAY, but the notion is quite different in the two signs. The motion of the sign DISTRACTED occurs, however, in the ASL sign for SEPARATE. Thus, the Chinese sign has primes which occur in ASL and are used in the same way in forming signs, but that particular combination of primes is not an ASL sign. The Chinese sign for OFTEN has a movement and location like the ASL sign for CARELESS, but the hand shape is different. The ASL sign for UNCLE has the same hand shape as the Chinese sign OFTEN. Again, the primes are recurring shared features used the same way as in ASL signs, but they do not occur in ASL in that particular combination.

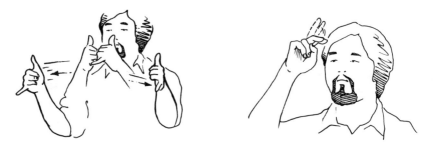

Chinese: DISTRACTED   Chinese: OFTEN

Other Chinese signs which might be considered possible but not actual ASL signs are ARGUE, MISJUDGE, PROSTITUTE, REASON, EXPERIENCE.

IMPOSSIBLE SIGNS

Finally we come to an important group of signs. These are Chinese signs which seem very different in formation from ASL signs. These are signs that do not appear to be part of the system of signs and sign formation in ASL. We have already described one case. We noted that the three extended fingers of the "pinching" handshape are never used in ASL as the focus of activity or the point of contact for the active or the base hand, and thus the Chinese sign TOPIC is not a part of the system of formation of American signs. The Chinese sign for SUSPECT uses a movement which does not occur in ASL. The Chinese sign for ELDER BROTHER uses a hand shape which does not occur as a prime in ASL. The primes in the sign for DISCIPLE all occur in ASL signs, but the particular way in

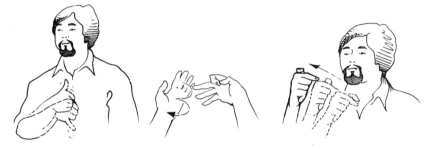

Chinese: SUBJECT   Chinese: TOPIC   Chinese: INCREASE

which they are combined does not. Other Chinese signs which are different from ASL signs include INCREASE, CONTROL, BOTH, INTRODUCE.

We are planning an experiment which will test the intuitions of deaf American signers with respect to these three groups of Chinese signs. Clearly we are just beginning to be able to define the notion of "systematic" within a sign language. The issues raised here merely point to the possibility that there is some degree of structuredness to the signs of a sign language. Few of the details have been worked out, but our evidence is strong that signs are processed, remembered, stored, on the basis of recurring parameters, simultaneously organized. The degree to which this will constitute a tightly structured system still remains to be investigated.

Summary

In summary, we return to some of the questions raised by Kavanagh in his introductory letter for this conference. The body of our paper is concerned with what new avenues of inquiry suggest themselves when such questions are asked about visual symbols in general, and about the sign language of the deaf in particular. In this light, we have focused specifically on the internal nature of the signs of American Sign Language. From historical change in the form of signs, the behavior of signers in the controlled situation of short-term memory experiments, from the form of errors occurring in casual, everyday signing, we find evidence that the signs proper of American Sign Language are not simply signals which differ uniquely and holistically from one another but are, rather, highly coded units. Despite the transparent relation of sign language to a nonlinguistic form of communication—pantomime—we find in American Sign Language a great deal of restructuring. The particular form that this restructuring has taken seems to be in large part dependent on the change in modality: from the ear to the eye and from the vocal apparatus to the hands. It does seem that our research presents some evidence that grammatical processes indeed bear the marks of the particular transmission system in which the language developed.

References

Bellugi, U., and S. Fischer. 1972. A comparison of sign language and spoken language. *Cognition,* 1: 173–200.

Bellugi, U., and P. A. Siple. 1974. Remembering with and without words. In *Current Problems in Psycholinguistics,* Paris: Centre National de la Recherche Scientifique.

Bellugi, U., P. A. Siple, and E. S. Klima. Manuscript. Remembering in signs.

Conrad, R. 1962. An association between memory errors and errors due to acoustic masking of speech. *Nature,* 193: 1314–1315.

Conrad, R. 1972. Speech and reading. In *Language by Ear and by Eye,* J. F. Kavanagh and I. G. Mattingly (eds.). Cambridge, Mass.: MIT Press.

Friedman, L. A. 1974. On the semantics of space, time and person reference in American Sign Language. Masters' thesis, University of California, Berkeley.

Frishberg, N. 1973. From iconicity to arbitrariness. Paper presented to the Linguistics Society of America.

Fromkin, V. A. 1971. The non-anomalous nature of anomalous utterances. *Language,* 47: 27–52.

Fromkin, V. A. 1973. Slips of the tongue. *Scientific American,* 229: 110–117.

Furth, H. G. 1966. *Thinking without Language.* New York: Free Press.

Furth, H. G. 1971. Linguistic deficiency and thinking: research with deaf subjects, 1964–1969. *Psychol. Bull.,* 76: 68–72.

Furth, H. G. 1972. *Deafness and Learning: A Social-Developmental Psychology.* Belmont, Calif: Wadsworth.

Furth, H. G., and J. Youniss. 1969. Thinking in deaf adolescents: language and formal operations. *J. Comm. Disorders,* 2: 195–202.

Goldman-Eisler, F. 1968. *Psycholinguistics.* New York: Academic Press.

Goodstadt, Rose Yin-Chee. 1970. *Speaking with Signs.* Hong Kong: Government Printer.

Klima, E. S. 1974. Sound and its absence in the linguistic symbol. This volume.

Long, J. S. 1918. *The sign language: a manual of signs.* Iowa City: Athens Press.

Mattingly, I. G., and A. M. Liberman. 1969. The speech code and the physiology of language. In *Information Processing in the Nervous System,* K. N. Leibovic (ed.). New York: Springer.

Schlesinger, I. M. In press. Some aspects of sign language. In *A New Dictionary of Sign Language,* part I, E. Cohen, L. Namir, and I. M. Schlesinger (eds.). The Hague: Mouton.

Stokoe, W. 1960. Sign language structure: an outline of the visual communication system of the American deaf. In *Studies In Linguistics,* occasional paper 8 (Reissued Washington, D.C.: Gallaudet College Press).

Stokoe, W. 1972. *Semiotics and human sign languages.* The Hague: Mouton.

Stokoe, W., D. Casterline, and C. Croneberg. 1965. *A Dictionary of American Sign Language on Linguistic Principles.* Washington, D.C.: Gallaudet College Press.

Wickelgren, W. A. 1965. Distinctive features and errors in short-term memory for English vowels. *J. Acoustic Soc. Amer.,* 38: 583–588.

Open Discussion of the Paper of Bellugi and Klima

Further Comments on Sign

For the record Alvin Liberman emphasized that there appear to be at least three different kinds of sign language: natural sign, signed English, and finger spelling. Obviously, signed English and finger spelling are not natural sign; they are parasitic on the spoken language. Thus it is really only the natural sign that is peculiarly interesting in terms of revealing, by indirect means, the role of speech in language. However, many deaf signers do all three types of sign and have contact with people who use each of them. An important question arises: To what extent has the natural sign that one studies been influenced by contact with spoken language, in this case English, and with forms of sign which are parasitic on English?

Edward Klima suggested that one way to look at this question is to observe the effects of specific attempts to "enrich" sign by the spoken community. In France, for example, there was an attempt to add various endings to signs, endings which are analogous to those found in spoken languages like French and English. Interestingly, these tacked-on elements were quickly rejected. A similar attempt was made in SEE (Signing Essential English). Here additions were made to a natural sign root, yielding sign constructions like verb + *ing*, among many others. Again, these accretions did not "take"; they were not "natural" elements which could be added to natural sign. There may have been many forces which contributed to the rejection process. One certainly is the fact that these additions take too much additional time to sign. William Stokoe added that there have been many such attempts, presumably to make sign "look more like language," and that generally they have all failed. Thus, natural sign is considerably resistant to contamination from certain forms of spoken-language influence.

Ursula Bellugi added that the learning of sign language is a very interesting process. At first one's eyes are riveted to the hands of the signer, looking for intricate differences between gestures. This nearly unavoidable habit is wrong. Fluent signers watch faces, not hands. Faces obviously carry much important information, especially in terms of affect modification, but nowhere near all signs take place on or near the face. Thus, many signs must occur in the periphery of the visual field. The importance of eye contact cannot be overemphasized. In fact, as long as eye contact is maintained the gestures involved in sign can undergo some fairly radical changes and still be understood. Consider the sign language counterpart to whispering. Imagine two fluent signers sitting over lunch and discussing a topic which they do not want "overheard." Their sign gestures are small and all of them are directly in front of them, perhaps near the surface of the table. It appears that in "whispered" sign the torso referents of the signs are projected forward as if onto an imaginary doll in front of the signer. In some ways the "whispered" sign is to sign as whispered speech is to speech: the message can be understood, but the signal is noisier, and does not "carry" very far. In sign, eye contact helps to "carry" the message.

Paul Kiparsky noted that whereas spoken language has little iconicity—basically in the form of phonetic symbolism, which appears to be the exception rather than the rule—sign language appears to be rife with iconicity. Neither situation seems to be entirely necessary. One can imagine on the one hand a spoken language in which iconic elements play a much more important role, and on the other a sign language in which gestures might be entirely arbitrary. Perhaps one reason sign is so iconic is that, in its present form, it is too new. During the course of its existence of two hundred years or so there seems to be a trend away from icons. Perhaps in several hundred more years icons will play a much less prominent role. Such a trend should still cause us to wonder why the oral languages that we have developed use icons so little. Is there an advantage to noniconic language? If there is it would seem to be in making certain types of relational notions. Kiparsky then asked William Stokoe how to sign *a small elephant*. Stokoe appeared to have some difficulty but promised that he would give a rendering during his presentation which followed. Ursula Bellugi then added that a signer would not append the sign for *small* in conjunction with the sign for *elephant*, perhaps because of the clash of icon and meaning.

Klima mentioned that Roman Jakobson has commented on the natural necessity of music and language being basically noniconic whereas in art (but not abstract art) there is more iconic representation.

The Shape of Soundless Language

WILLIAM C. STOKOE, JR.

This morning Paul Kiparsky asked me a very important question: "How do you sign "small elephant"? I am not a native signer and it took me the luncheon break to get into the frame of reference that the answer requires. If I were seriously expressing to a signer that I was talking about an elephant that was small, I would sign *elephant* first, then hold my hand up above my head where you might expect an elephant's back to be and bring it down to eye level, or lower.

Kiparsky's question touches an important point: if one looks at signs one at a time, if he considers them in isolation, if he has a native signer make one sign at a time, and if he asks other signers to do the same, then he will see considerable *iconicity* in signs. However, if he makes a videotape recording of rapid sign conversation, it would be quite difficult to note particular shapes or actions. Furthermore, the process of deiconization of signs goes on continually in American Sign Language (ASL). Consider the sign for a bird's beak, which is not a bird beak, of course, but a thumb and finger configuration used to mean *bird, bird beak, print,* and many other things. A similar two-hand sign means *awkward.* People may say that the awkward sign stems from the duck's webbed feet and waddle; but it is the same handshape used for *rooster* (a three-finger hand on top of the head). Notice that the hand is now an icon for the cockscomb. It can also mean *car* or *ship* (three-finger hand on edge in other palm). The point about "icons" in sign is that many are not as iconic as we might think; that is, they can represent a great many different things. There is no one-to-one relationship between gesture and meaning.

At the beginning of this conference Liberman presented a framework for us with intellect at one end of the transmission system and the vocal tract (the hand) and the ear (the eye) at the other end. Nearly everything between is a mystery, but the ends of the system must be linked by some kind of grammar. In dealing with sign language, people generally start with grammar—not with the use of vision and motor activity for transmitting, nor with the intellect where concepts are formed and related, but more towards the middle (but still near the lower end of the system) where there seems to be a sign-referent relationship, or more specifically a set of gesture-meaning pairs. Gestures and meanings may look like precisely fixed pairs, and many observers get no farther than that observation. If they begin with signs they come to a dead end. Starting with gesture-meaning pairs one may find iconicity and exclaim: "Aha, that is it, a natural system of icons and their denotata, one of the simple semiotic systems in which signs and meaning closely match." One may go further, and some have, by pretending that the dead end was not going toward language anyway. One may reason that such is the nature of sign languages: expression of emotion in man and animals has always been iconic and no one can arrive at language through simple sets of gesture-meaning pairs. One needs a grammar, and sign language has an intricate grammar.

It is possible to consider the composition of a sign and not just its meaning. Here I differ a little from Bellugi and Fischer [1972] in how I see the relationship between a sign and the syllable. A simple sign is quite syllablelike in that it has, not a consonant-vowel-consonant pattern, but hand shape, location, and movement. Those three are all transmitted by visible motor signals as distinct as the mechanisms for vocalic and consonantal production. Perceived by one who knows sign, they are recognized as elements that contrast in minimal ways. The elegant short-term memory experiments done by Bellugi [Bellugi and Siple, 1974] show that sign language users store information in short-term memory as shape, location, and movement. Furthermore, looking at a sign as composed of the relatively meaningless elements of location and motion and hand shape does not contradict the obvious truth that many gestures are iconic.

I am not sure that I would recognize the upright arm with its elbow resting on the other palm as an icon for tree unless I were told so; and were I a user of some other sign language than American, I am sure I would be able to accept the sign for some totally different meaning. It is possible gesturally to represent trees in different ways, but there seems a kind of syllablelike composition of the three basic parameters of a sign. Some time ago it seemed to me [Stokoe, 1960] that the difference between a syllable in speech and a sign in sign language was that the constituents of a sign are made and seen more or less simultaneously while the segments of a syllable are spoken and heard sequentially. But, as I said yesterday, the work of those at the Haskins Laboratories [see, for example, Liberman et al., 1967] shows that speech is much more simultaneous, much more like sign language than it might appear.

When the sound of a syllable is interpreted by a hearer and given phonetic representation, the hearer is actually segmenting a signal in which the consonant information has been folded into the vowel information. Much of the input signal is in fact simultaneous, and gets sorted into a proper sequential order only by the hearer.

What Bellugi calls parameters and I have called *cheremes* [Stokoe,

1960] are called "phonemes" by my young colleagues who, as I have, usually put quotation marks around the word. However these elements are called, they are the discrete categories into which a sign receiver sorts the incoming visual information with its constant flow and its simultaneous display. It is possible to recognize constraints on the arrangement and use of these basic parameters as Bellugi terms them. Siple [1973], one of her former associates, has shown that visual acuity constrains a signer to keep small changes in parameters close to the center of a signer-receiver's gaze, the face. Just as there are other physical constraints, there are also linguistic constraints. Some of my colleagues, Battison, Friedman, Markowicz, and Woodward, have found regular ways in which the hand shape and location are constrained by such things as morpheme boundaries and the occurrence of other "phonemes." Linguistic context, in fact, determines which signs go together; and if anything must give way, iconicity is first to go.

This discussion has taken us some way from gesture-meaning pairs in a simple discrete signaling system. In considering fluent sign language we may be looking at a transmission code which is like the speech code in that its units are relatively meaningless and the information needed to discriminate these units is presented simultaneously. The visual display which a human receiver of sign must segment into discrete units is as messy as a speech signal. It consists of what looks like vague motioning, but this input is categorically received and transmitted. One can give a signer a seemingly undecipherable flow of visual information on tape or film and ask him what is there. He can give it back as clear-cut and clean as one may desire it to be—in citation form with canonical formation, in paraphrased sign, or in English translation.

It is noteworthy that there is no such thing as the right way to form a sign. Of course deaf mothers do correct deaf children who try, for example, to make the sign for "egg" in nonstandard ways, as Bellugi and Klima [this volume] showed us. But the mother will correct the child *to the particular way the mother makes the sign;* and as Woodward [1973a, 1973b, 1973c] has shown there is not only much variation in the rules for making and putting signs together in phrases but also a regular relation of these variations to social parameters.

It is also possible to move from the level of grammar where a sign is a construction of relatively meaningless parts to a level where the signs themselves are the constituents of semantic and syntactic structures. When that move is made, one finds a number of differences that distinguish sign languages from all the other languages that I am familiar with. In other words, the grammar of sign is not like the grammar of speech. One reason I think it worth comparing both forms of language is statistical. The proportion of native speakers to native signers is about ten thousand to one. General estimates find one completely deaf person in each thousand of population, but only one deaf person in ten is the child of deaf parents. It is thus this one in ten thousand who learns sign as if it were his first, native and natural language. But the other nine also use it, and learn it from him directly if they are lucky, since they cannot usually learn it from their parents. The existence of this tiny fraction of total population, a community of persons who use sign as their language, means that we have an alternative to looking at the grammar of spoken language. Grammar is something we are all interested in when it is defined as Liberman defined it: the interrelationships of the transmission system with intellect through all of the systems and subsystems between. There seems to be enough difference between sign and speech to give a whole new perspective to grammar.

One very interesting difference is that the infant with deaf parents begins putting wordlike signs into sentencelike structures at an earlier age than the child making two-word or three-word sentences in speech. Deaf or hearing, the infant with deaf parents whose language is American Sign Language will also have been making recognizable signs before the hearing child of hearing parents produces recognizable words [Schlesinger and Meadow, 1972].

Such hints from ontogeny suggest a new look at phylogeny and the problem of the origins of language. If, as Hewes has proposed [1973a, 1973b], our species got hold of the ability to use language by developing a property of the information capacity in gestural transmission, the whole developmental picture might be that the acquisition of speech as the prime transmission system for language had a great cost and occasioned quite a setback—as if speech slows development. The observations of Huttenlocher [this volume] indicate that such setbacks do occur; specifically, a child who has developed the ability to respond to the speech of adults may lose some items while adding others to its repertory of comprehension.

All children *communicate* visually before they learn speech, but many of the deaf parents of hearing children say that they signed sentences to the parents before they were talking. All the testimony is that children with deaf parents make two-sign and longer sentences at around 12–14 months. One possible explanation is that deaf people's hearing children lack auditory stimulation, but in families where they have hearing siblings they still sign first.

Gesture Has Uses in Acquiring Speech

Let us say that the whole developmental pattern does not make it look as if the child with hearing has little built-in capacity for recognizing phonetic distinctions. Rather, it seems that before he is able to exploit that capacity to the extent of producing acceptable speech, he has to spend a lot of time using his experience and comprehension and every other faculty to learn how to speak. Part of the time he is probably relating things to the speech-language system with tactile and gestural ways of coming to grips with whatever it is he wants to talk about when he talks. I observed that my own granddaughter, at the age of two and a half years, was perfectly able to deal with three or four names for herself (her name, the diminutive of her name, *me,* and *baby*). She could also handle three labels for her mother and had several names for others in the family. But if someone talked to her and put more than normal stress on *me:* "You are *you,* and *I* am *me,*" that was the end of the conversation. That was too upsetting. She could understand synonyms but not a bunch of labels that changed meaning according to who was using them.

To us these are simple rules: speaker is *I* or *me,* and person spoken to is *you;* then with a change of speaker the words belong to the person they didn't belong to before. And the only way you can make sense of this, I believe, if you are a two-and-a-half-year-old child, is to do it with looks and gestures while listening and speaking. Somewhere along the way to growing up, the child gets to that next level of competence where it is perfectly easy to handle a pronoun system that switches forward and back with each change in turn. I submit that gesture, looking, and pointing are very important aids in that progress.

We need more information about what is going on all at once in the tactile, the gestural, the visual, the vocal transmission systems and how they converge and are sorted out, both in normally hearing children and in deaf children in various language environments. One of the ways of exploring the large *terra incognita* there between intellect and what is otherwise noise, is psycholinguistics. A new colleague at Gallaudet, I. K. Jordan, has done some interesting experiments in referential communication. Pairs of subjects, both deaf or both hearing, used sign and English, respectively. One subject, after the experimenter pointed out one picture in an array, conveyed to the other member of the pair the information needed for the second to pick out the identical picture in a similar array. Unlike any other psychological experiment I know of, this one resulted in the deaf communicator pairs scoring higher than the hearing pairs on some tasks. The best deaf subject pair put together amazing phrases, if one can call them that. For instance, when the pictures all were of men of similar appearance, one deaf subject signed, *black eyebrows like glasses*. *Black* is signed by drawing the edge of the index finger across the brows; *eyebrows* is much the same but with a touch instead of a slide. *Glasses* are indicated by the thumb and fore-finger as if grasping the frames by the hinge; but *like* is signed by bringing together the two index fingers side by side. However, in this phrase, *black eyebrows like glasses,* the signer simply made half the sign on the brows, following the light touch for *eyebrows* with a further withdrawal of the finger and a marked laying of it against the brows as an emphatic *like* would be made by laying one finger against the other.

When Jordan debriefed his subjects after the experiment, he asked one of the members of that signing pair, signing literally, "Know her how long, you?" She answered that she had known the other subject since they were babies. One sign was made by putting the thumb in the mouth, the other simultaneously by raising the palm-downward hand from tot height to teen height [Jordan, personal communication]. The ability of people to use this kind of language at very rapid rates and to communicate propositionally with it depends to some extent on the amount of exposure to each other's idiolect. There is also in this "since-babyhood" example an unusual truth about sign language grammar.

Sign does not make the same separation between things and acts that is characteristic of most languages. The noun/verb distinction may be a language universal; but in sign, using signs to name persons or objects and using signs to depict actions, processes, and changes in state are not so clearly distinguished. In sign language for *We grew up together* and *I saw a man over there and he approached as I was looking* the same sign does both naming and predicating duty. From such hints we may get ideas about how to formulate questions about the part gesture may have played in the evolution of syntax and semantics, of language. Once the species (an individual, a few individuals, or the whole group) began to use a gesture that combines noun and verb—and there still are many such in American Sign Language—it would not have been such a long step to separating the part which supplies the name from the part which describes the action, process, or state. In 1965, when I thought I knew enough about American Sign Language to put together a dictionary, I said that the sign for *suitcase* was the pantomime of holding a suitcase. That is true enough, but the sign also means *carry* as to carry something with a handle, like a suitcase or briefcase. The same sign is noun, or verb, or both together. This sort of surprise, the indeterminacy of word and phrase and sentence boundaries, happens often in the study of signs;

but it makes the work interesting because it gives all of us a second way of looking at how experience, the contents, in part, of the intellect, gets put into symbols. Even if this language is found among only a statistically very small part of the human population, it may help us find out more about how language is transmitted by speech.

Kinds of Language Contrasts

A one-sentence definition by Dunn and Byrnes [1973, p. 11] is a good starting point for our more detailed examination of language in which speech has no role:

Language is a signalling device dependent on an interconnected system of six different kinds of contrasts: phonemic contrasts between discrete sounds, both vowels (*bat*/*but*) and consonants (*bat*/*cat*); morphemic contrasts between forms (*cat*/*cats*); syntactic contrasts between constructions (*This is a cat*/*Is this a cat?*); semantic contrasts between words (*cat*/*dog*); stress contrasts between syllables (I'll per-*mit* you/I'll give you a *per*-mit); and intonational contrasts between sentences (*This is a cat*/*This is a cat?*)

The authors add that "English uses no contrasts other than these six (pitch provides intonational contrast but does not, as in Chinese, provide semantic tone contrast)." To simplify this for present purposes, I would like to define phonemic contrasts as between consonants, vowels, and tones (when used).

Of these six kinds of contrasts only two, phonemic contrasts and intonation contrasts, are directly signaled by speech sound. The other four are of course integral parts of language, but they or something very much like them are to be found in other systems as well. Phonemic contrasts and intonational contrasts belong to language and speech by definition and name, yet they are not functionally equivalent. The example Dunn and Byrnes use for intonation contrast distinguishes "between sentences (*This is a cat*/*This is a cat?*)," but the basic distinction of declarative and interrogative sentences is signaled by syntax "(*This is a cat*/*Is this a cat?*)." In varieties of English most familiar to me, the declarative order with marked intonational contrast signals surprise or irony or imputes aberration to whoever considers *this* a cat.

One difference between phonemic and intonational contrasts is the length of speech output they operate over. Phonemic contrasts may be made at rates up to thirty or forty a second; but intonational contrasts mark whole utterances, as long as sentences or as short as a syllable or two (*John?*/*Marsha!*) or even shorter paralinguistic or nonlexical sounds (*mmm* . . . I'm not really interested/*mmm* . . . That feels wonderful). These two kinds of contrasts differ in another way. Abbott [1973, p. 5; see also Liberman, et al., 1967] has proposed that a measure he calls "the degree of encodedness" be applied not only to whole systems but also to parts of systems as a way to determine which are more linguistic than others:

> For example, the steady state vowels are far less encoded than the consonants; they show less variation in different contexts; they can be perceived more continuously and less categorically; and they can be transmitted alone without any other sound segments. In the sense that encodedness is a measure of linguistic structures, we can say that these vowels are less linguistic than the consonants. Still less encoded are the prosodic features of speech.

There may be several explanations for the smaller degree of encodedness in prosodic features, that is, intonational contrasts. First, they are more primitive in the sense of earlier in ontogeny. Children acquiring language can signal with intonational contrasts quite competently before they reach the two-word or pivot-open stage of grammar and long before they master the phonemic, semantic, and morphemic contrasts. Listening supplies evidence enough of this, but Braine's [1963] original tapes of Andrewese give elegant proof. Second, intonational contrasts are used to signal stylistic, social psychological, and idiosyncratic distinctions as well as linguistic differences; hence they present or represent [Wilden, 1973] as well as encode. Third, intonational contrasts, unlike phonemic contrasts, can be experimentally removed from otherwise natural communication with little or no loss in propositional content. Finally, it should be possible to show experimentally that intonational contrasts relate to other nonvocal systems in ways that phonemic contrasts signaled by the speech code cannot.

A nonlinguistic acoustic carrier (*mmm, uh*) can be contrastingly modulated with intonations to transmit intelligible messages; and, such is the redundancy of the human system, intonation contrasts may be completely replaced by visible behavior with no loss of information transfer. This may easily be tested; hearing subjects trained to lipread sequences on the order of difficulty of *This is a cat* should be able to distinguish the import of intonational contrasts signaled by speakers behind soundproof glass. Of course this is not to say that visible behavior is unencoded. On the contrary, many speakers of American English have kinesic as well as intonational and paralinguistic contrasts between such sentences as *I did enjoy it!* and *I didn't enjoy it.* A hearer may be too far away or in too noisy a location to perceive and decode the contrast between [dɪd]-

enjoy ≠ [dɪdnt]-*enjoy* but it is likely that if the speaker were in full view the hearer would not have to ask for a repeat. Kinesic details redundantly supply the same contrast.

However, there are subtle differences in the kinesic coding, not only between deaf and hearing groups, as might be expected, but also between deaf persons natively competent in sign and deaf persons to whom sign is a second language. Among the sign sentences performed by a native signer on a videotape recording made in our laboratory is one which translates *did enjoy*. A salient visual feature is the gesture-sign glossed *enjoy* (right palm rubs left breast); it appears simultaneously with a complicated face and head gesture (of short duration and small positional displacement). Every hearing person who has some acquaintance with signing or who has been told the meaning of the *enjoy* sign and every deaf person not a native signer, when shown the taped sign sentence, interprets it as negative: *I didn't enjoy it*. Every native signer shown it takes the meaning as positive and emphatic, often in translation giving the emphasis lexical or semantic coding: *I really enjoyed it!* or *I enjoyed it, wow!* Simply stated, this identical kinesic signal encodes negative for one group and emphasis for the other.

It seems reasonable to conclude that despite the obviously vocal nature of intonational contrasts, they are not necessarily linguistic and have more affinity with other systems that signal affect than with phonemic contrasts. There remain then only phonemic contrasts between consonant and consonant, vowel and vowel, and tone and tone (when so used) as the indisputably linguistic, basic features of language.

The separation of the other five kinds of contrasts from the speech code has primary importance for dealing with language that does not depend on speech encoding. Semantic contrasts can be made by a nod and a headshake [Jakobson, 1972]; morphemic contrasts are signaled by many formal differences; stress contrasts are made by various physical mechanisms; syntactic contrasts, as differing arrangements of elements, may be most generally distributed of all; and intonational contrasts, besides doing language duty, form interfaces between language and paralanguage, between the auditory and the visual modalities, and between message systems defined as animal, affective, and nonlinguistic.

Recent movements of the van in two parts of the whole field support this attempt to describe language that is not speech-encoded. Lieberman [1973] argues for removal of the academic separation of linguistic and paralinguistic phenomena. Yngve [1973] proposes a broader base, "human linguistics." Sarles [1973] demands still wider scope, "a human ethological approach to communication." Their arguments seem to favor treating all the kinds of contrasts, except phonemic, in wider contexts than linguistic theory presently allows. But a concentration of keen scientific curiosity precisely on the speech code has the same strategic effect. Liberman et al. [1967] and Mattingly and Liberman [1969] present details of the structure and function of the speech code, which I take as further evidence that phonemic contrasts belong to a different order of neurophysiology, of information processing, and of code complexity than do morphemic, syntactic, stress, semantic, and intonational contrasts. If this accurately describes the current situation, the objective is clear: in order to show that human language is possible without basis in the speech code, some other system of encoding must be shown to be comparable. If that can be done, the interconnection of this nonvocal encoding system with the other five kinds of contrasts follows easily.

Before asking what else has the structure of and can match the information-processing function of the speech code, it may be well to consider why and how such a duplication should and could have come about. Deafness, in a word, sufficiently answers why. Evolution may be the one-word answer to how.

In What Sense Is Gesture Primitive?

Deafness since the beginning of written records has been remarked both as a condition for humanitarian concern and as an interesting test case for theories of knowing, thinking, and speaking. While it has many causes, deafness is also one result of the genetic pool of our species. Given the regularity and stability of genetic inheritance, deafness always, as now, has affected an appreciable fraction of the whole species (≥ 0.1 percent). Deafness provides both biological and social causes for emergence of sign languages, but the definition of social causes may vary. Some time ago I argued [Stokoe, 1960] that one or two hundred thousand deaf Americans sufficiently constituted a linguistic community, and described their system of sign communication as having the structure of any language, substituting *cheremic* for *phonemic* contrasts. The *Dictionary of American Sign Language* [Stokoe, Casterline, and Croneberg, 1965], based on recognition of these cheremic contrasts, has become a symbol of the solidarity of the group whose language is sign, besides providing a means of introducing the language to other deaf populations and nonhuman signers [Gardner and Gardner, 1971]. But now Kuschel [1973] has discovered that the existence of one deaf-mute person on a Polynesian island led to the invention of a sign language which mediates his almost complete integration into that island's culture. Population numbers have less weight in sign language emergence, it seems, than do several other factors: (*a*) man's species-specific capacity for language, often remarked in recent linguistics, but to be distinguished from the species-specific capacity for the speech code, to use which requires full auditory functioning; (b) the species-specific social need for language even when the physical channel for phonemic contrasts is blanked out; (c) the enormous potential for information processing in the visual, motoric, and cerebral systems of *Homo sapiens.*

Evolution, of language and of the one species that encodes it in speech, quite properly concerns the norm, which includes all the higher neural capacities of the animal kingdom, including hearing. In such a context, deafness is treated as pathology and excluded from consideration, and the sign languages that deaf groups use are thought to be irrelevant. But this may be oversight. Recent anthropological activity has emphasized social and ecological rather than the simpler physical aspects of evolution. Tool use [Hewes, 1973*a*, 1973*b*], group hunting activities [Peters, in press; Kortlandt, 1965], and social structuring in changing environmental conditions [Hewes, in press] bear interestingly on early language or protolanguages. The whole process of evolutionary change in social animals must have included constant feedback and amplification, amounting to a regenerative transfer between ethology or culture and the communicative systems. It seems clear that increased efficiency in interactive behavior would heighten adaptive and survival success and that changes in the latter would be reflected in the interactive systems. Ethology and primatology both support the view that, except for the speech code, most features of human interactive behavior have morphologically similar but less elaborated counterparts in other primates.

Despite the kind and amount of anthropological evidence Hewes assembles, the theory that a system of gestural signs played a major role in the evolution of speech and language does not command general belief. Yet many observers would describe a sign language such as the deaf use as being more primitive than spoken language. There seem to be three senses attached to the term *primitive* in such use.

First, gestures that signal basic emotional states derive, as Charles Darwin clearly noted, from physiological systems common to many animals. Hence kinesic, nonverbal, tone-of-voice, and all the other semiotic systems more directly affective than propositional in the human species are taken to be more primitive because derived from animal expressive systems [or zoosemiotic: Sebeok, 1963, 1970] and not from human speech code contrasts.

Second, sign languages, even contemporary, elaborated systems with duality of patterning, such as ASL, are taken to be primitive on specious structural grounds. There can be no denying that sign functions for the deaf as other languages function for their hearer-speakers, but often those who take sign language to be primitive are linguistically naive and ethnocentric to an extreme. Many writers on sign language follow exactly the processes described by Bloomfield [1944] and by Hill [1952]. They point to lack of verb inflection for tense in ASL, to lack of definite and indefinite articles, of a copula, or of regular inflection of sign nouns for number. They note the freedom of order in particular sentence types or the relative prevalence of onomatopoeia, which Wescott [1971] more properly terms iconism, in the ASL lexicon. But all those who attribute primitivism to sign languages seem to be unaware that any of these features or these lacks of particular features are common enough if one surveys the languages spoken by mankind instead of taking one's own language as equivalent to grammar, truth, and logic.

A third sense seems to derive from the use of *primitive* to characterize not language but thought. A young child's ability to perform mental operations may be called primitive if contrasted with his later achievement; hence the language the child uses to talk about these Piagetian operations may be more primitive than his language later on. This use of "primitive" is a valid generalization from individual performance and from the acquisition of competence; but when a variety of ASL is used by young pupils but not by their teachers and is prohibited by the school, their sign language is often called primitive by the educators and their textbooks and is equated with the cognitive and linguistic competence of its least competent users.

As a contrast, consider a fourth sense of the term and concept *primitive*. The supralaryngeal tract of primates, Neanderthal man, and human infants is primitive because from it develops the tract of adult *Homo sapiens* with its full capability for phonemic contrasts [Lieberman, 1973; Lieberman, Crelin, and Klatt, 1972]. Both phylogenesis and ontogenesis warrant this use of primitive as a description. Yet one cannot say that the sound patterns of Middle English (or of Old English or Indo-European) are more primitive than the sound patterns of English in the twentieth century (though it may be suspected that there has been some progress in the combination of ideas and in their *literary* expression by optional transformations of syntactic strings from King Alfred to Winston Churchill). In any strict sense of primitive (x is primitive if it is true that $x \rightarrow y$, but not true that $y \rightarrow x$), ASL cannot be more primitive than English. (Interestingly, Bloomfield thought that English was more primitive than the sign languages of the deaf: that is, the latter derived from the former.) ASL in fact derives from French Sign Language after 1817, precisely as American English derives from British English from about 1620.

Despite the foregoing caveats and refutations, there is a valid sense in which sign language may be primitive. If, as Hewes theorizes [1973a, 1973b], a hominid species, possibly *Australopithecus,* made and used a protolanguage of gesture signs, the species could have exploited many of the potentials of signal contrasts short of the phonemic. Not only would such a primitive gesture-encoded language add advantages in all aspects of existence, but it would also, Hewes reasons, have made cross-modal and cerebral connections—brain capacity increments—that would be needed for speech encoding and decoding apparatus.

Five Seconds Plus of Signing: Toward a Sign Code?

Speculation about causes and a possible course of sign language development, however interesting, do not furnish direct comparison of signed and spoken contrasts. The earlier rough analogy of *dez* (designator—the active hand), *sig* (signation—the action it does), and *tab* (tabula—the place where the sign is made) cheremes to consonant and vowel (and now tone) phonemes needs testing against the newest information about the speech code. A detailed, and as far as possible quantitative, analysis of a short but entirely typical stretch of sign language activity makes a first step in the large task of comparison.

The utterance chosen for analysis opens an informant's relation to a friend (both native signers) of his vacation plans. Intuitively I judge it both typical and somewhat closer to "pure" ASL than to Signed English on "the deaf diglossic continuum" [Woodward, 1973a, 1973b, 1973c]. This utterance is just 5.5 sec long. It contains 14 signs and 2 finger-spelled words glossed as follows:

"tomorrow morning I group friend several-will-go to *ocean city* for interview and find place sleep."

Englished it might read:

Tomorrow morning I am going to Ocean City with some friends to look for summer jobs and a place to stay.

Glossing and translation are among the least satisfactory ways to deal with sign, but are often necessary first steps. Examination of the visible phenomena which may parallel the acoustic representation of the speech code is made possible and convenient by a helical-scan videotape recorder (VTR).

Visible as narrow black bands moving from top down across the picture, when the VTR is set to "pause" and the tape advanced by hand, the raster lines are recorded (in effect invisibly) at the rate of 60 per second. Viewed thus, the utterance 5.5 sec long is crossed by 330 horizontal markers 16⅔ msec apart in actual time. It might seem that these lines would allow a reasonably precise timing of the segments of sign activity. However, what does appear turns out to be somewhat analogous to what is found when recorded speech is analyzed.

First, no record of movement appears in an instant of time (1/30 sec = 2 lines = 1 "frame"). If the signer happens to be relatively inactive during that whole instant, the picture is well defined. If any part of the signer happens to be in rapid motion, that part of the picture is blurred. Although many books that purport to describe sign language give single or sequenced drawings or photographs, sign activity does not consist of static positions followed by clearly defined motion (nor vice versa). Like speech, sign activity is a flow. The greatest difference seems to be that most of what the muscles move in speech remains invisible, and all of what the muscles move in signing shows plainly.

Stop motion photography, then, no matter how sophisticated, cannot reveal the elements of sign language contrasts. When the tape is slowly moved past the heads moving at normal speed, a slow motion picture results; but it is no easier than at normal speed to identify particular parts of the recorded action with particular elements of the signs. Native signers, in fact, read and transcribe taped performances more readily at normal speed (though with many stops and rewinds when making written transcripts) than slowed—exactly as native speakers find normal audio recordings easier to understand than recordings played back at slower than normal speed.

What the slowed videotape does reveal surprises both the native signer and the hearing investigator. This unexpected revelation has two aspects: sign elements, particularly dez cheremes, are not at all clearly separated; and the time taken in transition from one dez chereme to another may be much longer than the visible duration of either chereme. Native signers and trained hearing investigators alike, viewing the visible representation, completely disregard the transitions and categorically respond to the dez cheremes as if they were presented in citation form.

Table 1 shows glosses for the signs in the first 5.5 sec of the recorded utterance plotted against time as marked by raster lines (irregularly) and on the right by 1-sec intervals. An immediate disclaimer must be made. The line number used to represent a transition point between the dez of the sign above and below the number is approximate and has been

Table 1. Five and One-half Seconds of a Sign Narrative; Signs and Manual Letters Plotted against 16 msec Intervals

0		
	tomorrow	Begin
17		
	morning	
40		
	I	
58		
	group	1 sec
90		
	friend	
116		(Between lines 116 and 140 the *plural* element, the *future*
	(together)	element, and the *central verbal* element of a sign intuitively
121		perceived as one by native signers appear successively) 2 sec
	(will)	
140		
	go	
145		
	to	
160		
	o	(The finger spelling rate here, approximately 12 charac-
167		ters/second, seems about normal for spelled sequences
	c	this length)
174		
	e	
176		
	a	3 sec
184		
	n	
187		
	c	
190		
	i	
196		
	t	
197		
	y	
210		
	for	
230		
	interview	4 sec
249		(The taped signer can be clearly lipread saying "and,"
	and (?)	but viewing at all speeds is inconclusive about hand here)
273		
	find	
291		
	place	5 sec
318		(Something happens between "place" and "sleep": it
	to (?)	may be finger spelled *to* or signed 'to' or just a messy
320		transition)
	sleep	
330		5.5 sec

determined only within ±7. This is not because the lines are hard to count but because it is no easier to see exactly where, for example, the A-dez of *tomorrow* changes to the B-dez of *morning* than it is to hear exactly when the formants of [p] change to the formants of [ɪ] when *pit* is spoken in normal conversation.

Besides this uncertainty about what is on the tape, and that indicated by the notes in parentheses, the most surprising revelation is that no more time is used to encode (and by native signers to decode) the finger-spelled word *ocean* than to encode the sign glossed *group*. Obviously much more study will be needed to determine exactly the range and mode of the duration of signed and finger-spelled lexical units; but despite vast theoretical difference between signs as units of ASL and finger-spelled words as manually encoded representations of orthographically represented units of English, there seems to be little doubt that to native signers whose competence includes sign varieties with English vocabulary, sign words and finger-spelled words look and feel alike and fit time in similar ways.

The 25 entries in the second column of Table 1 record 24 successive dez appearances (the single sign glossed *together-will-go* begins with open C-dez and ends with closed G-dez;[1] future tense morpheme *will* is sufficiently signaled by the motion of the forearm). The average rate of dez chereme appearance is 4.36 per sec. But the average is misleading: the dez hands either do not show clearly as they do in citation forms, or last only about 0.02 sec (for example, 174–176), or appear simultaneously or with partial overlapping. The table does not show simultaneous appearance; but on the tape between lines 190 and 210, *i* remains visible as *t* is formed and changes to *y* (the little finger forming *i* remains to form one branch of *y*). Thus while the average rate of 4.36 dez cheremes per sec is low compared with phoneme discrimination rates, the dez change rate in *city* approches 12 per sec. More important than direct comparison of rates, the visual representation of sign activity that a native user converts into two distinct dez cheremes may be simultaneously present.

We have known for a long time that dez, sig, and tab aspects of a sign are often simultaneously or overlappingly signaled; but difference between an articulator, a location, and an action make conversion of visual signal to cheremes less remarkable than the parallel transmission and sequenced conversion of vowel and consonant material. Now, however, it appears that a signer receiving sign may see visual material for as short a time as 30–40 msec, convert some of it into one dez, some into another, and sequence the two in the cherological representation.

[1] See Stokoe, Casterline, and Croneberg [1968] for dez, sig, and tab types.

Slow viewing of the tape shows also that dez formation leads. Not only is there perceptible time during which a hand assumes dez configuration, holds it, and relaxes or changes to another, but there is also visible evidence that the dez appears more or less recognizably several (16 msec) lines before it reaches tab region or begins to perform sig action. On the other hand, tab lags. The nondominant hand, when it serves as tab marker, assumes its configuration or reaches its place or both, sometimes appreciably after dez is in mid-sig, sometimes so late as not to appear at all; and therefore, much information in citation-form performance may be missing from contextual signing. (The problem of 318 *to* (?) 320 in Table 1 may be missing tab.)

It is impossible to calculate the overall rate of chereme contrasts encoded in the Table 1 utterance or any sign utterance because the present state of the art is one of uncertainty about how to assign chereme and morpheme boundaries. The sign between lines 116 and 145 has clearly distinguishable plural (*concord*), modal (*will*), and action (*go*) semantic content. It can be seen to begin with upward spread fingers and upright forearm and end with the closed hand across in front of the signer. One question is, how many sigs? The hand swings in an arc from the elbow. The forward component of the motion looks like, and by native signers is perceived as, the future element in *will, tomorrow, next week,* and so on. Closing action of the hand distinguishes one sign language verb *go-to-a-place* from a more general *going, moving.* And the oblique movement and pointing (around line 145) establishes the destination. One to three signs for this one sign may be counted [discussed in full in Stokoe, 1972, pp. 21–45]. Further questions; what and how many tabs? The dez hands between lines 116 and 145 do not touch or approach any marked body part and so [Stokoe, 1960, 1966] may be taken as zero tab. But the upright forearm contrasts with the more relaxed oblique forearm (high-O/mid-O). And as Friedman [1973] has shown, a great many semantic distinctions are signaled by subtle differences in spatial designation. This sign may have from one to three or four tab cheremes; but I do not for the moment accept Friedman's elevation of orientation to cheremic status, with an immediate 25 percent increase in chereme classes [Stokoe, 1974, in press *a,* in press *b*] because I believe orientation can be treated as a vector of dez and sig, which are both of course analytical constructs until proven real.

With these caveats, some 60 cheremic contrasts may be very conservatively counted (3 each for 11 signs, 2 each for *together, will,* questioned *and, to,* and the 9 manual alphabet signs whose tab does not change from 160 to 210). This yields an average rate of 10.9 cheremes encoded and to be discriminated per sec—still not as high as the phoneme discrimination rate may be in speech. But this signer was hesitant, and as the performance was impromptu, probably it was slower than his normal rate.

Some of the difference Bellugi and Fischer [1972] have accounted for as the heavier semantic and syntactic loading of signs than of words. They show faster word/second than sign/second rates compatible with equal information carrying rates. This is confirmed by Woodward's study of ASL variation [Woodward, 1973a, 1973b, 1973c]. He shows that a negative incorporation rule and a verb directionality rule provide semantic and syntactic contrasts without increase in number of obvious cheremes (for example *have* [ ]B_x^T versus [ ]$B_\eta^\perp$ *don't have;* *I tell you* $G_T{}^\wedge \iota$ versus *you tell me* $G\iota{}^\wedge_T$). Making precise rate comparisons is also complicated by simultaneous signs, as in the "since we were babies" example cited previously.

Obviously a great deal of analysis remains to be done and earlier findings rechecked before the case for sign language as a genuinely linguistic sign-stimulus system is complete. Besides problems already noted there are some important neurophysiological matters to be probed. But the work of Hubel [1972] indicates that the quantity and intricacy of neural interconnections, visual field discrimination, and behavioral correlates found in cats' eyes make it most likely that primate vision and cerebral controls [of, for example, Sarah in Premack, 1971] have the capacity for language with at least as much potential for development as the first hominid speech.

Examination of what actually occurs in five seconds of signing, then looking back at what has been thought about sign language, reveals the psychopathology of everyday language study. The layman's notion that language is a simple matter of words and meanings gave way long ago to early grammar; words, grammarians said, are really strings of letters, *grammata,* for sounds. But as the simple matter proved to be dual—patterns of sounds and patterns of sound strings—gesture beckoned to an escape. If language couldn't stay simple, gestures must. Body language provides the magic. The message is unclear, is it, in all the gramarye of words? Just slip on the magic ring and look at what the foot or the little finger or the left end of the right eyebrow is doing, and all will be plain!

Careful observation of what in sober fact happens when deaf people use gesture as language destroys the sanctuary gesture was supposed to afford from the uncertainties of speech. The first readjustment to this puts many serious students of sign language into positions held by linguists of the past. Signs they see as patterns of visual aspects of behavior [*cheremes:* Stokoe, 1960, 1966, 1970; *formational parameters:* Bellugi, 1972]. Like sounds, these aspects pattern contrastively; and as in language generally, patterns constructed from these aspects (signs, morphemes, lexical units) serve as links with meaning.

However, while sign language was becoming respectable, with duality of patterning, linguistics was discovering that language was still less simple than it seemed. Instead of existing as sequential bundles of sound (for example, [h] + [ɛ] + [n] = [hɛn]), the acoustic output of a speaker in fact is a blend of energy spread over portions of the sound spectrum in mightily confused ways. New knowledge about the speech code, about formants and transitions, and about how these get sorted somehow categorically into vowel and consonant representations makes the actual operations of language more, not less, mysterious.

The layman has no need to escape from the mysterious reality physics describes—except when bombs drop. He can inhabit the seeming world of solid substance and leave to the physicist the real world of vast internuclear spaces traversed by electrical changes in obedience to non-Newtonian laws. The question, which is real, which fantastic, here remains academic.

But language is nearer at hand than nuclear research. Layman and linguist alike grow uncomfortable when deep probing of the speech code reveals our ignorance of language nature faster than it adds to our knowledge. And both may seek to escape to sign language, where, presumably, a hand is a hand and a cheek is a cheek, when they find that in speech the same acoustic information encodes [d] in one case, but [n] in another. Yet a look of five seconds of sign language activity shows very similar uncertainty.

The uncertainty principle, which first came to light in atomic physics and is now found in the relation of acoustical to grammatical information, also obtains in sign language. Simple judgments about a sign's parameters (this is correct/this is an error) will not stand sociolinguistic scrutiny— one signer's *pumpkin* is another signer's *watermelon*—nor close visual examination. What converts the continuous flow of visual activity into sign language categories cannot be found in precisely defined positions, places, movements, and times any more than in the competence of the native signer. We do not know whether acoustic cues determine the conversion of speech into phonological representation or knowledge or phonology determines how the sound will be converted. We are likewise ignorant about the sign code, but reasonably certain that the study of language in general will be better served by careful inquiry instead of comforting assumptions about sign language.

References

Abbott, D. F. 1973. Linguistic encodedness. Working paper, Linguistics Research Laboratory, Gallaudet College, Washington, D.C.

Bellugi, U. 1972. Studies in sign language. In *Psycholinguistics and Total Communication,* Terrence J. O'Rourke (ed.). Washington: National Association for the Deaf, 68–84.

Bellugi, U., and S. Fischer. 1972. A comparison of sign language and spoken language. *Cognition,* 1: 173–200.

Bellugi, U. and Klima, E. Aspects of sign language and its structure. This volume.

Bellugi, U., and P. Siple. 1974. Remembering with and without words. In *Current Problems in Psycholinguistics,* F. Bresson (ed.). Paris: Centre National de la Recherche Scientifique.

Bloomfield, L. 1944. Secondary and tertiary responses to language. *Language,* 20: 45–55.

Braine, M. D. S. 1963. The ontogeny of English phrase structure: the first phase. *Language,* 39: 1–13.

Dunn, C. W., and E. T. Byrnes. 1973. *Middle English Literature.* New York: Harcourt, Brace.

Friedman, L. A. 1973. On the semantics of space, time and person reference in American Sign Language. M.A. thesis, University of California, Berkeley.

Gardner, R. A., and B. T. Gardner. 1971. Two-way communication with an infant chimpanzee. In *Behavior of Nonhuman Primates,* Schrier and Stolnitz (eds.). New York: Academic Press, chapter 4.

Hewes, G. A. 1973a. An explicit formulation of the relationship between tool-using, tool-making, and the emergence of language. *Visible Language,* 7: 101–127.

Hewes, G. W. 1973b. Primate communication and the gestural origin of language. *Current Anthropology,* 14: 5–24.

Hewes, G. W. In press. Language in early hominids. In *Language Origins: A Symposium,* R. W. Westcott, G. W. Hewes, and W. C. Stokoe, Jr. (eds.). Silver Spring, Md: Linstok.

Hill, A. A. 1952. A note on primitive languages. *Int. J. Amer. Linguist.,* 18: 172–177.

Hubel, D. H. 1972. Specificity of responses of cells in the visual cortex. In *Recent Contributions to Neurophysiology,* EEG Supplement no. 31. Amsterdam: Elsevier, 171–177.

Huttenlocher, J. Encoding information in sign language. This volume.

Jakobson, R. 1971. Motor signs for "yes" and "no." *Language in Society,* 1: 91–96.

Jordan, I. K. 1973. The referential communication of facial characteristics by deaf and normal hearing adolescents. Unpublished Ph.D. thesis, University of Tennessee.

Kortlandt, A. 1965. Comment on the essential morphological basis for human culture. *Current Anthropology,* 6: 320–325.

Kuschel, R. 1973. The silent inventor: the creation of a sign language by the only deaf-mute on a Polynesian island. *Sign Language Studies,* 3: 1–28.

Liberman, A. M., F. S. Cooper, D. Shankweiler, and M. Studdert-Kennedy. 1967. Perception of the speech code. *Psychological Review,* 74: 431–461.

Lieberman, P. 1973. On the evolution of human language: a unified view. *Cognition,* 2: 59–94.

Lieberman, P., E. S. Crelin, and D. H. Klatt. 1972. Phonetic ability and related anatomy of the newborn, adult human, neanderthal man and the chimpanzee. *American Anthropology,* 74: 287–307.

Mattingly, I. G., and A. M. Liberman. 1969. The speech code and the physiology of language. In *Information Processing in the Nervous System,* K. N. Leibovic (ed.). New York: Springer.

Peters, C. R. In press. On the possible contribution of ambiguity of expression to the development of protolinguistic performance. In *Language Origins: A Symposium,* R. H. Wescott, G. W. Hewes, and W. C. Stokoe, Jr. (eds.). Silver Spring, Md.: Linstok.

Premack, D. 1971. Language in chimpanzee. *Science,* 172: 808–822.

Sarles, H. B. in press. A human ethological approach to communication. *World Anthropology,* Proceedings of the Ninth International Congress of Anthropological and Ethological Sciences, Chicago, 1973.

Schlesinger, H. S., and Meadow, K. P. 1972. *Sound and Sign: Childhood Deafness and Mental Health.* Berkeley, Calif.: University of California Press.

Sebeok, T. A. 1963. Zoosemiotics. *Language,* 39: 448–466.

Sebeok, T. A. 1970. Semiotics and ethology. In *Approaches to Animal Communication,* T. Sebeok and A. Ramsay (eds.). New York.

Siple, P. A. 1973. Constraints for a sign language from visual perception data. Working paper, The Salk Institute, La Jolla, Calif.

Stokoe, W. C., Jr. 1960. Sign language structure. *Studies in Linguistics,* Occasional Paper 8. Buffalo: University of Buffalo Press.

Stokoe, W. C., Jr. 1966. The linguistic description of sign language. Georgetown University, Monograph Series in Languages and Linguistics, 19: 243–250.

Stokoe, W. C., Jr. 1970. *The Study of Sign Language.* Washington, CAL/ERIC: ED 037 719.

Stokoe, W. C., Jr. 1972. *Semiotics and Human Sign Languages.* Approaches to Semiotics, 21, T. Sebeok (ed.). New York: Humanities Press.

Stokoe, W. C., Jr. 1974. Classification and description of sign languages. In *Current Trends in Linguistics,* Vol. 12, T. Sebeok (ed.). The Hague: Mouton.

Stokoe, W. C., Jr. In press a. Sign syntax and human language capacity. *Florida Foreign Language Reporter.*

Stokoe, W. C., Jr. In press b. Face-to-face interaction: Signs to language. In *World Anthropology,* S. Tax (ed.). The Hague, Mouton (IX, ICAES, Chicago).

Stokoe, W. C., Jr., D. C. Casterline, and C. G. Croneberg. 1965. *A Dictionary of American Sign Language on Linguistic Principles.* Washington: Gallaudet College Press.

Wescott, R. W. 1971. Linguistic iconism. *Language,* 47: 416–428.

Wilden, A. 1972. Analog and digital communication. *Semiotica,* 6: 50–82.

Woodward, J. C. 1973a. Implicational lects on the deaf diglossic continuum. Unpublished Ph.D. dissertation, Georgetown University.

Woodward, J. C. 1973b. Some characteristics of pidgin sign English. *Sign Language Studies* 3: 39–46.

Woodward, J. C. 1973c. Inter-rule implication in American Sign Language. *Sign Language Studies*, 3: 47–56.

Yngve, V. in press. Human linguistics and face-to-face interaction. In *World Anthropology*, Proceedings of the Ninth International Congress of Anthropological and Ethnological Sciences, Chicago, 1973.

Encoding Information in Sign Language

JANELLEN HUTTENLOCHER

Much of the discussion of natural language during this conference has concerned the nature of the speech code itself. In this context, the contrast between natural language and American Sign Language (ASL) has focused on how the form of a code might be affected by the fact that it involves the visual rather than the auditory modality. Indeed, not only do speech and ASL involve different modalities, but, in addition, speech involves a highly specialized aspect of the auditory system which is specifically devoted to the perception of speech sounds and which is closely coordinated with a specialized motor system for producing those same sounds. The fact that certain areas of the human brain are apparently especially equipped for the perception and production of speech suggests that codes which rely on other sensorimotor systems, like ASL, might not be of comparable structure or internal complexity. As we have seen from the papers presented by Stokoe and by Bellugi, such a comparison is not possible at present because the structure of ASL is not clearly understood. Indeed, attempts to analyze the syntax of ASL suggest that the problem may be a particularly elusive one.

I want to shift the focus from contrasting ASL and natural language as codes per se, and to consider instead whether these alternative types of code differ in what information they preserve about events. Admittedly, it is premature to try to deal with such an issue. Although it is obvious that linguistic codes derive their function from the fact that they allow listeners to obtain new information about events, and speakers to encode information about their experiences, the manner in which this is accomplished is only dimly understood at present. For our purposes here, we can stick closely to observables, departing only slightly from the position of the logician who treats the meanings of sentences by specifying the states of affairs which render them true. Let us make just a few obvious assumptions concerning the internal structure which underlies people's knowledge of what sentences are appropriate to what states of affairs.

Clearly, two different types of knowledge must be mentally represented in order to account for people's ability to use language systematically in relation to events. First, the *code* itself must be mentally represented. I will refer to this knowledge as the *code schema*. Second, the *events* which people encounter must be mentally represented. I will refer to this knowledge as the *event schema,* used here as a shorthand expression to designate the information about events which is stored in people's memories. The nature of these event schemas is determined by the perceptual-cognitive structures which process and store incoming events. Finally, in order to account for people's ability to use language in relation to events, the code schema must be mapped onto aspects of the event schema.

Those aspects of events which are dealt with by a code constitute its *reference field*. To maintain parallelism I will refer to the mental representation of the reference field as the *reference-field schema*. To anticipate the following discussion, the reason for making a distinction between reference-field schemas and event schemas is that particular codes may not be mapped onto all aspects of people's experiences. The use of the term reference-field schema is deliberately ambiguous here. I have not specified whether the reference-field schema consists of just concepts encoded by particular words and conceptual relations encoded by the syntax, or instead consists of all those meanings which potentially could be communicated given knowledge of the code. The issue is complicated, and I cannot discuss it here. In the terminology of Goodman [1968] a code (called a *symbol scheme* by Goodman) when taken together with its correlated field of reference constitutes a *symbol system*.

A code schema by itself preserves no information about events. Rather, a code schema is mapped onto a reference-field schema that preserves information about events. Thus one can differentiate two types of mental operations involving language. First, there are operations concerned with the *perception* and *production* of the code itself, and second, there are operations concerned with the *decoding* and *encoding* of messages. The former have to do with, for example, the identification of particular sound patterns as instances of particular word schemas, and the latter have to do with the mapping of particular words and word sequences onto particular states of affairs. It is frequently claimed that thinking involves linguistic processes. Since the code schema alone preserves no information about events, such a claim can make sense only if it postulates that thinking involves activation of the reference-field schema as well as activation of the code schema.

The issue to be considered here is whether ASL and natural language codes have different reference fields. Even if the mental representation of events is a direct result of people's perceptual-cognitive structure, and is unaffected by what code they use, the reference field for ASL might still differ from that for natural language. That is, because of the differing natures of these two codes, they might be mapped onto different aspects of events. There remains the alternative possibility, argued most forcibly by Whorf [1956], that the way people conceptualize events is significantly affected by the code which they habitually use in relation to those events. While no strong evidence in favor of this hypothesis has emerged by contrasting different natural languages, it is possible that one would observe significant differences in event schemas when one of the codes is not a speech code at all. The possibility of answering such questions about the relation of language and thought is one reason why investigation of the acquisition of ASL as a native language seems especially worthwhile.

Several problems stand in the way of examining these questions. First, the nature of the reference-field schema for natural language has not yet been clearly delineated. For certain symbol systems, one can easily specify what information is preserved by a particular code. For example, writing systems preserve information which permit people to recover the words of the spoken language. This is true for ideographic or pictographic schemes which preserve words as units, as well as for syllabaries or alphabetic schemes which preserve such component sound patterns as syllables or phonemes. Mathematics also involves a clearly definable reference-field schema; the symbols of mathematics are mapped onto specifiable aspects of people's notions of quantity, arithmetical operations, and so on. Contrary to such symbolic systems, natural languages are mapped onto an amorphous reference-field schema involving a vast variety of experiences. Many natural language categories involve poorly specified or "fuzzy" notions, and furthermore, systematic attempts to analyze concepts and conceptual organization are only beginning.

Second, it is not clear at present what characteristics a code must possess in order to be able to preserve particular types of information. There seems to be considerable flexibility in the form which natural languages can assume, as Klima notes [this volume]. He has described a language which involves very few lexical items, but nevertheless serves all the communicative needs of a people. However, there are surely certain minimal characteristics which a code must possess in order to preserve particular types or quantities of information about events.

On the face of it, different symbol schemes seem to vary in their suitability for preserving different sorts of information. Thus maps and pictures preserve information about the shapes of objects and about the spatial relations among their parts which is difficult or perhaps impossible to preserve in natural language. Similarly, one may be able to indicate how to assemble a puzzle or how to carry out a complex act via demonstration, pantomime, or other means in cases which would be difficult or impossible to describe in natural language. Since ASL is visual-spatial in nature and involves bodily movement, it seems possible that it might function in certain ways as do maps or pantomime.

In what follows I will contrast the reference fields of ASL and natural language only with respect to spatial information. There are two reasons for focusing on this particular issue. First, there is some evidence about the nature of event schemas for spatial information. Second, there seem to be fundamental differences in the manner in which spatial information is preserved in ASL and in natural language.

In the discussion below I will suggest that ASL is intermediate between natural language and such devices as maps and diagrams in that it is only partially categorical in nature. Natural language is categorical in that particular sound patterns either are or are not tokens of particular words, and these words designate conceptual categories to which particular objects, events, and so on either do or do not belong. While many individual signs in ASL are categorical, as in natural language, this does not seem always to be the case. The departure from natural languages seems clear in the encoding of spatial information where in some cases ASL is analog rather than categorical in that continuous variation within the code is mapped onto continuous aspects of people's spatial experiences.

How People Deal with Spatial Information
The first issue is to delineate the event schemas for spatial aspects of the world of objects and events. Although the experiments to be described were done with hearing subjects, that poses no problem, since the picture of event schemas for spatial information which has emerged from this research suggests that these are more directly coded by ASL than by natural language. Introspectively, when one thinks about the appearance of objects, or about rearranging them in space, one seems to be dealing with imaginary objects of particular shapes, or sizes or to be carrying out imaginary sensorimotor processes with objects. However, many psychologists have argued that as incoming stimulation passes from momentary availability to more permanent storage it becomes "encoded," that is, represented in a manner which differs from its initial icoinc form. This encoding process is sometimes described as if it were linguistic in nature [for example, Neisser, 1967].

As was pointed out above, the code itself preserves no information about events except in conjunction with a reference-field schema that represents aspects of those events. Thus such a claim could reasonably mean only that the event schema for spatial aspects of experience is identical with the reference-field schema for natural language; that is, that the ways spatial information is encoded in natural language directly reflect how that information is mentally represented, and that we store no more spatial information than what can be encoded in natural language. Such a conclusion, however, does not seem consistent with recent findings on spatial representation.

Consider first some demonstrations by Roger Shepard and his colleagues [Shepard and Metzler, 1971; Shepard and Feng, 1972; Metzler and Shepard, 1974]. In one series of studies, subjects had to determine whether pairs of geometric figures were identical to one another. The figures were two-dimensional projections of three dimensional forms involving a main stem with two arms jutting out from the ends. Pairs of figures were presented which differed in their axes of orientation. Sometimes they were identical, but sometimes the arms were mounted to the stems differently. The time required for subjects to judge whether the two figures were identical was found to be linearly related to the axis of separation between the stems of the two figures. The authors concluded that people solve this problem by imagining rotating one of the figures until the stems of the two figures are parallel, an imaginary process which takes time, just as if one were actually turning one of the figures. Another study dealt with mental paper folding involving drawings of two-dimensional folded-out cubes. Subjects had to indicate whether two particular sides would meet if the paper were folded into a cube. The time required to solve such problems varied with the number of necessary folds and surfaces folded, just as if the actual work of folding the cubes were being carried out in imagination to solve the problems.

The mental operations used to infer how arrays of objects appear when viewed from different vantage points are in some ways analogous to those involved in the rotation problems of Shepard and his colleagues. We had one group of subjects infer how a spatial array would appear if it were rotated about its own axis, and another group infer how an array would appear if they were themselves moved to some new viewing position [Huttenlocher and Presson, 1973; Huttenlocher and Presson, in preparation]. These two problems are parallel in that in each case the viewer sees an array from one particular vantage point and must infer its appearance from some other vantage point. While the problems differed markedly in difficulty and in error patterns, in both cases people's strategies involved imaginary sensorimotor acts of rotating the array. When asked to imagine the array having moved, people report "seeing" a continuous change in the appearance of the array as they imagine rotating it. When asked to imagine themselves having moved, people report a more complex strategy of rotating the array together with the imaginary viewer until the position of that imaginary viewer is superimposed on their own present position. Subjects' error patterns and reaction times are consistent with their introspections.

There is also evidence that people may use spatial representations of information in certain reasoning problems, in particular, in ordering syllogisms: for example, "Tom is better than Harry. Joe is worse than Harry. Who is the best?" [Huttenlocher, 1968; Huttenlocher and Higgins, 1971]. When subjects are given a series of such problems, they claim to construct imaginary spatial arrangenents of the items. From the first premise, they arrange the first two items. From the second premise, they set the third item (Joe) into the array among the other two. They claim to answer questions about the order of the items by consulting their mental representation of the array.

One kind of evidence for the claim that spatial representations are used in solving these problems is that there is a close correspondence between the difficulty of solving certain forms of the syllogism and the difficulty of arranging real objects spatially according to parallel sets of instructions. Another kind of evidence has been gathered by Potts [1972] and by Trabasso, Riley, and Wilson [in press] in analogous reasoning problems involving more premises. Even though the premises in such problems necessarily describe adjacent pairs of items, the ease of answering questions about the order of a pair of target items such as "Is Tom better than Joe?" increased with the number of items which intervened between those target items. In addition, it was easier to answer questions involving items from the ends of the series, just as when subjects are asked comparable questions about actual items in a real spatial array. These findings certainly suggest that people consult an imaginary spatial array of items in answering these questions.

In addition to these findings concerning the existence of spatial representations of information, there is also evidence that thinking about spatial information is in certain ways like actually looking at objects. The evidence is from a set of studies by Lee Brooks which indicate that thinking about spatial information interferes with processing incoming visual stimuli. In one of Brooks' [1968] experiments subjects were shown a block letter F with an arrow pointing at one of its corners. They had to report the sequence of inner and outer corners of the F one encounters as one moves around it clockwise. Subjects indicated whether each corner was an inner or outer corner either by announcing the sequence of turns aloud, or by marking them off on a check list. The problem was more difficult with the checklist. Evidence from a second experiment [Brooks, 1968] indicates that this finding is not because it is in general more difficult to read than to speak while thinking. In this second study, people memorized a sentence, and then had to indicate the parts of speech of the successive words; for example, "noun" or "nonnoun" or alternatively, "verb" or "nonverb." To carry out this task, the subject had to "think about" the words in a sentence rather than about a visual form. In this case it was more difficult to announce the answers aloud than to use a checklist. Thus Brooks's findings suggest that the mental representation of spatial information involves specifically visual processes.

The Symbolic Encoding of Spatial Information

All the studies described above indicate that people may generate images in representing spatial information and may carry out imaginary acts in transforming that information. The question of what status should be assigned to these imagelike representations of spatial information cannot be taken up here, but is treated more fully elsewhere [Huttenlocher, in press]. Let me just note that such mental representations certainly should not be regarded as "movies in the mind," since the ability to represent information in the manner shown in the studies above is surely the output of a highly complex system for processing information.

If one assumes that the mental representation of spatial information is "visual" in the sense shown in Brooks's studies, certain questions arise concerning the decoding of ASL for messages which involve spatial information. In particular, since the code itself is visual in nature, one might expect interference between processing the code and setting up a mental representation of the state of affairs being described. At least if the visual processing involved in decoding ASL is comparable to that involved in reading English, Brooks's studies suggest that such decoding difficulties might occur. Consider, for example, a signed description such as "from the doorway of the living room one can see a couch on the left with a chair to the right of the fireplace facing the couch." The decoder of such a message must continue to watch the signer while also attempting to set up a mental representation of the state of affairs being described.

Of course, for printed English, the words bear no obvious relation to the objects, acts, or properties which they represent, and since the spatial relations among the words on the page are simply left to right, they are in no way isomorphic with the spatial relations which they represent. If, instead, the nature of the visual code were in some way consistent with people's mental representations of such spatial information, the case might be quite different. Processing the code might even facilitate rather than interfere with setting up the mental representation of the events being described.

In attempting to familiarize myself with the way spatial information is encoded in ASL, I asked Ursula Bellugi and William Stokoe to sign for me certain descriptions of spatial relations among objects. I asked Bellugi to sign various simple descriptions such as "The bird is above the tree," and I asked Stokoe to sign a description of a room like the one just mentioned.

Bellugi was puzzled by my requests, saying that it was so obvious how to sign such descriptions that she could not imagine why I would ask. When I finally persuaded her to sign various descriptions of vertical relations between objects, she in each case made the two signs one above the other.

Stokoe signed the description of the room by distributing the signs for each of the items spatially to correspond to their described spatial location.

In the descriptions of spatial relations which I elicited, the setting up of the representation of the spatial information seemed to have already been done *for* the decoder because of the nature of the relation between the code and its reference field. Indeed, the relation between the ASL code and its reference field is such that these signed messages concerning spatial relations seemed like instances of those spatial arrangements rather than like descriptions involving processes of encoding or decoding. Not only is the spatial arrangement of items preserved in such ASL messages but, according to my informants, it is also possible to convey metric information concerning the distance among objects by varying the physical distances among the signs (as in a picture). In a way, my questions about how to sign the spatial relations among objects were as foolish as the question "How does one draw two objects, one on top of the other?"

Descriptions of spatial relations in ASL are not always of the form of this example. There are individual signs for "on," "under," and so on. One of the constraints on this type of signing comes from the fact that the location in which signing occurs is a critical feature for the identification of certain signs. Thus it may not be possible to locate the signs freely for one or more of the items which one might want to place in particular spatial relations to one another. Similarly, the ability to sign simultaneously the positions of two items is constrained because one or more of the constituent signs may require use of both hands.

In any case, it is not possible to ask questions about how to encode *any* state of affairs in natural language which are foolish in the same sense as were my questions about how to encode spatial relations in ASL. The relation between the natural language code and its reference field is, as is frequently said, arbitrary and conventional. That is, descriptions in natural language do not seem like instances of what they encode, nor do they automatically call to mind those states of affairs which they encode. One reason for this is that while natural language involves a sequence of speech sounds, its reference field rarely involves sounds at all, except for a few isolated lexical items such as "noise," "bark," "talk," and so on. In contrast, sign language is spatial in nature and involves bodily movement. Thus many aspects of the reference field can be encoded with mimicry and pantomime.

The encoding and decoding of information about spatial relations from natural language descriptions is far from a trivial problem. Indeed, many aspects of one's visual-spatial experiences are so difficult to preserve in natural language that they are typically omitted from descriptions. When a person describes a spatial layout involving several items, he may choose an item as the grammatical subject of his initial sentence and relate it to one or more of the other items using spatial relational terms like "above," "below," or "between." Several sentences may be used if the array is complex, each of which involves a subject term and a relational term which encodes its position relative to one or more other items as grammatical object. Ratio and metric information about distance among items is not ordinarily preserved in such descriptions of the spatial relations among objects, although such information can be added, as in "A is twice as far from B as it is from C."

There are several points to be considered in contrasting ASL and natural language descriptions of spatial relations among objects. First, the format of the ASL code differs from that of natural language in that the former need not involve sentences which include grammatical subjects about which predictions are made. When the signs for a pair of items in a vertical array are made simultaneously, there is no more differentiation between the grammatical subject and what is predicted of it than there would be in a pictorial display. Furthermore, relational terms need not be used in ASL. ASL can encode spatial relations in a manner which seems to be as continuous as the spatial relations which people can perceive and remember. In natural language certain spatial relations are honored by the existence of particular lexical items such as "above." In ASL, there is not a finite set of particular relational terms. Rather, in the types of descriptions we are considering all of the infinite number of alternative possible relations are equally honored. When one does not use lexical items to encode particular categories of spatial relations, one does not need syntactic devices like those required in natural language to preserve information as to how the component items enter into such relations. That is, in natural language word order or inflectional endings are used to indicate which item is, for example, "above" the other.

Of course, relational terms are used more regularly in ASL for encoding information in other domains of experience. However, it is not clear the extent to which ASL has a syntax which encodes the conceptual relations among items so as to preserve information about directionality; for example, "The boy hits the girl" versus "The girl hits the boy." In a communication study with signers in Israel, Schlesinger [1970] gave to an encoder and a decoder an equivalent set of pictures showing a particular type of relation such as "giving." There was an exchange among the roles of the various participants in the relation being portrayed, in the different pictures within a set. The decoder had to pick the appropriate picture out of the set on the basis of a signed message. The encoders used variable order of signs, and apparently they did not provide other cues about the directionality of the relation, since the decoders performed very poorly. This finding suggests that syntactic devices which encode the direction of a relation are not well established features of that type of sign language which is used in Israel. I am not aware of any comparable studies involving ASL.

Even for individual lexical items in ASL there may be continuous variation in how the sign is made which is correlated with continuous variation in the reference field. Thus the sign for "big" can be modulated, so that its size varies with the degree of bigness of an object being described. While in natural language there is the possibility of expressing variation in degree through paralinguistic devices, like saying "big" slowly and with emphasis, such devices can be sharply differentiated from linguistic devices themselves. In ASL, such devices do not seem to be as clearly separated as being paralinguistic, and quite possibly, they should be regarded as inherent parts of the ASL scheme.

Insofar as continuous variation is part of the ASL code, ASL would have a vocabulary which is, in principle, infinite. Consider the term "big." In natural language, the word either is or is not used depending on whether the object being described is noticeably above average for its kind. In ASL the sign for big may be made in an indefinite number of ways. In addition, as we saw various elements of meaning which may be encoded with single lexical items in natural language, notably those concerned with spatial relations, can also be encoded in ASL in an indefinite number of ways.

Given the incorporation of analog devices in ASL, there would seem to be the potential for ambiguity as to which aspects of the signer's behavior are symbolic and meant to preserve information about events, and which are nonsymbolic aspects of the signer's movements. Such ambiguity surely arises in pantomime and playacting. For example, consider a pantomime involving two different acts, one carried out when the pantomimer was sitting and the other when he was standing. It would be unclear whether the mimic was doing pantomime as he moved from the one position to the other. Similarly, in ASL, to sign that a particular item is above another, one must place the one at some particular distance from the other. This is true whether or not the signer wishes to preserve metric information about the distance between the objects. Thus, there must either be conventions concerning neutral uses of space in signing or ambiguities will arise as to whether or not metric information is being encoded.

In summary, the fact that ASL is spatial in nature and involves movement no doubt affected how it has evolved as a code. There are two different factors which may have led to the use of iconic representation and pantomime in sign language. First, such ways of encoding information are probably "natural" with a symbol scheme that shares so many elements of the reference field which it is used to encode. This is true not only for the encoding of spatial relations, but for the encoding of perceptible action sequences as well. Second, as we saw above, an arbitrary visual code might be difficult to decode, especially when visual-spatial information is to be conveyed. One would expect such a code to gravitate toward a form which could be decoded easily.

As we have seen, the reference field of ASL differs from that for natural language in several ways. The question arises as to whether the event schemas of signers may not also differ from those of the users of natural languages. That is, since information about relative spatial position apparently may be preserved in ASL without requiring notions such as "above" or "below," one wonders whether concepts such as these evolve as distinct categorical notions to the same extent in signers as in those who use the speech code. Hopefully, the answers to questions like these will emerge from research with the deaf such as that being carried out by Ursula Bellugi and by William Stokoe.

References

Brooks, L. 1968. Spatial and verbal components of the act of recall. *Canad. J. Psychol.*, 22: 349–368.

Goodman, N. 1968. *Languages of Art*. Indianapolis: Bobbs-Merrill.

Huttenlocher, J. Constructing spatial images: a strategy in reasoning. *Psychol. Rev.*, 1968, 75: 550–560.

Huttenlocher, J. In press. Language and intelligence. In *New Approaches to Intelligence*, L. Resnick and N. Glaser (eds.). New York: Lawrence Earlbaum Associates.

Huttenlocher, J., and E. Higgins. 1971. Adjectives, comparatives and syllogisms. *Psychol. Rev.*, 6: 487–504.

Huttenlocher, J., and C. Presson. 1973. Mental rotation and the perspective problem. *Cognitive Psychology*, 4: 277–299.

Huttenlocher, J., and C. Presson. In preparation. The coding and transformation of spatial information.

Metzler, S., and R. Shepard. 1974. Transformational studies of the internal representation of three-dimensional objects. In *Theories in Cognitive Psychology*, R. Solso (ed.). New York: Lawrence Erlbaum Associates.

Neisser, U. 1967. *Cognitive Psychology*. New York: Appleton-Century-Crofts.

Potts, G. 1972. Information processing strategies used in the encoding of linear orderings. *J. Verbal Learning and Verbal Behavior*, 11: 727–740.

Schlesinger, I. M. 1970. The grammar of sign language and the problem of language universals. In *Biological and Social Factors in Psycholinguistics*, J. Morton (ed.). Urbana: University of Illinois Press.

Shepard, R., and C. Feng. 1972. A chronometric study of mental paper folding. *Cognitive Psychol.*, 3: 288–293.

Shepard, R., and S. Metzler. 1971. Mental rotation of three-dimensional objects. *Science*, 171: 701–703.

Trabasso, T., C. Riley, and E. Wilson. In press. Spatial strategies in reasoning: a developmental study. In *Psychological Studies of Logic and its Development*, R. Falmagne (ed.). New York: Lawrence Erlbaum Associates.

Whorf, B. 1956. *Language, Thought and Reality*. Cambridge, Mass: MIT Press.

Open Discussion of the Papers of Stokoe and Huttenlocher

Further Aspects of Sign Language

The role of icons in sign was of great interest. How important, for example, is it that an upstretched forearm with fingers spread wide is a visual representation of a tree as well as the sign for *tree?* Gordon Hewes suggested that it might not be important at all: such icons are automatized very quickly and most signers are probably unaware of the iconic origin of most signs. Stokoe agreed with this view, noting that this lack of insight about etymologies is typical in speech; speakers rarely realize the origins of the words they use. Why should we expect sign to be different in this respect? Hewes expressed surprise that some dictionaries of sign languages, such as that of the Plains Indians of North America, even bothered to give etymologies of sign in terms of possible iconic antecedents. Bellugi then noted that when deaf mothers teach ASL to their deaf children, they are never concerned about explaining the iconic origin of signs. Mothers never tell their children that the sign for *egg* is made like the breaking of an egg for cooking purposes. Instead they are concerned most about proper "pronunciation," proper hand-gesture articulation.

Marler disagreed with this view and reintroduced the notion of features. The work of Eimas and his colleagues [see Cutting and Eimas, this volume] appears to demonstrate the existence of (phonetic) feature detectors in young infants. One might ask why an infant would be given such capabilities for his development. One answer is that they may make language acquisition easier. This is particularly important when one compares speech with sign. Surely there are no sign feature detectors in the visual system of the infant. Sign language, in some sense, may have to make up for this deficit and root itself in some other system or set of devices. Perhaps iconicity serves exactly this purpose.

Bosma reemphasized that sign appears to be acquired *before* speech. Perhaps the auditory feature system is tied to a larger inhibitory system which delays speech acquisition, but perhaps there is no corresponding inhibitory system for sign. Such a situation might explain why a ten-month-old child could perceive sign, produce sign, perceive speech, but not produce speech. The delay of onset in speech production might serve the purpose of language acquisition in the long run. Perhaps the feature detectors useful for speech sound discrimination organize themselves fully during this period of nonlinguistic babbling. When the system is fully developed speech production is no longer inhibited and the child ventures into the spoken world with a preprimed system ready to begin performing miraculous feats of language acquisition.

The discussion then centered on a comparison of linguistic structure in sign and in speech. Liberman noted that in speech there is the breath group, the largest phonological segment which marks the sentence or phrase; there is the syllable, the number of which can be determined for any given language—about 3000 for English and about 60 for Japanese, for example; there are the phonemes themselves, and they too can be counted for any language; and there are phonetic features, which never number more than in the teens. Liberman then asked Bellugi and Klima to outline the corresponding "phonological" units in sign. Bellugi resisted enumerating them but assured the conference that most but not all linguistic structures exist in sign. For example, prosodic features occur in sign for the sentence, the phrase, and even for the compound. Klima noted that compounds analogous to *blackbird* (as opposed to *black bird,* a bird that happens to be black) appear to be marked by rhythmic cadence much as they are marked by stress and intonation in speech. Phrases appear to be marked with pauses, and, as Stokoe pointed out, larger units such as sentences and paragraphs are often marked with shifts in body position.

Liberman pursued the issue asking for the number of meaningless elements in sign. Stokoe and Klima said there were nineteen "features" that are frequent, and ten which are easily distinguished and carry much information in the sign context. All signs can be constructed, more or less, out of sixteen. Studdert-Kennedy then interceded, expressing concern at the notion of features. Researchers took an unjustifiably long time in distinguishing between distinctive features, phonetic features, and auditory features. The addition of more "features" in the realm of sign may be unwarranted at present. It appears that sign features are partly empirical and partly metaphorical. Klima concurred with this view and stated that exactly this concern has led him away from the term *features* to the term *parameters,* which is linguistically neutral. One reason for this change is that while phonetic features are typically considered to be binary, sign parameters are not. Sign parameters are also not strictly like phonemes in the sense of being segments. For example, they do not appear to be perceived sequentially like the phonemes of a syllable, but rather in a more simultaneous fashion.

Studdert-Kennedy and Cutting were interested in possible hemispheric specialization underlying the perception of sign. Would sign be perceived primarily in the left hemisphere because it is linguistic, or would it be primarily perceived in the right hemisphere because it is spatial? Many felt sure that sign would be processed in the left hemisphere just like speech. Cutting noted that since sign language involves so much eye contact we may begin to draw inferences about underlying specialization. One would expect most signers to be right-handed, probably in the same proportion as in the speaking population. Moreover, one would expect most signers to make more signs to the right side of the midline of the body than to the left. When facing a right-handed signer, however, the signs appear on the left side of the focal point of the sign receiver. We know from extensive visual work that what is presented to the left side of the visual field is projected to the right hemisphere. Thus, perhaps by this circumstance alone, sign is primarily perceived in the hemisphere opposite from speech. Studdert-Kennedy added that the right hemisphere may then have to act as a waystation, shipping the neural representations of most signs over to the left hemisphere for linguistic analysis. Such a two-hemisphere process may be time consuming and might account for the fact that signing is slower than speaking. Liberman suggested that the answer to the specialization question might be found in the intersection of the aphasia and sign language literature. Jenkins and Stokoe stated, however, that they knew of no pure instances of brain damage in an adult native signer who had been deaf from birth. Bellugi added that fortunately for the deaf community, but perhaps unfortunately for science, the deaf have never been conscripted into war where many brain injuries occur that lead to aphasia.

Reading, Sign, and Speech Together; Syntax and Semantics

If sign is in some psychological sense a language, Mattingly suggested, there ought to be some carry over from early experience with sign. If so, then one might expect reflections of this experience in the acquisition of the skills of reading and writing, which are of course skills parasitic on language but often thought to be primarily parasitic on speech. Stokoe outlined some efforts to determine empirically the extent of carryover from sign into reading. In one study deaf children whose native language was sign and hearing children whose native language was not English appeared to acquire the skills of reading and writing English in the same fashion. This result suggests that deaf children with deaf parents who sign learn English skills as if they had another language to work from. On the other hand, deaf children of hearing parents who did not use sign appeared to do considerably worse on such tests. It should be noted that the signing children do not perform nearly as well as the foreign children, but the general pattern of acquiring the skill appears to be the same. Hirsh then noted that the general reading retardation in both groups of deaf children, those with and without deaf parents, is extensive. There has been a long history of controversy over whether a deaf child should be taught to speak or be taught to sign. Neither approach holds all the answers and a current pedagogical principle is to teach both in hope of opening up both systems and in hope of aiding such skills as reading and writing.

Gordon Hewes has written extensively on the possible gestural origin of language, and Peter Reynolds noted that in some sense it is puzzling that man developed speech at all if sign language is nearly as adequate. Half-jokingly Ursula Bellugi commented that if man had four hands instead of two, speech might never have developed. Noting the apparent primacy of sign language in the development of language in man, and noting the ease with which the child acquires sign, Philip Lieberman suggested that hand gestures and speech were meant to be used together. In support of this notion, he pointed out that all members of the conference gestured when speaking, often as if to punctuate and modify what they were saying. Verbal language is very strong in the sense that all visual information can be deleted, as in a telephone call, and the message can be understood. Nevertheless, the fact that this conference was called and that everyone gathered from great distance at great expense and great inconvenience, instead of making a conference telephone call, suggests that the visual input is also very important. Of course the verbal information is still present, but it may be subordinated to become more on a par with the visual message.

Premack suggested that one reason for the move out of gestures into the spoken word may be in the development of syntax. Perhaps extensive iconicity impedes the development of syntactic relationships. With this notion he then asked Stokoe and Klima to outline the syntax of sign. Both nearly blanched at the prospect of giving a thumbnail sketch of syntax in sign. Klima said that it is very difficult. If anything the study of syntax in sign has made the notions of syntax in speech appear to be on shaky ground. One must consider what is the essence of syntax at the conceptual and behavioral level. One approach is to consider the forms language could have taken. Language could consist, for example, entirely of expressions like *the animals, the hunters, the kill.* Such an example is an expression, it has significance, and it could be used for certain communications. It might suggest to us that some animals were killed by hunters, but it does not have the underlying structure of the sentence *the hunters killed the animals.* This second statement is an assertion; it has truth value. *The animals, the hunters, the kill,* on the other hand, is not an assertion and we cannot make judgments about whether or not it is true, and it may not even be appropriate to do so. One of the functions of syntax is to structure, but the "asyntactic" expression does have a structure without the usual syntactic niceties. In ASL both statements could be made, and they would be roughly equivalent to their English counterparts, but it causes Klima to wonder if the standard approach to syntax is relevant to sign or if it is even relevant to speech. Fodor agreed with this view and suggested that what syntax does is to define the domain of semantic relationships that are stressed by a language. Syntax may be intimately related to vocabulary; it allows an infinite number of statements with a finite number of specifiers. However, there is nothing natural about syntax except the persistent idea that semantic relations for a language are defined over the lexicon rather than the sentence. That notion may be wrong.

Ira Hirsh then injected the suspicion that it cannot be too difficult to look at syntax in sign. There are obviously two very important questions with regard to syntax of sign; does it exist, and, if so, what is it like? The first question could be answered in two ways: (a) get two linguists to agree on what are the minimum essentials of syntax in all natural languages (not a likely task) and then see if they apply to sign, and (b) determine whether or not it is possible to generate syntactically improper sentences. Stokoe and Klima both have begun to collect agrammatic sign statements. A problem arises, however, in that native signers appear to have a high tolerance for accepting signed English which has a syntax very different from sign. Both readily agree, however, that sign has a complex syntax. The next question is: what is the syntax like? Hirsh suggested that this might be answered in assessing the influence of the syntax of the spoken community on the syntax of the signing community. If American English and British English have the same (similar) syntax one would expect that ASL and British Sign Language would also be similar. Stokoe and Klima attested that the two sign languages are very different, but perhaps in some abstract sense the syntaxes might be similar.

Earlier Huttenlocher had commented on the discreteness of semantic systems in natural language. John Ross then noted that semantic categories are fuzzier than we often think. For example, consider the concept "bird." There are criterial birds such as robins and eagles, slightly off-center birds such as chickens, more off-center birds such as penguins, and quasi-birds such as bats. The distinctions here are not clear; there appears to be a continuum of "birdness." Fodor injected a word of caution, however, about pursuing the psychological reality of such continua: they are difficult to define and perceptual distances between member items are difficult to pin down in Euclidean space.

Sculpting Space with Sign

Gordon Hewes suggested that one reason that gestures probably preceded speech is that gestures are much more useful in relaying information about the topography of terrain. For early man it was probably much easier to gesture the equivalent of "go down the path to the big rock and turn left" than to speak it. Mental mapping is quite easy with gestures.

Ursula Bellugi then commented that it is just this mapping property which is important in sign. A sign sentence is literally laid out in space for the signer and the sign receiver to refer to. This aspect of sign has little to do with iconicity. Instead temporal and spatial relationships are created through the sculptured use of the space in front of the signer. Consider how time relations are made. A signer giving a narrative will use the space in front of her, but when refering to past events or past signs she will move all signs backwards in space toward the body or even gesture over the shoulder. It is tacitly understood by the sign receiver that time advances forward from the body of the signer, so that the future is far to the front and the immediate past is just to the rear. Stokoe then noted that this use of space makes it impossible to mix up third-person references in a discourse. Third persons are spatially set in particular positions by the signers and are "there" to refer to throughout the conversation.

III. Phonology and Language

Sound and Its Absence in the Linguistic Symbol

EDWARD S. KLIMA

The Sequential and the Simultaneous

At a 1965 conference entitled "Brain Mechanisms Underlying Speech and Language," Noam Chomsky gave what has become the standard characterization of "having command of a language": "a language is a specific sound-meaning correspondence. . . . Command of a language involves knowing that correspondence" [Chomsky, 1967a, pp. 75–76]. At one point during the meeting, Chomsky was asked how he would consider the sign language of the deaf in terms of this general characterization. Chomsky replied that he would rephrase his characterization so as to read "*signal-meaning correspondence.*" The next question addressed to Chomsky was one very central to the topic of the present meeting, language with and without speech. Is sound a crucial aspect of language? Chomsky's answer: "It is an open question whether the sound part is crucial. It could be but certainly there is little evidence to suggest it is" [Chomsky, 1967a, p. 85].

It is clear that there is a *glottocentric* bias among most of the hearing population and indeed among many researchers involved in language studies that somehow sound *is* central to language or at least that sound insinuates itself into the essential structure of language. So much, even, of organized propositional thought seems to be in terms of "inner speech." Of course, languages like English can also be presented visually in terms of orthographic presentation, but this is secondary and derivative. A really interesting question is what sort of difference, if any, the output mode of language really makes. The eye is very different from the ear; the hands are very different from the tongue; but what is the effect of these differences on the various levels of language structure?

For the past four years, our research group at the Salk Institute and the University of California, San Diego, has been investigating the nature of sign language,[1] its internal structure, and the way it is perceived and processed by native deaf signers [see Bellugi and Klima, this volume]. Of course there are similarities between sign languages and spoken languages but for the moment I would like to concentrate on some of the differences between them. In fact, I will focus here on that aspect of the two languages where the differences are most obvious; namely, on

---

[1] The following distinctions are important throughout the paper: *sign language* is the generic term, like *spoken language;* there are individual *sign languages* as there are individual *spoken languages;* one of the sign languages is *American Sign Language* (referred to commonly as ASL).

the formational level of the *signal,* the manual gesture which is perceived by being seen versus the vocal articulation that is perceived by being heard.

Let me delineate the general frame of inquiry in the following way: The existence of a language which (at least for those deaf users who are congenitally deaf) is clearly a primary language, not based on spoken language, allows us to ask some questions which might otherwise have remained merely speculative and hypothetical. Of course, both sign language and spoken language have a realizational level, some system of rules that realizes the more abstract levels of linguistic structure as units to be perceived. But with the existence of sign language, one can reasonably ask: What would language be like with a realizational system other than phonology, where phonology is understood as "the system of rules that relates the syntactic and *phonetic* representation" [Chomsky, 1967*b*, p. 102], or, more technically, the set of rules which "take the transformed terminal string which consists entirely of special kinds of *segments* [italics my own] and boundaries and completes the assignment of phonetic features of these symbols" [Halle, 1959, p. 26]. The notion of the sequencing of units and, in particular, that of the sequencing of the special kinds of units called phonological segments will figure centrally in the discussion that follows. While the signs in the sign phrase are conceived of as separate units following one another in sequence just as the words in word phrases of spoken language follow one another in sequence, the individual sign itself—unlike the individual word—while having a durational aspect is none the less not conceived of as consisting of *segments* following one another. This is not to say that the sound structure of spoken language is exclusively sequential. As Roman Jakobson aptly observed, "though the predominantly sequential character of speech is beyond doubt," it cannot be considered as unidimensionally organized in time. Spoken language is conceived of as a "successive chain of phonemes," but the phonemes themselves are *"simultaneous* bundles of concurrent distinctive features" [Jakobson, 1971, p. 340]. When considered at all their levels of linguistic structure, both sign and spoken languages have a sequential dimension and a simultaneous dimension. The sequential aspect, however, goes one level lower in the hierarchy of unit types for spoken language in that it characterizes the individual meaningless units and their occurrence in and as morphemes and simple words.

In spoken language phonological features (such as nasality, presence of voicing, and stridency) occur simultaneously in constituting the phonological segment, and phonological segments in turn occur *sequentially* in constituting the morphemes and words of the language. The words in turn occur sequentially in constituting the various phrases which form the sentences of the language. In sign language, on the other hand, as I will specify in greater detail below, representatives (primes) of each of three or four major formational parameters (hand formation, place of articulation, movement, and perhaps orientation) combine *simultaneously* to constitute the individual signs (that is, the sign language equivalent of free morphemes), while the individual signs combine *sequentially* to form sign phrases and sign sentences.

Table 1 schematizes some of the essential differences between the organizational principle characterizing the morphemes of spoken language and that characterizing the signs of sign language. I do not mean to suggest that the temporal dimension has no relevance in terms of the individual sign. The parameter of movement involves processes and changes that very clearly take place over time, but what appears as the

Table 1. Comparison of Organizational Principles of a Sign and a Morpheme

ASL Sign That Translates as *Blue*

1. One from at least 133 *hand combinations* (analyzable into various combinations of 19 basic *hand configurations* involving one or both hands: the hand configurations themselves may turn out appropriately to be analyzed into a small number of digital-manual traits)
2. One from at least seven *relationships* that one hand can bear to the other hand in two-handed signs
3. One from at least sixteen different *orientations* that one or both hands (the fingers and/or the thumbs) can have with respect to the body. (Note: Items 1–3 I refer to collectively as *manual arrangements*.)
4. One from about twelve *locations* (on the body or in space) where the manual arrangements are articulated
5. One from well over one hundred different *movements* of the hands (which may be appropriately analyzed as combinations of more basic kinetic traits)

English Word of Three Segments ([b-l-u] blue)

First Segment	Second Segment	Third Segment
1. One from 2 values of the *feature: consonantal* 2. One from 2 values of 3. the *feature: voiced* [and 4. so on for the total inventory of thirteen bi- 5. ventory of thirteen bi- 6. nary (or ternary?) val- 7. ued features] 8. 9. 10. 11. 12. 13.	1. 2. 3. 4. 5. 6. 7. 8. 9. 10. 11. 12. 13. The same as the preceding but with some different values occurring	1. 2. 3. 4. 5. 6. 7. 8. 9. 10. 11. 12. The same as the preceding but with some different values occurring

dominant organizational principle of morpheme structure in spoken languages (recurring segments which are, at least in principle, permutable) is replaced by the *concurrent* presence of representatives of a very limited number of parameters. These parameters represent very large inventories of alternative choices.

Not in American Sign Language, any more than in any spoken language,[2] are all the million combinatorial possibilities realizable as possible signs—and, of course, only a fraction of possible signs appear as actual signs. Some combinations of representatives (primes) of the parameters are simply imcompatible with one another for physical reasons; others seem to be excluded on the basis of language-specific patterning in ASL. It obviously would be wrong to conclude—as some might have been tempted to conclude—that because of the special organizational principle of the sign there is some significant lack of potential in terms of the number of formally distinct signs that are possible in a sign language. This contrasts to the segments-in-sequence principle that characterizes the organization of the morpheme of spoken language. The following rough estimates may give some idea of the potential richness of ASL in terms of possible, though not necessarily actual, signs. The estimate is indeed very approximate and only suggestive of reasonable lower limits of magnitude. The merely suggestive nature of the approximations results from the lack of any careful analysis of the restrictions on co-occurence of the individual primes of the basic formational parameters of signs in ASL—and, in particular, from the lack of detailed information (to say nothing of the theory) of the parameter of movement in sign languages.

There are at least 19 distinct hand configurations—the number given by Stokoe et al. [1972].[3] Other researchers suggest that the number of

[2] When the sound segment is further analyzed as a complex of features (for example, the thirteen or so "distinctive features" of the Jakobsonian tradition), then spoken language certainly falls far short of anywhere near a full use of the richness in different segments possible: In the abstract, 13 binary classificatory categories are sufficient to describe a "language" of 8192 (2^{13}) "phonemes" —over 200 times the number of distinct segments in English and well over 100 times the number of phonemes in any known language. This is due in part, of course, to the fact that certain of the acoustical and/or articulatory correlates of the features in the current distinctive feature system are mutually exclusive. Nonetheless, it is obviously the case that there is great redundancy in the segmental structure of spoken language and a great deal of this redundancy is due to language-particular restrictions. In addition, of course, the sequential organization of segments into morphemes also results in great redundancy.
[3] The number of representatives (primes) of the individual parameters specified by Stokoe et al. [1965] will be low because of Stokoe's methodological bias at the time of compiling the dictionary: insistence on the discovery of actual minimal pairs to justify the postulation of each independent prime of any parameter. Stokoe's inventory thus sets the extreme lower limit.

significant variations on these nineteen brings the total number closer to 40. The hand configuration which figures most often in the signs found in Stokoe, Casterline, and Croneberg [1965] consists of the flat hand, fingers not spread and thumb close in. The gesture that a traffic officer uses to stop traffic—the flat hand with fingers up and palm facing away—is an approximation. Any one of the nineteen hand configurations may be assumed by one hand alone or—with a difference that distinguishes one sign from another—it may be assumed symmetrically by both hands. In addition to the resultant 38 different hand combinations, the 19 basic hand configurations formed by one hand (the dominant hand) can also be articulated on one of at least five hand configurations formed by the other hand (nondominant hand). The 95 hand arrangements that result from the latter combine with the previous 38 to yield a total of 133 distinct hand arrangements.

In addition, the full specification of the possible manual arrangements includes about seven significant differentiations concerning the relation of one hand to the other in two-handed signs (one hand in front of the other, above the other, behind, crossed, or interlocking). Because of the nature of certain hand configurations, many of these relationships are limited in distribution, but certainly the variations at least triple the forms constituting possible two-handed signs. On top of this, two-handed and one-handed signs can differ from one another in their orientation to the signer, specifically in terms of whether the palm of the signing hand or hands faces right (to the center) or left (to the side), up or down, away from the signer or toward him. The orientation of the fingers along the same axes is also significant in distinguishing different signs. There are 16 to 18 such orientations possible for each hand configuration located in the "neutral" space directly in front of the signer's chest. Even if restrictions imposed on these orientations by places of articulation on the head and body should reduce the possibilities by a half and the asymmetrical two-handed signs by another half, there would be more than 1700 possible manual arrangements (differentiated according to hand configuration, one-handedness versus symmetrical and asymmetrical two-handedness, varying relationships of the hands to one another and to two-handed signs, and the orientational possibilities of all hand configurations).

All of the more than 1700 manual arrangements could play a part in possible signs articulated in neutral space giving an initial 1700 manual arrangements with location. In addition, the 608 one-handed and symmetrical two-handed "manual arrangements" (including differences attributable to distinct hand relationships and distinct orientations) can be differentially articulated in any one of at least seven significant locations on the face, on or in front of the head, and on the rest of the upper body. There are in addition four distinct locations on the arm. Thus the total possible "manual arrangements with location" is over 6000.

There remains one very important parameter to be accounted for in our gross estimate of possible signs in ASL, that of movement. The parameter of movement is not only the most distinctive in terms of its structural properties but also the most elusive in terms of standard paradigms of linguistic analysis. There are at least 12 simple movements possible with any manual arrangement in any location. There are another 12 simple movements restricted as to orientation, hand configuration, or whether one or two hands are involved in the sign. The 12 simple movements which occur anywhere include upward, downward, up and down, rightward, leftward, side to side, movement toward, movement away, to and fro movement, bending of the hand at the wrist, twisting of the hand, and finally simple circular movement. A search through the approximately 2500 entries in the Stokoe dictionary reveals more than a hundred complex movements where one direction merges into another or where the nature of one movement changes in one way or the other. There are, for example, at least 25 distinct complex movements which involve circular action. There are at least 11 distinct movements which involve two contacts on the body or on the base hand with distinct movements intervening between the contacts. These 11 are distinct from the at least 36 complex movements in which the contact occurs first followed simply by some movement.

Thus, the number of possible manual arrangements with location and with movement (that is, the number of possible signs)—not counting the possibility of compounding—will be very far above 72,000 (the 6000 possible manual configurations with location times the 12 simple movements assumable by all the manual arrangements) and could conceivably go to over ten times the amount. Thus in saying that the structural principles of a sign language result in a very rich vehicle for providing differentiated form, the richness implied far exceeds any practical needs that a language may have.[4]

[4] It is, of course, an empirical question whether or not the sequencing (in differing orders) of a relatively restricted inventory of units (let's say the 30 or so phonemes of English) is more easily processed and/or stored when the *auditory* mode is involved than is the occurrence of one of a large inventory of primes from each of, say, five formational parameters when the visual mode is involved. The picture is not changed substantially when the individual phoneme of spoken language is considered itself in terms of the co-occurrence of, for example, one binary value from each of, say, 13 distinctive phonological features.

There remains, of course, the very crucial question: Are signs really processed according to the parameters by which they have been analyzed?[5] What is the structural nature of the organizational principle of the sign? Where, for example, does the sign lie along the structural continuum between units as totally separate gestalts, each more or less equally different from all the others (each perceived in terms of its own "template") and the other extreme of a tightly structured feature system with minimal redundancy?[6] What, furthermore, is the nature of the transition zone in perceptual space between what is recognized as one sign and what is recognized as another? And finally, if there are areas of no-man's land in the perceptual space between signs are these areas relatively large or small?

The contrast between the predominantely sequential character of the constitution of words in spoken languages on the one hand, and the predominant simultaneity in the internal organization of the signs of sign languages, is repeated in the differing ways that each prefers in systematically modulating meaning. In spoken language, the modulation of meaning within the word is carried out predominantly through affixation—again the sequencing of units before, after, or between others. Such a word as *bluish* is, after all, the lexical morpheme *blue,* followed by the derivational morpheme *ish.* In sign language, when there is modulation of meaning within a given sign, this modulation typically takes the form of some *simultaneous, concurrent* systematic variation in, for example, the direction, intensity, and/or other formational parameter of the sign. The sign in American Sign Language which has as its translation *blue* has the following formational description:

The sign is single handed; the Hand Configuration is the flat hand (with thumb against palm). The Location is the neutral space in front of the signer's chest. The Orientation of the active hand in fingers away from signer, palm inward (i.e. facing the left when the sign is made with right hand). The Movement is a repeated twist from the wrist, the blade of the hand moving up and down.

The meaning of this sign can be modulated as "more or less blue," that is, approximately, "bluish," by superimposing concurrently a laxness of

[5] The question of the psychological reality of the constructs that have been developed in current studies of sign languages has been one of the main concerns of our research group. The general thrust and rationale of those investigations is sketched in the contribution by Bellugi and myself in this volume. Some particular experiments are reported in Bellugi and Siple [1974] and Bellugi and Fischer [1972].

[6] Not that any real human language is expected to lie at the latter extreme. As Halle [1954, pp. 79–80] puts it: "Real languages are not minimal redundancy codes invented by scholars fascinated by the power of algebra, but social institutions serving fundamental needs of living people in a real world."

hand configuration and a "suspendedness" in the quality of movement
(a wrist twist but in sort of suspended animation). Significantly such
modulations of meaning in sign language are typically achieved by just
such concurrent superimposition of additional gestural characteristics.

As with any other language that has been studied for only a very short
time, by only a few researchers (and those with linguistic interests seldom
centering on the lexicographic), the compilation of a reasonably comprehensive dictionary of actual signs is probably a long way off. There does
exist a *Dictionary of American Sign Language,* compiled by Stokoe, Casterline, and Croneberg [1965], giving a collection of signs from ASL and
their English word equivalents. This is the first attempt to construct a
dictionary according to a notation meant to reflect significant and distinctive characteristics of the *form* of the signs of a sign language. There
are about 2500 entries in the dictionary. This dictionary makes no claims
of completeness or of representing even the sign vocabulary of the "average deaf signer." It is generally felt that ASL easily contains three or
four times the 2500 entries. The estimates of entries here refer to individual basic signs; that is, not counting the systematic modification in the
form of sign that reflects the sort of modulation in meaning so typical
of sign language.

The Actual and the Possible in English
Let us turn now in some detail to the potential richness in distinct
forms provided by a language organized according to a structural principle
whereby a relatively small inventory of segmental phonemes[7] is con-
catenated in various orders, though certainly not in all logically possible
orders, and where strings of varying length may occur. Such relative
freedom in the distribution and number of phonemes possible in the
morpheme certainly characterizes current English. In terms of permuta-
bility take the three segments that occur in the English word *pass:* [p],
[æ], [s]. Of the six logically possible permutations, four are actual words
of English (*pass, sap, apse, asp*). The other two permutations are simply

---

[7] Hawaiian, with thirteen surface phonemes, is commonly cited as a language
with strikingly few segmental phonemes. At the other extreme, in Chipewayan,
there are 45 surface segmental phonemes. Hockett found that from a sample
of 69 different languages the average number of phonemes is 27 [Hockett, 1958].
Presumably, there are Caucasian languages with up to 70 segmental phonemes.
The number of segmental phonemes postulated for English varies according to
the methodology used to work out the figure for the vowels in particular. Hockett
[1958] and Francis and McDavid [1958] assume 33 (24 consonant phonemes
and 9 vowel phonemes). Other linguists like Trnka [1968], who considers the
diphthongs and triphthongs as unit phonemes, can go as high as 44, including
6 stressed short vowels and 14 long, diphthongal, or triphthongal vowels.

not possible words of English: (a)*[spæ] is excluded because English words do not end in a lax vowel; [spa], spelled *spa,* with a permissible final vowel, is, of course, not only a possible but an actual word in English); (b) *[psæ] is excluded both because it ends in a lax vowel and because [ps] is not a permissible initial cluster in English. The addition of one more segment [t] makes 24 possibilities of which only five are actual words: [sæpt], that is *sapped,* [spæt], [pæst], [tæps], [pæts]; another three are clearly possible words: [æspt], [stæp], [tæsp]. The status of a fourth possibility is not absolutely clear: [æpts]. The other 15 are clearly impossible words as far as the sound structure of English goes. Although the majority of the most frequently used words are monosyllables, the language as a whole has more polysyllabic words than monosyllabic words, and in any running text a good number of polysyllabic words are likely to occur. Many polysyllabic words are of course also polymorphemic, but there are also in English many words consisting of a single polysyllabic morpheme.

The number of words in an unabridged English dictionary of course is very great. The *Century Dictionary* listed 530,000; the *Oxford English Dictionary* has over 400,000; and *Webster's Third New International Dictionary* lists more than 450,000. These figures, while they do not include the various inflectional forms of the words (for example, plural, past tense, possessive) do include compounds. According to Ramsay [1933] the total number of lexical units is really "something like 250,000" (and of these over 50,000 are obsolete). Obviously, no individual speaker of the language has anywhere near this number of items in his active vocabulary—or, for that matter, in his passive vocabulary. According to one test mentioned by Miller [1951] the "average college student" has a recognition vocabulary of nearly 60,000 different lexical units (or a total of about 156,000 words including inflectional forms). It is hard to say, however, how many words would be in the active vocabulary of such an "average college student," but of course it would be much, much smaller. Hall [1944, p. 378] claims: "The complete vocabulary of any full (not minimum or pidgin) language, regardless of the cultural level of its speakers, is at least 20,000 to 25,000 words," but again the vocabulary of any given individual would tend to be far below this. McKnight [1928, p. 186] refers to a vocabulary test made at Princeton University in 1916 that showed that the "upperclassman at that institution had at his command 16,500 words." By 1926 the figure had jumped to 17,500—purportedly reflecting "the rapidly expanding vocabulary of modern times."

Of course, the real richness of the system is reflected by the possible forms it can generate. But the task of trying to estimate the number of possible words or possible morphemes in English is made very difficult by the fact that English words may be polymorphemic and English morphemes may be polysyllabic. Jespersen did, however, make a calculation of the number of possible monosyllabic words in English (including monosyllabics which are polymorphemic, like *sixths*, [sɪks + θ + s], *twelfths*, [twelf + θ + s]). The structural possibilities for such monosyllabic forms in English include as many as three consonants clustering at the beginning and, as exemplified by *sixths*, as many four consonants clustering at the end of the monosyllabic word. According to Jespersen, the number of such possible words is 158,000 [Jespersen, 1960].

Trnka's *Phonological Analysis of Present-Day Standard English* provides a comparison between actual and possible forms from several points of view [Trnka, 1968]. Trnka sets the number of monomorphemic monosyllabic forms occurring as actual words in English at 3203. The most common pattern is consonant-vowel-consonant (CVC), which is the shape taken by 1346 actual monosyllabic, monomorphemic words. The next most popular pattern is CCVC (714 actual words), and then CVCC (445 actual words). These three patterns (out of fourteen total patterns of a single vowel or diphthong with up to five consonants) account for over 78 percent of all the actual monomorphemic monosyllabic words in English; or, more precisely in his source, the *Pocket Oxford Dictionary of Current English,* Trnka estimates the number of *possible* monomorphemic, monosyllabic words (that is, different word shapes) in English to be 89,165. However, because his data of actual monomorphemic words do not contain any in the patterns CCCVCCC or VCCC (although he does include the pattern CCVCC, as in *sculpt*), he erroneously excludes them from the possible word shapes. The inclusion of these two patterns brings the total number of possible monomorphic monosyllabic words to 90,765—thirty times the actual number of such words that Trnka found in the *Pocket Oxford Dictionary of Current English.* Trnka's figures for the number of actual bisyllabic monomorphemic words is 2451 (2221 of which occur with first vowel stressed—about 90 percent). By far the most frequent bisyllabic pattern is CVCVC (as in *ballot, fathom*), with 668 actual forms representing actual monomorphemic words. Trnka figures that the actual words in this favorite pattern are only about 0.1 percent of the possible words. Accordingly, there are 668,000 possible monomorphemic words of the form CVCVC alone!—a greater number than the entries in any unabridged dictionary.

When we compare American Sign Language and English, there is no question that English, with its relatively full utilization of the possibilities inherent in the sequencing of phonological segments, represents a much richer system. But here the richness is of such outlandish magnitudes and is so conspicuously underutilized that we cannot attribute any serious poverty to the system, as such, underlying American Sign Language. Nor, however, do we hesitate to add that these considerations of systems in the abstract leave open completely the very important questions about differences in the ease, rate, and methods of processing signals organized according to such different principles. At any rate, it seems to me that with even the little knowledge we have about the structure of one sign language, we cannot be quite so matter-of-fact as Wang is when he writes:

Visual signals have several obvious limitations which phonetic ones do not have. . . . They have a much lower ceiling as to the number of distinct signals and as to the rate at which these signals can be transmitted. . . . While it is true that a class of concepts can be associated with a class of signals of any medium or make, human language derives its tremendous wealth by having evolved along phonetic lines. . . . [It is] hard to conceive of any other system of bodily signals that could have been evolved that could function adequately as the carrier of man's rich stock of concepts. . . . Man's sounds are a crucial ingredient in the emergence of his language, and should be studied in that perspective. [Wang, 1973, pp. 84–85.]

The Phonetic Side of the Phonological Segment

As a final part of these all too informal reflections on differences in the organizational principles of languages in significantly different modes, it seems to me appropriate to focus on the functional and structural nature of this purportedly crucial entity—the sound segment—which, when favorable circumstances allow it to occur freely in number and distribution within the word (as it obviously does in English), produces such prodigious richness in possible forms. Ironically, however, as will be seen in the next section, the phonological segment has inherent in its nature as speech sound the potential for its own degeneration.

The phonological segment, from the point of view of the higher levels of grammatical structure, has a purely differential value. Each of the three words *sip, zip, lip,* for example, is simply different from the other two. It is immaterial whether two of the words are less different from one another than from the third. In terms of higher levels of structure it is a matter of all or nothing. The segments *s, z,* and *l* simply count as different in initial position in English. From this point of view they might just as well be arbitrary digits. Nothing would follow as far as higher grammatical structure is concerned, if the word *sip* were more similar to *zip* than to *lip*. But in terms of lower levels of structure, there are significant generalizations to be made that cannot be captured when segments are not further analyzed. Some of these generalizations have to do with language-specific characteristics, some with general tendencies, others with linguistic universals. The generalizations which are pertinent here are those that are correlated with phonetic facts. In terms of phonetic processes like assimilation, *s* bears the same relation to *z* as *p* does to *b* and as *t* does to *d*; the first member of each pair is identical to the second member except with respect to the phonetic feature of voicing. The past tenses *ceased* [sis + t] and *seized* [siz + d] bear the same relation as the past tenses *napped* and *nabbed* (i.e. [næp + t] and [næb + d]).

Let us go even further; in terms of higher grammatical structure nothing follows from the fact that one morpheme *bill*, meaning a bird's beak, and a different morpheme *bill*, meaning a demand for payment, are the same in form, whereas a third morpheme, *pill*, differs minimally from the first two in form. All that counts at higher levels of grammatical structure is that these three are indeed different morphemes. (Notice that this is not identical to the differences in what the three actually refer to—for in the word *object* we do not have three different morphemes but only one, despite the fact that *object* can refer to the same things as *pill* and the two distinct morphemes with the single form [bil]. Ambiguity and vagueness are not the same in language.) Again, in terms of the highest levels of grammatical structure the morpheme itself, like the segment, is purely differential. That *can* meaning 'be able' and *can* meaning 'to put in a container' have the same form does not prevent them from being differentiated in their past tenses as *could* and *canned*. The same holds for *fit* meaning 'to measure out' and *fit* meaning 'to be appropriate for' which have as their respective past tenses *fitted* and *fit*. On the other hand, morphemes do have a form, and when morphemes, through their sequencing, come in contact, phonetic factors come into play—although otherwise regular phonetic processes may be modified to preserve the identity of the morpheme (a desideratum insuring effectiveness of communication) and the invariance in the form of the morpheme (a desideratum promoting economy of expression). Such considerations suggest that the role of phonology in spoken language is to bridge the interface between the level at which segments and morphemes have purely differential function and the level at which factors involving phonetic form become paramount. The irony is that while the segment as purely differential unit leads to the richness of differentiated "beads on a string," the actual phonetic constitution of the segment has in itself the potential for the reduction of this richness. Sounds affect surrounding sounds. The natural phonetic processes postulated by linguists predict that the changes will in fact be in the direction of simplification.

The function of sound in language is to differentiate in form what is different in meaning, but the tendency of sound to simplify, to assimilate to its environment, is in conflict with this function. Sounds strive to change: morphemes strive to assume and maintain a single constant uniform shape. The two are in conflict, a conflict that can result in what Kiparsky [1972, p. 213] characterizes as "the conflict between a paradigmatic condition and the simplicity of the phonological rules." A conflict, a mismatch—one of a series of mismatches that find an interface in the various systems of "grammatical recoding that reshapes linguistic information so as to fit it to the several originally nonlinguistic components of the system" [Liberman, 1974]. "Why," Liberman asks "must the linguistic information be so thoroughly restructured if it is to be transmittable in the one case and storable in the other?" Liberman offers as an answer that "the components of transmission and storage are grossly mismatched . . . they cannot deal with information in anything like the same form." Kisseberth [1973, p. 4] describes the conflict in the following way: "The existence of morphophonemic variation, which undermines the semantic pole of language, is a consequence of the opposite force in language, the phonetic pole. . . . Sounds and their chaining together to form words and sentences are subject to the forces that are basically independent of meaning—assimilation, vowel reduction, truncation. . . ."

Schane [1972] sets up the dichotomy between "naturalness conditions" and "uniqueness conditions." According to the criterion of uniqueness, lexical morphemes have a single underlying form; Kiparsky [1972] elaborates such criteria even further as "distinctness conditions" reflecting a tendency for semantically relevant information to be preserved in surface structure and "leveling conditions" reflecting the tendency toward the elimination of allomorphy in paradigms. The other side of Schane's dichotomy consists of "naturalness conditions"—reflecting the tendency for *natural* phonological rules to resolve the clash that may result when one morpheme comes into contact with another yielding a sequence of sound segments that are incompatible either by their inherent nature or because of the language's specific distribution constraints.

When phonological segments are thus looked at in terms of performance factors (at least in terms of the production and perception of speech), their behavior shows certain definite tendencies which have not escaped contemporary phonologists. Postal [1968] has spoken about what certain segments "normally are": Segments are normally nonimplosive, that is, there are "no languages with only implosive segments, although languages with only nonimplosives are found everywhere." "Vowels are normally non-nasal . . . there is no language with only nasal vowels." Front vowels are normally nonrounded, nonlow back vowels are normally rounded, "consonants are normally followed by vowels, vowels by consonants, etc." [Postal, 1968, pp. 81–82]. Except for the last, which is contrast-maximizing, the naturalness conditions considered by Postal are distinguished by Schane [1972] as "rules" (and by Stampe as "processes" [1972]) that have to do with the inner nature of the segment itself. Schane and Stampe distinguish the above from rules or processes reflecting the effect of one sound upon others in its environment, the various assimilations and agreement phenomena that have been well known in linguistic literature. These include (*a*) assimilatory vowel nasalization (whereby a vowel preceding the nasal consonant is nasalized as it is in English, for example); (*b*) voicing agreement in clusters; (*c*) assimilative intervocalic voicing of obstruants; (*d*) assimilative homorganization of nasals. The two general types of phenomena involving inherent nature of segment or context are further differentiated from phenomena which provide maximum differentiation. These include preferred syllable structure rules and the devoicing of obstruants in word final position. A natural phonological phenomenon of one type can have exactly the opposite result as a phonological phenomenon of another of the three types; this is the case in the assimilative process of nasalization where a following nasal consonant nasalizes a vowel (but does not as such make it phonemically distinctively nasal). On the other hand, there is exactly the opposite segment-internal tendency of denasalization whereby nasality is phonemic in vowels only if phonemically non-nasal vowels are also part of the system. Where might it all lead? "The end result of unbridled phonetic processes," Kisseberth maintains, "is total merging of phonetic contrasts, and thus of semantic contrasts as well" [Kisseberth, 1973, p. 4].

The Other Extreme

There does turn out to be a real example of a language where phonetic processes like the ones mentioned above have, in the history of that language, actually been so "unbridled" that the language has taken the extreme form that would be predicted by natural phonology. The language is the Li Jiang dialect of Southwest Mandarin Chinese. My colleagues, Matthew Chen and Benjamin T'sou of University of California, San Diego, led me to this interesting dialect and helped me interpret the facts. According to the *Report on a Survey of the Dialects of Yunnan* [Yang, 1969], Li Jiang dialect has 24 consonantal phonemes, nine vowels, and four tones. The nine vowels occur alone or in twelve possible diphthongal combinations. The morpheme structure constraints are extremely severe. The morpheme may consist of a vowel or diphthong alone or preceded by a single consonant. No initial consonant clusters are permitted and every morpheme ends in a vowel. Furthermore, aside from a few exceptional cases consisting mostly of foreign borrowings, every morpheme is monosyllabic. There is only a handful of bound morphemes with purely grammatical function (function morphemes as opposed to content or root morphemes). The structure of the Li Jiang morpheme is thus simply $C'_0 V$,[8] where V represents a single vowel or a diphthong. This already narrow range of structural possibilities is further narrowed by constraints on the co-occurrence of segments. In the end, there turn out to be only 550 distinct syllable types (including the distinctions attributable to the four tones), which means essentially only 550 possible indigenous morpheme shapes. The amount of homophony is enormous. The shape LI with second tone represents seven different morphemes: *pear, to separate, forest, neighborhood, knoll, soul, peace.* Out of a 600-word sample vocabulary, there are five different words taking the form *ǰi* (first tone) ; one word *ǰi* (second tone) ; nine words *ǰi* (third tone) ; and seven words taking the form *ǰi* (fourth tone).

Chen [1973, p. 38] observes that "the number of distinct syllables has been reduced by a factor of three to one from Middle Chinese (3612 possible distinct morpheme shapes) to some modern dialects" (to about 1800 possible monosyllabic morpheme shapes in current Cantonese and about 1200 in present day Pekinese, and finally to the mere 550 in the Li Jiang dialect). If we consider 5000 words to be a minimum standard functional vocabulary, then it is obvious that if the words were represented by single base morphemes, then homonymy would be very troublesome for Cantonese and Pekinese Chinese and would be intolerable for the Li Jiang dialect. For modern standard Mandarin with slightly under 1200 distinct syllables available for its possible monosyllabic morphemes, "given a core vocabulary of about 5000 lexical items, each identical syllable (including tone) represents an average of 4.15 different characters or graphs," (4.15 semantically independent morphemes). And of course "the degree of homophony increases as the size of the lexicon grows." [Chen, 1974, p. 16]. What would the situation be like in the Li Jiang dialect? Each morpheme shape would represent an average of nine homonyms!

---

[8] In the following discussions of Chinese, C'_0 refers to a single consonant or none at all; V refers to a vowel or diphthong; N refers to a nasal consonant; $\bar{V}$ is a nasalized vowel or diphthong.

On the basis of comparative historical grammar, internal reconstruction, and cross-dialectal latitudinal reconstruction, Chen has been able to sketch the development of the morpheme structure from earlier Chinese to the current Li Jiang dialect [Chen, 1973]. Although reconstructions of prehistoric Sino-Tibetan suggest a parent language which may have had some suffixes, prefixes, disyllabic stem words, and perhaps even stems with consonant clusters, by the time of ancient Chinese the consonant clusters had been reduced. This of course would follow from one of the putative phonological universals: consonants are ordinarily followed by vowels. By the time of ancient Chinese, whatever prefixes and suffixes might have existed had dropped and the morpheme had taken on its typical Chinese form consisting of a vowel nucleus optionally preceded by a single consonant and optionally followed by a single consonant: $C'_0 V C'_0$. It is estimated that in archaic Chinese there were 4000 possible syllable types (that is, 4000 possible different morpheme shapes) and that by Middle Chinese this had already been reduced to 3700. Further historical development down to the Li Jiang dialect consists of added restrictions on possible morpheme-final segments. These restrictions find a very natural framework for discussion in the context-sensitive, context-free, and contrast-maximizing processes that are included in the "natural phonology" of Schane, Kisseberth, Stampe, and Postal. It will be recalled that in earlier Chinese the morpheme could end in one of three stop consonants: [p], [t], [k] or one of three nasals: [m], [n], [ŋ]. According to Chen [1973] some current Chinese dialects maintain six contrasting stops in morpheme final position. Let us consider first the development of the three nasals, after they had been simplified to a single nasal (this situation also exists in several current Chinese dialects). First of all it is natural to assume a contextually determined process of assimilatory nasalization (the vowel tends to become nasalized when followed by a nasal consonant): $C'_0 V N \rightarrow C'_0 \tilde{V} N$. But there is, in addition, a syllable structure tendency across languages predisposing languages to have an open syllable structure. That is, $C'_0 V C$ tends to become $C'_0 V$ rather than the other way around. Under certain conditions, this could be expected to result in a surface contrast which in fact does exist in a few Chinese dialects; that is, the contrast between morphemes of the structure $C'_0 \tilde{V}$, where nasality in the vowel or diphthong is phonemic, contrasting with morphemes of the form $C'_0 V$. Furthermore there is an observed tendency for nasalized vowels to become simplified as oral vowels; that is, vowels are in themselves normally oral rather than nasal: $C'_0 \tilde{V} \rightarrow C'_0 V$.

The reduction in the richness of possible morpheme final segments follows an analogous pattern, according to Chen, involving such phonetic processes as the shortening of vowels before voiceless stops, the tendency toward open syllable structure, and the simplification in the direction away from having phonemically distinct long and short vowels. The very restricted 550 distinct morpheme shapes that the Li Jiang dialect is left to operate with are the end effect of the extreme in the realization of such natural processes, processes which have to do with the fact that while at upper levels of structure, segments may indeed be purely differential, at lower levels of structure the segments represent sound. Sound as it is articulated and as it is perceived. However, this hazardous—and, in the case of the Li Jiang dialect, intolerable—potential for ambiguity is, in fact, mitigated by mechanisms that are not purely phonological: mechanisms that systematically build self-disambiguating compounds.

One of the commonest methods of compounding for disambiguation is through synonym compounds, coupling two morphemes which have more or less the same meaning.[9] There are a few isolated instances of this sort of compounding used in very special linguistic contexts in English: For example, when someone or something is referred to as *funny,* it is not unusual for the hearer to ask for an elucidation of the ambiguity by asking whether the thing or person is *funny-ha-ha* or *funny-peculiar.* Similarly if food is referred to as *"hot"* it is not uncommon in English for the hearer to request a disambiguation by asking whether what is meant is *spicy-hot* or *hot-hot* (where in the latter expression the first instance of *hot* is understood to have its most basic meaning).

One might well ask to what extent the individual morphemes comprising these synonym-compounds are felt synchronically by the speakers of language to be independent elements in terms of meaning. The question is, of course, an important one, not only from the point of view of the very narrow, restricted phenomena being dealt with here. More generally, one can ask to what extent morphemes are purely distributional units and to what extent they are not only that but also meaningful units in terms of the synchronic structure of the language. Whether or not the particular morphemes entering into the synonomous doublets of these dialects of Chinese are actually felt to be semantically independent by native speakers is an empirical question, a question inviting perhaps psycholinguistic experimentation. There are, however, at least anecdotal indications that the elements of these compounds may indeed count as individual semantic units. T'sou, a colleague of mine, whose native language is Cantonese Chinese, has expressed the impression that Chinese

---

[9] Examples from Modern Chinese: *péngyǒu* 'friend' (*péng* 'friend' and *yǒu* 'friend'), *jiěfàng* 'to liberate' (*jiě* 'to untie' and *fàng* 'to release'). For discussion of Chinese grammar, see Kratochvíl [1968] and Karlgren [1962].

children, when learning their language, begin by using not the "correct" polymorphemic (compound) form of words but rather by using the simple, monomorphemic forms in their simple utterances. It is only later that they restructure their language in terms of what must appear to them to be the correspondents of the synonymous doubles so characteristic of modern colloquial Chinese dialect. The first approximation of these doublets, however, is an error on the part of the children, but one which is interesting from a systematic point of view. The children tend simply to reduplicate one of the elements of the compound—thus creating the simplest form of doublet, the parts of which are the same in meaning. That is, following the imprecise analog in English (*funny-ha-ha* as opposed to *funny-peculiar*) the child in learning the Chinese dialects begins by using a simple term *funny*, then extends this according to the bimorphemic principle, to *funny-funny* and then only later correctly differentiates between *funny-peculiar* and *funny-ha-ha*. In terms of the grammar of the adult, it is my impression that these doublets lie somewhere between the petrified idiomatic compound and the purely productive compound. The native Chinese whom I have consulted feel that the individual elements of these compounds have a very strong and pronounced semantic individuality. And yet, it hardly seems to be the case that this is merely an instance of one ambiguous form seeking for any synonymous form whatsoever. As for the prognosis, the situation may well be as Karlgren puts it. "These expressions will gradually cease to be felt as compounds; they will be felt as simple words, and thus the monosyllabic Chinese will develop into a polysyllabic language." [Karlgren, 1962, p. 23].

It appears that in these Chinese dialects, the greater the homonymy, the more abundant the compounding. At least this would suggest itself from a study conducted by T'sou [1971], who shows that in spoken narrative, disambiguating synonym compounds are significantly more frequent than in written narrative and that furthermore in Mandarin Chinese, which has greater simplification of morpheme structure and therefore more homophones than Cantonese, significantly more disambiguating compounds appear in extended spoken narrative. One would predict that in Li Jiang the compounding would be even more frequent. It is appealing to consider this interesting state of affairs in terms of the original function of sound: to provide distinctions in form corresponding to distinctions in meaning. Because of regular phonetic processes, the sound segments as such no longer perform that function in a way that is sufficiently effective for communication. Other devices have been developed.[10]

---

[10] Compounding, including synonym compounds, is not the only sort of elucidative device that functions to disambiguate; a rich classifier system has also developed.

The connection between sound and meaning is, of course, essentially arbitrary, and since it is arbitrary there is no particularly strong bond between the meaning of the word and any individual segment that partakes in its sound form, but as the bond is so weak there is also no particular resistance as such to the loss of any particular, individual segment.

At this point it will be instructive to examine in some detail the extent of homophony in a language like English, where, in contradistinction to the Li Jiang dialect, there is such potential richness in the possible shapes that base morphemes may assume—not only in terms of the distribution of phonemes within the morpheme but also in terms of the sheer number of phonemes that may occur in the morpheme.

Trnka [1968] gives the following comparative figures for monomorphemic monosyllabic words in English: only 5.86 percent are of the Li Jiang type (a vowel or diphthong along or preceded by a single consonant, that is, CV or V). The 42 percent representing the most common pattern in English show a consonant followed by a vowel (or diphthong) followed by a consonant (CVC). The patterns consisting of V alone or CV (the Li Jiang type) represent a total of 186 actual word shapes in English, which include 96 homophonic forms (a single shape representing more than one actual morpheme) according to Trnka's figures. In fact, in some cases a homophonic form may represent three or more distinct homonyms.[11] I have calculated that the 96 homophonic forms presented by the patterns consisting of V alone or CV actually represent a total of 255 homonyms. Of the 1346 CVC combinations assumed by actual words in English, 292 are, according to Trnka's calculations, homophonic. That is, while 51 percent of the forms represented by V and VC are homophonic, the percentage if down to 22 percent within the favorite pattern in English, CVC. The percentage of homophonic forms drops to 13 percent or the pattern CCVC and to less than 7 percent for the pattern CCVCC.

In Summary

At this point, I would certainly be the last to argue that speech does not constitute part of the biological foundations of language. How else can one explain the relative ease with which any normal human being with the faculty for hearing can produce and perceive such a subtle signal? But if speech is specially selected, if sound constitutes such a natu-

[11] The homophonic CV form [lei] represents the following 4 homonyms: *lay*, past tense of *lie* 'to recline'; *lay* meaning 'a song'; *lay* meaning 'nonprofessional' or 'of the laity'; and *lay* meaning 'to place or put' (with various extensions of meaning possible); for many speakers of American English *lei* meaning 'a wreath of flowers' is a fifth homonym.

ral signal for language, then it is all the more striking how the human mind—or perhaps "mind" makes the process seem too conscious, too much a matter of intellect—let's say, rather, how the human disposition, when deprived of the faculty that makes sound accessible, seizes on and perfects an alternate form to enable the deeper linguistic faculties to give expression to ideas. Even at what may be the rather superficial level of providing distinct signals (capable of serving as symbols for concepts) and providing them in some more or less systematic fashion, sign language is clearly very rich in potential. There may indeed be some substantive difference in the nature and utilization of the two types of signals—but after all, seeing is different from hearing. One would be no more successful in seeing with the ear than in hearing with the eye. When sign languages use space in a blatantly nonphonetic way (in a way that perhaps speech never could), when they favor the concurrent over the sequential, is that not just what we would expect? Especially, given what insightful observers have already noticed about the general differences between the visual and the auditory: that in vision things tend to be patterned in space, while in hearing, the patterning tends to be in time [Hirsch and Sherrick, 1961; Jakobson, 1971].

Once again, it may well be the case that spoken sound constitutes the most natural signal for language, but that is not at all necessarily the same as saying that sound and speech are ideal. If the levels of grammatical structure are as complex as linguistics insists, then the match that the signal is making could hardly be ideal. After all, if the notions of natural phonology are correct, and if data like that presented by the Li Jiang dialect truly do exemplify what results when forces emanating from those aspects of language most intimately associated with speech and sound get the upper hand, then speech and sound—"natural" as they may be for human language—are certainly very far from ideal.

References

Bellugi, U., and S. Fischer. 1972. A comparison of sign language and spoken language. *Cognition,* 1: 173–200.

Bellugi, U., and E. S. Klima. 1974. Aspects of sign language and its structure. This volume.

Bellugi, U., and P. Siple. 1974. Remembering with and without words. In *Current Problems in Psycholinguistics,* F. Bresson (ed.). Paris: Centre National de la Recherche Scientifique.

Chen, M. 1972. The time dimension: contribution toward a theory of sound change. *Foundations of Language,* 8: 457–498.

Chen, M. 1973. Cross-dialectal comparisons: A case study and some theoretical considerations. *J. Chinese Linguist.,* 1: 38–63.

Chen, M. 1974. Natural phonology from the diachronic vantage point. To appear in *Proceedings of Chicago Linguistics Society,* a special volume on *Natural Phonology.*

Chomsky, N. 1967*a*. The general properties of language. In *Proceedings from Princeton Conference on Brain Mechanisms Underlying Speech and Language, 1965,* F. Darley (ed.), Grun and Stratton.

Chomsky, N. 1967*b*. Some general properties of phonological rules. *Language,* 43(1): 102–128.

Francis, W. N., and R. I. McDavid, 1958. *The Structure of American English.* New York: Ronald.

Hall, R. A., Jr. 1944. Language and superstition. *French Review,* 17: 377–382.

Halle, M. 1954. Why and how do we study the sounds of speech? Georgetown University, *Monograph Series on Languages and Linguistics,* 7: 73–80.

Halle, M. 1959. *The Sound Pattern of Russian.* The Hague: Mouton.

Hirsh, I., and C. Sherrick, Jr. 1961. Perceived order in different sense modalities. *J. Exp. Psychol.,* 62(5): 423–432.

Hockett, C. F. 1958. *A Course in Modern Linguistics.* New York: Macmillan.

Jakobson, R. 1971. About the relation between visual and auditory signs. In *Selected Writings II: Word and Language.* The Hague: Mouton.

Jespersen, O. 1960. Monosyllabism in English. In *Selected Writings.* London: G. Allen and Unwin, Ltd.

Karlgren, B. 1962. *Sound and Symbol in Chinese.* Hong Kong: Hong Kong University Press.

Kiparsky, P. 1968. Linguistic universals and linguistic change. In *Universals in Linguistic Theory,* E. Bach and R. T. Harms (eds.). New York: Holt, Rinehart and Winston.

Kiparsky, P. 1972. Explanation in phonology. In *Goals of Linguistic Theory,* S. Peters (ed.). Englewood Cliffs, N.J.: Prentice-Hall.

Kisseberth, C. W. 1973. The interaction of phonological rules and the polarity of language. To appear in *Proceedings of the Indiana Rule Ordering Conference,* 1974. (Also appeared as distribution of Indiana University Linguistics Club in mimeograph form, March 1973.)

Kratochvil, P. 1968. *The Chinese Language Today.* London: Hutchinson and Co.

Liberman, A. M. 1974. The specialization of the language hemisphere. In *The Neurosciences: Third Study Program,* F. O. Schmitt and F. G. Worden (eds.). Cambridge, Mass.: MIT Press.

McKnight, G. H. 1928. *Modern English in the Making.* New York: Appleton-Century-Crofts.

Mencken, H. L. 1963. *The American Language.* One-volume abridged edition. New York: Knopf.

Miller, G. A. 1951. *Language and Communication.* New York: McGraw-Hill.

Postal, P. M. 1968. *Aspects of Phonological Theory.* New York: Harper & Row.

Ramsay, R. L. 1933. Taking the census of English words. *American Speech,* vol. 8.

Schane, S. A. 1972. Natural rules in phonology. In *Linguistic Change and Generative Theory: Essays from the UCLA Conference on Historical Linguistics in the Perspective of Transformational Theory, Feb. 1–2, 1969*, R. P. Stockwell and R. K. S. McCauley (eds.). Bloomington, Indiana: Indiana University Press.

Stokoe, W., Jr. 1972. *Semiotics and Human Sign Languages.* The Hague: Mouton.

Stokoe, W., D. Casterline, and C. Croneberg. 1965. *Dictionary of American Sign Language on Linguistic Principles.* Washington, D.C.: Gallaudet College Press.

Stampe, D. L. 1972. An essay on phonological theory. Ph.D. dissertation, University of Chicago, Chicago, Illinois.

Stampe, D. L. 1969. The acquisition of phonetic representation. *Papers from the Fifth Regional Meeting, Chicago Linguistic Society.* Chicago: Department of Linguistics, University of Chicago, 443–454.

Trnka, B. 1968. *Phonological Analysis of Present-day Standard English.* University, Alabama: University of Alabama Press.

T'sou, B. K. 1971. Homophony and internal change: the Chinese case. Paper presented at the First May Day Linguistics Conference, University of California, Berkeley. Unpublished.

Yang, S-F. 1969. *Report on a Survey of the Dialects of Yunnan* (Chinese). Taiwan: Academia Sinica.

Wang, W. S-Y. 1973. How and why do we study the sounds of speech? *Project on Linguistic Analysis,* 17: 82–100. *Proceedings of the International Conference on Computer and the Humanities,* L. Mitchell (ed.). Edinburgh: Edinburgh University Press. In press.

Comments on the Role of Phonology in Language

PAUL KIPARSKY

I should like to discuss here, from the linguist's point of view, some questions relating to the role of phonology in language. By "phonology" I
mean the system which relates syntactic surface structures and phonetic
forms. Though I shall not be concerned directly with such questions as
the function or evolution of vocal (as opposed to, for instance, gestural)
transmission of language, which have received much attention at this conference, it appears to me that their discussion might in some ways be
helped along by a look at where phonology fits in with language as a
whole.

First, what does it mean to say that a language has a phonology as
distinct from a morphology? We might first want to answer this by saying
that it is necessary to describe a language as made up out of elementary
units called phonemes, which are then put together in various combinations into larger units called morphemes. But suppose now that there
was a language in which each morpheme contained just one phoneme,
where consequently each phoneme also constituted a morpheme. (Some
Caucasian languages, remarkable for their enormous phoneme inventories, have actually been analyzed this way [Kuipers, 1960], though the
analysis is controversial and in some ways gives the impression of a *tour
de force*). Would we be justified in saying that here the phonological
and morphological levels coincide? I think not. In such a language the
phonological units would still be organized from a phonological point
of view, by distinctive features, and the morphological units would fall
into morphological classes on the basis of their grammatical behavior.
We would still have to distinguish between phonological (phonetic or
morphophonemic) rules and morphological rules, though the line between them might not be clearly drawn in all cases, as indeed it often
is unclear in a language like English. In short, a phonological component,
or its equivalent, is intrinsic to the grammar of any language in which
the sentences are given some real-world expression (in effect, any language which is used for purposes of communication), for that mode of
expression will always have its own aspect of organization.

The question then arises whether the phonological component of the
grammar is structured purely autonomously, or whether it interacts with
the rest of language in some way. This was a matter of fierce debate
between schools of linguistics for nearly a century. It is today widely ac-
cepted that phonology is in some respects dependent on syntax, but the
extent and formal character of this dependence continue to be an open
question.

But even this was a hard-won insight. For a long time, the dominant view was that phonology is an autonomous level of linguistic structure, independent of morphology, syntax, or semantics. This view was first put forward by the positivist school of historical linguists that came to be known as the "neogrammarians." Their slogan, "sound changes have no exceptions," summarized the belief that phonological changes are at bottom physiological phenomena which cannot be caused, or in any way conditioned, by either structural, functional, or semantic factors. The synchronic counterpart to this historical conception was the autonomous phonemic level which developed in post-Bloomfieldian structural linguistics, in part as a direct outgrowth of neogrammarian ideas.

Generative grammar, developing earlier ideas of Jakobson and others, abandoned the idea of autonomous phonology and provided a framework in which the relationship of phonology and syntax was explicitly allowed for, and in which the precise nature of this relationship could be productively investigated. It can now be regarded as established that phonological rules can be sensitive to syntactic constituent structure, as well as to morphological constituent structure inside the word. Promising hypotheses about the formal properties of this interaction are beginning to be formulated [for example, Selkirk, 1972; Bresnan, 1971; Brame, 1974]. A few examples will make this clear.

Phoneticians had long observed that even such purely mechanical-seeming processes as the slurring and elision of vowels in monosyllabic function words in speech is syntax-dependent. The phenomena of phrase phonology have been often investigated by generative phonologists in recent years, most thoroughly by Selkirk, with instructive results. Compare the sentence pairs

(1) a. Where's Bill?
    b. *I wonder where *Bill's.*
(2) a. I wonder where John's going.
    b. *I wonder where *John's* today.
(3) a. John's in Boston.
    b. *Bill's happier in Portland than *John's* in Boston.

The (b) sentences in each pair (1–3) are odd because of the contraction of *is* in the underlined places: we can only say *I wonder where Bill is, I wonder where John is today, Bill's happier in Portland than John is in Boston,* even though we do not intend to put any particular emphasis on the *is.* Most speakers recognize this as a fact about their own usage when it is pointed out to them, though few are likely to have noticed it before. These facts assume a special significance in the context of the discussion about the dependence of phonology on syntax. Not only is contraction syntactically conditioned, it depends on a rather abstract context whose explication requires the concept of a syntactic transformation. It is that of a *removal site:* contraction is blocked before the empty slot left by a deletion or movement transformation, for example, the operation denoted by the arrow in diagrams (4–6), which correspond to the embedded sentences of (1b) and (2b) and the *than*-phrase of (3b) :

(4)

(5)

(6)

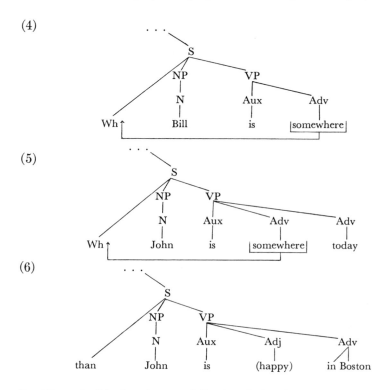

In (4) and (5) the element following *is* has been moved, and in (6) it has been deleted. Sentence (1a) is derived from the structure in (4), but nonembedded. In this case (as in direct *Wh*-questions generally) the Aux (*is*) moves into second position, where it no longer is followed by a removal site and is therefore free to contract. In (2a) and (3a) a removal site is never present, and so contraction is again possible.

Another type of interaction of deep syntax and phonology has been investigated by Bresnan [1971], who concludes that the rules for sentence stress are applied after the syntactic transformations at the end of each transformational cycle. This makes it possible to account for such contrasts as (the accent indicates the main stress of the sentence):

(7) a. He has pláns to leave.
   ("plans which he must leave")
   b. He has plans to léave.
   ("plans of leaving")
(8) a. Helen left diréctions for George to follow.
   ("directions which George should follow")
   b. Helen left directions for George to fóllow.
   ("directions telling George to follow")

If we assume that "normal" stress contours are assigned by a rule which weakens by one degree all stresses except for the last primary stress in a string, Bresnan's assumption that the stress rules are in the transformational cycle predicts the right stress patterns as follows (1 = primary stress; 2, 3 . . . = successively weaker stresses):

```
        1    1    1        1     1     1
(9)  [Helen left [directions [for George to follow directions]  ]  ]
     S        NP       S                               S NP S
                       [     2     2     1     ]         First cycle:
                       S                       S         stress
              [                          Ø     ]         Second cycle:
              NP                               NP        syntactic
                                                         deletion
     [  2    2    1        3     3           ]           Third cycle:
     S                                       S           stress
        1    1    1        1     1
(10) [Helen left [directions [for George to follow]  ]  ]
     S        NP       S                   S NP S
                       [     2     1     ]               First cycle:
                       S                 S               stress
              [  2             3     1     ]             Second cycle:
              NP                         NP              stress
     [  2    2    3        4     1           ]           Third cycle:
     S                                       S           stress
```

The cyclical derivation in (9) gives the correct stress difference because the word which is most highly stressed in the first cycle is deleted in the second cycle, so that the rightmost 1 stress comes to be further to the left. In (10) no syntactic deletion affects the stress pattern.

Note that in both cases the dependence is unidirectional. This appears to be true in general: phonological rules must be able to look at the syntactic derivation, but syntactic rules need never look at the phonological derivation. (Some cases which may marginally contradict this generalization are thoroughly examined in Zwicky [1969], who there concludes that they are not real counterexamples.) A more recent challenge to it is presented in Cook [1971]. The assumption is built into the theory of generative grammar by assigning to phonology the role of an interpretive component of the grammar, whose input is the set of representations generated by the syntactic component.

There is at least one type of interrelationship between phonology and semantics which is not strictly compatible with the standard versions of generative grammar. This is the phenomenon of sound symbolism, which plays a minor role in the lexicon of languages, especially in affective vocabulary, and is systematically exploited in the grammar of a few, such as Dakota and other Siouan languages, where the triple contrast of dentals, palatoalveolars, and velars is used to form verb triplets with diminutive, normal, and augmentative meaning, respectively [Boas and Deloria, 1941; Matthews 1970]. Matthews cites the following examples:

(11) a. bláza   'torn in a straight line'
         bláža   'forced apart producing strain'
         bláǧa   'spread apart in all directions'
       b. mnúza   'makes a crunching sound'
         mnúža   'makes a crackling sound'
         mnúǧa   'makes a noise like breaking'
       c. sóta   'clear'
         šóta   'muddy'
         xóta   'gray'
       d. súza   'slightly bruised'
         šúža   'badly bruised'
         xúǧa   'fractured'
       e. ptúza   'bent'
         ptúža   'pieces cracked but not broken off'
         ptúǧa   'pieces broken off'
       f. zí   'yellow'
         ží   'tawny'
         ǧí   'brown'

This apparently has to be formulated as rules of semantic interpretation sensitive to phonetic features, as Matthews suggests, or phonological rules sensitive to semantic features of the word. Either way, some revision in the theory of grammar is required.

Given these intimate links between phonology and the rest of the system, it would be surprising if sound change were the purely agrammatical, quasi-physiological phenomenon the neogrammarians made it out to be. Observations by Labov and his collaborators suggest a vastly more intricate picture of this historical process. There is some question as to how their findings should be interpreted, but some essential points are clear. Sound change happens in two stages. It enters a language as an optional rule. The variability in the application of optional rules is at least in large measure, if not completely, determined by a complex interaction of factors, which can be divided into three groups: (1) speech performance factors (psychological state of the speaker, such as fatigue, excitement, and so on), (2) social factors (class and sex), (3) functional factors (requirements of speech production and perception). This third type involves applying the rules so as to favor easily pronounceable and easily interpretable surface forms. For example, speakers who can delete word-final [s] and [z] (for instance, Black English speakers) have been found to apply this rule more frequently after consonants than after vowels, and more frequently before consonants than before vowels (thus, rarely in *bees are* and relatively frequently in *dogs came*). The second perceptual factor calls for retention of semantically important information in surface forms and so inhibits deletion of plural *-s* as opposed to the redundant genitive or third singular markers.

At the second stage of sound changes, the rule becomes obligatory in some contexts, and ceases to be applicable in others. Generally, the context in which the rule remains in operation is one of the functional conditions, or a combination of them, which boosted its application at the first, optional stage. In societies where social differences between classes or sexes are very sharp, the division may take place along social lines, resulting in class (caste) dialects (found, for example, in India) or sex dialects ("women's speech," found in some American Indian languages and in others).

Consider an example from the history of English. The present-day rule for the plural and genitive ending in English states that a vowel [ə] or [ɪ] appears before the sibilant after [š, ž, č, ǯ, s, z]. Historically, this is a retention of the Middle English ending, whose vowel was dropped except after strident consonants. Looking back at the earlier stages of this change, we find a period of fluctuation before the emergence of the modern stable system. In the sixteenth century, vowel deletion could still take place even after strident consonants (as in Shakespeare's *my mistress' eyes*), and on the other hand, it sometimes failed to apply in the cases where it is today obligatory. The conditioning environment which was established on the modern rule is explicable in the case of stems in palatals on articulatory grounds. It serves to break up the articulatory complex clusters [šs, žz, čs, ǯz] which would arise if the suffix vowel was deleted there. In the case of stems in [s, z], deletion of the vowel would have no such consequences, for the resulting [ss, zz] would be reduced to simple [s, z] by a general rule of English phonology. This, however, would yield seemingly uninflected genitive and plural forms, such as *his horse back* (Shakespeare), with unwanted ambiguities. The inclusion of [s, z] in the context of the rule prevents such morphologically opaque forms from arising.

Not surprisingly, similar considerations hold for the lexicon. Homonymy which cannot easily be resolved in context is dysfunctional and tends to be eliminated. A well-known example is older English *let* 'hinder, prevent,' from Old English *lettan,* which was ousted by its homonymous antonym *let* 'allow.' Gilliéron discovered striking proof of this tendency in cases where the geographic area in which a word disappeared coincided with the spread of the sound change that rendered it homonymous with another word.

Language must not only remain capable of being spoken and understood with some degree of facility, it must also be mastered by each new member of a speech community. Learnability is the most important (though not the only) factor determining the type of change known as "analogy." It involves a continual ironing out of wrinkles in the linguistic system. Nonfunctional rules are dropped from the grammar, rules are generalized, exceptions are eliminated, the relation between underlying and surface forms is made more transparent. Of course, in the case of pervasive features of grammar this elimination may be a slow process. The system of strong verb inflection, and the remaining case distinctions in the pronoun, are no doubt moribund in English, and they are in fact sites of ongoing analogical change, but they are probably well-entrenched enough to linger on for a great many centuries.

Language change, then, involves an interplay of social and functional motivation, where the latter has to do with making language easier to speak, easier to understand, or easier to learn. No system could ever be optimal from any single one of these three points of view, simply because they present mutually conflicting requirements. In designing a communication system, ease of encoding, decoding, and learning cannot be increased together beyond a certain point, but it is generally possible to effect an improvement in any one at the cost of the others.

This raises the question: Why do all languages keep changing all the time? Why is an optimal structure never attained at which the three conflicting factors reach an equilibrium? There are several answers which can be suggested to this question. First, functional determinants of change interact with social ones. Society is not static, and hence language is not static either, in so far as it reflects society. It does so to a considerable extent. This is true not just in obvious cases like systems of address and politeness levels, but in sex and class differences of linguistic usage in syntax, phonology, and lexicon. Secondly, the relative weight of the functional factors is not constant. This brings about a second stratification of speech (in English, but not in all languages, to a great extent overlapping the social one) into styles depending on which functional considerations dominate. Consider, for example, speaking over the telephone with a bad connection (maximization of perceptibility), extremely rapid speech (maximization of speakability) or speaking to a three-year-old (maximization of structural simplicity, or learnability). Features of any such style may then get stereotyped use outside of the conditions that originally brought them forth (compare the hyperarticulated pronunciations, such as disyllabic *nine,* that were formerly used by telephone operators, or lexicalization of fast speech forms, such as (*one*) *o'clock,* from **of clock*). A third, and crucial reason for linguistic instability is this: it is apparently true of linguistic change that optimalization with respect to any function takes place independently of its effect on the other functions. Thus, changes in the system are locally rather than globally teleological. There is no advance guarantee that any change will not have bad side effects, which then must be corrected by further adjustments. An example of this is the case cited by Klima where phonological change results in large-scale homonymy, from which the language must extricate itself through compounding. I should add that some linguists, such as Martinet, have disputed this view of change. They hold that, other things being equal, the more homonymy a given sound change would create in a language, the less likely it is to happen. For example, a devoicing of [ž], as in *Asia,* would in this theory be more likely than a devoicing of [ǰ], as in *Ajax* (assuming both to be equally plausible from the phonetic point of view), since [č]:[ǰ] but not [š]:[ž] distinguishes a large number of words in English (*cherry: Jerry,* and so on). But this view has failed attempts to verify it statistically [King, 1967] and is considered by many linguists to be mistaken.

Language, then, evolves as a self-correcting system, without ever reaching a state of equilibrium, but also without ever deteriorating to a point where it cannot function as a fully adequate means of expression. Languages are also in principle fully adaptable to the changing uses to which they may be put. Languages become extinct for political reasons, not because of any inherent deficiencies. Thus, the evolution of language differs in important ways from the evolution of biological species.

Some linguists, such as Jespersen [1922], imagined the history of language as a continuous progress of "simplification," by which they merely meant reduction of morphology. "Primitive languages" were thought to have had very long and morphologically complete words, and English and especially Chinese were thought to be the endpoints of a fixed general line of typological development. It is certain that this view is wrong. Finno-Ugric languages are known to have built up their complex morphologies from an earlier relatively simple stage, and Indo-Europeanists are now beginning to recover a simpler morphology antedating the complex system which can be most immediately reconstructed by a comparison of Greek, Sanskrit, and other Indo-European languages. There is no general unidirectional development towards reduction of morphology. The deeper point is that it makes no sense to measure the "complexity" of a language by its morphology alone. There is no way in which English could be called 'simpler" in any overall sense than, say, Latin or Sanskrit.

Other linguists have surmised a long-range cyclical pattern in the evolution of languages [see Hodge, 1970, and Givón, 1971, for two recent formulations of this old idea]. To explain this hypothesis, we can again take Klima's example as a starting point. The language, which is basically of the "isolating" type (poor in morphology) begins to enrich its lexicon by forming large numbers of compound words. Looking at overall patterns of change, we can see as a frequent development the stereotyping of compounding into "agglutinative" (loosely attached) prefixation or suffixation, as in *friendly* from *friend-like,* or *dreadful* from *dread-full.* Agglutinative morphology is apt to develop, by sound changes obscuring the morphological units, into an analytic (fused) morphology of the type characteristic of Russian or Latin, or, in reduced form, French. Further reduction could then lead to a complete loss of morphology, that is, to a return to the initial "analytic" stage, from which the cycle would start over again.

This hypothesis presupposes that languages are neatly classifiable into typological sorts such as "isolating" or "agglutinative." But this is plainly not the case. Most languages are mixed types, and to the extent that they are, they show several kinds of development in progress simultaneously. For example, the changes proper to each of the stages in the hypothetical cycle are abundantly exemplified in the recent history of English.

References

Boas, F. and E. Deloria. 1941. Dakota grammar. *National Academy of Sciences Memoirs*, 23: 2.

Brame, M. 1974. The cycle in phonology: stress in Palestinian, Maltese, and Spanish. *Linguistic Inquiry*. 5: 39–60.

Bresnan, J. 1971. Sentence stress and syntactic transformations. *Language*, 47: 257–81.

Cook, Eung-Do. 1971. Phonological constraint and syntactic rule, *Linguistic Inquiry*, 2: 465–478.

Givón, T. 1971. Historical syntax and synchronic morphology: an archeologist's field trip. *Papers from the Seventh Regional Meeting, Chicago Linguistic Society.*

Hodge, C. T. 1970. The linguistic cycle. *Language Sciences*, No. 13.

Jespersen, O. 1922. *Language: Its Nature, Development, and Origin.* New York: Holt, Rinehart and Winston.

King, R. D. 1967. Functional load and sound change. *Language,* 43: 831–852.

Kuipers, A. 1960. *Phoneme and Morpheme in Kabardian.* The Hague: Mouton.

Matthews, G. H. 1970. Notes on Proto-Siouan continuants. *International Journal of American Linguistics*, 36: 98–109.

Selkirk, E. 1972. *The Phrase Phonology of English and French.* M.I.T. doctoral dissertation.

Zwicky, A. 1969. Phonological constraints in syntactic descriptions. *Papers in Linguistics,* 1: 411–463.

Open Discussion of the Papers of Klima and Kiparsky

Phonology in Li Jiang and in Sign Language

Li Jiang is a remarkable variant of Chinese in that perhaps every one of its five-hundred-plus possible syllables generated by its phonological rules is in itself a meaningful unit. Thus, since all syllables are lawful, there are no phonological constraints, and there can be said to be no phonology. Obviously it is rife with homonyms. Ira Hirsh asked Klima if it takes longer to say something in Li Jiang than in Mandarin or Cantonese. Klima did not know, but noted that polymorphemic words in English are pronounced more rapidly than monomorphemes, at least in terms of syllable rate. If such constraints are found in Chinese as well, perhaps Li Jiang is more "wordy." Ignatius Mattingly then suggested that the next evolutionary stage for Li Jiang is that CVCVC compounds would form whose constituents, each of which is now meaningful, would be forgotten. Klima agreed and expressed surprise that this process was not already underway.

Kiparsky then commented that phonological systems need not be related to syntactic systems in a direct fashion, and vice versa. Phonological rules may be applied later than most syntactic rules in the casting of an utterance, and thus "upstream" cognitive effects may be minimal. Li Jiang may have no phonology, but that fact may not differentiate it from other languages in terms of higher linguistic attributes.

Liberman suggested that phonology be defined in broader terms. "Sound" may not be so important as having *any* meaningless structures at all. Liberman noted that, in his opinion, Li Jiang appeared to have a phonology—all its morphemes are made up of CVs, consonants plus vowels, and both these segments are meaningless. With this redefinition in mind, he suggested that there are three interesting questions here: (*a*) is there a phonology in sign, (*b*) what effects of phonology in sign or speech are manifested "upstream" in grammar, and (*c*) what are the tradeoffs between phonology and syntax?

Ursula Bellugi, in answering the first question, suggested that there is something like phonology in sign. As an example she noted a parallel between mimicking of a foreign language in speech and in sign. A speaker of English, for example, will, when trying to repeat an utterance in a language that he or she does not know, mimic the general syllabic structure but change the phonology into English. In a similar fashion an American signer (using ASL) will, when trying to copy an unknown Chinese sign (in CSL), fashion the gesture in the "phonology" of ASL [see Bellugi and Klima, this volume]. That is, certain hand shapes and thumb positions are altered to conform to those typically found in ASL. There are certain finger positions which occur in CSL but not in ASL, and vice versa, much the way certain places of articulation and certain voice onset times occur in some spoken languages but not in others. Another point of evidence is that there appear to be vertical and sequential constraints in sign, just as in speech. Certain cheremes go together better than others, and certain signs can be combined in sequence better than others. Klima emphasized that there are no segments in sign: sign is continuous. Metaphorically speaking, however, there are parallels to be considered. One, Stokoe suggested, is that in speech a final consonant is often dropped from a CVC syllable, as Klima noted in Li Jiang. Likewise, a signer may often drop the location of a particular brief statement, changing it to an easier gesture. Perhaps there is an evolutionary trend in sign (as suggested by Bellugi and Klima, this volume) which parallels phonological simplifications in speech.

Kiparsky had already spoken to Liberman's second and third questions, but there was general interest in how phonological and syntactic rules contribute to ease or difficulty in learning a language. Kiparsky dispelled the myth that all languages are equally easy to learn. Some are more difficult than others; for example, Navajo is more difficult than English, which is in turn more difficult than Spanish, even in first-language acquisition. In English, the less motivated phonological rules such as changing the [t] in *illiterate* to an [s] in *illiteracy* are late in coming. Some tense and gender agreements in languages such as Russian are not learned until very late, if at all. Fodor then noted that distinctions should be made between rules which are crucial, which are mastered by all members of a dialect group, and those which are more like icing on the cake. Moreover, perhaps one should not judge rate of acquisition against the standard of the adult dialect, but against the standard of internal consistency in a regularized dialect. In such cases differences between languages should disappear. Kiparsky maintained that differences might then still exist; for example, a Creole language would probably be easier to learn than some of the more regular Latinate languages.

Parallels in Phonological and Semantactic Organization

JOHN ROBERT ROSS

1

Until quite recently, I think it would be fair to have characterized the greater part of research in generative grammar—both in phonology and in semantax (this latter term being meant to describe a blended system concerned both with meaning and with form)—as a linguistic analog of deep-sea biology.

Why do I say that? Well, in my unburdened-by-facts-or-first-hand-experience conception of what the deep-sea biologist does, I picture him sitting in a ship anchored over, let us say, the Mindanao Trench armed with a basketlike trap and miles of cable. The trap is lowered into the deeps, and after an appropriate length of time, it is cautiously winched up to the surface again, whereupon its contents—weird creatures with huge jaws, or with hugely extendible stomachs, or with their own portable lanterns—are oohed and ahed at by all aboard.

In generative grammar, it was much the same. The analogy to cable and basket was the concept of *underlying structure,* or *source,* a concept arising from Zellig Harris's work in the 1950s on kernelization (see Harris [1957, 1965] for some details), but given added impetus in phonology by Halle, and in syntax by Chomsky. In the hunt for sources, a number of wondrous phonological and semantactic creatures came to light: for instance, α-switching rules, rule features, cycles, linking rules, NP*'s, distinctness conventions, Chomsky adjunctions, morpheme-structure rules, root transformations, feedings and bleedings, connections between meaning and more superficial levels of representations, and so on, and so on. This list is representative, perhaps, but it is orders of magnitude too short.

And during this collecting and gathering phase of generative grammar, it was often only possible to say "This type of beast appears to exist"—it was not possible to give any explanation as to why such beasts, and not other ones, should be being discovered. Why, for example, should α-switching rules [Chomsky and Halle, 1968] or rule features [Lakoff, 1970] exist at all?

Let me emphasize that by referring to this congeries of conceptual structures from linguistic theory as "beasts," I do not in the least disparage their discovery—far from it. I have stumbled on many strange beasts myself, still do,[1] and hope to continue to in the future. I *do* know, from first-hand experience, how hard it is to describe any single one of

---

[1] My present research on squishy grammar is a case in point. See Ross [1973].

them, and my sense of wonder at their intricacy, variety, and beauty grows constantly.

But now that generative grammar's bestiary has the impressive population that it does, more and more scholars are beginning to ask the *why* questions which the inherent difficulty of the task of description had necessitated postponing until now.[2] To wit, why should there be phonological rules? Why should there be transformations? The second section of this paper will be concerned with such teleological questions, and the third with pointing up some parallels between the phonological and the semantactic areas of the bestiary.

2

To the first question—"why phonology?"—I will have little that is novel to say. Here, probably because a high level of detail for phonological descriptions has been available for decades longer than anything comparable in syntax, the traditional answer seems so obviously right, in its broad outlines at least, as to require almost no comment.

This answer is that most types of phonological processes—assimilations, neutralizations, epentheses, deletions, metatheses—are to be explained on the basis of a need to adapt what we have to communicate to the structure of what he have to wiggle. For to simplify a language is merely an encoding of concepts into a sequence of movements—in oral speech, movements of the vocal tract; and in the visual language of the deaf, movements of the hands, arms, and head. There are some things that our vocal tract can do easily (like producing a sequence of obstruents which are either all voiced or all unvoiced), and some things that it either cannot do, or can do only with great effort (like producing a string of obstruents of alternating voicelessness). Physiological reasons can often be found for these difficulties, as well as acoustic and perceptual ones. Thus, the fact that oral phonologies the world over tend to output CVCV sequences[3] is understandable articulatorily (it's easy to open and close your mouth), acoustically (consonants and vowels are maximally distinct in acoustic terms), and perceptually (it's easy to hear someone opening and shutting his mouth).

The study of visual phonology—the way visual signs become smoothed and coarticulated in order to provide an easy-to-do-and-see chain of body movements—is just beginning, but many fascinating results have already

---

[2] It is of course too far to crass to say that no previous research in generative grammar has addressed itself to such questions. We are dealing here only with matters of emphasis.

[3] Where C stands for consonant, and V for vowel.

emerged (see, for example, Frishberg [1973] and Battison [1974] and the articles cited therein), and it is to be expected that this field will have a tremendous impact on oral phonology. One question that we can now raise, but not answer is this one: what corresponds to CVCV in visual phonology?

To say that ease of saying and hearing is one of the primary answers to the "why phonology?" question is not to deny that there are other factors—such as the drive for regular morphological paradigms—that play important roles. But for the present paper, I will not go into these others. Instead, let us turn to the second question: why semantax?

To reformulate slightly, who do we not perform our phonological streamlinings, our CVCVings, directly on semantic structures? Why do we not merely assign some random noises to all of the parts of the conceptual structures that constitute our messages and just send them through our phonologies? Why go to all the trouble of moving constituents around; adding and deleting small change elements like prepositions, cases, and complementizers; deleting and collapsing, creating ambiguities in the process? Thus note that *old men and old women* can become *old men and women,* even though this latter can have a reading (namely "women and old men") which the former could not.

While we are a long way from being able to answer teleological questions for all syntactic processes, I would like to suggest in this paper that the four principles I will single out here have a wide range of applications.

(1)   Four Bases of Semantactic Explanation
       A. Lazy Tongue
       B. Fat Things to the Outside
       C. Old Things First
       D. Clause Crunching

2.1 LAZY TONGUE

This principle is just a rewording of the injunction "Be concise." When something has already been said somewhere in a discourse, we can often avoid repeating it. Thus (2) can be answered by (3a), or more lazily by (3b).

(2)   When are you coming back?
(3)   a. I'm coming back on Tuesday.
       b. Tuesday.

Other processes can apply to remove the parenthesized portions of the sentences in (4)–(8) below:

(4)   I saw him outside and (I saw) her inside.
(5)   Though (he is) not yet completely stewed, Jake is feeling no pain.
(6)   They are more obnoxious than I thought (they were).
(7)   Harold began cutting the cheese, and Jason finished (cutting the cheese).
(8)   They said that he might have been fondled, and he might (have been fondled).
       (have been).
       (have).
       (_____).

Note that other principles will be necessary to specify exactly how laziness can operate to shorten sentences. Other things being equal, we might expect (8) to have yet other variants—say, one in which just the second occurrence of *fondled,* or just the second *might,* or just the second *been* was deleted. Yet as the ungrammaticalities of (9a), (9b), and (9c), respectively, show us, this is not possible.

(9)   a.   *They said that he might have been fondled, and he might have been being _____.
       b.   *They said that he might have been being fondled, and he _____ have been being fondled.
       c.   *They said that he might have been being fondled, and he might have _____ being fondled.

The generalization that seems to govern this kind of deletion is that it works from the bottom up, if we view *might* as superordinate to *have,* *have* to *been,* *been* to *being,* and *being* to *fondled.* That is, in this process, which is sometimes called VP Deletion, at least the two most subordinate items—*being* and *fondled*—must be deleted, with other superordinate items deletable only if all of their subordinates have been.

For a final example of the laziness of the tongue, consider (10).

(10)   Bill claims to want to avoid going to Moscow, and Sam claims to want to avoid going to Rome.

Here, the most subordinate verb is *going* (V_4). The next one up is *to avoid* (V_3), with *to want* (V_2) superordinate to it, and *claims* (V_1) superordinate to all others. If we call *Bill* the first subject ($Subj_1$), *Sam* the second subject ($Subj_2$), *to Moscow* the first object (Obj_1), and *to Rome* the second object (Obj_2), (10) has the schematic structure shown in (11).

(11) $Subj_1 + V_1 + V_2 + V_3 + V_4 + Obj_1$ *and*
        $Subj_2 + V_1 + V_2 + V_3 + V_4 + Obj_2$.

Note that we have the same chain of verbs—$V_1 \cdot \cdot \cdot V_4$—in both clauses, so our tongue looks for a lazy way out. The rule involved here has been called Gapping (see Ross [1970] for some discussion of this process); some successful and unsuccessful results of applying it can be seen in (12).

(12)   a. Bill claims to want to avoid going to Moscow, and Sam to Rome. ($Subj_1 + V_1 + V_2 + V_3 + V_4 + Obj$ *and* $Subj_2$ _____ Obj_2).
        b. Bill claims to want to avoid going to Moscow, and Sam going to Rome. ($Subj_1 + V_1 + V_2 + V_3 + V_4 + Obj_1$ *and* $Subj_2$ _____ $V_4 + Obj_2$).
        c. Bill claims to want to avoid going to Moscow, and Sam to avoid going to Rome. ($Subj_1 + V_1 + V_2 + V_3 + V_4 + Obj_1$ *and* $Subj_2$ _____ $V_3 + V_4 + Obj_2$).
        d. Bill claims to want to avoid going to Moscow, and Sam to want to avoid going to Rome. ($Subj_1 + V_1 + V_2 + V_3 + V_4 + Obj_1$ *and* $Subj_2$ _____ $V_2 + V_3 + V_4 + Obj_2$).
        e. *Bill claims to want to avoid going to Moscow, and Sam claims to avoid to Rome. ($Subj_1 + V_1 + V_2 + V_3 + V_4 + Obj_1$ *and* $Subj_2 + V_1$ _____ V_3 _____ Obj_2).
        f. *Bill claims to want to avoid going to Moscow, and Sam to want going to Rome. ($Subj_1 + V_1 + V_2 + V_3 + V_4 + Obj_1$ *and* $Subj_2$ _____ V_2 _____ $V_4 + Obj_2$).
        g. *Bill claims to want to avoid going to Moscow, and Sam claims to avoid going to Rome. ($Subj_1 + V_1 + V_2 + V_3 + V_4 + Obj_1$ *and* $Subj_2 + V_1$ _____ $V_3 + V_4 + Obj_2$).[4]

The laziest rewording of sentence (10) is found in (12a), where the entire verb chain is deleted in the second statement. Notice, however, that this is not the only option open to the speaker: (12b)–(12d) are also possible. The legitimate paraphrases of sentence (10) (with verbs

_____
[4] I have starred (12g) not because it is ungrammatical on all readings, but rather because it is not a gapped version of (10).

1-2-3-4) contain verb chains of 2-3-4, 3-4, 4 alone, or none. Sentences containing Verbs 1 and 3 (12e), 2 and 4 (12f), or 1, 3, and 4 (12g) are not acceptable paraphrases of (10). Thus, Gapping seems to operate in the opposite "direction" from VP Deletion. For here, a subordinate verb can be gapped only if all verbs superordinate to it have been. As yet, no one knows why sentences (12e–12g) should not be legitimate paraphrases; but clearly they are not.

Thus, we have seen that the principle of Lazy Tongue may well explain why such deletion processes should exist at all; but at the same time, it has been made clear that there are many idiosyncrasies about each kind of deletion which will be explicable only on the basis of additional, less gross, principles; principles which have to date, in fact, resisted adequate formulation.

2.2 FAT THINGS TO THE OUTSIDE

The second principle is analogous to centrifuging the constituents within an utterance. There are many syntactic processes which have the effect of removing awkward, or "heavy," constituents from an internal position. The relocations are to the front or to the rear. Consider the following set of sentences:

(13)   a. I consider that you fainted unfortunate.
       b. That you fainted I consider unfortunate.
       c. That you fainted, I consider it unfortunate.
       d. I consider it unfortunate that you fainted.

Although sentence (13a) is intelligible, it is somewhat indigestible. Somehow, *that you fainted* does not read well in the middle of the statement *I consider———unfortunate*. It is just too cumbersome, too fat to remain. There are at least three ways to remedy this situation. The first is to move the phrase to the front of the sentence by a rule of Topicalization, as in (13b). A second method is to replace the phrase with *it* and again move the bulky constituent to the front, as in (13c). The third and probably the most common remedy for (13a) is found in (13d), where the phrase is moved to the end of the sentence by a rule of Extraposition, with the pronoun *it* remaining behind as a kind of place marker. Regardless of which remedy we use, we seem to be motivated to get fat things (unwieldy constituents) to the outside.

This kind of centrifuging, which shows up in many languages, is doubtless to be explained on the basis of whatever kind of processing algorithm is used when a hearer starts to figure out the structure of a sentence. There must be something difficult about interrupting the process of parsing a clause to restart the same process.

2.3 OLD THINGS FIRST

This is a short way of stating a law that was discovered by Vilem Mathesius, one of the founders of the Prague Linguistic Circle. In comparing Czech translations of English texts with their originals, Mathesius noted that though Czech is a "free word order" language—that is, a language in which the major elements of clauses can be permuted in (almost) any order—when translating a particular English sentence in a particular discourse context, only certain orders of the elements were possible. The other logically possible orders would not be ungrammatical, merely bad translations. Separating the constituents of a sentence into two groups, the *theme* (those constituents that had been mentioned earlier in the discourse) and the *rheme* (that which was new information), Mathesius's basic law was that in unemphatic, normal word order, the theme must precede the rheme. As an example, consider the discourse fragment in (14):

(14)   It had been a lousy morning. Bill had woken up late, he had gotten a nasty letter from the IRS, and then he cooked his egg twenty minutes too long in the excitement. Then to top it all off . . . .

(15)   a. My pet cobra, Coral, bit him.
        b. He was bitten by my pet cobra, Coral.

While (15a) could be used to complete (14), (15b) would be more natural—smoother. This is because *he* = (*Bill*) is the theme of (15), and *my pet cobra, Coral* is rhematic.

Mathesius's law—the principle that old things come first—explains why (15b) is better than (15a), after (14), and, as Mathesius noted, it can also be used to explain an interesting fact about Slavic languages. Though these languages have a passive voice for sentences, it is seldom used, while English passives are extremely common. Mathesius explains this by noting that since English has a fixed word order, the only way it can shape its sentences so that they will be in conformance with the unmarked theme-rheme order is by making use of grammatical transformations, like the rule of Passive, which allows the rheme-theme (15a) to become the smoother theme-rheme (15b). But since Slavic languages have free word order anyway, they have no need of such additional reordering processes as Passive.

This line of explanation for reorderings of various kinds has generated a great deal of research, far too much for me to review here. The Prague Circle name for this area was *functional sentence perspective*—that is, the sentence viewed from the perspective of its function. An extremely important application of functional sentence perspective to the thorny problem of pronominalization, with a demonstration of the explanatory value of such theme-rheme considerations for detailed problems of analyses in a non-Indo-European language, Japanese, is given in Kuno [1972].

2.4 CLAUSE CRUNCHING

The fourth general principle that I will discuss is the following: presumably because single clauses are the semantactic equivalent of the phonological target CVCV, many processes exist which crunch two clauses into one. While the scope of this paper does not permit a justification of the following derivations, in fact, arguments can be given that in each of (16)–(21), the a version is more basic, with the b version being derived from it by some semantactic rule.

Whiz Deletion
(16)   a. [I know someone [who is tall.]]
          S_1 S_2
                                    $\Downarrow$
       b. [I know someone tall.]
          S_1

Possessive Formation
(17)   a. [A car [that he has] was at the corner.]
          S_1 S_2
                  $\Downarrow$
       b. [A car of his was at the corner]
          S_1

Raising and To Be Deletion
(18)   a. [I want [for you to be satisfied.]]
          S_1 S_2
                    $\Downarrow$
       b. [I want you satisfied.]
          S_1

Have Deletion
(19)   a. [I want [to have a bagel.]]
          S_1 S_2
                    $\Downarrow$
       b. [I want a bagel.]
          S_1

Slifting, Adverbialization
(20)   a. [It is alleged [that he dallied with Big Lew's board.]]
          S_1 $\Downarrow$ S_2

       b. [He dallied with Big Lew's board, allegedly.]
          S_1

Conjunction Reduction
(21) a. [I read *TIME* yesterday] and [I read *SPACE* yesterday].
      S_1 $\Downarrow$ S_2
      b. [I read *TIME* and *SPACE* yesterday.]
      S_1

In each of these cases, two clauses are fused into one, as indicated informally by the use of brackets. What is of interest is that it appears that there exists no case of the reverse process—a one-clause structure becoming a two-clause one. Presumably, then, the basis for this asymmetry will be found to lie within the structure of the processing algorithm: single clause sentences must be in some way easier to understand than multiple-clause sentences.

2.5
By and large, the bases of explanation in phonology and semantax seem to be quite similar. In phonology, the primary basis is *movability*—whether of vocal tract in oral phonology, or of hand, arms, and head in visual phonology. In semantax, it is clear that the deletions and shortenings stemming from the Lazy Tongue and Clause-crunching principles are aids to pronounceability—the less said, the easier. However, while it seems a fairly safe bet that sentences containing Fat Things in their interior or having many surface clauses are hard to *perceive,* there is as yet no evidence that they are harder to *say.* There are parallels to phonology here, too—phonological rules often seem to operate in such a way that their output will be easier to perceive than their input would have been (see Kiparsky [1972; this volume] for some examples).

The only principle in section 2 for which I can at present see no phonological analog is Old Things First.

3
In this section I will no longer be concerned with teleology. Instead, I will point out some rather apparent formal parallels between phonological and semantactic systems.

3.1
The first thing to note is that the processes in each kind of system must apply in a fixed order.[5] Thus dialects can differ phonologically with respect to the order in which their rules apply, and also semantactically.

[5] I hereby waffle on the question, which is presently being hotly debated, as to whether statements of extrinsic rule ordering are necessary in the grammars

A phonological example is the following. Many dialects of black English differ from white English in allowing a final consonant to be deleted. Thus, *test* is pronounced [tɛs]. There is a split among dialects of black English as to whether this consonant deletion happens before or after impermissible final clusters are broken up by an epenthesis rule, which inserts an [ə]. Thus, derivations for the plural form *tests* proceed as shown in (22) and (23).

(22)   Underlying form: /tɛst#s/
        Consonant Deletion: /tɛs #s/
        Epenthesis: /tɛs#əs/
        Output: [tɛsəz]
(23)   Underlying form: /tɛst#s/
        Epenthesis: (Does not apply—environment not met)
        Consonant Deletion: /tɛs #s/
        Output: [tɛs]

Such examples, which could be multiplied indefinitely, show the necessity of making it possible to specify that phonological rules apply in different orders in different dialects.

In semantax, the application of rules in different orders can also produce dialect differences. Consider the following set of statements:

(24)   a. He is smarter than I am.
        b. He is smarter than I.
        c. He is smarter than me.

The rule for the appearance of nominative pronouns such as *he* and *I* is, roughly, that they are the first constituent of a clause. In sentence (24a), *I am* is a clause, so a nominative pronoun appears. But this second clause in (24a) can be declaused, yielding (24b) or (24c). Just as in the phonological case in (22)–(23), these two sentences differ in the order in which the two semantic processes of Case Marking and Comparative Deletion are applied. In (24b), Case Marking occurs before Comparative Deletion, the rule that deletes *am* and declauses *I*, whereas in (24c), pruning applies before Case Marking, as can be seen in (25) and (26), respectively.

---

of particular languages, or whether all necessary rule orderings can be predicted on universal grounds. For the relatively minor formal similarity I wish to demonstrate here, the outcome of this controversy is not relevant.

(25)   Remote structure: [He is smrter [than I am.]]

S_1 S_2

Case Marking: $\begin{bmatrix} \text{He} \\ +\text{Nom} \end{bmatrix}$ $\begin{bmatrix} \text{I} \\ +\text{Nom} \end{bmatrix}$

Comparative
Deletion: [He is smarter than I.] = (24b)

S_1

(26)   Remote structure: [He is smarter [than I am.]]

S_1 S_2

Comparative
Deletion: [He is smarter than I.]

S_1

Case Marking: $\begin{bmatrix} \text{He} \\ +\text{Nom} \end{bmatrix}$ $\begin{bmatrix} \text{I} \\ +\text{Oblique} \end{bmatrix}$

Output: (24c)

3.2

The second parallel between phonological and semantactic processes is the following: not only must they be capable of being specified for the order in which they apply, but they must also both be capable of being applied cyclically, or recursively. Consider the phonological ramifications in the stress subordination of *remonophthongization*, to use an extreme example. The bracketing of this word is shown schematically in diagram (27):

(27)   [# [re# [mono + phthong] #ize]] # ation]
                     N   V V   N

To this underlying structure, cyclical stress rules apply in the following way.

First, rules of primary stress assignment place main stress on the unbracketed sequence of phones in (27), placing one occurrence of [1 Stress] in each subsequence of the form #X#, where X contains no occurrences of #. Thus, we get:

(28)   #re# mono + phthong # ize # ation #

The innermost constituent of this word is *monophthong*, which is produced from the representation in (29a) by a stress retraction rule which assigns

[1 Stress] to the leftmost vowel in the word, thereby automatically lowering all other stresses within the domain being stressed by one degree, producing (29b).

(29) a. [mono + phthong]
               1 N   Primary stress rule
      b. 1   2   Stress retraction

             1
On the next cycle, *ize* is "added to" (29b), as it were, and (30) is the resulting input.

               2   1
(30) [[mono + phthong] # ize]
                    N   V
       1   2   1

To this, a cyclical stress rule reassigns [1 Stress] to the leftmost occurrence of [1 Stress], with the resultant weakening of the other stresses in (31).[6]

(31) [[mono + phthong] # ize]
                    N   V
       1   3   2

Note that just as (29b) shows a pronunciation of *monophthong* in isolation that is roughly correct, phonetically (but see Chomsky and Halle [1968] for a fuller account), so (31) also gives a roughly correct pronunciation of *monophthongize*, in isolation.
               1
Now, when *re#* is "added" to (31), (32) results:

(32) [re # [[mono + phthong] # ize]]
                          N   VV
       1   1   3   2

To this structure, Chomsky and Halle's Nuclear Stress Rule applies, reassigning [1 Stress] to the *right*most occurrence of [1 Stress], with the

---

[6] This restressing is a generalized version of Chomsky and Halle's [1968] Compound Rule.

concomitant weakening of the other stresses shown in (33):

(33)   [re # [[mono + phthong] # ize]]
                          N   VV
       2   1   4   3

Again, this contour seems to be correct, in its essentials, as an account of the pronunciation in isolation of *remonophthongize*.
                                  1
Finally, when *#ation* is "added on," producing (34),

(34)   [[re # [[mono + phthong] # ize]] ation]
                           N   VV   N
       2   1   4   3   1

the Nuclear Stress Rule is applied one final time, reassigning [1 Stress] to the rightmost [1 Stress]-bearing vowel, in this case, the vowel of the suffix
 1
#ation. The result is (35).

(35)   [[re # [[mono + phthong] # ize]] #ation]
                           N   VV   N
       3   2   5   4   1

Again, the resultant contour is roughly on target, with the exception that it assigns a greater stress to *ize* than to *phthong,* which seems wrong to my ear. At present, however, I do not know how to modify these rules, or add new ones, to produce the observed result.

   Nonetheless, for our present purposes, the force of the example should be clear. The important fact of this derivation is that the two stressing rules—the Compound Rule and the Nuclear Stress Rule—apply to each other's output, working from an inner piece of the word outward, with the sequence of "additions" being controlled by the bracketing shown in (27). In summary form, the derivation proceeds as shown in (36).

(36)   [[re # [[mono + phthong] #ize]] #ation]
                           N   VV   N

1		1	1	1	Primary Stress
	1	2			Stress Retraction
	1	3	2		Compound Rule
2	1	4	3		Nuclear Stress Rule
3	2	4	5	1	Nuclear Stress Rule

For a semantactic parallel in recursive rule application, where rules apply to inner constituents before outer ones, consider George Lakoff's celebrated sentence about bagels [Lakoff, 1967]:

(37)   Irving expects that Max will believe that Seymour has eaten the bagel.

(38)

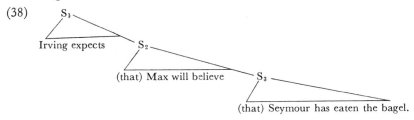

Here, two sentences are imbedded in a higher one, as suggested in the rough underlying structure shown in (38). For reasons of functional sentence perspective, we can front *the bagel* by the Passive transformation and the process of Raising:

(39)   a. Irving expects that Max will believe that the bagel has been eaten by Seymour.
          [from (38), by passivizing S₃]
       b. Irving expects that Max will believe the bagel to have been eaten by Seymour.
          [from (39a), by raising *the bagel* to make it a derived object of *believe*]
       c. Irving expects that the bagel will be believed by Max to have been eaten by Seymour.
          [from (39b), by passivizing S₂]
       d. Irving expects the bagel to be believed by Max to have been eaten by Seymour.
          [from (39c), by raising *the bagel* to make it a derived object of *expects*]
       e. The bagel was expected by Irving to be believed by Max to have been eaten by Seymour.
          [from (39d), by passivizing S₁]

The passivization/raising process for the sentence transformation from (38) to (39b) is suggested in diagram (40).

(40)

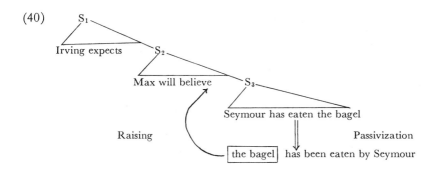

Such a process, when applied recursively, can front *the bagel* from its position as last constituent in sentence (37) to first position in (39e). A schematic illustration of this derivation may make this point clear, in (41).

(41)   Cycle 1 (S₃):   Passivize *eat*.
        Cycle 2 (S₂):   Raise the derived subject of S₃, *the bagel*, into the object of *believe*. Passivize *believe*.
        Cycle 3 (S₁):   Raise the derived subject of S₂, *the bagel*, into the object of *expects*. Passivize *expects*.

Again, we see a set of rules operating first on an innermost clause, then on clauses superordinate to that one, with the order of application being determined by the bracketing imposed by the sentence being processed. And just as it makes sense to say that the stress contour of *remonophthongization* "contains," or "is a product of," the stress contour of *monophthong* in isolation—thus note that in both, *mon* bears a higher stress than *thong*—so also it makes sense to say that sentence (39e) "contains" or "is a product of" the output of the first cycle of (41), which, if the derivation were to stop there, would produce (42).

(42)   The bagel was eaten by Seymour.

Many facts about (42) are "reflected" by facts about (39e)—thus note that in both, the *by* phrase must precede *eaten:*

(43)   *The bagel was by Seymour eaten.

and that the old subject of *eaten* shows up with the preposition *by*, instead of the *to* which can show up with *know* (44), and so on.

(44)   a. This was known $\begin{Bmatrix} by \\ to \end{Bmatrix}$ them.

     b. This was eaten $\begin{Bmatrix} by \\ *to \end{Bmatrix}$ them.

In short, just as the stresses of big words are (often) cyclically made up of the stresses of little words in them, so also is the syntax of big sentences cyclically made up of the syntaxes of their component clauses.

3.3

A third parallel in the rule structures of phonology and semantax is the occurrence of conspiracies. Conspiracies are groups of rules which are superficially quite different, but which have the same "target" in mind, in a way that is somewhat analogous to convergent evolution in biology. In English phonology, for example, there is a liquid conspiracy, whose function is to prevent two occurrences of the same liquid (either two [r]s or two [l]s) from occurring too close to each other.

First, there appears to be an attempt to avoid having the same liquid occur twice in the same syllable in a morpheme. Two [l]s appear to make uncomfortable morpheme mates, and, likewise, [r]-[r] combinations tend to be avoided. Thus, for example, while there are words such as *frill* and *flurry*, there are few words of the form **flill* and **frurry*. Of course, words such as *flail*, *lull*, *frier,* and *roar* do exist, but in general there seems to be a ban on such sequences.

In addition to this constraint on the classes of allowable segment sequences that can constitute English morphemes, there is a phonological rule which *changes* an underlying /l/ to an [r] in precisely such a way as to avoid the uncomfortable homoglottal liquid sequence [l . . . l]. This process operates on the output of the morphological rule which adds the morpheme *-al* to nouns and stems in order to make the appropriate adjective. Thus, *person* becomes *person + al*, and *minim + um* becomes *minim + al*. Obviously, this does not work for all noun stems, because *module* becomes *modular,* not **modulal;* and the adjective pertaining to the moon is *lunar*, not **lunal*. Similarly with **tabul + al → tabul + ar,* **pol + al → pol + ar, *stell + al → stell + ar,* and so on. Note that this process is formally of a quite different nature from the template, or filter, that rejects **flill*. There is no evidence that there exists a rule which changes **flill* to *flir,* while there is evidence, gained from words which do not contain [1], that the underlying form of the propheme is -*al*, not -*ar*, as suggested by the words in (45).

(45)   parental, anecdotal, pivotal, social

The generalization is that this morpheme never assumes the shape -*ar* except when following a word containing an [l]. Thus we postulate a *process* that changes [l] to [r] in these cases. What makes this a conspiracy is that both the morpheme structure filter and this phonological process cahoot to yield surface strings which do not manifest homoglottal liquid sequences.

Yet a third place where the conspiracy rears its head is in the restriction on the verbal affix -*al*. Briefly, this suffix can be added only to final-stressed verbs *which do not contain an* [l]. Thus, *refuse* goes to *refusal*, *avow* to *avowal*, *arrive* to *arrival*, *acquit* to *acquittal*, *refer* to *referral* and *try* to *trial*, but *apply* cannot go to **applial*, nor *collide* to **collidal*, nor *repel* to **repellal*. Note that **applial* is not "saved" by changing the final [l] to [r]—the form is irrevocably damaged.

For a final manifestation of this conspiracy, consider the behavior of the comparative suffix -*er*. While we find *smart-smarter,* and *noble-nobler,* *sober* cannot be compared as **soberer* but must appear as *more sober.* We do find *nearer, furrier, direr,* and *fairer,* but there are no cases of [. . . [consonant] + r + er]. Thus, in each of the four cases above, the liquids [l] and [r] do not appear to tolerate close proximity with replicas of themselves.

In semantax there are similar conspiracies. Consider, for example, the imperative conspiracy. For some reason, English and other languages seem to like to have sentences which start with a verb and have no subject: many quite dissimilar sources are converted by a group of conspiring rules to surface structures of the imperative form. For example, many requests or orders can show up in this form:

(46)   a. Go home.
        b. Go home, please.
        c. Go home, won't you.
        d. Go home, or else.

Another input to this imperative conspiracy is seen in sentences which are logically equivalent to conditionals (*if*/*then*) sentences.

(47) a. Have any fun, and the cops hate you.
          (= If you have any fun, then the cops hate you.)
      b. *Have any fun, and the cops hate you please.
      c. *Have any fun, and the cops hate you or else.

Notice that sentence (47a) is similar in appearance to sentences (46–46d). We can see, however, that it is not a true imperative, because if it were, (47b) and (47c) would be grammatical.

A third type of imperativelike sentence is found in statements which Postal has called dreckatives, such as:

(48) a. Go to hell./Ram it./Take gas./.
      b. *Go to hell, please.
      c. *Go to hell and the cops hate you.
(49) a. (Don't) have any fun, and the cops hate you.
      b. (*Don't) go to hell / ram it / take gas /.

Although (48a) has an imperative form, and may seem similar to either (46a) or (47a), sentences (48b) and (48c) show it to be different from either true imperatives, like those in (46), or from *if/then* imperatives, like those in (47a). The contrast in (49) indicates that while either true imperatives or *if/then* imperatives like those in (47) can be negative, dreckatives cannot. These three imperative types thus have partially similar surface forms, but they come from very different underlying representations, and have only minimal syntactic overlap. Here we see semantactic conspiracy guiding the production of similar surface forms, just as phonological conspiracies guide us to avoid (or hit) certain phonological targets. While we can hazard a phonetic guess as to why there should be a liquid conspiracy, for neighboring [l]s and neighboring [r]s seem difficult for the English tongue to produce, we have no idea why there should be an imperative conspiracy.

3.4

The fourth parallel is related, in an inverse way, to conspiracies. Consider the conditions under which liquids do and do not conspire. They appear to conspire within a word; thus *module* becomes *modular*. However, two-word phrases such as *small lemon* and *fatter ram,* do not become *small remon* and *fatter lam,* or *smar lemon* and *fattle ram.* Thus, the liquid conspiracy does not work across word boundaries.

In an analogous fashion, semantactic rules often do not apply across clause boundaries. This, in a rough sense, is an effect of the Primacy

Constraint. As an example of this constraint, consider the process of reflexivization in English, which is shown in sentences (50).

(50) a. He washed him.
      b. He washed himself.

English speakers must distinguish between coreferential and noncoreferential pronouns within clauses: *him* is noncoreferential with *he,* while *himself* is necessarily coreferential. In some African languages, on the other hand, sentences with meanings like (50a) and (50b) have the same syntactic form; no distinction is drawn between obligatory coreference and obligatory noncoreference. A single pronoun can be used to express either meaning.

In English, we must make such distinctions within a clause but cannot make them across clauses. Consider:

(51) a. He believes that he knows everything.
      b. *He believes that himself knows everything.

Statement (51a) is ambiguous. We cannot be sure if there are two individuals referred to here or just one. Furthermore, (51b), an attempt at disambiguating the first sentence, is not grammatical. In Japanese, on the other hand, the equivalent of (51b) would be entirely grammatical. In other words, reflexivization in Japanese can extend across clause boundaries, whereas in English it cannot.

Interestingly, there is not language which is the inverse of English in this respect: such a language would be able to make the distinction between obligatory coreference and obligatory noncoreference across clauses, but not within clauses. This constellation of facts with respect to reflexivization appears to follow from a general principle—the Primacy Constraint.

(52) The Primacy Constraint
      Elements of one clause *have primacy over* elements of clauses subordinate to this clause, and, while processes may be constrained to apply only within clause boundaries, no process may by constrained to apply only across clause boundaries.
      (See Ross [in press] for other examples of primacy.)

Why should English not have the power in reflexivization that Japanese has? It is as if the clause boundary poses an impenetrable barrier to the process of making *he* into *himself*. We have no idea why this is so. This constraint, however, may be intimately related to the notion of Clause Crunching which was mentioned earlier. For if single clauses are less marked semantactically than multiple clause structures, we can imagine that some semantactic processes will have the "zip" to penetrate into marked semantactic areas—will be able to cross semantactic barriers— while others will have too little "zip" to leave their own clauses. Japanese reflexivization would appear to have more zip than English reflexivization.

It is at present not clear to me what the precise phonological analog to (52) is. A first approximation is stated in (53) :

(53)   Phonological processes that apply from within one word to the inside of another can also apply within any word. While processes can be constrained to apply only within word boundaries, no process may be constrained only across word boundaries.

The problem with (53) is that there are many processes of external sandhi—processes which affect the beginning or end of a word under the influence of the immediately contiguous segments of the adjoining word. Thus, in French, word-final consonants delete if the following word begins with a consonant, but remain if it begins with a vowel: *petit̸ garçon* but *petit ami*. What (53) is intended to rule out is a process, say nasalization, in which a nasal would cause all vowels in an adjoining word to be nasalized, but which would not affect the vowels of its own word.

If no such processes exist, and I know of none at present, then we would have an extremely interesting analogy between the clause in seman- tax and the word in phonology. Terry Langendoen, who first suggested this possibility to me, also pointed out that a further phonological unit which may be found to bear functional analogies to the clause is the syllable, particularly in view of the way in which Stampe's rules of rapid speech operate. These rules, some optional, some obligatory, specify the possible phonetic shapes of syllables. After their application, words may be resyllabified, with the new syllables that result from this resyllabifica- tion also being shaped by the syllable-structure rule (see Stampe [1972] for details). This is a process that is highly reminiscent of the cyclical processes that were the topic of section 3.2. If the analogy clause = word = syllable can be maintained, it should be possible to find some generalization that is cognate to (53), but which specifies how syllable- shaping rules can and cannot affect neighboring syllables. At present, however, not enough is known in this area for such an attempt to be feasible.

4

To sum up, I have suggested above that four principles should be recognized to start us on the way to explaining why semantactic rules should be necessary. Roughly, these principles seem to make surface structures more speakable and more hearable than would be their underlying logical representations. These twin goals of speakability and hearability also seem to be desired for phonological outputs, so one parallel between phonology and semantax is a teleological one.

In section 3, I discussed some obvious and some less apparent formal parallels between the two subsystems. The rules from each system have to apply in specified orders, both kinds can cycle, and both kinds conspire to hit or avoid targets (and whatever word one might fancy to describe the opposite of a target) in their respective domains.

In my opinion the most interesting parallel of all, which is unfortunately simultaneously the most speculative one, is the one in section 3.4, in which a tentative analogy is drawn between clauses, words, and syllables—the domains of cyclical application for semantactic and phonological processes. If this last analogy can be more fully supported by future research, there will emerge a deep-running and far-reaching parallelism between both linguistic subsystems, and we will understand more fully not only that, in Ferdinand de Saussure's words, "tout se tient," but also how it does.

References

Battison, R. 1974. Phonological deletion in American Sign Language. *Sign Language Studies,* 5. The Hague: Mouton.

Chomsky, N. and M. Halle. 1968. *The Sound Pattern of English.* New York: Harper & Row.

Frishberg, N. 1973. From iconicity to arbitrariness. Paper presented at the December meeting of the Linguistic Society of America.

Harris, Z. 1957. Co-occurrence and transformations in linguistic structure. *Language,* 33: 283–340.

Harris, Z. 1965. Transformational theory. *Language,* 41: 363–407.

Kiparsky, P. 1972. Explanation in phonology. In *Goals of Linguistic Theory,* S. Peters (ed.). Englewood Cliffs, N.J.: Prentice-Hall.

Kiparsky, P. Comments on the role of phonology in language. This volume.

Kuno, S. 1972. Functional sentence perspective: a case study from Japanese and English. *Linguistic Inquiry,* 3: 269–320.

Lakoff, G. 1967. Deep and surface grammar. Unpublished paper, available from the Indiana University Linguistics Club, Bloomington, Indiana.

Lakoff, G. 1970. *Irregularity in Syntax*. New York: Holt, Rinehart and Winston.

Ross, J. R. 1970. Gapping and the order of constituents. In *Progress in Linguistics*, M. Bierwisch and K. E. Herdolph (eds.). The Hague: Mouton, 249–259.

Ross, J. R. 1973. Nouniness. In *Three Dimensions of Linguistic Theory*, O. Fujimura (ed.). Tokyo: The TEC Company, 137–257.

Ross, J. R. In press. Three batons for cognitive psychology. In *Cognition and the Symbolic Processes*. Washington, D.C.: Winston.

Stampe, D. 1972. How I spent my summer vacation. Unpublished Ph.D. dissertation (linguistics), University of Chicago.

Comments on Ross's Paper

JERRY FODOR

Ross' paper sticks pretty close to the facts and, by and large, I'm not inclined to challenge the facts he's sticking to. Nor do I want to go so far as actually to deny the inference he draws from the facts he cites: primarily that there seem to be convergences between the outputs of linguistic rules which, so far as one can tell, have nothing *but* the convergences in common; as though the rules were conspiring, by many different means, to bring about certain desired ends. To put the same point another way: derived linguistic structures are, by and large, less homogeneous than the forms that they are derived from; transformations function to produce heterogeneity of superficial structure. But derived forms are also, by and large, *less heterogeneous* than they ought to be given the implicit power of the transformations. That is, there ought to be more kinds of surface structures than there are. It looks as though some principle that the transformations do not express themselves militates to prevent the full range of surface forms that transformations could, in principle, produce. What is one to make of this?

I don't know. I so much don't know that I don't even feel confident about what the explanatory options are. The scattered remarks that follow are not, then, attempts to say what's going on; they're just an enumeration and criticism of some of the choices that one might want to consider.

1. It would be possible to argue that there is really nothing to explain. After all, to imagine a language in which every possible surface structure is well formed is ipso facto to imagine a language with a vacuous transformational component: that is a language in which any old operation on deep trees produces a phonologically interpretable derived form. Conversely, the more elaborate the transformational component is, the more kinds of surface structures it will filter out. In effect, then, for the claim to be substantive that there are indeed transformations, the transformations will have to select some set of well-formed outputs to the exclusion of others, and it will always be possible (post hoc, as it were) to impute a spurious air of teleology to the selection process. Looked at this way, the question "why are there conspiracies" is just the question "why are there transformations" since the transformational component *in toto* constitutes a conspiracy in aid of those surface structures that it generates and in opposition to those surface structures that it fails to generate. (Note that we don't think of deep structure rules as conspiracies to produce S-dominated, single-rooted, binary branching trees, and we

don't think of the morphophonology as a conspiracy to produce strings of phones. Why don't we?)

I think there's a temptation to meet this sort of argument by repeating doggedly that there is, nevertheless, less variety of surface structure than there ought to be; less than we might have expected from just looking at the kinds of rules that a grammar can contain. For all I know, there *is* something to this. But the trouble is: how do we tell if there is? How much convergence of surface structures would the transformations produce if they produced only a random amount of convergence? How much convergence counts as significant for the purposes of proving conspiracy. What is the null hypothesis in this area?

I should emphasize that the problem I'm raising isn't just the usual philosopher of science's worry about teleological explanation. That worry arises when, given a demonstrably nonrandom convergence of structures, we want to know whether the mechanisms that mediate the convergence can be characterized as *aiming* to produce it. In the linguistic case, however, we haven't even got the first step towards raising this problem since we don't know if there's enough difference between what a possible transformational grammar could produce and what actual grammars do produce to justify the claim that the output of the known grammars is significantly biased. To put the point briefly: the claim that there are conspiracies is at least the claim that there is more homogeneity of surface structure than would be predicted just from the universal constraints on transformations, whatever those constraints may be. But, of course, we don't know what those constraints are, so we aren't in a position to assess the claim.

2. It may be thought that a way out of this difficulty would be to show that the structures that grammars prefer are structures that they *ought* to prefer on nonlinguistic grounds. This would yield a nonstatistical (as it were, qualitative) ground for believing that the appearance of conspiracy is something we ought to take seriously. For example, Bever [1970] has argued that some of the transformations one finds in a language (hence some of the structures that the transformations produce) can be explained by appeal to the exigencies of the information processing mechanisms speaker/hearers use to encode/decode utterance tokens. Let's see how such an explanation might go.

Ross mentions, as one of the more striking conspiracies among syntactic rules, the phenomenon of Clause Crunching—a set of processes which take materials from a variety of distinct deep clauses and crunch them into the same surface clause. Now, it is striking that there is reason to believe that surface clauses have a special psychological role to play in the recognition/production of sentences; that they in some sense provide the processing units in terms of which sentence tokens are integrated/analyzed. I won't review the evidence for this claim here (but see Chapter 6 of Fodor, Bever, and Garrett [1974] where it is discussed extensively). So, then, on the one hand we have conspiracies on the part of the syntax to produce surface clauses wherever it can; and on the other we have a special salience of surface clauses in the sentence production/perception system. Wouldn't it be natural to explain the former fact by reference to the latter: to suggest that the grammar conspires to produce the structures which primarily engage the production/perception system, thereby improving the match between the structures that grammars enumerate and the ones that the psychological mechanisms compute?

Well, maybe. But, also, maybe not. To begin with, there has to be *some* sort of match between the structures that a grammar enumerates and the ones that the "performance" mechanisms produce/recognize or, by definition, the recognition/production system wouldn't be a recognition/production system *for that grammar*. It might, of course, be suggested that the match that actually obtains is better than it minimally needs to be, and that shows that the grammar is conspiring to placate the psychology; but, again, how good would the match have to be to be barely good enough, and *how much better* would the observed match have to be to be significantly better than the least that we could get away with? We don't know what the null hypothesis comes to for this kind of story any more than we did for the story that is told in sentence (1) in the following paragraph.

What does seem certain is that there are ways in which the grammar could be improved if optimizing the match to the psychology were the primary goal in view. Indeed, clause crunching is itself something maladaptive from the viewpoint of sentence processing. Thus, for example, Whiz Deletion (wh-is deletion) crunches clauses [as in pairs like (1) and (2)].

(1) [The lady [who is sitting on the shelf]]   is my last duchess.
                                          S NP
(2) [The lady sitting on the shelf]   is my last duchess.
                NP

In doing so, however, it sometimes abuts surface VPs and NPs in such fashion as to produce NPVP sequences which are *not* related as subject and verb. Now, there is reason to believe that an early-pass strategy in sentence perception presumes, precisely, that NPVP sequences are typically analyzable as subject-verb [see Fodor, Bever, and Garrett, 1974]. The interaction of Whiz deletion with this strategy produces such curiousities as (3):

(3)   The horse raced past the barn fell.
      The man kicked the ball kicked the ball.

This could be avoided by dispensing with Whiz Deletion wholesale, or after passivization. If grammar is concerned with the well-being of the psychology, why doesn't it do something about Whiz Deletion?

It may, of course, be answered that sentence crunching (or Whiz Deletion) is a Good Thing *überhaupt*. Perhaps what's gained by proliferating surface clauses amounts to more than what's lost by permitting sentences like those in (3). Once again, there may be something to this, but, once again, we don't have any way to tell. Roughly, we don't know why the recognition/production system is interested in surface clauses, so we don't know how to evaluate the total good that clause crunching does that system. *A fortiori* we don't know how to evaluate the claim that clause crunching does more good than (3) does bad. So, as things now stand, Scotch verdict.

3. I've argued that we're not, at least for now, in a position to explain the conspiracies by reference to the psychological processes involved in sentence production/perception. On the one hand, those processes must exhibit a minimal fit to the grammar and, on the other, we don't know how much better than a minimal fit the observed fit is, or even whether the conspiracies serve, in general, to make the fit better rather than worse over all. There is, however, a further possibility we might explore.

It may be that sentence processing procedures are just special cases of more general, nonlinguistic, information processes. That is, it may be that the recognition/production of linguistic tokens was, from an evolutionary point of view, imposed upon recognition/production systems which were specialized for purposes other than communication. If this is true, and if we could characterize the general properties of such systems, then we might be able to show that some of the features that grammars exhibit are determined by the need to satisfy the demands that such systems impose upon the objects they compute.

So, for example, Ross notes the special role of CVCV in the output of the phonetics, and it does seem plausible to argue that the centrality of such structures can be explained by reference to the open, close, open, close cycle of the vocal apparatus. Notice that this case contrasts with the one discussed above. We don't have facts about the *general* character of human production/perception systems which would imply that surface clauses ought to play a special role in communication. I can't, myself, imagine what sorts of facts such facts would be.

If, in short, we could show that the structures that conspiracies conspire toward were natural, not just for the purpose of sentence processing but from the point of view of psychological mechanisms at large, then we could plausibly imagine languages to have been "shaped" to accommodate those mechanisms. But, outside some of the strictly phonetic cases, I know of no clear examples of such convergences. On the contrary, there seems to be very little reason to believe that the speech production/perception system *is* just a specialization of general informational handling mechanisms. But if it isn't, then we're back in the bind of section 2 above.

So where the thing stands is this: there *appears* to be a bias in the grammar toward producing certain kinds of derived forms at the expense of certain other kinds; a bias, that is, over and above what the mere existence of transformational mechanisms implies. If that appearance isn't specious, then it is natural to try to account for that bias as a species of teleological convergence. The natural candidate for the biasing mechanism would then be some form of selection which increases the correspondence between the structures that the grammar enumerates and the computational demands of the data processing operations available to the organism. This would be an attractive kind of argument to make. I wish it well. But it seems to me, as things now stand, the discussion proceeds largely at the level of anecdote; the general claims haven't been tacked down at any point.

References

Bever, T. G. 1970. The cognitive basis for linguistic structures. In *Cognition and the Development of Language,* J. R. Hayes (ed.). New York: Wiley.

Fodor, J. A., T. G. Bever, and M. Garrett. 1974. *The Psychology of Language.* New York: McGraw-Hill.

Open Discussion of the Papers of Ross and Fodor

Lazy Tongue?

Ignatius Mattingly added to the list of motivations for linguistic maneuvers such as those given by Ross. If we dealt only with whole sentences and if there were no such things as paragraphs and other larger units, there would be little preservation of reference. Pronouns, for instance, would cease to exist except where referring to antecedents within the sentence. However, since a great many of Ross's transformations will apply only in the case where two nouns of the same reference co-occur, a paradox results in that the more transformations a sentence undergoes the tighter the connection between the references becomes. Ross agreed with this view and suggested that it is a sidelight of the principle of lazy tongue. Kernel sentences which have the same coreferential argument can easily be telescoped; thus, *I want, I try, I begin, I go* yields *I want to try to begin to go*.

James Jenkins then commented that such "laziness" is as relevant to the perceptual end of the speech chain as it is to the productive end. One might argue for a "lazy memory storage." Some of the work of Bransford, Barclay, and Franks [1972] and others demonstrates that adults and even small children will listen to related sentences and wrap them up into one sentence in order to get it nicely coded. This appears to occur because of a small short-term processing space rather than productive constraints, but the principle is the same. The listener makes the syntax of a sentence or group of sentences work for him to save space.

Alvin Liberman noted that the tongue is not just lazy, but is imperfect. This imperfection is exactly what appears to have caused the need for parallel transmission of information at the phonemic level and at the syntactic level. If there is a lazy, or perhaps somewhat passive, tongue there must be an active "something else" to compensate for it. Mattingly then suggested that an ultimate motivation in speech is to be able to say something in one breath: lazy tongue may stem from lazy lungs. Lieberman noted that the average length of an utterance is about two seconds, a duration found by the Bell Telephone Laboratories in average telephone conversations.

Michael Studdert-Kennedy balked somewhat at the notion of lazy tongue. In a strict articulatory sense the tongue is not lazy; the notion that inertia is operative in coarticulation is wrong. A more correct view is that there is a genuine adjustment in target that the articulators attempt to hit. Such a view, however, need not detract from Ross's main point. Transformational processes, for example, could be considered to be adjustments in targets as well. Ross then redefined his notion of lazy tongue to include only an abhorrence of the repetition of underlying constituents, not the phenomenon of coarticulation. Fodor suggested a better term would be "lazy ego."

Studdert-Kennedy and others then asked for a fuller explanation of the analogy between the CVCV phonological structure and the single-clause target in semantax. Ross explained that both are the end result of "crunching" processes. Since he had previously outlined the process in semantax, he then briefly addressed the process in phonology. Consider the word *divinity* as it might be pronounced in the phrase *divinity fudge*. By degrees this word may be crunched from a CVCVCVCV structure into a CVCV structure. The process, in abbreviated form, is outlined as follows:

(1) [də·ˈvɪn·ə·ti]
(2) [də·ˈvĩə̯·ti]
(3) [də·ˈvĩ·ti]
(4) [də·ˈvĩ:]

The [ɪ] vowel in the second syllable becomes nasalized, then through vowel harmony absorbs the schwa-like vowel [ə], leaving a CVCVCV structure. The crunching process has not ended since the [t] in the unstressed final syllable may become flapped, then nasalized, and then absorbed into the [ɪ] vowel, leaving a CVCV final form. Klima then gave another example: can't you [kænt·yu], roughly a CVCCCV structure. The process here is similar to that outlined by Ross. The [æ] vowel becomes nasalized, absorbing the [n], and the [ty] cluster becomes affricated into [č]. The end result is [kæ̃·ču], another CVCV.

Psychological Reality of Syntactic Units

Jerry Fodor then outlined some of his investigations into the determination of psychological reality of linguistic structures. One method is to place a click somewhere within a sentence. The instructions to the subject ask him to determine the location of the click within the sentence. The overwhelming result is that the subject reports the location of the click according to the structural organization of the sentence. It appears that the boundaries between deep-structure units attract the perception of the click. The most important units here appear to be clauses; internal constituent structures appear to make very little difference in the click mislocation.

The interesting question is: should we take this seriously; are these operationally defined clause boundaries those dominated in the surface structure of the sentence? This can be tested by using sentences with transformations. In a pair of similar sentences, only one of which is whiz deleted, one finds a large asymmetry in click displacement. That is, there is a much larger effect in the whiz-deleted sentence than in the other.

There is a strong suggestion here that there is something about the integrity and accessibility of surface clauses. Center-embedded sentences are relevant here since they outrageously violate clause integrity: *The dog that the horse kicked chased the cow* may be fine but *The dog that the horse that the boy rode kicked chased the cow* is intolerable. But why is this? One suggestion is that we have a surface buffer for centoids and we can hold only one of them while processing the main clause. This is certainly true for reading, but Jenkins suggested that in speech, clause integrity can be carried over center embedding by changes in pitch and speaking rate. Stokoe then noted that sign languages will often not even accept one level of center embedding; instead embedding is external in two senses. It occurs at the front or back of a main clause, and the subordinate clauses are often laid out in space so that the signer and the sign receiver can refer to them later.

Reference

Bransford, J. D., J. R. Barclay, and J. J. Franks. 1972. Sentence memory: a constructive versus interpretive approach. *Cognitive Psychol.,* 3: 193–209.

IV. Reflections on the Conference

Speech, Language, and Communication: Reflections on the Conference

IRA J. HIRSH

To reflect on the contributions to this conference and on the relations among them is to reflect on almost all of communication. Each of you in his field of expertise will have concluded on issues at a more profound level than can be represented here, but yet it may be useful for one person, perhaps any person, to reflect on the entirety.

It appears that we have discussed four general issues. The first concerns the formal characteristics of systems—systems of expressive behavior, of communication, of language, and of speech. Second, we have tried to set apart those systems that are uniquely human. Third, we have focussed heavily on interdependence—of speech on language, of perception on production, of language on memory and perhaps also on human knowledge. Finally, a fourth concern has been the genetic, both phylogenetic and ontogenetic, as opposed to the learned aspects of behavior under each of these systems.

I believe that in the early planning for this conference, Liberman suggested that one question for discussion would concern how necessary speech is for language. Such a question implies that we can state certain formal properties of language systems, and then ask whether or not there could be any such without speech. Put so badly, the question is almost trivial, for surely there are formal languages, of mathematics, for example, that need not be spoken. But are there languages used for communication to which we impute direction of thought or influences on motor and perceptual systems outside the natural, spoken languages of human beings? Discussion in this conference has been less philosophical. One starting point was a definition offered earlier by Lieberman [1973] that says: Language is a system of communication that permits exchange of new information. Such a delimiting definition implies that there are also nonlanguage systems of communication, like the signaling cries and chirps of chimps and birds, described so well by Marler. If these systems are not language, at least social contingencies and ensuing behavior indicate a communication function.

Of course, questions about what is in and what out can be avoided by a definition like that given by Liberman and Mattingly on the first day of this conference, namely, that linguistic communication requires that a string of phones be transmitted from one person to another. The problems about whether language communication must involve speech or must be uniquely human simply disappear. But we did reach beyond this kind of tautological constraint.

Marler's report and the Reynolds commentary suggested that these signals are not just yells, not just random noises or calls, but rather are associated with rather specific situations. Those situations do not elicit (in Skinner's sense) particular kinds of responses. Rather there appear to be circumstances under which such calls are emitted without one's calling into play any intention on the part of the animal doing the calling. Now Premack doesn't want us to conclude from those ethological studies about the nature of the chimp mind. That kind of signal communication, perhaps prelanguage, would be inadequate. He emphasizes other aspects of what might be a chimpanzee intellect in terms first of symbol function, in terms of an apparent organization of information, and, somewhat more tentatively, I thought, something about internal representation.

What seems to have been more emphasized in setting apart language system as opposed to a nonlinguistic communication system is that the information that, in Lieberman's definition, is transmitted, is so in discrete chunks—chunks that somehow emerge from signals, or in our case speech, that were originally continuous.

This brings us immediately to human language and persons. One of the fascinating parts of the conference from Lieberman, Hewes, and others was the kind of reconstruction and interpretation that people do from fossils that allow them to predict the sort of system that man was to produce.

I don't know quite how to avoid teleological comment in this context, although I would have liked to spend the first half hour of my half hour inveighing against mentalism, which now is in modern form. Although we no longer speak about mental aspects or even the mind, we speak instead about the intellect or knowledge. Then we can have machines knowing, and we have, in a couple of the commentaries from one corner, models both knowing and willing. However, I will not inveigh.

There appear to have been two strains of conversation about evolution. One followed the idea that a brain got big enough to permit the making of tools. The making of tools was not so much in and of itself the marker, as the implication that the fashion of tool making gave evidence not only for goal-directed behavior, but some notion of planning. This cast appeared to some at least to be the precursor of creating sentences before they got uttered. Perhaps that is my jump rather than the speakers' jumps.

The second idea about evolution was that of a change in the arrangement of bones and muscles and where they got attached so that man could speak. It wasn't quite clear to me what the stronger emphasis was to have been, whether it was the possibility of speaking or the possibility of a languagelike system, to be spoken. At any rate, man got a language, and in addition to that he spoke it, and we should keep those two notions separate, at least for a while.

More than that, for Mattingly what was uniquely human about the speaking was not so much the arrangement of the instruments of production but the encoding that went from sounds to phones. We heard about encoding rules at all levels in the language system from the phonological to the syntactic, and in fact this encoding function has appeared to be a kind of a keystone here, which was almost predictable.

I would like to comment about human language and its use of symbols, which, as Fodor argued with Premack, is not a sufficient condition for language. A useful distinction between signs and symbols was made quite carefully about 25 years ago by Charles Morris [1946]. The important criterion for him about symbol, as distinct from sign, was that it was arbitrary. Now may I translate loosely "arbitrary" into "noniconic" for our purposes. It doesn't naturally (iconically) stand for something, like a conditioned stimulus. If that is the case, I would suggest, as was almost done in a recent chapter on a comparison of visual and auditory perception [Julesz and Hirsh, 1972], that the spoken language, and thus the auditory language, is the one in which it is easiest to be noniconic, or to be arbitrary. Only a small fraction of the referents in our vocabulary make sound, and therefore the acoustic symbol in language cannot "sound like" any but that small fraction.

The main substance of our discussions yesterday and today had to do with interdependence. Actually, I prefer to break that word down into dependence of A on B. "Interdependence" often implies lack of knowledge of which is dependent on which.

The speech code tells us of the dependence of speech production and perception on the language. The dependence of spoken language on speech, and the dependence of such psychological functions as perception and memory on speech have been emphasized here. We haven't said enough, it seems to me, about the dependence of speech or the speech code on the characteristics of those same psychological functions. Is the fact that you don't put an [r] after another [r], mentioned in Ross's illustration this morning, a commentary on the system itself, or is it a commentary on the mechanics of speech production? It is hard to do. It can be done, as he illustrated, but it is hard to do.

Or take another example—and here I am going to really get into deep water—the location of the click in the sentence. Are those observations indicative of attributes of the language system, or are they corollaries of the fact that as language is spoken there are speech-produced markers for the ends and beginnings of clusters which are, from a strictly auditory perceptual point of view, the places where you would expect clicks to be targeted in memory? It is that kind of question that I think might be asked.

One of the reasons why I think this might be important is that our description of auditory perception is historically far behind our description of language. One of my principal concerns has been to move the description of auditory perception out of the realm of pitch discrimination and intensity discrimination into more temporally oriented functions. We don't now have all of them.

Let me mention further an illustration from Eimas's data and in connection with Studdert-Kennedy's paper. I am a little concerned about bringing this in now, because the Eimas data should be brought in under our fourth question about what is given and what is learned. But let me say, anticipating that discussion, that I believe that the Eimas data is the only case in which a predisposition for speech has been operationally defined. Otherwise "predisposition for" or "innate capacity for" means that the behavior eventually takes place and no antecedent conditions have been otherwise specified.

In Eimas's case, I think we are getting close. But again I don't know whether the fact of sharp discrimination across a phoneme boundary corresponds to what you mean, Peter Marler, by an almost wired-in auditory template or whether it is an example of a more general auditory perceptual fact, namely that two events have to be separated by something between 20 and 40 msec before a person can judge reliably in what order they occurred. So I am not yet sure that Eimas's data, so well presented by Cutting, are about speech. There will have to be many elaborations done.

There is another realm of interdependence discussed in an interesting manner this morning by Klima, by a kind of compensation between two levels in the language as changes at one level take place, and information transmission is presumably continued at the same rate.

Under human language, we skirted around the issue of sign language as described to us by Stokoe and, with some very illuminating experiments, by Ursula Bellugi. I should say parenthetically that American Sign Language is not typical of the signing that is taught in a great number of schools for the deaf throughout the United States. The schools' system is one in which the signing can go on while the teacher is saying the same sentence. American Sign Language is special and the population of users quite small. It is a minority, I would guess, of deaf people, but not a minority of that special group involving deaf parents with a deaf child. Certainly that system as described takes on many of the characteristics that had been imputed to human language, in general the spoken language system. We did then address the very interesting issue, through Klima's paper and others, about whether you could have a language without a phonology. Here, I take it, phonology was being used in a metaphoric sense, applicable to individual signs as well as phonemes.

I thought that discussion ended a little too quickly because it seemed to me that the three dimensions of signs that were discussed—the hand shape, the place, and the movement—were not like phonemes but rather like phonemic features. Thus various combinations of those features give rise to phones or expressed signs. The level that does not appear to exist in the sign language is the level of sounds, if I understand this dichotomy. It began with a "phone," not a signal to be coded, and thus it is less ambiguous. Yes, there are some variations within, as was indicated, but it seems to me that considerably less of the encoding function is to be provided by the signer from individual occurrences of signs, that is, signs as members of the language system, than is the case for individual speech sounds in their great variety and the implied phones that result in spoken transmission.

The things we want to hear about in the immediate future are some of the things on which Ursula Bellugi has already started, and that is a re-examination of many of those cases of dependence of psychological functions, like that of short-term memory on aspects of speech, redone as characteristics of human memory that depend upon different sign systems, or sign features. I have a bias, which you already know about, that many of the features that have shown up in short-term memory and in other psychological functions may be as much characteristics of an auditory system as they are of a speech system.

Finally, we have come to the fourth major issue, and that is the "givens" versus the "learneds." I have already spoken about the use by some of you of the terms "innate capacity" and "predispositions" as euphemisms for "I don't know how they got there but they are not learned."

Let me remind you, particularly the psychologists here, about a certain historical matter, the theory of local signs. In the case of visual perception—I'm oversimplifying now—you recognize an object because that object has certain local signs that permit you to identify it. That is a good way to get rid of a problem, and if all of our problems were thus solved a lot of psychologists would be out of work.

Early phonetic-system descriptions, going back in my own reading at least to a scholar by the name of Orminn in the twelfth century, described consonants and vowels, open vocal tract versus closed vocal tract, place and manner of articulation. The phonemes of language systems have been described in terms of articulation patterns ever since. Early they were positions and later on they were movements, dynamics, and so on.

That wasn't good enough and from about the middle 1920s through 1960 we decided we would get better descriptions of speech sounds by using the tools of acoustical analysis. So we started analyzing the speech sounds, producing a rich variety that seemed to be less languagelike than the original articulatory descriptions.

But yesterday, Liberman said in a discussion that if he were to build a phoneme recognizer he would rather have articulatory information than acoustic information. How do we perceive this articulation if we don't perceive the acoustic patterns, if there is too much variety there and too much ambiguity? Mattingly said that we have a tacit knowledge of the vocal tract. Now, the nature of that knowledge was interestingly approached by the question of whether the deaf child has such knowledge available. He has a vocal tract, after all. I would doubt it because I believe that that knowledge is not knowledge about the vocal tract. It is knowledge about the coincidence between anything that happens in the vocal tract and constant monitoring by the auditory system.

If I may bend my analogy—and why not, everybody else has—to some of Reynold's notions about play, here is vocal play that goes on from almost the very start. That is different from other kinds of motor-skilled activity, because is constantly monitored. You don't have to open your ears; you can't even shut them. There is a coincidence that is developing over the first couple of years that gives rise to a type of knowledge that is not so much about the articulatory processes themselves as about the coincidence between those processes and certain auditory impressions. Anyway, my guess is that the deaf child does not have such knowledge.

If you teach a deaf child to speak, as is done in some schools, what you find, as R. Monsen has found in our laboratory, is that, for example, some of the phonological rules don't work. These youngsters produce intelligible speech, sometimes only marginally intelligible. Their voice quality is distinctive and for some listeners at least is not acceptable; but no matter, the speech can be intelligible. You find, for example, that short vowels are short and long vowels are long. There is no evidence for whether there is a voiced or voiceless consonant following. That rule is violated. You can say, "Well, nobody taught it," and that is probably right. What was likely taught was that long vowels are long and short vowels are short. The monitoring system, which is the teacher, isn't there 24 hours a day and so is not the auditory monitor for all vocal behavior.

Now I return to Eimas's data and the notion of categorical perception. What is curious is that the categories are not isomorphic in the perceptual and productive realms. For example, from an articulatory point of view there is no continuum from [ba] to [da] to [ga], as there is from an acoustical point of view. You can make a continuum of [ba]s, rounding the lips more or less, but there is no continuous space between putting two lips together and putting the tip of the tongue against the alveolar ridge. There is a discontinuity there. But the acoustical continuum resulting from those manipulations appears to be more of a continuum.

On the other hand, in [ba] versus [pa], you can think of an articulatory continuum. You can manipulate it to a certain extent. The categorization, however, by the time it gets converted into auditory or perceptual recognition, is very strong, and as I understand Eimas's data, is stronger than the one corresponding to [ba, da, ga].

I haven't said anything about our discussions about physiology, partly because I don't understand them. I would remind you, however, that there is a kind of discrepancy. Reynolds' emphasis, for example, on plasticity, as we come to these higher forms of behavior, somewhat reflected by Jenkins's talking about the global nature of language function as represented in a variety of categories of brain damage, appears to be inconsistent with Marler's view that there must be some constraints built in for the learning to be efficient and rapid.

To summarize this conference would have been more difficult even than to summarize these reflections, but we should note how we have, by various routes, responded to questions raised by the chairman at the outset. We have focused on the importance of grammar to language systems, whether a grammar in the formal syntactical realm or a more metaphoric grammar of speech sounds and their coding for transmission. It appears, however, that the grammar and the required encoding, which appears to be uniquely human in this language communication, does in fact depend upon our language being spoken. With Kiparsky's reminder that such formal properties do indeed depend upon the modality, we note that a very general characterization of encoding or of the properties of a grammar is elusive because of our preoccupation with the right coupling between language and speech. There is no doubt but that formal properties can be described for language systems, like that of signs, or for communication systems, like that employed by animals. The distance between such formal properties and what we now understand to be the properties of grammar of human languages may in fact be related to the distance between those vehicles of transmission and what we know as human speech. Some of the effects of language on more general psychological properties of humans, like short-term memory, may more adequately be called properties of speech rather than of the language, and those in turn may turn out to be properties of the systems of production and of perception. We must agree with Mattingly's statement that what is uniquely human about spoken language is the encoding process, but it may also be that that very encoding is a human attribute only in its speechlike form.

Since the issues raised outnumber the problems answered, we still have much work to do.

References

Julesz, B., and I. J. Hirsh. 1972. Visual and auditory perception—an essay of comparison. In *Human Communication: A Unified View*, E. E. David and P. B. Denes (eds.). New York: McGraw-Hill, 283–340.

Lieberman, P. 1973. On the evolution of language: a unified view. *Cognition*, 2: 59–94.

Morris, C. W. 1946. *Signs, Language and Behavior*. New York: Prentice-Hall.

Name Index

Abbott, D. F., 214
Abbs, J. H., 141
Abramson, A. S., 11, 128, 129, 132, 135, 141, 173
Ades, A. E., 142
Aldrich-Blake, F. P. G., 12
Altmann, S. A., 64

Baddeley, A. D., 118
Bailey, P. J., 142
Baker, M. C., 34
Barclay, J. R., 118, 310
Bartlett, F. C., 70
Bastian, H. C., 156
Bastide, R. P., 86
Bateson, G., 47
Battison, R., 173, 209, 285
Beck, B. B., 94
Bellugi, U., 63, 168, 208, 209, 224, 225, 229, 235, 239, 241, 242, 244, 246, 249, 281, 318, 319
Bentley, D. R., 24
Berko, J., 151
Bernard, J., 127
Bever, T. G., 3, 306, 307, 308
Blakemore, C., 141
Bloom, L., 127
Bloomfield, L., 90, 218
Blumstein, S., 117
Boas, F., 275
Bogen, J. E., 162
Bogert, C. M., 86
Booth, A. H., 18
Bordes, F., 103
Bosma, J. F., 107–108, 109–111, 241
Brady, P. T., 139
Braine, M. D. S., 214
Brame, M., 272
Bransford, J. D., 310
Bresnan, J., 272, 273, 274
Broca, P., 84
Brooks, L., 234, 235
Brown, R., 127, 151
Bryan, S. S., 139
Byrnes, E. T., 213

Campbell, B., 22
Campbell, F. W., 141
Capranica, R. R., 39, 85, 86
Carmon, A., 121
Carroll, J. B., 161
Casterline, W. D., 173, 216, 253, 256
Chen, M., 262, 263, 264
Chomsky, N., 33, 63, 69, 89, 90, 92, 100, 102, 103, 249, 283, 294

Clark, E., 48
Cole, R. A., 141
Conrad, R., 183
Cook, E. D., 275
Cooper, W. E., 129, 141, 143, 144
Corbit, J. D., 141, 142, 143, 144
Crelin, E. S., 5, 68, 87, 89, 97, 107, 127
Croneberg, C., 173, 216, 253, 256
Crowder, R. G., 117, 118
Cutting, J. E., 11, 122, 149, 166–168, 241, 242, 318

Darwin, C., 83, 217
Darwin, C. J., 98, 118
Day, R. S., 30, 120
DeClerk, J., 66
De Laguna, G., 47
Deloria, E., 275
DeLucia, D. A., 129
De Saussure, F., 303
Dorman, M., 118, 129
Doty, R. W., 24
Dunn, C. W., 213
Durnford, M., 121

Eibesfeldt, I., 64
Eimas, P. D., 11, 29, 30, 122, 149, 150, 153, 166–168, 318, 321
Erickson, D., 93
Erulkar, S. D., 139
Evans, E. F., 136, 139
Evarts, E. V., 93

Fant, C. G. M., 32, 66, 87, 88, 128
Feng, C., 233
Fischer, S., 63, 173, 208, 224
Fodor, J., 3, 74, 166–168, 282, 310–312, 317
Fouts, R. S., 95
Franks, J. J., 310
Freud, S., 46
Friedman, L. A., 193, 209, 223
Frishberg, N., 173, 183, 285
Frishkopf, L. S., 85, 86
Fromkin, V., 133, 194
Fry, D. B., 115
Fujisaki, H., 116, 144
Furth, H. G., 173

Galanter, E., 161
Gardner, B. T., 95, 216
Gardner, R. A., 95, 126

Subject Index